# Case Studies
## *for*
# Organizational
# Communication

# Case Studies *for* Organizational Communication

*Understanding Communication Processes*

Third Edition

JOANN KEYTON

PAMELA SHOCKLEY-ZALABAK

New York    Oxford

OXFORD UNIVERSITY PRESS

2010

Oxford University Press, Inc., publishes works that further Oxford University's objective of excellence in research, scholarship, and education.

Oxford    New York
Auckland    Cape Town    Dar es Salaam    Hong Kong    Karachi
Kuala Lumpur    Madrid    Melbourne    Mexico City    Nairobi
New Delhi    Shanghai    Taipei    Toronto

With offices in
Argentina    Austria    Brazil    Chile    Czech Republic    France    Greece
Guatemala    Hungary    Italy    Japan    Poland    Portugal    Singapore
South Korea    Switzerland    Thailand    Turkey    Ukraine    Vietnam

Published by Oxford University Press, Inc.
198 Madison Avenue, New York, New York 10016
http://www.oup.com

Oxford is a registered trademark of Oxford University Press

Library of Congress Cataloging-in-Publication Data

Case studies for organizational communication : understanding
human processes / Joann Keyton, Pamela Shockley-Zalabak [editors]. — 3rd ed.
        p.   cm.
Includes bibliographical references and index.
ISBN 978-0-19-538672-1 (alk. paper)
1. Communication in organizations—Case studies.   I. Keyton, Joann.
II. Shockley-Zalabak, Pamela.
HD30.3.C367 2010
302.3'5—dc22        2009016794

Printing number: 9 8 7 6 5 4 3 2 1

Printed in the United States of America
on acid-free paper

# CONTENTS

*New to the Third Edition

# WEB CASES

## Available at www.oup.com/us/keytonshockley

### W1. Just Part of the Crop
*Joann Keyton*
> Having held jobs for one year, two friends disclose about their job-seeking experiences.

### W2. A Decision to Change?
*Theodore E. Zorn*
> A team charged with a significant knowledge management project runs into opposition and quick cancellation of the effort.

### W3. Celebration of Diversity
*Joann Keyton*
> An Asian manager questions why his new organization promotes workplace diversity by singling out one racial group.

### W4. Change, Coalitions, and Coping
*Joy L. Hart, Shirley Willihnganz, and Greg Leichty*
> Management change fractures a widely accepted family culture, forcing the retired founders to return.

### W5. Contemplating My First Year
*Joy L. Hart*
> A new employee discovers that what is said and what is done in the organization are vastly different, with the effect being the stifling of innovation in the organization.

### W6. Downsizing at Tata Steel
*Rajeev Kumar*
> Downsizing of an organization challenges management in communicating with employees and union representation.

## W16. Long-Distance Cultural Integration

*Gerald L. Pepper and Gregory S. Larson*

Human resources leadership is challenged to assist integrating different organizational cultures utilizing mostly virtual communication strategies.

## W17. Where Do We Go From Here?

*Edward C. Brewer*

During a period of rapid change, an email conflict replaces face-to-face discussion of the potential adoption of a new system.

## W18. Why Does This Always Happen?

*Philip Salem*

A low-performing employee resists feedback in an organization unable to confront issues and problems effectively.

## W19. The First Day at Work

*Julie Davis*

A new employee orientation session causes a new hire to question her decision to work for the company.

## W20. When a Good Thing Goes Bad

*Anne P. Hubbell*

A drug company faces a crisis over issues of creativity, differences in protocols, and disagreements among senior staff members.

PREFACE

# The Case Study Method as a Pedagogical Technique

Case methods have been employed at least since the 1920s to encourage reflection, integration of theory and practice, and problem solving. They have been widely used because they illustrate the nonlinear, complex, and context-specific reality of organizations (Kitano & Landry, 2001). Well-developed cases can offer insight into organizational practices, procedures, and processes that are not otherwise available for classroom use. Case studies allow students the opportunities to analyze critical incidents, translate their knowledge into practical applications, and develop strategies for their own organizational communication practice. Moreover, the case study method can enhance students' abilities in perspective taking, as well as highlight the communication process among multiple actors. Finally, this pedagogical technique helps students find the intersections among the communication issues, styles, and strategies of managers and employees (Mier, 1982). These benefits accrue because cases present opportunities to first observe and then discuss how people communicate in work settings.

New to this edition are 21 cases distributed among each of the types of cases: organizational culture, organizational technology (formerly virtual communication), teamwork and group processes, decision making and problem solving, the individual and the organization, and organizational diversity. New cases also appear in two new sections to this edition: organizations and their stakeholders and organizational crisis. Twenty cases from the first and second editions no longer available in the print edition are now available on the book's website www.oup.com/us/keytonshockley. 

Literally all of the undergraduate organizational communication textbooks now include cases as an in-text pedagogical technique. The cases here support and extend the use of cases in teaching organizational communication as they are longer and more complex. As a result, the cases will provide you with a richer set of assignment options. Instructor materials for both print and web cases are password protected and available online at www.oup.com/us/keytonshockley. There you will find:

1. A one-paragraph case overview (including type of organization, key actors, and issues in the case).
2. A one-sentence learning objective that identifies the central communication problem in the case.
3. A list of keywords and their definitions.
4. A series of questions for written essays and potential/probable answers.
5. A series of discussion questions.
6. Other teaching ideas including assignment alternatives, audiovisual materials, and websites that support the case.
7. Short paragraphs describing any conceptual analysis that could aid in understanding and teaching the case.
8. Bibliography of resources for the instructor.
9. Bibliography of resources for students.
10. Epilogue of the case (if appropriate).

Also on the website are 20 cases from the first and second editions. Please contact your Oxford University Press representative for password information.

Discussion of cases can foster students' reasoning, enhance development of theoretical and practical knowledge, and increase awareness of personal beliefs and values (Lundeberg, 1999). We believe this happens most effectively when students are encouraged to develop multiple alternatives as case solutions. Critical learning occurs when students analyze each solution, compare and contrast plausible solutions, and then choose one believed to be most effective at improving communication or sustaining effective communication.

We believe cases are most effectively used when there is both independent and interdependent learning. Not only should students be assigned to independently analyze the case and make recommendations, students should also learn to listen and respond to other students' ideas about the case. Cases can augment or extend content presented in class or in the text you use.

Because cases are complex and realistic depictions of organizational communication, the same case can be approached from a number of perspectives. Consider assigning different groups of students to take the roles of different characters, or to make recommendations based on competing theories or perspectives.

We believe that instructors should be actively involved in the case analysis process. Here are some methods for using cases to create interdependencies with your students:

1. Let students generate questions about the case for you to answer in class.
2. Help students generate criteria for deciding if the recommendation or alternative chosen will be effective.
3. Cases can be used to improve critical thinking skills. Ask students: What's the evidence for your claim? What are your assumptions? Biases? Emotional responses?
4. At the end of case discussion, give closure by summarizing:

- What was learned?
- What communication skills would students need to implement recommendations?
- To what other settings would recommendations apply?

There are a variety of methods for using cases as a pedagogical technique. Here are some of our favorites:

1. To enhance the communicative aspect of the case, ask that students practice effective communication in their case discussions. You could assign students to practice a particular communication skill (i.e., a specific listening or speaking strategy) during their discussions with one another.
2. Cases can be used as the basis for oral presentations. Assign two students or two groups to debate alternative recommendations and then take questions from other students.
3. Assign students to write a one-page position paper describing the overarching communication problem that needs to be addressed in the next 3 to 4 hours. Next 24 hours? Next week?
4. Use the case as stimulus for a test. Given the case before hand, the exam can be a test of the degree to which students understand and apply communication principles and concepts.
5. As a group assignment, each group is responsible for delivering the following as written or oral presentation:
   - A statement that defines or describes the communication decision, dilemma, or problem.
   - A procedural statement for addressing or solving the problem.
   - A list of resources (physical, monetary, human resources) needed for implementation of the proposed solution to the problem.
   - A timetable for implementation.
   - A statement of expected benefits or expected impact of the proposed solution.
6. Assign students to one role in the case and have them develop a communication plan for themselves, their team, or their organization.
7. Assign students to develop a training program to respond to the communication problem or challenge in the case.
8. Use the case as a stimulus for students to design an organizational communication assessment.
9. Based on the organization presented in the case, assign students to develop a selection or recruitment interview for one or more of the jobs described in the case.
10. Use the case as a basis for developing a team meeting procedure.
11. Using the key character as the stimulus, assign students the project of designing a leadership development program (e.g., training, coaching, counseling, mentoring).

12. Use the case as a basis for developing a code of ethics for the organization or a profession.
13. Use the case as a basis for developing a public relations or external communication plan.

## ACKNOWLEDGMENTS

We wish to thank the following colleagues for their insightful reviews of our book:

### Third Edition Reviewers

Elise J. Dallimore, Northeastern University
Martha J. Fay, University of Wisconsin–Eau Claire
Bethany Crandell Goodier, College of Charleston
Michael P. Pagano, Fairfield University
Suchitra Shenoy, Purdue University
Kami J. Silk, Michigan State University

### Second Edition Reviewers

Amy H. Amy, University of Central Arkansas
Michael Fairley, Austin College
John W. Howard, East Carolina University
Steve May, University of North Carolina, Chapel Hill
John C. Meyer, University of Southern Mississippi
David E. Weber, University of North Carolina, Wilmington
Toni Whitfield, James Madison University
Cory Young, University of Wisconsin, Oshkosh

## REFERENCES

Kitano, M. K., & Landry, H. (2001, June). Instructional cases: Learning from the dilemmas of practicing teachers. *Roeper Review, 23,* 206–218.

Lundeberg, M. A. (1999). Discovering teaching and learning through cases. In M. A. Lundeberg, B. B. Levin, & H. L. Harrington (Eds.), *Who learns what from cases and how? The research base for teaching and learning with cases* (pp. 3–23). Mahwah, NJ: Erlbaum.

Mier, D. R. (1982). From concepts to practices: Student case study work in organizational communication. *Communication Education, 31,* 151–154.

# Using Cases to Learn About Organizational Communication

Nearly everyone who works can tell at least one story about his or her work experiences. Funny, disgusting, sad, motivating, amazing–some stories are about the mundane day-to-day events at work; other stories are about pivotal events, or turning points, in a person's work life. The cases in this book are stories, or narratives, about the work experiences of individuals and teams in a variety of organizational settings. As you learn about organizational communication, you can use cases to (a) broaden your perspective on what it means to work, (b) gain an understanding of work settings or occupations with which you are unfamiliar, and (c) develop greater understanding of the ways in which communication is central to getting work done. Cases are also useful as a guide to identifying and developing your competences to determine actions appropriate for a variety of work situations.

## WHAT ARE CASES?

Cases are examples or illustrations of organizational problems or challenges. A case gives information about the organization–its people and its performance. By itself, a case is a good story. A case becomes a learning experience when we apply the theories we study in an effort to determine the best solutions for resolving the issues presented in the case. The case study approach to organizational communication provides an opportunity to blend theory, analysis, and practice in our efforts to better understand how communication processes create and shape organizational events. Case studies provide rich opportunities to apply theory to organizational practice. They bridge the gap between reading about organizations and theory and knowing what to do in actual organizational situations. They also expand our analytical and critical capabilities as we examine dynamic and complex events for their impact on organizational behavior. And they help us develop strategies and approaches for application to real organizational problems or challenges. The primary purpose of the case study approach is to develop our abilities.

Developing a one-paragraph summary will help you as you complete the assignment given by your instructor.

With the case read and summarized, reflect back on the case to identify the character in the case most like you and the character least like you. Acknowledging the perspective from which you read the case will help you challenge and test solutions that you eventually develop. Second, develop a list of statements about the case that you can defend. Be sure to note which information in the case you could use as data in the defense of your conclusions. Third, develop a list of questions you have about the case. A good place to start developing questions is to ask what the case reveals that is interesting and unique. Fourth, what organizational communication theories, perspectives, or research support your conclusions? Which theories, perspectives, and research challenge what is presented in the case? With these steps complete, you are ready to identify appropriate strategies for solving problems illuminated by the case.

## A Practice Case

The case that follows was written about a group of friends—Sherry, Arly, and Deb—who met at their first jobs after college. Sherry is the central character and the case reveals her knowledge, emotion, and attitudes about her job as a store manager of a large national women's clothing boutique. As the three women talk over lunch, the conversation focuses on two organizational tensions where Sherry is employed. The first is Sherry's role in the hierarchical structure of a family-owned business. The second is how the company owner manages sale events and his expectations about Sherry's performance during those events.

The case allows you to eavesdrop on the conversation and hear how Sherry explains her work environment to her friends. Notations in the column of the case illustrate key turning points in the conversation, identify points at which Sherry reveals information and uncertainty about her role in her organization, and illuminate instances in which her interaction with others reveals communication challenges or opportunities of which not even she may be aware. As suggested above, an example case analysis follows that includes a summary providing a contextual description and time line of the case, as well as a description of the key characters and their communication styles and relationships, the salient issues and problems of the case, symptoms and root causes of the communication problem described by the characters, and effective elements of communication. The example analysis also includes a list of statements about the case, a list of questions about the case, and a list of organizational communication theories, perspectives, or research that could be used to analyze the case. The practice case demonstrates that multiple perspectives can be taken on reading and analyzing case material. Different theoretical perspectives will suggest different strategies for different characters. By privileging different character roles, it will be easier to see the simultaneous, yet different, processes that comprise organizational communication.

# The Sale

## Joann Keyton

Sherry* sat down with a sigh, "Thanks for meeting me for lunch on such short notice. Work has been crazy. I just cannot plan ahead. For anything."

"It's okay, Sherry," said Arly. "We understand how new jobs can be. But haven't you been there six months already?"

"Yeah," said Deb. "I thought you took that job shortly after I went back to work after having Caden."

Sherry nodded her head in agreement and launched into her explanation. "It's far more complicated than I expected. I manage the Benson store, but I completely underestimated what it would be like for the company owner to have an office in the same location. The back of the store is pretty big—he has an office, Bill the designer has an office, and so does Gary."

Deb jumped in, "Who's Gary?"

"Good question," Sherry continued. He's the owner's son-in-law and I think he's in charge of operations. You

This part of the conversation sets the context for lunch and Sherry's revelations to the other women. This section also introduces Sherry as the primary character in the case.

---

*This case has been developed based on real organization(s) and real organizational experiences. Names, facts, and situations have been changed to protect the privacy of individuals and organizations.

know—scouting the country for new locations, negotiating with our manufacturers. He seems to be there when Charlie is there and not there when he isn't. If I had to guess, I would bet that Charlie is grooming him to take over the business when he retires."

"But what about you?" Arly added. "I thought you were hired to help with the succession of the company."

"I was. But it's a family business—and, of course, I'm not family—as everyone there reminds me. It's just very difficult for me to figure out my role. I manage the Benson store and Charlie's made sure to let me know that I'm 'completely responsible for it,' as he says. And, I think Charlie wanted a female presence. It's just not clear to me yet how I figure in his plans for the future." Sherry looked down at the menu. "Let's order and eat. I'm famished!"

The waiter took their lunch order. Waiting for lunch, the women, who had met at their first retail jobs working for a national retailer after college, caught up on their personal lives and friends they had in common. Lunch was served and Sherry took her first bite of the sandwich. "Gosh, this is good. I wish I had more time to meet you for lunch. But Charlie insists that I bring lunch in when there's a sale. But today, I just had to get out of there for a while. Traffic had slowed down. They can handle it."

Sherry works for Charlie who owns Threads, a women's fashion boutique that specializes in two-tone color combinations. Threads is in over 20 upscale markets, and their clientele is loyal. Rather than being located in large shopping malls, Threads stores are situated in neighborhoods, often in a strip mall, fairly inconspicuous for the price tags on

Sherry's response describes the communication context and the relationships among other central figures at Threads.

Interestingly, this part of Sherry's description reveals how little she knows about where she fits into the larger organization.

Sherry has broken an organizational norm by having lunch away from the store while a sale is in progress.

Deeper background on Threads and on Charlie's level of control of the organization.

the clothes. Women who find Threads come back often. The clothes are made in the U.S. and are size-consistent. As owner, Charlie has kept strong control over both design and manufacturing. As a result, the clothes last through many seasons—and that's where the design came in. Bill, the designer, has a knack for combining the season's new colors in a flattering way. Thus, to be in style, women buy items from each new season's collection. With colors rotating every six to eight weeks, Threads has a constant flow of traffic. And traffic is especially high when they have their weekend sales.

Having worked for a national re-tailer, Sherry was accustomed to working all weekend when sales were on. Like other national retailers, Sherry's former employer heavily promoted its sales in the newspaper—often with coupons. Dates and times of the sales were well identified. Sherry liked that approach as it made it easy to tell the sales staff she managed when and how to merchandise the floor, and how to handle sales at checkout. But at Threads, having a sale was a different matter. Without any notice, Gary or Charlie would walk in during a sale and tell Sherry where to move the merchandise or to add more items to the discounted racks.

This section describes how the Threads store facilitates sales; more importantly, it is possible that Gary and Charlie only involve themselves in the store where their offices are located. How does their involvement reflect on Sherry as a manager?

Sherry, Arly, and Deb were about finished with their lunch when Sherry's phone beeped. "Oh good grief," she exclaimed. "Can't I eat lunch in peace?"

Arly and Deb rolled their eyes and laughed. "It's okay. Take it," said Arly.

Immediately Sherry's face became tense, her body posture stiffened, and she sat straight in her chair. Still holding the phone to her ear, she stood up and rushed out the door of the restaurant. Now pacing on the sidewalk while she was talking

Notice how Sherry continues to break the organizational norm, even after it's been brought to her attention. Her report back to the other women also signals Sherry's emotional reaction to the issue and the phone call.

on the phone, Arly and Deb were speculating about who Sherry was talking to. The women could see Sherry talking very infrequently; when she did say something, it seemed to be just a yes or no answer.

Sherry was outside for more than 10 minutes—long enough to allow the waiter to clear away the lunch plates.

Finally, Sherry came back inside, and sat back down. "Sorry, we're having a sale and that was Gary. He's completely freaked that I'm not at the store. 'We're having a sale, Sherry,'" she said mimicking his voice. Of course I know that. But that doesn't mean I can't stop long enough to eat lunch. Let's order dessert."

It is clear that a call from Bill is unexpected. How will this call facilitate or hinder the further development of their relationship? Was it right of Bill to call her?

Not under any time pressures, Arly and Deb agreed. But no sooner than the waiter appeared to take their orders, Sherry's phone beeped again. Before answering it, she looked at the display. It was Bill, the store's designer. He seldom called Sherry— in fact, they really hadn't developed much of a relationship yet, as he was often gone to market or at the manufacturers.

"Sherry, it's Bill. I think you need to get back here. Gary is really mad that you're gone. And Charlie walked in a few minutes ago. You really need to get back here," he said emphasizing the "really."

The other women could see the confusion on Sherry's face. Sherry responded, "Okay, Bill. Thanks. But why are you calling me?"

"Just trust me; you need to get back here. We're having the sale."

"I know that, but the store is fully staffed."

"But Gary and Charlie are here."

Defeated, Sherry thanked Bill for the call.

"Sorry, can one of you get my part of the check. I've got to get back to the store."

The case ends without knowing what Sherry will do when she gets back to the store. What are the possible alternatives? What is your recommendation for dealing with this issue with Gary and Charlie?

# PRACTICE CASE ANALYSIS

The following presents a case summary and contextual description, a timeline, key characters, and information about their communication styles and relationships, salient issues raised in the case, symptoms and root causes, and effective elements of communication.

Sherry is friends with Arly and Deb. The women became friends when each was hired by a national retailer. The women no longer work together, but have remained friends. Meeting for lunch is a way for them to stay in touch although it has been some time since they've been able to do this. Arly and Deb know few details about Sherry's job.

Sherry is the primary character. She works for Threads, a women's fashion boutique, which is owned by Charlie and is a family business. Charlie's son-in-law Gary directs operations for the boutique, which has 20 stores in upscale markets throughout the U.S. Bill, the other Threads employee, is the boutique's clothing designer.

At lunch, Sherry is visibly rushed. As the lunch conversation unfolds, Sherry talks more than Arly and Deb. Venting about her job, she describes how the store works and the roles of Charlie, Gary, and Bill. In response to questions from Arly and Deb, Sherry explores her role at Threads. Her disclosures reveal uncertainty and ambiguity, and also that she has broken a store norm by going to lunch during a sale. Sherry's inability or unwillingness to further explain how the store operates relative to the owner who has an office in her store location is the symptom for the root problem of not having established effective communication relationships with Charlie and Gary. It appears that Sherry does not understand the reason for the norm. She also does not appear to be concerned that she chose not to follow the norm—even after a warning phone call from Gary.

Despite Sherry's lack of a relationship with Bill, the boutique's designer, he calls her and encourages her to return to the store. Her uncertainty about this relationship is revealed.

# STATEMENTS ABOUT THE CASE

1. Sherry, Arly, and Deb are good friends. Conversation among them is comfortable and relaxed. Their friendship is strong enough to withstand significant periods of time between contact.
2. Sherry works for Threads, an upscale women's fashion boutique. Threads is owned by Charlie; its operations are managed by Gary, Charlie's son-in-law; Bill is the boutique's designer.
3. Sherry manages one retail store of a chain of boutiques. Charlie, Gary, and Bill have offices at that location. The three men are often absent.
4. Charlie has exerted strong control over Threads' operations; he appears to be grooming Gary to succeed him when he retires.
5. Although warned by Gary to return the store, Sherry mimics their conversation and decides to stay for dessert.

6. Bill calls Sherry to let her know that both Gary and Charlie are in the store; he encourages her to return.
7. There is a norm in the store of salespeople and the manager staying at the store during sales. Lunch is brought or catered in; no one takes a lunch break during a sale.

## QUESTIONS ABOUT THE CASE

1. How does a relatively new employee learn organizational norms? Is Sherry in a position to break or change the norms?
2. How would you characterize the communication relationships among Sherry, Charlie, Gary, and Bill? How would you characterize their communication network? What role does Bill play in the network?
3. How should Sherry handle the situation? With Bill? With Gary? With Charlie? How does Sherry determine to whom she should pay the most attention?
4. What are your recommendations to Sherry for handling the situation? What specifically should she say to whom? Or should she say nothing?
5. Sherry has communication responsibilities to both the store's owner (and management team) and to her sales staff. What is your advice for communicating those responsibilities?
6. Should Sherry talk directly with Charlie about her role in Threads? Why or why not?
7. Should Sherry talk directly with Bill about his phone call? Why or why not?
8. Should Sherry accept business calls while on a lunch break? Why or why not?
9. Is there any way Sherry's friends can help her with this situation?
10. Is Sherry managing her communication responsibilities effectively?

## THEORIES, PERSPECTIVES, OR RESEARCH THAT COULD BE USED TO ANALYZE THE CASE

1. Communication network theory
2. Uncertainty reduction
3. Organizational assimilation
4. Supervisor-subordinate relationships
5. Leader-member exchange
6. Work-life balance

# Organizational Culture

CHAPTER 1

# How Do You Get Anything Done Around Here?

## Marian L. Houser and Astrid Sheil

Kate Elliott,* a new product development specialist at Donaldson Family Foods, Inc., paced in her office and shuffled papers on her desk. She had a lot of work to do, but she couldn't seem to concentrate. It had been one month since she presented a comprehensive proposal for product testing to SMART, the Senior Management Action Review Team. She needed an answer on whether she could move forward on test-marketing an all-in-one insulated portable cooking bag that had been developed as the anchor product for a new line of high-end, quick fix, specialty picnic foods. The planned product launch and the portable cooking bag were scheduled to coincide with Memorial Day weekend, the traditional start of picnic season. Although Memorial Day was still six months away, Kate knew that her window of opportunity for completing the test-marketing was closing quickly. If she missed the time frame scheduled for Memorial Day weekend, there was a good chance that annual sales projections would fall short. She didn't want to think about the consequences. Kate wondered why she could not get a straight answer. Could their dallying be the result of the famous "Black Hole" she had been warned about when she first joined Donaldson Family Foods ten months earlier?

### THE BEGINNING

When Kate received a call from an executive recruiter about a "great opportunity" at Donaldson Family Foods, her immediate reaction was "No thanks, not interested." A recent MBA graduate with two years' experience under her belt at a *Fortune 500* food-manufacturing company, Kate was primed for the fast track. Her goal was to become one of the youngest national brand managers in the country by

---

*This case has been developed based on real organization(s) and real organizational experiences. Names, facts, and situations have been changed to protect the privacy of individuals and organizations.

the time she was 28. All that Kate knew about Donaldson Family Foods was that it was a privately held family company that had been canning vegetables since 1899. The products had not changed in over 100 years–even the labels had not changed in 50 years. To Kate, Donaldson Family Foods was a low-growth, low-margin commodity business. It was stale and old, and she had no interest in applying there. Then she received a phone call from Jeff Donaldson, the president and CEO of his family business. Stunned by his forthright candor in calling her directly, Kate agreed to come for an interview.

Jeff Donaldson was the fourth generation to lead the family business. A graduate of Duke University with an MBA from Michigan, Donaldson was groomed from birth to take over the company. During high school and college he worked summers at the canning plants, driving forklifts, hosing down equipment, and changing the glue canisters for the labeling machines. After graduate school, he started as a shift supervisor, eventually working his way up to plant manager. Before rising to the office of the president, Donaldson had done a tour of duty in the marketing department and served as chief financial officer for six years. At 45, the man knew his business.

Kate was impressed by Donaldson's charisma and sincerity. "You're just the type of person I want on my team," he had told her. "I'm ready to move into the high-growth, prepackaged, specialty foods market. I need bright, energetic, and creative people who can take ideas from concept to completion without a lot of interference from management." It was that last phrase, *without a lot of interference from management*, that caught Kate's attention. Kate was ready to manage a portfolio. Donaldson dangled the ultimate carrot in front of her. "If you come on board with me, your first project will be to handle the introduction of our new portable cooking bag at the same time we launch our new prepackaged specialty picnic foods next year. You handle this right, and you'll be a national brand manager before you know it." Kate was hooked.

She liked everyone she met at the company, the money was good, the on-site workout facility and juice bar were an immediate bonus, and the opportunity to become a national brand manager was definitely the trump card. Kate could not think of one reason she should not join the company.

## EARLY WARNING SIGNS

One of the first things Kate noticed during her first weeks at Donaldson Family Foods was how lax everyone seemed to be about office hours. At 7:30 every morning, her car was generally the first in the parking lot. Most of the marketing and new product development people did not arrive until 9:00 A.M. By 5:15 P.M., the parking lot had cleared out, except for a few cars. Kate chalked up the late start and the early departures to the emphasis on family that Jeff had stressed in their first meeting. "This company was founded by my grandfather 100 years ago on the simple premise of neighbors working together to make a better life for themselves,"

Donaldson had told her. "No one is expected to put in a 70-hour workweek. Time with the family is important. Even our plants close on Sundays and major holidays so workers can be with their families."

It did not take Kate long to feel comfortable. During her first few weeks on the job, someone in the main office dropped by her office nearly every day to chat and welcome her aboard. The place was full of nice people, so it caught her by surprise when, after offering a problem-solving remark, she was singled out at a staff meeting for being "too aggressive."

Rick Clark, her immediate supervisor, told her, "Now, Kate, that might be how you talked to others at your last employment, but around here, we do not attack each other in staff meetings."

Embarrassed, Kate stammered, "I'm sorry...I wasn't trying to hurt anyone's feelings...was just trying to look at what the objections might be if..."

Clark cut her off with a wave of his hand. "We know you don't know any better yet, but you'll learn. We keep it nice and friendly around here in all our conversations. It's the Donaldson Family Foods way."

In her office later that morning, Kate replayed the exchange over and over in her mind. She was confused. Tom Kadzinsky, a veteran product development specialist, poked his head in the door. "Mind if I talk to you for a minute, Kate?" he asked.

## THE CULTURE CONTRADICTION

Kate motioned for Tom to sit down. "Tom, what just happened to me in that meeting?" she queried.

"Ah, that was the official 'Welcome Aboard and Don't Rock the Boat Lecture' from Rick," he replied. "All of the relatively new people have gone through it, Kate." Kadzinsky shrugged.

"Do you mean we're not allowed to criticize or challenge anything in a staff meeting?" she asked.

"Yeah, that's pretty much it," he replied dryly. After a long silence, Tom continued, "I can see the wheels in your brain turning. You're trying to figure out what's going on here, right?"

"How do you get anything done around here?" she asked.

"Things get done eventually," Tom stressed. "This is a privately held company in a low-growth business. Because there's no big hurry, SMART–the Senior Management Action Review Team–always takes its time making decisions."

Kate was incredulous. "Wait a minute. Jeff Donaldson himself told me that the company was positioned to move into new, high-growth markets. If we're going to be competitive, we're going to have to make decisions in real time and get new products to market faster than our competition. All of that suggests decentralized decision making."

Tom smiled. "Yeah, it's even in our mission statement, but that's not the way things really work around here."

"Then why would they hire people like us? It makes no sense." Kate sighed. "I came here for the chance to be a national brand manager, to do cutting-edge work. I didn't come here to baby-sit a bunch of hundred-year-old products."

Tom looked out Kate's window onto the manicured lawn and landscaping in front of Donaldson Family Foods. "In my interview," Tom continued, "Donaldson promised that I would be in charge of branding a new line of Latin foods. I've been here three years and I have yet to roll out a single new product."

Kate sat silently, taking in this new disclosure.

"It's because of the Black Hole," Tom stated.

"What's that?" Kate asked.

"The *Black Hole* is the nickname the employees have given to the SMART group. In those weekly meetings of SMART, all initiatives, ideas, and proposals come to a grinding halt. Nothing moves forward until SMART has given its approval."

"How could there be a black hole when, according to Donaldson, the company hierarchy has been flattened to shorten the decision-making time?" she asked.

"Look, Kate," Tom offered as he turned to leave, "it's always a little frustrating at first here, but you'll get used to it, and why sweat it? The money's good, the hours can't be beat, and there is no pressure to perform. No one ever gets fired from Donaldson Family Foods."

Kate reached for her company manual. It was the first thing she had been given by the human resources manager when she joined the company. She opened to the inside cover and stared at the smiling, tan face of Jeff Donaldson. Even in photographs, he was charismatic, she thought. She reread the vision statement, next to his picture:

> At Donaldson Family Foods, we are committed to being the number one innovator of high-end, specialty food products. We will reach this goal by employing the best and the brightest, adhering to the best management practices, and offering the best value for our customers, suppliers, and vendors. To this end, we strive to provide a safe and congenial workplace for all employees, offer personal and professional improvement programs, and compensate generously for performance. We provide a business environment in which innovation and creativity can flourish, and people at all levels of the organization are empowered to make decisions as if they owned the company.

She agreed with every word in the vision statement. It sure looked good on paper.

## THE PROJECT

The day after Kate's conversation with Tom, Jeff Donaldson dropped by her office. He flashed his winning grin as he sat in the plush visitor's chair across from her desk. "I just wanted to check up on you and see how you are getting along," he started.

"I'm doing great," Kate offered hurriedly.

"Good!" he replied. "I know you are ready to break out from the back of the pack and become a lead sled dog for Donaldson Family Foods!" Kate made a mental note of how Donaldson always peppered his conversations with metaphors about dogs. "She's a greyhound," he had told Kate when describing the CFO, Katherine Halburton. "I hired her straight out of business school. She made it to the front of the pack in less than five years."

Donaldson seemed to have a rating system for all his employees. He referred to some as greyhounds (fast, with a strong desire to win), St. Bernards (loyal, but not very productive), or strays and puppies. Kate wondered if he had already settled on a dog rating for her.

Donaldson continued. "I think it's time for you to take on the cooking bag project we talked about during your interview." Kate took out a pad of paper and jotted down notes while Jeff Donaldson shared his ideas with her. As he left her office an hour later, he offered one more suggestion. "Call Angie, my secretary, and make sure she puts you first on the agenda. Can you have the numbers ready in three weeks?"

"I'll be ready," Kate said confidently. All concerns regarding Tom's warnings about the Black Hole went out of her head.

Kate worked tirelessly, putting together the numbers and rationale for the new portable cooking bag. The centerpiece of the plan was the focus group research. She could not recommend the company move forward with production of the bags without strong evidence from the focus group research. With calendar in hand, she estimated when everything had to be completed to make a Memorial Day kickoff. Kate called the focus group research company and told them to have everything ready in one week. "This shouldn't take long," she told the owner of the research company. "I've got the budget, the timeline, and the rationale all worked out. I know it's a 'go.' I just need to get the final green light from Mr. Donaldson."

During her presentation, Kate fielded questions from the senior vice presidents. At the end, Donaldson announced, "Kate, this is really excellent work. We will have an answer for you shortly." She departed the meeting confident about her performance and the plan. She went back to wait for the answer from SMART. Inwardly, she laughed at how gullible she had been to believe there was a black hole.

## THE BLACK HOLE MAKES ITS APPEARANCE

At the end of the week after Kate had made her presentation to SMART, the phone rang in her office. It was the president of the research company. "Hello, Kate? This is Dave Seavers at Independent Research. I've got a squad of people on standby waiting for your signal. What's the word? This is starting to cost me money." She felt terrible as she tried to stall for time. "I'm sorry, Dave. Jeff Donaldson has been out of touch this week with an emergency at the northern plant. I'll call you as soon as I have an answer. To be on the safe side, you better let everyone go for now."

Now, one month later in her office, Kate was lacking confidence with every breath. "This has got to be bad news," she fretted. "How could I have missed the mark so badly? Why doesn't one of them call me and at least tell me something?"

Kate drove home frustrated and tired from the lack of communication at Donaldson Family Foods. "This is not what I signed on for," she thought bitterly.

Monday morning, Kate called the president's secretary, Angie Parker, trying to sound confident.

"Hi, Angie. This is Kate Elliott in new product development. I need to set up an appointment with Mr. Donaldson as soon as possible."

"What's this regarding?" the president's secretary and gatekeeper asked coolly.

"Well, it's been one month since I presented the test marketing proposal at the weekly senior management meeting. I have a very tight deadline, and Mr. Donaldson assured me that he would get back to me promptly. I'm just following up because I have a lot of people on standby, waiting for the signal to begin. I don't have much time to spare if we're going to make the rollout in May. I just need to know where we are on this."

"Kate, if Mr. Donaldson said he would get back to you, I'm sure he will. Mr. Donaldson is in the Bahamas this week with clients and cannot be disturbed. When he returns next Monday, I will let him know you called."

"Monday! Angie, I really need an answer before then. Can't somebody else on SMART give me an answer?"

"I'm afraid you'll just have to wait until Mr. Donaldson returns."

Kate felt totally adrift. With each passing day, the chances of her making the Memorial Day weekend kickoff were fading quickly. "How could I have been so wrong about Jeff Donaldson and this place?" she thought. "Is he the consummate liar or was I naive to think I could make product development decisions on my own?"

Kate walked into the spacious break room, complete with fireplace and television, where employees gathered to chat, exchange pleasantries, and sample new products. The place looked the same as the day she started, but now she saw things with different eyes. "Jeff Donaldson may have flattened the organization, but he never empowered his people," she thought bitterly. "We're all just hanging around waiting to be told what to do."

Kate walked up to Tom Kadzinsky, who was pouring himself a second cup of coffee, the newspaper under his arm. "Does anything ever come out of the Black Hole?" Kate asked.

Tom looked at Kate sympathetically and said, "Yes, but generally not until you have completely abandoned the project and given up all hope on it."

Kate felt defeated. She stammered, "Why do you stay, Tom?"

"Kate, I may be here physically, but my heart and soul have left the building," Tom replied flatly. "I got my hand slapped so many times my first year, I quickly learned to keep my mouth shut, my thoughts to myself, and just do as little as possible. I have two kids in grade school, a wife, and they all like it here. There are worse things in life than not being fulfilled professionally. And I am one of many—just look at the parking lot. There are a lot of people with this organization who check out early every day."

There was a lag in the conversation and finally Tom said, "Come on, Kate. You'll get used to it, especially when you realize there's really nothing you can do about it."

Kate had given up a lot to come to Donaldson Family Foods. She thought about the friends and family she had left when she moved halfway across the country to take this job. What had seemed like such a promising career move now felt like a big mistake. "I don't know, Tom. I just don't know...." Her voice trailed off.

## CHAPTER 2

# Communicating and Leading
# Change in Organizations

### Christina M. Bates

### THE RIGHT DECISION?

As she pulled into a parking spot and wiped her moist brow from the Texas heat, Kathy Fuller* thought about the decision she had recently made. She had just moved with her family from a small town outside of Chicago to southern Texas for an assistant vice-president position with Third Bank. She had spent weeks convincing her two boys and husband that the move was "worth it" because she would finally have the chance to run her own site and make changes in a sometimes splintered, challenged organization.

"Of course this is what I want," she said out loud as she stared through her windshield at the large, dull brown building in front of her. Inside, several hundred people were processing customer payments to ensure that when John Doe in Vermont mailed his check to the cable company (a customer of Third Bank), that check would be processed for the cable company and accurately reflected on John Doe's account.

Looking at the dashboard, she saw that the time had gotten away from her–it was nearly 8:30 A.M. "I'd better go in," she muttered as she reached for her briefcase and the cold coffee she had forgotten to drink on the ride over. Staring at the building one last time, she pulled the large glass door open and proceeded to the security desk.

### CHANGES AT THIRD BANK

"Kathy Fuller," she said as she fumbled through her briefcase to locate her security badge.

---

*This case has been developed based on real organization(s) and real organizational experiences. Names, facts, and situations have been changed to protect the privacy of individuals and organizations.

"Good morning, Ms. Fuller. I'm Wes. Work the first shift here on security. Pleased to meet you. First day, huh?"

"Yes. Pleased to meet you too, Wes. Ah, can you help me out, which way to my office?"

"Down the hall, second door on the left," Wes said with a chuckle as he dangled his finger towards the hallway. "Great to meet you and good luck."

Kathy turned on her heels and gave Wes a doubtful, crooked smile.

"Good luck," she repeated to herself, wondering what he meant. Why would I need luck, anyway? I know this business. I've been with this Bank for eight years now. Survived three mergers. Came up through the ranks–processor, team lead, shift supervisor, assistant site manager, and now site manager. What's luck got to do with it? As she reached for her office keys, a cheery "hello" broke her train of thought.

"Hello, you must be Ms. Fuller," a tall, thin man who looked to be in his early twenties, said with a cautious smile.

"Yes," Kathy laughed to herself. "I think so. It's been that kind of morning."

"I'm Matt. I'm the business lead for the frontline employee quality teams. I couldn't wait to meet you. Heard lots of good things. You know you're really needed around here."

"Nice to meet you, Matt. I think I have a meeting on my schedule with you and the three shift supervisors later today."

"Yes, we thought it would be a good idea for us to get together–you know, talk about Carson (Carson, Texas). Fill you in on how things are here."

"Great. I need all the help I can get. See you at eleven?"

"Will do. I'm looking forward to it."

As she sat down behind her new desk, Kathy thought about Matt's words–"fill you in on how things are here." Kathy was no newcomer to this business. She had experienced all the ups and downs at Third Bank. Most recently, she had had more ups than downs. Third Bank had recently embarked on a massive quality improvement initiative and had begun the process of transitioning to what Damon Hauss, CEO of Third Bank, referred to as a "participative organization" with self-directed teams and a "flatter structure where ideas from every corner of the organization are valued."

Kathy knew Mr. Hauss had long grappled with what he called "the big, lumbering, bureaucratic giant" that Third Bank had become after several years of mergers and acquisitions. Kathy recalled his speech at a management retreat held earlier in the year.

"We've become a slow-moving, red-tape-littered, splintered organization," Hauss exclaimed with his arms outstretched across the podium as if reaching out to touch the more than 200 managers seated in the large ballroom. "Communication and interaction across divisions and functional units are poor, at best. Folks in check processing have no idea what the folks handling customer service do on a daily basis. How many of us really talk to the folks who are doing the work–processing the checks, running the sorter machines?"

Kathy recalled the embarrassed, uncomfortable smiles that appeared on so many of the managers' faces seated in that ballroom when they pondered the answer to Mr. Hauss' pointed question and she recalled how he continued to describe the changes he wanted.

"We need to flatten this organization, strip away the bureaucracy and red tape, tear down the silos, open the channels of communication, and allow those who do the work to be involved deeply in making this organization a better place for all of us. Self-directed teams are part of our answer."

## THE TEAMS: 'TAKING OFF' OR 'TROUBLED'?

The sound of Kathy's cell phone vibrating on her desk interrupted her thoughts of the CEO's presentation. Dismissing the message for a moment, her thoughts turned to the self-directed teams she had worked so hard to nurture while in her old position in Chicago. Pat, the Chicago site manager, and Kathy had given the teams breathing room to develop a culture of accountability, respect, and empowerment. The Chicago teams were making good progress. It was fair to say, they had "taken off," to say the least. Kathy had challenged the teams to reduce their error rates by 50% within four months and when they exceeded the challenge in just three months, she purchased, as promised, a combination television-DVD for the lunchroom. The Chicago teams then challenged themselves to increase internal and external customer satisfaction by 75%. When they met the challenge four months later, Kathy provided them with a team budget a part of which they could use to have a pizza party complete with team member prizes and awards. By year-end, employee morale was at its highest ever at the Chicago site. It was becoming clearer each day that frontline employees were beginning to trust management, to feel empowered and fulfilled, and to take ownership for improvements.

But Kathy knew, from talking to colleagues who were at other Third Bank sites, that most of the other teams weren't doing nearly as well. Most teams still deeply distrusted management and considered Third Bank's new plan to become a participative organization to be the "flavor of the month" that would soon blow over and things would be back to normal: do something wrong, you get yelled at…management stepping on your neck…little or no communication about the day-to-day.

Kathy began to reflect on what many of Third Bank's management referred to as the "troubled" teams. These teams did not receive the necessary management support. She knew of several Third Bank managers who believed in, and lived, the classical management structure and approach–hierarchy, separation of power, bureaucracy. These managers were not the least bit interested in being part of a participative organization. Rather than encouraging and nurturing the teams at their sites, these managers merely paid "lip service" to Mr. Hauss' vision for Third Bank. Consequently, their teams suffered. Performance improvements were lacking. Morale was dangerously low.

"Wow," she thought. "Already quarter to eleven. I'd better get my mind on things around here. I have a feeling this meeting is going to be interesting." She spun around to flip on the coffee maker on the shelf behind her desk and picked up her cell phone to check the message she had just received.

## THE MANAGEMENT TEAM MEETING

At a few minutes before eleven, Matt knocked on Kathy's office door.

She looked up from her computer monitor and said "Oh, hi Matt. Come on in. Are the others with you?"

"Yes," Matt said with a smile. "Are we meeting in here or would you like to go to the conference room?"

"I think we can meet in here. Let's sit around the table."

The three shift supervisors walked into Kathy's office, following Matt. Debbie Borders, a tall, thin woman in her early forties, Christy Flynn, a petite woman in her early thirties, and Sean Cooper, a tall man in his late forties, introduced themselves to Kathy and sat down at the round table in the corner of her office.

"Well, it's so nice to finally meet all of you," Kathy said with a reassuring smile. "I am hoping to use this time to get to know each of you a bit more and to learn more about Carson. Why don't you each just tell me a bit about yourself and your time at this site?"

"Okay, I've lived in Texas all my life and began working at this site 10 years ago back when it was Second Bank," Debbie said. "I began as a processor, then a team lead, and two years ago I was promoted to shift supervisor."

Then Sean spoke up. "I moved here from the East Coast six years ago. I began my career in the banking industry with Main Street Bank in downtown Dallas and transitioned to this job three years ago. I like this place so much better than my old job at Main Street!"

"Well, as you know Kathy, I am the business lead here and have been in this role now for about two years," Matt shared as he sat forward in his chair. "I work closely with the frontline employee quality teams to help them schedule and plan for meetings, develop performance metrics, and generally boost morale around here. I joined Third Bank just about three years ago as an assistant shift supervisor and was moved into my current position shortly after joining when the former business lead moved to a position at Third Bank headquarters. Christy, you're up."

"Hmm. Let's see. I've lived here all my life and I began my position here two years ago," Christy said in a thoughtful tone. "I started like Debbie, as a processor, and then jumped to shift supervisor. I'm really glad you're here. This place needed a change."

"That's the feeling I'm getting, Christy," Kathy said nervously. "I am counting on you four to fill me in. What's going on?"

The team then told Kathy their perceptions of the previous management team at Carson. The previous management team ran a very hierarchical, traditional organization. All decisions were made at the management level and no one on the shop floor dared to even knock on the site manager's door. Kathy listened intently as the team continued.

"You know, Kathy, it has been pretty bad here," Debbie said in a serious tone. "The frontline employee quality teams have long since abandoned any desire to excel. They haven't had a team meeting in months. Carson's quality measures, such as error rates and defect rates, are at an all time high—we are not even close to where we need to be. If you walk around Carson, you'll notice that the morale here is the lowest of the low."

Kathy could feel her breakfast like a lump in her stomach. What have I gotten into? she thought to herself as her mind raced.

"As the business lead, I've listened to the quality teams' concerns," Matt interrupted. "They feel that their voices are never heard. They don't feel like they have a role or a place in this organization. They've lost their will to come in here and do good work. They think that management doesn't care and that the self-managed teams are just another management ploy. I can't seem to get through to them that things are changing for the better around here. I've really tried—offered my help, tried to boost morale, tried to be open and listen. But, they are so down because of the previous management team, that I don't know that we can change things now. I don't know how we can get their trust back."

"You know, Kathy, with all of the changes at Third Bank—mergers and management changes—I sometimes feel like I don't know what to expect next," Christy said as she leaned her elbows on the edge of the table. "And I'm more in the loop than the frontline employees because I'm a supervisor. But, the previous manager wouldn't let us do anything without her oversight and permission. We couldn't even discuss the employees' work performance with them—this went through her as well. It really was tough and it's still tough because the employees have lost faith. In some ways, I think we have too."

Matt, Debbie, and Sean nodded in agreement as Christy sat back in her chair.

## KATHY'S CHALLENGE

"Well," Kathy said as she sat with her chin resting on the palms of her hands, "this is not good. Senior management is watching this site closely because of its poor numbers and low ranking. I was recruited because they felt I could change things. I knew the previous management team didn't really work out, but I couldn't have anticipated this. I think we need to get our heads together to figure out how to approach change. I want the people at this site to be happy and to enjoy coming to work each day. I don't see why we can't have that. But, I know it's going to be tough—it's not going to happen over night, but we've got to start working at it. I value everyone here and I want to hear their concerns—my door is open."

"Thanks, Kathy," Sean said in a relieved tone. "I think we needed to hear that."

"Yeah," Matt agreed, "we really did."

"The time has flown," Kathy responded as she glanced at the clock on her office wall. "Let's plan to meet tomorrow to discuss this further. Can all of you make it, or should we shoot for another time?"

The team agreed to meet the next day, thanked Kathy, and walked back to the shop floor. Kathy remained seated at the round table and reviewed their discussion in her mind. She slowly moved back to her thoughts in her car earlier that morning.

After a few minutes, Kathy stood up and walked over to her desk. As she sat down in her swivel chair, she felt pangs of doubt. Could she really bring about the change that Carson desperately needed? How would she do it? Would it work?

"Yes," she said out loud. "This was the right decision. I'll help my team to change the culture here. I know we can do it."

Kathy opened her email and began to go through her overflowing inbox.

CHAPTER 3

# Managing a Merger

### Cheryl Cockburn-Wootten, Mary Simpson,

### and Theodore E. Zorn Jr.

The buzzer went off on Peter's alarm clock. Today was *not* the day to hit the snooze button. Peter knew he was going to have a long day–if not year–ahead of him with his next managerial assignment for his company, Glass X. Glass X had recently merged with another glass manufacturing company called Krys Klear, and Peter's new role was managing the "new" Hamilton branch. Years previously, after his graduation with a Communication Studies degree at Waikato University in Hamilton, New Zealand, Peter had applied for a position at Krys Klear. He was unsuccessful but the company had initially appealed to him because he knew that they had a long and successful retailing and distribution history in New Zealand. But that was years ago and now Peter knew that in the domestic market Krys Klear had lost its competitive edge and was finally taken over by–or "merged with," as the official announcement had said–Glass X.

As Peter picked at his breakfast he mulled over what reaction he might have from the staff at the Hamilton branch. For the staff it all happened so quickly, and he was worried how he might manage this situation and turn this branch around into a successful outlet for Glass X. The merger was announced to the Krys Klear staff four weeks ago and many of their branches were in the process of being closed or merged with Glass X branches. The Hamilton branch of Krys Klear had merged with Glass X. Most of the Krys Klear staff members were made redundant (laid off) on Friday, although some were given the option to take a new position or leave the company. Both Hamilton managers were also made redundant because each had been operating an underperforming branch. Individually they were told by senior management, "Sorry, but you don't have the skills or experience to manage the new merged branch." Because Peter had already "turned around" two

*This case has been developed based on real organisation(s) and real organisational experiences. Names, facts, and situations have been changed to protect the privacy of individuals and organisations.

underperforming branches for Glass X, he now had the unenviable role of branch manager at Hamilton.

Peter wasn't daunted by the task before him as he remembered his dad saying to him, "The things you can't control don't waste time worrying about. Only focus on the things you can actually change." So with this advice Peter felt reasonably confident he would succeed as he had done the other times for this company. Growing up he had been involved in many of his parents' business ventures–one of which had been a glass company. Peter liked and understood the glass business.

On the drive to work, a sudden rainstorm brought floods into the Hamilton streets and traffic came to a standstill. Although, as Peter recalled, this traffic jam was nothing like the ones he had experienced while working in the UK and USA. While stuck in traffic, his mobile phone caught him off guard with its sharp and loud ring. Laurence Browne, the Area Manager, called to wish him luck in turning this underperforming branch around. Peter reassured him that he could do it: "Don't worry mate, this is not the first time I've had this kind of thing–nor the last." But Peter knew it would be a challenge and added, "The main aim is getting the staff working together within a very short time. And I know I'm on my own."

Still, sitting in the traffic jam Peter recalled saying to his wife Alice, "The companies have two different ways of doing everything and the management in both of them hasn't been very strong. It's going to be really tough working with the two different cultures." The traffic began to move forward.

On arriving at work, Peter called in Samantha, his new secretary, and asked her to call everyone to a staff meeting that evening. "And make sure there is food and drink, Samantha, we want people as relaxed as possible–including me!"

Peter spent the rest of the day familiarizing himself with the branch layout, and introducing himself to staff as he went checking to see if they could make the meeting. When he approached groups of staff, conversations would stop, and he had to speak first. It was clearly awkward for everyone.

That evening in the staff room, Peter began: "Welcome everyone and thanks for coming. I met most of you today, but for those whom I missed, I'm Peter Franks, the new manager of the branch. I called this meeting because I think it's important that we start off on the right foot. It's been tough over the last week, and we need to get a sense of direction from here. So we'll start with a few words from Laurence Browne, our area manager, who then has to leave straight away for another meeting in Tauranga. And then I'll talk for a bit. Feel free to ask questions."

A short wave of murmuring crossed the room as Laurence stood up to speak. He talked about the history of the organisation before moving onto the more recent events. "The merger was the easy decision, but how to implement it was tough for us because we knew that one way or another people were going to lose jobs. In the end our analysis was that the overall performance for both operations wasn't very good. Neither has been profitable for some time, and the assumption was that if we could hang on to the majority of the business with fewer overheads we should make money in theory. We've done our best to merge as many branches as possible. Peter's charged with turning this branch into a successful business, and it can only be done with your input. Obviously the important part is that everyone does their own part, their own little bit to get there."

After Laurence had finished and left, Peter began to talk. After a few preliminary words he said, "My main aim is to get everyone working together so that we are profitable. And an important part of that is to retain the customers of the two branches. We can't afford to lose them. We hardly know each other, so tonight spend a little time meeting new people–because you'll be working together within a very short time. I know many of you have questions, and are upset about the changes, but at my level [of the organisation] I am not party to a lot of the workings or the reasons for things happening, so I can only focus on what I do know and just try and deal with other problems. Same goes for everyone here." After a noticeable silence, Peter went on, "I can't do it all by myself. I can't go out there and fix the broken windows, serve customers, and answer the phone. Everyone has to do their little bit and if we all work as a team in doing what was required individually the results will follow. If we don't perform as a branch, the whole branch will go, and it won't be one job, it will be everyone's. Glass X expects this new combined branch to make a profit and we're very lucky to have survived this merger."

The staff were still silent, so Peter finished, "I'm treating the merger as a fresh start for everyone. We can't change the past–it's been, it's gone, these are the new rules and we have to work within them. So rather than focusing on what's happened let's look to the future and get on with it."

Despite this emphasis on a new outlook, in the first few weeks that followed Peter found staff often approaching him with their frustrations and anger about the merger. He would listen as best he could and then say, "Look mate, the best you can do is put the past behind you, and get on with the job."

## MAKING CHANGES: MONITORING WORK PRACTICES

Late one Friday, having had an afternoon of heavy discussion with some members of staff regarding the branch's inability to reach sales targets, Peter called into his favourite bar on the off-chance his mate Finn would be there. After a couple of beers Peter was talking about his work problems to Finn. "The previous managers were hopeless–I'm left cleaning up. They employed people who don't know what they're doing–no technical skill, no people skill, no business knowledge–NOTHING! And they didn't manage them–they're getting away with murder, using the system to suit themselves."

Finn responded, "Hey mate, sounds like you've got to put in strong controls and work out roles and responsibilities."

"Yeah, don't I know it!" said Peter, "That's this weekend's work for me!" A few beers later Peter got a taxi home.

Over the weekend Peter considered his options. With his previous experience in the industry he was well aware of what could be achieved in one day's work. He spent Sunday morning going over branch job descriptions. On Sunday night he said to Alice, "I know what I'm going to do with this lot: I'll work with each staff member one-to-one and apply the pressure on those who aren't up to speed." So, in the weeks that followed, Peter began to monitor the employees' work and quickly became aware of who was not achieving the expected daily outputs of window repairs.

Two auto-glaziers (workers who repair automobile windshields and windows) stood out as "non-performing": Dave Smith and Barry Morgan. Peter knew that an auto glazier could complete between six and eight jobs in a normal working day. For example, windscreen (windshield) repair should take two hours while a door should take only 30 minutes. Peter met with Dave and Barry to make sure they knew these performance standards, and both men agreed to try and meet them. It was part of the company customer service policy that customers were always given a price and estimated time for the jobs. Peter noticed that over a three-week period Dave and Barry consistently failed to meet the set standards.

Dave and Barry had been long-time employees of Krys Klear. They had each worked for the company for nearly 15 years, but before the merger they had worked in different departments. After the merger they had been brought together as a team. As in most New Zealand firms, Glass X had a 15-minute morning and afternoon break. Dave and Barry took their breaks from 10 to 10:15 A.M. and 3 to 3:15 P.M. While walking around the branch, Peter noticed that Dave and Barry were often in the staff room when he stopped in at 20 past the hour. "Hey guys, it's past your break–time to get back to work." It was beginning to sound like a broken record; he was getting increasingly irritated at having to tell them to get back to work.

The final straw came at the end of the month. The telephone rang and it was Andrea, the Customer Services Manager. "Peter, we've got another customer on the phone complaining about her car not being ready. This customer is really annoyed as her first appointment wasn't kept."

Peter replied, "I'll deal with it, and try to placate her with a big discount." He groaned and contacted the angry customer. When he called Andrea to confirm the customer's discount, she told him, "Hey Pete, more bad news. This months' branch earnings are down and 20% short of target–seems the office staff have been booking fewer jobs because Dave and Barry aren't completing their jobs on time."

Peter decided to talk to Dave and Barry individually about their work. In their respective meetings with Peter, Dave and Barry challenged Peter. Barry actually shouted at him, "You combined windows and doors into one workshop–what do you expect? Of course we give a hand to each other–what's the problem? We're working together–just as you asked."

Peter thought to himself, "Oh no! The two of them doing one job and getting half as much done." Peter calmly said, "I don't mind you helping each other, pro-vided it's after you've finished your own work."

But despite the individual talks Peter found that the men continued their prac-tice of working together. In the end he said to them both "Each time we talk about working independently, you say 'yeah, yeah, yeah,' and then the next day nothing changes. What is it with you guys?" After many more frustrating meetings, and after several occasions where they were paid overtime so the jobs could be completed on time, Dave and Barry began to meet the set standards.

Andrea walked into Peter's office having just completed the figures for the month. "Well done!" she said, handing him a box of chocolates. "We've improved the margin–only 5% short of targets this month; still a wee way to go for a full celebration."

"Excellent timing," said Peter, picking out a hard caramel, "I've just this afternoon received two resignations–one from Dave and one from Barry. I put them under pressure to perform, and after eight weeks they leave. I am so relieved; I reckon when we replace them we'll double our output."

Peter advertised and interviewed two new replacement staff. This time he reviewed the employment policies and job descriptions and made clear his expectations from the start.

While monitoring the work of the other employees Peter found a number of employees who exceeded his expectations. One of them was Joe McGinty, a long-term employee from the old Krys Klear company. Peter called Joe into his office and said, "Joe, you're an excellent employee and I know that in Krys Klear you were an excellent foreman. We need a good man here too, Joe. Do you want to continue in a foreman position with Glass X?" Peter was surprised by Joe's response–a flat "No thanks!" In the following weeks, Peter noticed with sadness that Joe became increasingly uncooperative; he didn't work any overtime and would not mix with the other staff members during breaks or social activities. After six months Joe transferred to one of the Auckland branches.

One month later, Peter was called to an area meeting at this branch and while there he bumped into Joe. Joe greeted Peter with enthusiasm and Peter thought, "He's a changed man!" Surprised, Peter asked, "What's happened to you, Joe–won the lottery, have you?" Joe laughed and answered, "No mate. I'm enjoying being here–you know this branch is mostly staff from Krys Klear. I didn't like it when everything changed to Glass X. I'm really happy here–name's different, but the people haven't got the Glass X influence. It's a great place to work."

Peter returned to Hamilton, but found out that a couple of months later the Auckland branch where Joe worked had been closed. Peter hoped that Joe would accept a transfer back to his branch, but was told by Laurence, the area manager, "Joe accepted redundancy–like most of the staff there. Pity, he was a good foreman."

## MAKING CHANGES: IMPROVING STAFF RELATIONS

Peter and Laurence had just finished their three-monthly audit of the Hamilton branch. "Well, Pete," said Laurence, "it's been just over six months and I can't believe what you've done to this place! You've done it again–the impossible–this branch is doing well for the first time in a long time."

After Laurence had left, Peter, quietly pleased with himself, reflected on his achievements. Even though after six months 60% of the original staff had left, the branch was now one of the top performing branches for the company. Peter called in Samantha, his secretary, "Sam, I think it's time to celebrate. Let's have a social evening. Can you organise it please? Make sure there's plenty to eat and drink, and get some kind of music: Time to spend a bit of what we've earned!" The branch was now performing so well that there were funds to support social activities for the staff.

A staff social club was formed with regular social events including fortnightly 10-pin bowling with drinks and pizzas. However, 10 months after the merger, Peter received a call from Laurence, "Sorry mate, Glass X now has a policy that all social clubs must stop. We can't afford to get liquor licenses."

"Oh what!!" replied Peter, "That kind of policy will put a damper on everything we've achieved here! The branch is starting to jell quite nicely and now all of a sudden we get told by head office, no more drinking!"

"Sorry, Peter, we've got to think of our image and sales. We can't be seen as a bunch of boozers now, can we?" With this Laurence hung up. Peter thought a few minutes. "Well, I guess there is nothing stopping me from turning the staff meetings into a social event, with some food and a few beers."

With drinks and nibbles at staff meetings, Peter found they lasted longer. There was more time for chatting. As well as including some social fun at the staff meetings, Peter also introduced staff feedback sessions as part of the staff meeting agenda. These sessions focused on improving work flow, work environment, and occupational health and safety, which included the number of accidents, lost time, and injuries.

In the bar one evening after work Peter met up with his old mate Finn. He recounted what had happened at the branch since he saw Finn that evening many months ago. Finn was interested in the staff meeting and feedback sessions: "So what do you do in those feedback sessions, Pete?"

Peter told Finn, "On the whole they went pretty good. There's one guy who always has a better way who says 'I don't think we should be doing it this way.' And so on. He tends to try and rule and take over those sessions, but because we're running quite smoothly at the moment not a lot comes out of it–thankfully!

"I try to focus on positive things in the meeting. Normally at the start it's all good news rather than bad news; maybe the odd time but hardly ever do I try and bring up negative issues in the staff meeting. Any negative issues I leave to be dealt with one-by-one and in private rather than in a group set-up. I always feel that I wouldn't want to be rapped over the knuckles in public, so it's my policy not to do it to anyone else either."

"Sounds like you enjoy them," said Finn.

"Yeah–funnily enough," Peter continued. "I enjoy the feedback sessions and the staff contribute so many suggestions. I just listen to each idea, and then rather than saying 'Good idea' at the time, I take it away from the meeting, investigate what is possible, and then report back at the next meeting. Often this means that I have to say, 'I've talked to so-and-so about this but no, good idea but not the right time.' Also, I find that sometimes staff approach me individually at other times–straight after the meeting, for example–to mention something that has gone wrong on the job. So I ask them how they would resolve the problem and how they could help. I figure staff talking about their problems is better than hiding them–like they used to! And I make sure that I thank everyone for their contribution, because obviously everyone contributed to the result, not just one person."

"You know," said Finn, "most managers seem to always focus on the problems, to get people to work harder, to do a better job, to be nicer, to dress cleaner, or to get a haircut because you look scruffy. But staff recognition is just as important. When you get a letter or a phone call from a customer saying 'well done,' you need to talk to the staff member, tell them the customer was really pleased with the service. Sounds like that branch is coming along! Let's hope it keeps going that way. Have a beer on me, then it's my shout for dinner." The evening finished with Peter resolving to meet with Finn more often.

## CHAPTER 4

# Merged, Incompatible
# IT Cultures

## Jeanne S. McPherson

"What a challenge!" Tom Bannister* thought as he assembled his notes for a bi-weekly staff meeting. As manager of Computeam, Tom directed a computing services supervisory team in the new Information Technology Department of a large state university. He knew team members were threatened by the recent merging of the telecommunication and computing services departments. Specializing in computer design and engineering, Computeam had survived the merger intact and continued to provide customary computing services to the campus. However, team members nervously awaited news of department changes, and Tom was the newsbearer.

A long-time campus employee in his late thirties, Tom's easy-going manner was usually reflected in a slight smile and a twinkle in his eyes. He presented an attitude of seriousness toward work, yet with a touch of humor. But today he had little to make him smile.

Technological convergence made an integrated information technology (IT) department a reasonable university goal. In addition, *reinvent government* trends promoted accountability and efficiency throughout the state university system. Unfortunately, the traditional work approaches of the merged technical units clashed. Even more disturbing to some Computeam supervisors was the emerging dominance of the telecommunication unit, with its commitment to standardized IT customer services. Most Computeam members preferred customized computer services that provided targeted solutions, rather than standardized or off-the-shelf programs.

Tom's attention returned to the upcoming Computeam meeting. He considered his choices in presenting new changes to the team. He knew efficiency and

---

*This case has been developed based on real organization(s) and real organizational experiences. Names, facts, and situations have been changed to protect the privacy of individuals and organizations.

cost effectiveness were driving management decisions. How could he make the changes palatable for his staff while promoting camaraderie, individuality, and highly valued customized computing services?

Taking one last look at the agenda, Tom walked into the conference room to meet with his Computeam members. After highlighting the agenda for the meeting, he passed around some photocopied material, casually commenting: "These are two articles we're circulating around the building. One is called, 'How to Get Into the Academy: How to Survive the Higher Learning (Arguing) Culture.' It's very interesting. And then the other one, if you're interested, talks about organizational management, and some of the factors that either enable or disable an organization from responding to changes."

"Does that mean you're expecting a change?" a team member asked.

Tom grinned in response. "It's a smooth and subtle way of saying, 'Hold on to your seats—the big one's coming!'"

## CONTRASTS IN OCCUPATIONAL PRACTICES: REFLECTING ON CLASHING SUBCULTURES

After the meeting Tom asked himself, "Why is this so difficult?" He had worked with the key players throughout the merged department and knew that they were all committed to providing efficient IT services for their campus customers. "It's not a matter of finding the right message," he reasoned, "and it's not that people differ in their view of customers. It just seems like their work cultures negate each other's way of doing things."

The merged technology units provided campus users with voice mail, Internet, computer laboratories, training, and related IT services. To ensure consistent quality of these services throughout the campus, the IT department director, George Mitchell, had decided to introduce into the university an organizational model similar to the best practices in the private sector. However, competing ideas between telecommunication and computing units for providing IT customer service threatened this goal.

Tom considered the subcultural distinctions between computing and telecom services, remembering a colleague's description of the computing techies:

> People sprawled all around a small room discussing options for solving a user's problem. The leader, an eccentric, computer genius from Berkeley University–a 60s-era, high-tech innovator–calmly clips his toenails. A dog roams from person to person for a pat or a snack. The office, as well as its occupants, appears disheveled, just like home.

Tom smiled to himself as his colleague's description of the telecom style came to mind:

> A long-distance call to the service center from Europe with questions regarding a variety of offerings from the university. A new professor needs a telephone and voice mail, equipment and connections. A student makes a long-distance call from an open

dormitory telephone–an issue of security. An environment of efficiency is needed here, a mini AT&T.

These contrasting images triggered the thought of a department manager's recent assessment, sarcasm evident in his tone of voice: "Telecommunications was a very directed, business organization, while computing was a very free form, you know, wear your shorts into work, flip flops, work out during the lunch hours. Sure. Exactly!"

Tom reflected on a meeting he attended not long ago in the telecom group. Teleteam was charged with implementing a campus upgrade in voice mail, and its members included specialists from a private-sector contractor.

The Teleteam meeting had proceeded according to a written agenda. Bill, Teleteam's project manager, reviewed the schedule and efficiently moved into a checklist of problems: "OK. If you are associated with task notes, review them, shoot me an email. Any questions about task schedule? Now, to our problem list. Server 4?"

A technician from the contracted organization quickly replied, "It wasn't Server 4. I checked it, it tested out."

Bill nodded and moved to the next item on the agenda. "IVR Financial Aid."

The contractor's project manager urged an immediate response. "Kathy?"

"Yes," Kathy replied, "I was on the phone with John Jacobson. I tested it, no problems since 9:30."

Bill moved to the next agenda item: "DNA."

No one replied, and there was an uncomfortable gap. "Oh, that's me!" announced another technician. And the group burst out in laughter.

"I was looking right at you!" Bill scolded.

The technician promptly responded on task, "I'm waiting to see...."

"How different those meetings are from ours," Tom thought. "We tend to interact spontaneously, freely digressing from the agenda, and sometimes squabbling like professional siblings." He was reminded of the different work styles between telecom and computing services at his next staff meeting.

## HIGH-TECH CONFLICT: STANDARDIZATION VERSUS CUSTOMIZATION OF IT SERVICES

Until the merger, Computeam members had supervised technical experts assigned to specific areas of the campus, developing relationships with users, and providing customized solutions to meet their needs. However, shortly after the merger George Mitchell introduced a telecom-based, centralized customer response system called the Tier 4 Help System.

The Tier 4 system required university customers to call a one-stop troubleshooting number, starting at Tier 2, or lowest level of difficulty. (Tier 1 is self-service, where the user solves the problem.) The Tier 2 troubleshooter on the telephone line would evaluate the problem and either resolve it or refer the caller to another expert, up to the highest level, Tier 4.

Computeam members claimed customers would try to jump immediately to Tier 4, preferring the highest-level experts to solve their particular problems, no matter what the difficulty might be. In addition, customers often called individuals they knew and trusted rather than an anonymous help desk. In the Computeam meeting where Tom introduced the Tier 4 model, he encouraged a discussion of these issues.

Supporting the Tier 4 model, Kim affirmed the need for centralized IT services: "In today's world, it makes absolutely zero sense to focus service on individual departments. It has to be central or it's a *total waste of time. It really is.*"

Steve objected, "I think the only thing we're dealing with here is there's no Tier 2 person within a building. I call some number and say, I'm so and so, I have such and such service, and our file services are currently unavailable, and you hand it off to IT services Tier 2–no personal help."

"Yeah, there's a real issue here," Jack chimed in.

Understanding that department leaders had already embraced centralized IT support services, Kim attempted to redirect the discussion: "OK, but take Microsoft, or take Dell. Take any of those companies. *They* have centralized support services. They've got millions of users!"

Jack wailed, "I'm not *talking* about them, I'm talking about *us!*" And the entire team burst out in laughter.

Tom took advantage of the light moment to underscore the new departmental direction. "Well, I think you can divide this problem along the lines of a business model that makes sense. We can only provide the level of customer service that is funded in our budget. Is there a way we can support the Tier 4 model and possibly still be available for special user needs?" As the meeting continued, he successfully averted a team breach while setting the stage for a change in client-provider interactions. At the end of the meeting Tom sighed in relief, thinking, "Things may work out yet."

## DEPARTMENT RESTRUCTURING AS A MEANS OF CULTURAL CHANGE: THE TENSIONS ESCALATE

The next Computeam staff meeting brought further challenges, however. George Mitchell had decided that the Educational Technology group should be absorbed into Computeam, arguing that in today's university environment, educational technology emphasizes computer-aided classroom instruction. Tom knew that the restructuring plan would further decrease the independence the computing workers had enjoyed.

At the staff meeting, Tom attempted to announce the change neutrally. "The thing we're gonna have to keep in mind is that Education Technology is gonna be under us. The campus doesn't have any more money to support them. So, what will *probably* happen, if I had to see in a crystal ball, is we'll push resources back into labs that are more directly in support of instruction. That's what I see on the horizon. It doesn't matter, really, if we agree with it philosophically or not, I think that's the only way the campus will be able to go."

Team members were uncustomarily silent as Tom spoke, reacting in shock to this announcement.

"I'm meeting with George and the senior management team after lunch, today," Tom continued, "I will give them our perspective of this decision. Carla, Ben, I'd like you to be there as resources to provide your perceptions of the effects on users with this plan. Any other thoughts?"

No one responded. As the meeting ended, team members filed out quietly.

"Yeah, what a challenge!" Tom Bannister thought later as he gathered his notes for the meeting with George and the senior management team. "What are our choices in this changing IT work environment?"

## CHAPTER 5

# Your Attitude Determines
# Your Altitude

### Erika L. Kirby

### WEDNESDAY, JULY 25TH

As Kalee* methodically packed for the Colorado "team-building" mountain climb sponsored by We-R-Radio for its management team, she remembered the first week of January. Her mother Lena (a manager at one of We-R-Radio's many stations) had called in a panic: "You won't believe what I have to do for work. I just got a letter from Jack Welton that we are definitely going to climb a fourteener as a company-sponsored activity!"

Jack Welton was the owner of We-R-Radio who conceived of the mountain-climbing trip and created 95% of the correspondence with affiliate station managers about the climb. A "fourteener" was any of the 55 mountains in Colorado that has a peak of over 14,000 feet above sea level.

Lena's voice shook as she read from the letter: "There are several objectives: bonding, enjoyment, teamwork, and health. Most of all, we want it to be fun and a reward for your hard work. It is also something you have to take seriously beginning RIGHT NOW. The idea is to get you in shape." Lena continued, "But there is more; the letter says 'Spouses or significant others are not required to make the climb but are encouraged to participate; *you, however, are required to make an effort.*' What constitutes an effort? What if I can't do it because I don't get in good enough shape? Do you think I could get fired over this?"

Kalee reassured her mother, "Of course you won't get fired if you aren't able to summit a huge mountain. That's ridiculous–and if you do get fired, that would have to be a lawsuit! This feels a little unethical for them to make you do this Mom.... Your job is to be a sales manager, not a mountain climber."

---

*This case has been developed based on real organization(s) and real organizational experiences. Names, facts, and situations have been changed to protect the privacy of individuals and organizations.

Lena replied, "I know…but you know what people in radio are like, Ka-you've been around them all your life. The lifestyle is to eat, drink, and smoke a lot and stay up late…a lot of radio people are heart attacks just waiting to happen, so I can understand their concern." Kalee agreed, but still felt uncomfortable with what she considered to be a mandated wellness program. When Kalee's dad decided early on not to accompany Lena on the Colorado trip, Kalee jumped at the chance and began reading through frequent emails from Jack Welton and his wife about the trip that had come to be known as *"Mountain Madness."*

In his correspondence, Welton frequently chided the We-R-Radio managers: "Is everybody on board? Does anybody care?" Welton's most common motivation was that "your attitude determines your altitude," a slogan he introduced because it "will serve you well every day of your life." Additional email attempts at motivation included:

*January 22nd*: EVERYBODY is capable of making it to the top…but you have the responsibility to put yourself in the condition to succeed…it's time to get serious.

*March 5th*: Time keeps marching on. Remember, your attitude determines your altitude. And we're going to the top!!!!!

*March 28th*: We can control the quality of our lives and it is NEVER too late to start to improve our chances…climbing a fourteener is as good excuse as any. If you haven't gotten serious yet, you need to NOW! Get with it! Get ready! No excuses!

*May 26th*: The more you work out, the better you ought to feel about climbing those daily mountains you face…only you will know your body and what you've done to prepare.

*June 13th*: You have to be prepared! Hope you're ready: mentally, physically, with the proper equipment…Crank it up! Your attitude determines your altitude!

*July 8th*: Three weeks from tomorrow, "My Friend," we're going to the top of Colorado! Here we go, ready or not! Aren't you excited?

*July 12th*: CRANK IT UP! You'll be on the bus two weeks from today.

As much as Kalee was aware of the motivational purpose of the emails, she also read them for their concrete tips on what "fellow mountaineers" (as the We-R-Radio group was now called) needed to buy and to do in order to prepare themselves. From resources provided by Welton, she had learned about first aid, bears, lightning, avalanches, altitude sickness, sun exposure, hypothermia, insects and parasites, clothing choices, drinking water, and personal sanitation. She had also read some of the additional novels about mountain climbing that Welton had assigned in that first January letter, because he had warned "There will be a test over the above readings." At the same time, she had "buffed up" her workout routine and was on the treadmill and elliptical about two hours a day. All this physical and mental preparation had taken a lot of time–and she did not even have the pressure of *needing* to attempt the climb as part of her job. Kalee wondered how the managers felt about learning all this information and building in extended amounts of time to exercise in addition to doing their normal job–running radio stations. Her mom told her one manager had quit over the expectation to climb a mountain. Kalee wondered how many other managers were secretly resenting the mandate.

Kalee also wondered how her fellow mountaineers had reacted to the waiver attached to Welton's email two days ago. All individuals who planned to attempt the climb were required to sign the waiver "releasing Welton, individually, and We-R-Radio, it members, its managers, its independent contractors, its directors, officers, employees and agents from liability of any sort or nature whatsoever" for individuals pursuing the activity of "hiking and climbing Colorado mountain peaks." She found this timing interesting. Employees had been preparing for seven months. They were finding out less than a week before the climb that We-R-Radio could not "officially" force them to attempt the climb and indeed accepted no responsibility or liability if something went wrong on the climb.

## THURSDAY, JULY 26TH

Kalee walked around the bedroom in her hiking boots to further break them in as she double-checked her packing job from the night before. She compared Welton's packing guides to the contents of her suitcase and backpack, and wondered aloud, "OK...besides my normal clothes and gear, I have gore-tek pants that zip off into shorts, a backpack, a baseball hat, a new rain jacket, a fleece vest, hiking boots, a wicking shirt, socks, several water bottles, aspirin for altitude headaches, band-aids, sunglasses, and sunscreen. I hope this is enough–I can't afford to spend upwards of $1,000 for hiking gear like Mom's manager Dallas did." Just then, she heard Lena pull in the driveway and walk in the door.

"Hey, Mom, are you ready for this *Mountain Madness* adventure?" Kalee called from the bedroom.

Lena replied, "I am certainly going to give it my best shot. As Welton says, 'your attitude is your altitude!'"

Kalee responded "And we're going to the top!" Both women chuckled as they recalled seeing that phrase at least 10 times since January. They loaded Kalee's gear and headed to Caravan City, where they would get on the bus with the other We-R-Radio managers bound for Colorado. In the car, Kalee and Lena reviewed the schedule Welton had created:

> You will arrive at our house by a bus on Friday, July 27th, to begin the acclimatization process and complete the test on the reading materials....We'll have some frosty libations around our firepit. Saturday we'll go higher in the mountains–above 9,000 feet–and the acclimatization process continues. On Sunday we'll summit a fourteener together and the bus will head home with a lot of self-satisfied and very tired people.

Kalee joked, "Mom, I hope my test scores over the readings don't embarrass you too much because I'll tell you right now I did not read all six books." Lena just rolled her eyes at her daughter.

As they drove, Kalee talked with excitement about climbing Mount Elbert, because "we'll be able to say we climbed to the highest point in Colorado,

Mom–14,433 feet!" When her excitement was met with silence, she looked over and realized how anxious her mom was. Kalee reminded Lena that "Welton sent a book chapter that rated Mount Elbert as a 'great summer hike for novices'– You'll do great!" Lena nodded, but Kalee knew her mom was nervous as to her physical readiness for the climb. Although she had been working out regularly for seven months, she had not lost as much weight as others at We-R-Radio who had received Welton's public praise of "FANDAMNTASTIC!"

Since Welton was upfront that part of this trip was about getting in shape, he took great pride in publicizing the weight-loss achievements of We-R-Radio employees in his emails. On January 27th, he had reported "hearing from people that the pounds are starting to come off." In early February, Welton's email high-lighted those who had lost the most weight to date and gave an exercise science lesson that muscle is heavier than fat "so don't get frustrated if the pounds start becoming harder to take off." In March, he had forwarded an article from ABC-news.com on toxic weight caused by stress. Later in March, Welton reported "the latest good news" of "someone who has lost 14 pounds since starting in late January and crossed a weight threshold they haven't seen in years." In April, he told a story of receiving a four-inch strip of someone's belt in the mail. In late May, Welton took great pride in announcing his wife's 38-pound weight loss. But in mid-June, Welton made the most direct call to arms regarding weight loss: "Are you in shape? It's now or never. Hate to see anybody embarrass themselves...José has lost over 30 pounds and says this challenge has changed his life." Given this public discourse equating weight loss with being a valuable employee, Kalee understood why her mother was a little nervous. She changed the subject to cute stories about her own kids to put Lena in "grandma," rather than climbing, mode.

When they arrived in Caravan City to meet the other managers, talk almost immediately turned to weight loss. Attention turned to José and how he lost over 40 pounds in six months; his wife explained his eating regimen of a large breakfast and lunch and then soup for dinner...and Kalee gave Lena a knowing glance to say "can we talk about something else *please*?" Over dinner, talk of weight loss dissipated and was replaced with conversations about "what a party" this trip was going to be. When Kalee asked her table how they thought it would increase team-work, one manager characterized it as "team drinking and team excuse-making at the base of the Rocky mountains." She thought, "Only time will tell if and how this team-building will work."

## FRIDAY, JULY 27TH

Kalee, Lena, and the rest of the We-R-Radio group boarded the bus at 6:00 A.M. Friday morning to leave Caravan City. Although the bus stopped occasionally for food and gas, it was pretty much a straight journey on the interstate to Colorado, so Kalee had a lot of time to talk. As she conversed with people on the bus, she tried to get a read for what people thought of *Mountain Madness*. One manager said, "This challenge is like lots of things we run into as managers. We're faced with something we can't totally predict the outcome of." While one accompany-ing spouse was "psyched to see how one of these outdoor team-building exer-cises really works," another spouse articulated Kalee's own concerns: "I think it is unethical to *make* managers do this...even if it is not legally framed as a condition of employment, I think it is perceived that one *has* to go, and in some ways, has to make it." Kalee was further struck by a manager who "questioned why we are doing this. They are very dictatorial and micro-managing in their leadership style, *which now has bled into our private lives*." A third accompanying spouse was perhaps even more cynical: "Most of these people have no clue as to what they are about to attempt. I think at the end of the ordeal there'll be a lot of disappointed people, including Welton, because I think he is expecting team building one for all/all for one, people exceeding their limits, and people preparing for a challenge. I think he'll use this to see who goes the extra mile."

In talking to her fellow mountaineers, most seemed excited about the oppor-tunity, but a few others admitted thinking "they can't be serious" and "you've got to be kidding." Some expressed concerns about the physical aspects of the climb, such as whether their knees would hold up and especially how they would react to the high altitude and thin air (Kalee had asthma, so that was a concern to her as well). Kalee's conversations kept her busy, and so she was surprised how quickly it seemed that the bus arrived at Welton's Colorado home. After a round of quick introductions, the group was invited to get some drinks and socialize—and it was at that point that everyone who was going to make the climb absolutely had to sign "the waiver."

The fellow mountaineers then hopped on a bus and went to several touristy sites, including a horse ranch and a museum that was created in an old horse barn. The bus then headed to Welton's country club for a high-carbohydrate pasta din-ner and an Awards Ceremony. The ceremony began with Welton introducing (and presenting gifts to) his invited guests outside of We-R-Radio. He then explained the actual mountain climb process:

> This is not a race, but to make the process more efficient I have divided us into three subgroups. Alpha, or A group, will be the group of people I expect to get up the moun-tain first, and so they will leave last [Kalee was assigned to this group]. Bravo, or B group, will be in the middle [Lena was here], and Charlie, or C group, will take off first on our climbs because I anticipate they will need the most time to ascend.

Then the We-R-Radio employee awards began; Welton "was happy to report that as a group, you managers sold $26,000 in radio advertising and sponsorships for *Mountain Madness*."

At the end of the awards ceremony, Welton proceeded to make a speech that next year, this event would last for four days of physical activity to include rafting and climbing another fourteener, and "While we're going to take a vote about this, I'm the majority *and we're doing it*." Then when most were exhausted after the dinner and suggested going to the hotel, Jack Welton replied "that's too damn bad, I'm having a party" and so the group begrudgingly went to his house for drinks.

Eventually, the group retired to their hotel to get some sleep in anticipation of Saturday's "practice" hike.

## SATURDAY, JULY 28TH

On Saturday morning, Kalee found most of the group to be fairly relaxed as they ate breakfast and loaded the bus to travel to Welton's house. In their seats, Lena again asked Kalee, "What if I just can't do it, Ka? What will others think of me?"

She replied, "Mom, you will do just fine. I got moved to Bravo to be with you and I will hike with you."

Lena then said, "And I'm worried about my manager Dallas as well. He has stopped smoking, but is still not all that fit. What if he doesn't make it?" She asked Kalee if she had noticed the Welton email that highlighted them a few months ago: "Dallas and Lena have joined a new YMCA in River City. Will wonders never cease??????? Those of you who had them in the pool to be the last to start have just lost the pool!" She confided, "I just didn't know what to think of that—if it was motivational or derogatory...are they just waiting for us to fail?" Kalee no longer knew how to verbally comfort her mother, and so she squeezed her hand. The bus stopped briefly to pick up Welton, his wife, and children, and the fellow mountaineers were off to do a "practice" hike.

Kalee and Lena were in Bravo group, with Welton's wife as their guide. Almost as soon as the group got off the bus, she took off at a very fast pace and half of Bravo was left behind because they were going to the bathroom. The group did not wait for individuals who were struggling, and early on Lena started having trouble breathing and got winded. Kalee was hiking with her for a while, and then Dallas caught up and they encouraged her to go on ahead. While Kalee did, she was quickly disappointed because she found the experience to be extremely competitive for a "practice" hike. She watched as individuals vied for position versus staying together as a group–to the point where walkie-talkies had to be used to rejoin members of Alpha and Bravo. Kalee tired of this dynamic quickly, and decided to go back and find Lena and Dallas. She found her mom alone at the side of the trail; Lena began crying and sobbed that "they (the staff Welton had hired to organize the climb) won't even let me try to climb Mount Elbert tomorrow–they said I won't stand a prayer of making it." Kalee took her mother's hand and as they walked back toward the bus, fellow mountaineers who passed by expressed how sorry they were Lena was having such a hard time.

The We-R-Radio group loaded back on the bus to see more tourist sites, and hushed whispers spread through the bus. "Could you believe how competitive Welton and his son were on that *practice* hike? It was out of control, and yet he tells US it's not a race? I thought this was supposed to be team-building, not individual best times...."

Kalee, Lena, and Dallas went out for dinner with a small group of closer friends to try to forget the day. Dallas and Lena had both been told they could not even attempt the Mount Elbert climb, and they commiserated about how unfair it felt.

A manager from a nearby station consoled them, "I can't understand why you two aren't at least being allowed to try for tree line, because I know you're both goal-oriented and would get some satisfaction out of at least trying....I think people who don't make it to the top are going to feel isolated so I feel bad for you."

At that point, Lena broke into tears and said, "I am so disappointed because I have been training for seven months and now I can't even try. I can't breathe up in this altitude whether I am exercising or not. I feel like such a failure, and I just hope this failure is not considered as part of my job performance!"

Kalee comforted her mother, "Any ethical supervisor should recognize that you did make big improvements in your physical condition in the spirit of this *Mountain Madness* challenge, Mom. Go shopping and have fun tomorrow and don't even think about the climb."

Back in the hotel, Kalee said "good night" to Lena and tried to get a good sleep in preparation for the physical ordeal she knew was coming in the morning.

## SUNDAY, JULY 29TH

Kalee boarded the bus at 5:00 A.M. and was promptly handed a bag of gorp and her breakfast to eat as they drove. People seemed quietly apprehensive as the bus drove to the North Trailhead of Mount Elbert. Welton reminded the group of the process by which Charlie would leave first, followed by Bravo and then Alpha, with the expectation that Alpha would pass the other groups and be waiting for them at the summit. As day broke, Welton gave a pep talk: "I want you to remember your attitude determines your altitude. Your attitude should have enabled you to get in shape; being in shape, mentally and physically, will help get you to the top! Talk is cheap, the proverbial 'rubber meets the road' takes place within the hour."

At the trailhead, Kalee waited for Bravo to leave and made small talk and accepted condolences on behalf of her mom who was still back at the hotel. She donned all her layers and strapped on her gear, and then made her way up the mountain with Alpha group. She left about 6:45 A.M., and slowly put one foot in front of the other. Her asthma and allergies gave her fits, and at one point in time she just stopped and started to cry, sobbing that "This is as bad as childbirth, and I want to stop." However, a woman who was one of her climbing buddies reminded Kalee that "slow and steady wins the race" and they pushed each other to finish. She watched others turn back, and was mindful of the clock because they had been told that if they had not reached the summit before noon, they would have to turn back without getting to the top in order to move out before the afternoon storms hit. Kalee suffered another mental blow when she reached a "false summit" that looked like the top, but was still about half an hour from the summit. She was therefore thankful when the "noon turnaround rule" was slightly modified in an effort to let all who had the perseverance to make it to the summit accomplish their goal.

Kalee looked at the majesty of Colorado from its highest point around 12:45 p.m. After her picture was taken sitting on a rock at the top with a sign reading "14,433 feet," Kalee borrowed a cell phone to call the River City radio station on behalf of Lena and Dallas to describe the climb and her view from the top. As she hung up the phone, she was silent with her thoughts for a while on the mountaintop. Although the experience was physically exhausting, she was grateful for the opportunity; she would never have done this on her own. Yet she thought about Lena and how her mother must be feeling about this "team-building" climb. Kalee hoped her mom would get word soon that she had made the summit–that news would hopefully make Lena's day a little better. She remembered one of the last memos Welton had sent in July:

> You're all CHAMPIONS in my book for dedicating yourselves to making the attempt. I'm proud of everyone who has made an effort to take on this challenge. Getting ready for the attempt is what it's all about and if we make it to the top that will just be the icing on the cake. The fact that you have faced this new challenge with enthusiasm makes me proud to have you as a part of this organization.

Kalee hoped that Welton was serious, and that other managers followed suit in taking pride in everyone who embraced the challenge, whether they successfully reached the summit or not. She expressed her concerns to a fellow mountaineer, who replied, "I will definitely be interested to see how this plays out in terms of the supposed goal of 'team-building,' because for those of us who reached the summit, we will always have that common accomplishment. For those who did not, they will always feel left out." Kalee knew her mom and Dallas had worked hard to prepare and did not want them to be ostracized or treated differently because of a physical challenge that was certainly NOT a part of the job description of "radio station manager." She hoped for the best as she began her descent down the mountain.

## CHAPTER 6

# Growing Pains

## Jessica Katz Jameson

When Eileen Ramsay* was asked by a previous colleague to serve on the board of directors of Helping Others, she said yes with almost no hesitation. She had lost her mother the year before, and Helping Others volunteers had made all the difference in her mother's last few months of life. Having no relatives nearby, Eileen was grateful to have had others to help her get her mother to doctor's appointments or pick up prescriptions on days when Eileen just couldn't get away from the office. Despite her gratitude, she realized she knew very little about the organization. She hoped that her expertise as a human resources and benefits specialist could allow her to make an important contribution to the board and the organization.

Eileen wanted to be a productive board member and immediately began reviewing orientation materials. She read the history of Helping Others and learned that it opened in 1980 with the mission to provide social and instrumental support for the senior population of a growing county in North Carolina. The organization offers assistance to seniors who live independently but are largely home-bound due to failing health or limited mobility. The organization was founded by the first executive director (ED), Abigail, and three staff members. Abigail served as the ED for 25 years and grew the staff size to 15 full-time and 8 part-time employees. Over that time the organization went from 100 to over 2,200 volunteers. Several current staff members were hired by the original ED. Another ED took over for a brief period, and the current ED, Brian, was hired in 2006. Eileen continued to read about all the people Helping Others supports and the growth in services from 200 to over 1,300 seniors a month. She was more committed than ever to the mission of the organization but felt like the orientation packet told only part of the story. She looked forward to the first board meeting, when she could learn more about the organization's members.

---

*This case has been developed based on real organization(s) and real organizational experiences. Names, facts, and situations have been changed to protect the privacy of individuals and organizations.

## STRIFE OVER STAFF CHANGES

Eileen's curiosity was piqued at her first board meeting when Brian announced Helping Others had hired someone for the new staff position: a finance director.

One board member, Dan, asked, "Is this person going to do more than our current accountant, or is this just a fancy title?"

Before Dan's question could be answered, another member, Kim, asked, "Why are we replacing Joe?" (the organization's accountant for the last 20 years).

Brian explained that Joe is only part-time and has been doing the books the same way for 20 years. "Helping Others has grown to where we need someone with computer experience who can centralize our volunteer and donor databases and update the way we manage finances."

Eileen overheard Dan make a side comment to Kim about how loyal Joe had been over the past years. John, the board president, clearly heard it, too, as he jumped in and said, "Look, we need someone who can take care of the day-to-day finances so that Brian's time isn't tied up here and he can get out into the community."

Several board members nodded in agreement, while another member, Charlie, commented, "Thank heaven for loyal staff like Joe and Becky" (the assistant director). "I don't know how this place would run without them." While some members enthusiastically agreed, Eileen noticed that a long-time board member, Joan, rolled her eyes. This ended the discussion of this topic as Brian announced they would meet the new hire at the next board meeting.

After the meeting ended, Brian approached Eileen and said, "I guess you noticed that we have some tension related to our current staffing situation."

Eileen nodded.

"We could really use your expertise to look over our personnel policies and compensation package and make sure we are making the right moves. Would you be willing to chair the personnel committee?"

Eileen had assumed she would be asked to do this given her background but felt cautious given the brief exchanges she had just encountered. "I would be happy to help the board with this important work," she said, "but since I am so new to the board I think it would help me to meet the staff and get a sense of their view of things. Would it be appropriate for me to meet them and ask them some questions?" "Absolutely, we can set up a day to introduce you to everyone, and then you can talk to the staff as it suits your schedule."

Eileen made a note in her appointment book to follow up with Brian and started to head toward her car. Before she got to the door of the building she was stopped by John, the board president. "I hear you are going to head up the personnel committee for us—that's great."

"Thanks, John. I'm looking forward to putting my experience to work for the organization."

"Well, we have a lot of people around here who are reluctant to change, so try not to let them dampen your spirit. You need to know that Joe is being paid a very nice salary plus vacation for the 10 hours a week he puts in." With a smile he added, "This could be a challenging assignment."

"I suppose change is always difficult, especially if people don't understand the reasons behind it. I appreciate the heads-up and hope I can help make the transition go more smoothly."

## STAFF MEMBERS SPEAK OUT

About two weeks went by before Eileen was able to schedule time with Brian to meet the staff. She went in on a Friday morning and found that several staff members were not in the office, but she talked to those she could. She started with Maryanne, who had been there for seven years and helped train volunteers. Eileen asked her what she enjoyed about working at Helping Others and why she had stayed so long.

"I love helping our clients, and we all work together so well here in the office. It's not like some places where everyone does their own thing and doesn't help anyone else. We are always there for each other, and if my kid has a school play, I know I can go and someone will cover for me. If a volunteer doesn't show up, I will get in my car and go visit one of our clients. We all pitch in and make sure everything gets done."

"What do you know about the board of directors?" "Not much," said Maryanne. "I honestly don't think I would know most of them if they were standing right in front of me. I think it used to be different years ago, but I don't know what they do, and I'm pretty sure they don't know what I do either."

"Is there anything about working at Helping Others you would like to see improved?"

"Well, it seems like they are creating more rules, and I'm not sure I like that," Maryanne replied. "It takes away from the caring, family feel I have always liked about this place."

Eileen thanked Maryanne and then went to speak with Laura, the fundraising coordinator. Eileen asked her what she thought about the current staff situation.

"It's a bit of a mess," she laughed. "There is very little communication between staff members, and I don't even know what some of them do."

"But I thought I saw that there are monthly staff meetings. Doesn't that help?"

"They could, but they are practically nonexistent. Half the time we don't have one, and, even when we do, whoever happens to be there that day shows up."

Eileen reflected on the several empty cubicles she had seen and had an idea what Laura meant.

"It's not Brian's fault," Laura continued. "We have a lot of staff that have been here a long time, and they got used to the way things were under Abigail. Even though there was another ED in between, many of them still talk about the days when Abigail was here. Abigail founded Helping Others, you know."

"Do you have a sense of why everyone liked Abigail so much?"

"I'm not sure, just that the atmosphere was a lot different. We were a much smaller organization, and the staff were very close, like a family. Some of us are, maybe, well, more professional than they are used to? They seem really resistant to change and to new authority. For example, some of them seem very loyal to Becky. She has been here a long time, too, and some people thought she should have been promoted to executive director."

"Wow," Eileen thought to herself, "there's a landmine she hadn't been aware of. Hmm." "So what would you like to see happen to improve the current personnel situation?"

"Oh, I have lots of ideas on that," Laura said, "and I have shared them with Brian. Mandatory monthly staff meetings for one," she began. "I also think this new financial director is going to be a big help because we have no policies on days off, vacation, sick leave, or anything like that. People pretty much show up when they want to right now, and we can't continue to work like this—so that is going to make a big difference in getting things organized around here."

"Well, those are exactly the kinds of things the board is going to be looking at as well," Eileen said. "Thanks for your candor, and I hope we can talk again soon."

"Any time. I'm very anxious to see things change around here."

After that conversation Eileen decided to stop and take some notes. She was amazed that the first two people she spoke with had such completely different views of the organization. Maryanne loved the staff members and spoke about how warm and collaborative they are, while Laura characterized it as a mess. As Eileen was thinking Brian walked by and asked how things were going.

"Oh, very enlightening" she said. "Who do you recommend I speak with next?"

"I think Diana is in her office. She is our most senior staff member, so she should have an interesting perspective."

"Perfect," said Eileen as she headed in the direction of Diana's office.

Diana was an RN before she joined Helping Others 20 years ago. She started as a volunteer and was there so often Abigail had eventually convinced her to join the staff as its health specialist. Eileen asked Diana why she stayed so long, and her answers echoed Maryanne's earlier comments.

"I really enjoy the interaction with everyone. We have a lot of face-to-face communication, although, of course, the newer ones use email. Everyone is very friendly, and we have an open-door policy. We celebrate birthdays and are very people oriented. There is almost no turnover here."

"Wow," Eileen smiled. "It sounds like a pretty wonderful place to work. What about interaction with the board. Do you have any?"

"No, not at all. I know the ones who have been on the board since the beginning. When Abigail was here we used to take turns making presentations to the board, and they used to come around and meet us, but I don't know the new ones at all."

"Do you have any interest in going to a board meeting?"

"Oh, no. We used to have them during the day, but I don't need to stay until 6:30 to go to a meeting. Of course, I'd go if they asked me to, but they never have."

"Is there anything else you particularly like or would like to see changed in the staff situation?"

"Well, Becky is wonderful to bounce things off of, so it is great to have her as a resource. Brian seems like a good leader. He is much younger than our past directors, and he is still establishing himself. Other than that, it is just sad that we are losing the feel of the agency. It has been such a great place to work for so long, and it is changing. I wish it were different."

Eileen thanked Diana for her time and said she hoped to talk to her again. After leaving Diana's office, Eileen spoke to two more employees, each of whom had been at Helping Others for about 10 years. From them she heard many of the same refrains: the importance of the mission of the organization and the need for its services, the flexible and humane atmosphere that made Helping Others a nice place to work where they were understanding of personal needs and not too nit-picky or legalistic. One staff member said she had very good job security and never felt her job was threatened. She added that she was out of the office in the field a lot, and more monthly staff meetings would help her stay in touch with what was going on at the office and what others were doing. She also concurred with those who said they did not know the board members and only saw them at the annual holiday party, "If they even show up for that." She thought it might be a good idea if there was some direct contact between staff members and the board so that the board did not know the staff only through the executive director's eyes. When asked to whom they reported, one woman said Brian, while the other was pretty sure she reported to Becky. Eileen made a note about the difference between staff members who felt Brian was the go-to person and others who were more likely to seek out advice from Becky.

Eileen's head was spinning at this point, and she decided she had done enough research for one day. When she thought about the emphasis many staff members placed on the informality of the Helping Others organization she realized why John had warned her there would be resistance to change. Yet, she also understood the argument that the increase in Helping Others' client base required a larger organization with more staff, electronically managed databases, and a more formal structure. She believed the key to successful buy-in from the staff was going to be communicating the need for the change and how it was going to improve the organization's ability to serve its clients.

## THE BOARD'S PERSONNEL SUBCOMMITTEE MEETS

When Eileen realized the next board meeting was rapidly approaching she decided to call a meeting of the personnel subcommittee so it would have some progress to report at the next full board meeting.

The subcommittee consisted of Eileen, Brian, and three other board members. While she had met each of them at the last board meeting, Eileen wanted to learn a little more about their perspectives on the staff situation before she shared what she had learned from the staff members she had spoken to.

"Thank you all for coming today. Just a reminder that I am new to the board, and Brian and John asked me to chair this committee due to my background in human resources. Since I have only attended one board meeting, could you each tell me a little about your role on the Helping Others board?"

"Hi, I'm Allison. I'm in the second year of my three-year term on the board, and I'm a public relations consultant. I have mostly been involved with fundraising events but thought this committee would be good because I need to work with staff on the special events. I hope we can continue to hire more full-time, professional staff to help with event coordination and volunteer management."

"I'm Charlie. I've been with Helping Others for 12 years now, as a volunteer and three-time board member. I'm concerned that the organization might be taking on more than we can handle. In these days of increased competition for funding, I am not convinced we can continue to provide services at the level this board seems to expect."

Brian jumped in and said, "This is a very important discussion, and it should be on the agenda for the next full board meeting. This is exactly the kind of strategic decision that is part of the board's governance role."

Finally there was Sheila. "I've been with Helping Others for many years now and have previously served as the board president. I feel strongly that this organization's mission is to provide services to everyone in the county, and our volunteers expect us to do that. My main concern is that some of our current staff are holding us back by living in the past and not accepting the fact that we have to change."

Eileen realized that the differences she saw in the staff members' views were apparent in this group as well. Although Charlie seemed to hold the minority opinion in this group, she didn't know where the rest of the board members fell. For her part, she still did not know enough to decide how she felt about the organization's growth, but she felt strongly that some new policies were needed to reduce the current level of ambiguity among the staff members. She told them the committee's goal for this meeting was to come up with a set of objectives for the committee to achieve this year. She also let them know that she had spoken to some of the staff members to get their views on how the office was running and their level of job satisfaction. This seemed to arouse everyone's curiosity, and Eileen realized they probably would not be able to focus on the task at hand if she did not provide some report of what she had learned. She explained that in her view the staff members seemed to fall into two camps: the old-timers who were somewhat nostalgic for Abigail's leadership and resistant to the changes that were happening and the newer employees who were a bit patronizing of the old ways and eager to make the organization more professional. Charlie immediately chimed in to say that this organization's strength was its laidback atmosphere that helped everyone feel like a family, while Sheila countered that what made them successful in the past was not going to allow them to achieve their full potential, especially in this new era of nonprofit accountability.

Brian suggested that he was doing his best as executive director to maintain the existing family culture while adding staff to increase Helping Others' capacity but admitted there were challenges to making everyone happy. Eileen reminded them that it was their job as a committee to examine current personnel policies and benefits and make certain that the organization was making good decisions that would contribute to staff recruitment, retention, and performance in support of the Helping Others mission. She felt confident that they could develop some goals that would help them meet what she articulated as the organization's most pressing challenge:

> "How do we keep the supportive, flexible, family feel of the organization while creating an organizational structure that will improve internal communication and allow us to effectively achieve our mission?"

## CHAPTER 7

# How Dare He Try to Manage Our Talk

## Ryan S. Bisel and Amber S. Messersmith

"What's going on?" Tami\*, a hospice nurse in her mid-40s, asked the receptionist as soon as she got back from seeing patients on a Friday afternoon. She knew something was wrong because the office was utterly silent.

The hospice nursing organization, New Day Hospice (NDH), was made up of 70 nurses, social workers, and physical therapists. These employees worked together to provide medical and emotional care for dying patients and their families. Employees at New Day Hospice loved their work and took pride in providing their community with health care for the dying. Although nurses could make more money at hospitals or doctors' offices, there was just something special about working for New Day Hospice—something that Tami deeply valued and that had kept her working there for 11 years. NDH was a close-knit group. In fact, nurses frequently called the NDH office, "the sorority house."

The receptionist shook her head, pressed her lips tightly, and rapidly whispered to Tami, "After work, we're meeting at Johnny's." Then the receptionist sat back down at her desk, began to type, and avoided more eye contact with Tami.

Tami's face felt hot. "This is so strange. What could have possibly happened?" she wondered. In the time she had worked at New Day Hospice, she had never known it to be so quiet around the office. Laughter and chatting frequently filled the halls and cubicles of the sterile building. New Day Hospice *was* a social place, just not today.

While Tami worked on completing a stack of medical and insurance forms, Linda, Tami's friend and supervisor, quietly passed Tami's cubicle, locked eyes with her, and nodded at the door. Tami had known and worked for Linda for seven of the 11 years she had worked at New Day Hospice. The eye contact and nod were enough to make Tami quickly file the forms, put on her coat, and walk 10 steps behind Linda. Tami felt a sense of relief as they made their way outside because she

---

\*This case has been developed based on real organization(s) and real organizational experiences. Names, facts, and situations have been changed to protect the privacy of individuals and organizations.

could hear the sound of traffic—a welcome change from the unnerving silence so uncharacteristic of New Day Hospice.

"Linda, what is going on in . . . ?"

"Wait. Meet us at Johnny's." Linda interrupted. Tami nodded and walked briskly toward her car.

Johnny's Tavern was an old bar with local appeal. New Day Hospice employees would often meet at the bar for drinks on Fridays after work to socialize and discuss humorous patient interactions that happened during the week. The stress of helping patients and their families cope with death created a bond among them. And, while it might seem like the nurses, social workers, and physical therapists' socializing should be filled with serious talk, the truth was the Friday night happy hours were normally filled with laughter and joking.

Tami arrived at the same time as Linda. She parked, and the two greeted one other with a hug. Linda had tears in her eyes.

Tami tried again, "What is going on, Linda?"

"Come on inside. We need a drink," Linda explained.

They stepped inside and sat at their usual place in the back. Six other New Day Hospice employees were already sitting around the table. Linda grabbed a waiter and ordered before they sat down.

"Hi, everyone," Linda said to the others at the table in a defeated tone accompanied by a shrug of her shoulders.

"Hi, Linda. Hi, Tami. Did you get drinks?" Carly asked.

"Yeah, they're on their way," Tami said to speed up the greetings. "Why is everyone so down? What happened? The office was eerily silent when I got back from seeing patients. It has never been that way before."

"Ugh. We have a story for you," Carly groaned.

Linda explained, "While you were gone on calls, our high and mighty chairman Bill comes in with two of his cronies. They march into Patricia's office and close the door. About 15 minutes later Patricia was walking out with a box full of her personal belongings and a bright red face."

"Oh, no! Not Patricia! Did they fire her? They can't fire the executive director, can they? She's been with New Day Hospice for years," Tami's heart was in her throat. Patricia was the best boss—and fellow nurse—Tami had ever had the pleasure of working for.

"Well, apparently they can fire her and did," Linda said with an angry tone.

"If they can fire her, they can fire anyone. Who's going to run New Day Hospice now? What exactly did she do to get fired? She just won an award for outstanding leadership in the community. It just doesn't add up." Tami's head was swimming; nothing about what she heard seemed to make sense.

"I know." "Yeah," chimed in a couple of others sitting at the table.

"You haven't even heard all of it," Linda said.

"What else could there be?" Tami replied.

"After Patricia walked out, a couple of nurses ran after her and asked what was happening. Within minutes a crowd starting forming around Patricia. Then Bill comes over and orders everyone to meet in the conference room immediately. At this point, I was half convinced that he was going to fire all of us. Patricia leaves choking back tears, and we all head to the conference room. We are all talking to one another about Patricia being fired and getting really angry when Bill walks into the conference room. He says, 'This organization has been in the red for three years, and it was the decision of the board to remove Patricia as executive director. My law office has given me leave to be interim executive director until I find a replacement. Now, you are not to talk about this matter. I know you ladies love nothing more than to start juicy rumors. So if I hear you discussing it, you will be fired, too. Everybody get back to work.' "

"You're kidding," Tami said with wide eyes. "How dare he tell us what we can or cannot say! He has no right! He can't go around dictating who says what."

"Apparently, he can," said Carly.

"Unbelievable. I feel so sorry for Patricia," Tami said.

"Who knows, maybe Patricia will be the lucky one. At least she doesn't have to work for Bill," Linda said.

## THE NEXT WEEK

Tami dreaded returning to work on Monday. The idea of New Day Hospice without Patricia seemed alien. Monday morning she walked into New Day Hospice and was immediately angered by the site of Bill Rogers sitting in Patricia's office. Tami gathered her daily schedule and left as soon as she could just to be out of the place she once loved.

When she returned from seeing patients late in the afternoon, Tami was disappointed to hear from the receptionist that Bill had called a mandatory meeting, which would begin at 4 o'clock—in ten minutes.

Who's he going to fire now? Tami thought to herself.

Tami arrived in the conference room a minute early. The room was nearly full of the 70 employees but almost completely silent—a sound that made Tami sick to her stomach. Tami was disappointed to see that the only remaining chairs were in the front of the room. She wished she could put as much distance between her and Bill as possible. Bill entered the room with a big smile.

"Ok, ladies, and—um—a few gents," he said as he nodded at the three men in the room, "let's get started."

Tami immediately resented that he pointed out the gender differences in the room. Furthermore, his chipper attitude made it seem as if the events of last Friday never happened.

"I'm here to turn this *failing* organization around, but I need your trust, and I need your input. Any ideas about where we can cut costs or increase revenue?" Bill questioned.

If the room was silent when Tami entered, it was even more silent now. Tami was angry that Bill called New Day Hospice a failing organization. New Day Hospice was extremely well known in the community as the premier provider of hospice care. Frequently the mayor, city commissioners, chamber of commerce, and local newspaper praised New Day Hospice for its contribution to the community. Besides, Tami thought, New Day Hospice is a nonprofit. Cutting costs and increasing revenue were not even the point of New Day Hospice—providing the best care to dying patients and their families—that was the point.

"Well?!" Bill said loudly with annoyance in his tone.

The room remained silent.

# Organizational Technology

## CHAPTER 8

# Caught Online

### Jensen Chung

J ean Kopel* was stunned, staring blankly at the computer screen. She looked at
the email again. Yes, it was about her. President Scott Longman of the Tempflo
Asian-Pacific branch was admitting in public that, in hiring Jean, he had hired the
wrong person to be director of the Engineering Department.

The Tempflo Company had set up a new email system three months before.
Since then, several blunders had occurred. Because the IT group used a different configuration for the email *REPLY* command, several colleagues had inadvertently sent personal messages to the entire company. Jean had been amused
initially, especially by romantic or flirtatious notes sent to her and everyone else
by mistake. But, with this latest blunder, she was no longer amused. Apparently in
response to complaints about her from the engineers in the Browser Group, Scott
had sent an email saying:

> ...Thank you for your information and feedback. I was surprised to know that a man-
> ager from the U.S. headquarters would have such a level of incompetence. I will see
> to it that she improves. As the Asian-Pacific branch's president, who was instrumental
> in bringing her over, I apologize to you. We will be more careful in the future when
> selecting managers from headquarters....

"This is horrendous," Jean thought. She reflected on how Scott had appeared
so nice to her from day one. She had solved so many problems for him. Yet, as soon
as a few employees ganged up on her, he yielded to their pressure. All along, she
had believed that with the two of them working together, they could transform
this branch. How naive she had been, Jean suddenly realized.

Jean resisted the impulse to send Scott Longman a nasty message. She decided
to take a shower and wait until the next day to get more information before reacting.

---

*This case has been developed based on real organization(s) and real organizational experi-
ences. Names, facts, and situations have been changed to protect the privacy of individuals and
organizations.

She told herself to just cool down and sleep before dealing with the humiliation. But Jean could not stop worrying about what Scott had done. How could she?

## WAS I SOLD OUT?

Jean pondered her working and social relationship with Scott Longman. The day she arrived in this Pacific Rim country, Scott had taken her to dinner and told her that she was the first woman to be hired by the branch since headquarters had delegated the authority to hire and fire managers of local branches. He also said that he had argued on her behalf to convince the hiring panel that she was the best choice to head the Engineering Department, which consisted of the software section and the hardware section. To help her settle in, Scott had asked the Department of Human Resources in the branch to assign a person to take care of her housing, transportation, and other adjustment needs. He had been so thoughtful, even bringing hangers from his own home to her.

Jean had been trying to reciprocate by supporting Scott. For example, employees in the hardware section (called "Hardies") had accessed a lot of files that had not been made public before. Hardies started expressing particular interest in many policy issues, including opposition to the proposed collaboration project between the Asian-Pacific branch and a local semiconductor provider. In several IM chats, they had become unusually vocal, and Jean had been striving to come up with all kinds of arguments to support Scott's proposals.

About 30 expatriates from the U.S. headquarters had been transferred to the local branch, and they often socialized after work but also online discussing both job-related business and social topics. They gradually formed a clique, communicating much more frequently than before. President Scott Longman had not been included in their chat group. Jean was in the group but never initiated and seldom joined the conversations.

Most of these expatriates, particularly supervisors, managers, and engineers, did not like Scott's management style. For example, they often made fun of Scott's habit of routinely inviting individual employees to lunch with him at a nearby restaurant. "Who goes to lunch?" had become an often-cracked inside joke among the expatriates, who ate their homemade sandwiches at their desks. They argued that Scott should spend the money and time in social functions with local businesspeople, not with employees. "Scott should lunch with clients, not us," a supervisor once whined.

Furthermore, since the online system now allowed employees more access to shared files, lower level employees could now browse the spreadsheet analyses on the electronic resources. Engineers in the software section ("Softies") pointed out that rank-and-file colleagues knew more about clients' problems than Scott did.

After hearing this complaint about Scott's not having enough contact with clients, Jean had managed to connect her engineering department with a local university and cosponsored two open-to-the-public workshops. The two workshops attracted media attention and were successfully publicized. Three hundred people, including Tempflo employees, attended the workshops to learn about state-of-the-art animation techniques, audio file resources, and network administration. As far as Jean knew, at least one business deal was struck as a result of the workshops, even though generating businesses had not been the main purpose of the workshops. She gave sole credit to Scott by purposefully working behind the scenes while Scott hosted the workshops.

One week after the workshops, Jean was browsing the branch president's monthly reports to headquarters, which she had never accessed, and came across Scott's report to headquarters about the success of the workshops. She noticed that her name was left out. Although somewhat disappointed and a bit suspicious of Scott's motivation, Jean didn't make a fuss. She told herself that she should be a good team player and it was all right to let the leader take the credit.

Now, however, having re-read this most recent and damaging email, Jean reconsidered her earlier suspicions. Perhaps they were reasonable. Other curious incidents had occurred. Two months ago, for example, she had expressed to Scott some reservations about Lucy, who supervised the Browser Group (the "Browsers"), a special task force consisting of engineers from both the software and the hardware sections, who were researching and developing browsers. Jean had casually mentioned to Scott that Lucy lacked enthusiasm in conveying to Jean the needs and expectations of the new browser interfaces. Coincidence or not, a couple of days after Jean had made this remark to Scott, Lucy became quite cold to her.

Jean had hoped to have a good relationship with Lucy. Lucy, a local-born employee, was the most senior in the hardware section and was the only local in the Browser Group who had ever worked in U.S. headquarters, albeit for only a year. Jean had noticed that many engineers would look up to Lucy when making decisions at the project group meetings. Jean also observed that, unlike other locals, Lucy always spoke English at work (which was appreciated by this group of multinational colleagues), but she spoke the local language with her resident colleagues after work. Indeed, Lucy provided a bridge between cultures. A week before the incident of Scott's damaging email, Jean had inadvertently learned that Lucy had invited all the local Browsers to her home for a party celebrating a culture festival, a fact Jean had learned because of another misdirected email–a Browser had mistakenly included Jean in his emailed apology to Lucy for not being able to attend the gathering.

Jean reflected more upon this. Although the spoken and written language used in the Asian-Pacific branch was English, local employees spoke their own language among themselves. Scott had been living in this Asian-Pacific country 10 years and could speak the local language fluently. Jean had once mentioned to Scott that she was not fluent in the local language, but he reassured her, "Oh, forget it. No need to spend time on that. I would rather you learned more programming languages." At the time, she had thanked him for his reassuring words. But in light of this new evidence, she suspected that he was being cagey, perhaps keeping her separated from the local employees by language so that he could solidify that role for himself.

After a long shower, Jean tried to put herself to sleep. Instead of counting sheep, she worked on translating an executive summary into the local language. The translation didn't succeed in putting her to sleep, either.

At 4 A.M., jean took a tablet of melatonin, provided by Scott, who said it would put her to sleep when work anxieties caused insomnia. He had said, "Guess what, its antioxidants can keep you young, too." However, the melatonin didn't work. She got up and did some yoga stretches, a practice that she had taken up also at Scott's recommendation.

Jean decided to read the email again when she discovered a new message appeared right after Scott Longman's "apology" to the group A former U.S. colleague, now in the hardware section, was forwarding Scott's apology message to her. In the postscript to the message, the man explained to Jean that employees in the Browser Group had obtained some of Jean's personnel evaluation criteria from a presumably secure server and had subsequently complained to Scott that Jean evaluated subordinates "solely on results, ignoring their effort."

"Evaluating based on how hard they work rather than how the job gets done?" Jean pondered, bewildered. The company manual never mentioned effort but rather results. "Is that an unwritten practice in this branch? How come I have never heard of it?" Jean was perplexed.

## THE PRESIDENT PROMISED TO FIX

At work the next morning, Jean could not concentrate. At 11:00, she received a phone call from the colleague who had forwarded Scott's message to her last night. After speaking with him, Jean decided to write Scott a very simple email, saying:

> Scott, I was shocked by a colleague's phone call informing me of your response to the complaints of a few Browser group members about me.

Upon pressing the *SEND* button, Jean had second thoughts as to whether it was wise to communicate through email instead of confronting Scott face-to-face. She then calmed herself by the thought that her message was crafted tactfully: She had made no mention of knowing the Browsers' complaints. Nor had she mentioned having read the entire content of Scott's message, thinking this would test his candidness. She had been polite in her wording.

Half an hour later, Scott replied:

> Jean, I'm terribly sorry. I apologize. After answering hundreds of email messages, I was so tired last night when I responded to the complaint from the Browser Group that my message was quite hasty. I realize that my reply to them was a big gaffe. Let's talk. I will cancel my lunch engagement today. Let's have lunch together and discuss this matter. Scott

Scott's email struck Jean as insincere. She reasoned, "If he was so sorry, why hadn't he picked up the phone and called me?" But then, by the same token, she had to question her own motivation for emailing rather than phoning Scott.

Jean did phone Scott's direct line. She declined his offer for lunch, saying she preferred to meet in his office.

With a mask of a smile, Jean walked into Scott's office past two secretaries, who didn't return her smile. This struck Jean as unusual. Normally, the secretaries would have greeted her with broad smiles. And normally Jean would have had a mug of coffee in her hand when walking into Scott's office, particularly when discussing relatively trivial business. This time, she went empty-handed.

Scott opened his office door to greet Jean before she could even knock. He started to invite her into his private conference room but hesitated. He instead asked Jean to sit down on the sofa by his desk. Again, he apologized. He explained that he had piggybacked the wrong message for replying to the Browsers, and the *REPLY* command in that email system had been set up to reply to all employees in the company, so unfortunately everyone had read his message demeaning Jean. Jean demanded a second message from Scott to the Browsers retracting his statements. She had also come in planning to demand a formal letter of apology, but she decided to hold off that demand for the time being. For his part, Scott, although clearly embarrassed, argued that as the Browsers were still very upset, he should let them calm down before he sent them the message Jean demanded. "I promise to write the second message after Christmas. It's only three weeks away anyway," Scott lowered his voice beseechingly. Jean reluctantly agreed.

## IT WASN'T A REVOLT, BUT...

Returning to her office, Jean found several email messages from friends at the U.S. headquarters asking "What the heck's going on?" Obviously, Scott's "hired the wrong person" message to the Browsers had reached other parts of the company. Jean fell into depression again–until getting a phone call from Nancy Mooney, inviting her to meet for dinner.

Nine years older than Jean, Nancy had been Jean's classmate in communication classes during their college years together. At that time, Nancy was a software engineer, Jean a communication major. Later, after working as a human resources officer for a few years, Jean had studied computer programming. With Jean's move to Tempflo, the two had found themselves working together again; Nancy Mooney was the director of human resources. During an IM chat, one engineer in the branch had nicknamed Nancy "The Moon," as opposed to "The Sun" for President Scott and "Star" for Jean. Nancy accepted the nickname by using it as her email signature.

That evening at the restaurant, the first question Jean asked Nancy was if she had read Scott's message to the Browsers.

"That's why I called you....I could understand how you must be feeling," answered Nancy. "On a positive note, if you had heard other people's comments about Scott's message last night, you certainly would feel much better. Jean, it's not your fault, this whole faux pas. I would focus now on how to repair the damage."

After Jean explained that Scott had promised to send a second message of correction, Nancy suggested that Jean look into the cause of the complaint.

"I already did," said Jean, beaming. "This afternoon I wrote myself a 12-page memo trying to identify the root causes of the mutiny. They can be a potential list of complaints, too."

"You go, girl! That'll be another chapter of the textbook you said you've been writing for yourself, right?!"

Jean smiled in agreement. Her friend Nancy was like a beloved older sister.

"Jean, I'm reminded of the days when we were in that corporate communication class together. When a bunch of guys were arguing with the professor about her grading scale, you were busy writing down several options for managing the conflict from the perspective of a professor. What an attitude!"

Jean's expression showed her appreciation for Nancy's compliment on that long-past incident. After a pause, she returned to the present matter, saying, "To avoid similar reply-all blunders, I'm proposing reprogramming of the email system and stronger online security measures."

Nancy praised Jean's problem-solving ideas and leadership skills and asked her if she went out to lunch with colleagues.

"Don't we folks from America bring our sandwiches for lunch?" Jean sighed.

"Yes, but not every day. Besides, you are different from other Yankees, especially from other techies. You are leading all kinds of people. I mean, folks from all kinds of backgrounds. Most Yankees don't have the same role as you do. They don't need to communicate as much as you do."

Taking a deep breath, Jean looked up to the ceiling, laughing. "Com-mu-ni-cate!" She raised her voice, almost shouting. "Compared with senior colleagues or senior professionals, I spend more time exchanging information and opinions with professionals in other companies. Now with 24/7 access, it allows us to communicate with a whole range of people throughout the company. Sharing information has sparked more dialogue, as we both know."

"And more power to employees, too," Nancy intoned.

"There you go. The more information employees share, the more questions they raise, and the more managers have to justify.

"That's all right, Jean. Remember managing up?"

"Yes, managing-up bosses... there is another new big boss."

"Who?" Nancy raised her eyebrow.

"These online systems. I feel these communication tools are increasing our communication needs! We thought we had brought in servants; we actually have brought in masters–making us do more."

"I agree. The online system is like laundry machines and microwave ovens. They save us a whole lot of time but at the same time push us to do even more work."

Nancy continued, "What the Browsers were complaining about is debatable, but if you chatted with them over a lunch or a dinner, don't you think debates might become discussions? Most of them are locals after all, you know; thus they are people of consequence to this branch location."

Resting her chin on her hands, Jean contemplated Nancy's suggestion. It sounded a familiar ring. Suddenly she remembered that a colleague had told her that Scott spent half a year eating out with local colleagues when he assumed his duties as president. "Maybe," she thought, "he was doing the smart thing, even though some of our Yankees made fun of it."

The two friends conversed throughout dinner. On parting that evening Nancy said, "Since Scott has given his word to send a corrective message, you should continue in good form." She added, "The revolt won't bring you down. After all, it isn't a revolt."

## HE IS MY TRUSTED PRESIDENT NO MORE

A month after Christmas, Jean went to Scott's office with a gloomy look. She asked when he would write his promised overturn message.

He looked perplexed. "Oh, I'm sorry. I thought we had put that matter to rest when you said 'It's all right' the other day."

"When did I say that?"

"When I mentioned the issue to you in my email message about my contact with the Browsers."

Now she remembered. In that message, Scott had admitted to her that, according to his individual interviews with the Browsers, not every Browser had agreed to the complaint about her that was sent to him. Scott had then repeated his apology to Jean, adding his intentions to make it clear that some Browsers disagreed with the complaint. Jean had emailed back, "That's all right."

Apparently "That's all right" had been misinterpreted by Scott. What she had meant was that it was all right for him to clarify the issue in his retraction.

The following day, all concerned finally received Scott's email, as promised to Jean. She read the long-awaited message with some relief, but her distrust of Scott remained. She forwarded his email to Nancy, with a brief note mentioning her reservations about Scott's character.

## A TURNING POINT

A month later, Jean was suddenly transferred back to the U.S. headquarters with the tentative title of senior programmer, pending a new position. The title was a demotion back to the position she had held for six years prior to going to Asia. Scott appointed Lucy, the head of the hardware section and the leader of the Browser Group, to be acting director of the Engineering Department.

To ease her transition back to headquarters, Jean was granted a two-week vacation.

When Jean returned to work, a friend at the headquarters' Human Resources Department told her privately that, in an earlier proposal by the personnel vice president, Jean had been in line to succeed Scott Longman when he retired. After the two successful workshops, headquarters has been very impressed with her accomplishments.

"The vice president overseeing your department learned of your accomplishments through some IM chats," the friend said, "but then that email incident caused a series of personnel chain reactions." The friend then added, "Thanks to our technology, folks here know pretty much about what's going on out there in the branches."

Jean was frustrated and angry, but then she learned more developing news that lifted her spirits. While Jean was on vacation, her friend and mentor Nancy was also transferred back to U.S. headquarters and promoted to become one of three vice presidents overseeing Human Resources, Training, and Corporate Communication for the entire company.

Physically rejuvenated by the two-week vacation, Jean returned to her office and logged on the computer.

She went first to a message from Nancy that read:

Hi Jean,

I have nominated you to be one of the candidates for the position of the Director of Human Resources. You will need to be interviewed and to make a presentation pretty soon. Come by ASAP for details.

Nancy

CHAPTER 9

# The Difficulties of Virtual Leaders

## Alexander Lyon

"**I** read your report, Max, and I agree. Your analysis verified what I had already assumed," said Sarah, an in-house executive in charge of human relations at Zi-Learn,* an Internet startup company. "The virtual executives are hardly in contact with the in-house executives. How can we expect to work well together?"

"I see your point," replied Max, a Zi-Learn training coordinator, as he stirred his coffee.

Sarah met with Max on a sunny day at a trendy café across the street from Zi-Learn, to discuss the difficulty that Sarah and other in-house executives were having communicating with the company's virtual executives who worked out of state.

She continued. "The virtual execs are near the clients, and that's good. But boy, they sure are a different breed, aren't they?" Sarah sipped her drink and thought for a moment. "Still, we've got to do better at keeping them on the same page as we are. I'm going to solidify a plan to get the virtual execs communicating more regularly with the people here in Front Range City. I just hope they go for it," she concluded.

This conversation with Sarah echoed in Max's head for months.

### LIFE AT A DOT-COM

Zi-Learn prepared online courses for healthcare providers, such as hospitals, who employ nurses and other medical professionals. Nurses, in particular, were required to continue their education even after an organization hires them, to stay current with the latest medical advances, treatments, and techniques. To meet this need, Zi-Learn developed interactive courses available through the Internet.

---

*The case is based upon an actual organization and real organizational experiences. Names, facts, and situations have been changed to protect the privacy of individuals and the organization.

Zi-Learn members considered the organization a "dot-com" company because of its startup status, informal culture, and use of the Internet to deliver its services. About 100 of Zi-Learn's 120 members, including three in-house executives, worked at a downtown office building in Front Range City. "In-house executives" were the company's high-level managers who worked day-to-day at the organization's main offices along with most of Zi-Learn's employees. The in-house executives included the chief human relations officer, chief knowledge officer, and a finance executive.

In contrast, five *virtual executives* worked mostly away from Zi-Learn's main offices in various out-of-state locations and were hired primarily for their expertise and relationships with Zi-Learn's main client and other potential clients. The virtual executives included the chief executive officer (CEO), chief technology officer, marketing executive, sales executive, and chief financial officer. Virtual executives managed small staffs at their own out-of-state locations. Technically, they also supervised many of the mid-level managers and their staffs in Front Range City. However, most virtual executives visited Zi-Learn's main offices only about once every month for one to two days each trip. The rest of the time, they communicated with members in Front Range City through occasional phone calls or emails. This virtual arrangement provided few opportunities for most employees to interact with virtual executives on a regular basis.

Steve had been recently hired as CEO of Zi-Learn. He was selected for the post by Omnicorp, Zi-Learn's majority stockholder and primary client. (Omnicorp was a large healthcare corporation that owned numerous hospitals in various cities.) Upon accepting the position, Steve announced that he would not be relocating to Front Range City to lead Zi-Learn. At an all-staff meeting following his appointment, he stated, "I'll be working virtually and will remain out of state to be close to our clients. However, I'll be here with you as much as I can to make sure things stay on target." His announcement surprised employees who were more accustomed to the hands-on leadership approach of the former CEO.

When the company was founded, the leaders typically recruited through their relationships. As the company grew, other, managers and employees continued this practice. This approach to hiring helped to develop many strong relationships at Zi-Learn. Sarah, an in-house executive who was hired by Zi-Learn's founding CEO, supported relationship hiring. She told Max and others, "We've grown so fast, we literally have to recruit through our network of people. When we hire, the first thing we do is ask, 'Does anybody know any programmers or illustrators who are looking for work?' When we've hired like that, new employees have usually been a good fit because they know what to expect."

"Nepotism *is* a blessing," one manager replied with a smile.

"Yes," responded Sarah, "but things are changing lately."

Max, who had been at Zi-Learn for a few weeks, noticed how close personal relationships seemed to be, how hard everybody worked, and how good they appeared to feel about working at Zi-Learn. The only exception was the in-house members' difficult relationships with the virtual executives, who were recruited and hired by Zi-Learn's main out-of-state client and majority owner, Omnicorp.

## LET'S "KEEP IN TOUCH"

Max listened in as Sarah teleconferenced with a few of the virtual executives. Sean, an unpopular virtual executive, kidded Sarah over the phone, "So, Sarah, I've heard you're going to *fix* us and solve our *communication* problems."

Sarah leaned toward the conference phone with a positive tone, "Well, Sean, we're workin' on it." With a raised eyebrow, Sarah glanced at Max to communicate her negative feelings about Sean's comment. Max agreed with her reaction. Sean sounded rude.

In the coming weeks, Sarah launched her communication plan to keep the virtual executives in touch with the rest of the organization. She scheduled regular group email updates, one-on-one phone conversations, and conference calls between and among the in-house and virtual executives. Additionally, Sarah and the other in-house executives expected the virtual executives to visit Zi-Learn's main office in Front Range City at least once a month.

A few weeks later, Max asked Sarah, "How are things going with the communication plan for the virtual execs?"

"Well, it was okay for a few weeks, but they've had meetings with clients and other things came up that conflicted with our scheduled phone conversations and their visits here. So, we're basically back where we started," Sarah replied, sounding a little frustrated.

The distance between the virtual executives and Zi-Learn's employees in Front Range City grew in the coming months. "We used to have a Monday morning breakfast with the execs and we'd all hang out after work and on the weekends," Christine, a long-time employee, told Max. She went on to note, "The former CEO would come around to our desks and ask us about our projects and our lives. That said a lot. The virtual executives, though, they're hardly ever here. They don't put the time in."

"When they do visit," Max replied, "they just whisk by our desks aloofly with their travel bags rolling in tow. It seems so elitist."

Sarah talked to Max about the problem. "We've got a lot of well-educated, bright professionals here. Our employees aren't going to 'jump' just because somebody's title has the word 'executive' in it."

"Well, why don't the virtual execs spend more time and energy here to bridge the gap?" asked Max.

"They won't relocate and they don't think it is necessary to be here more often. They figure that we're grownups. We don't need babysitters, right? But it really helps when they do find the time to hang out with us more. Like two months ago, I begged Steve [the CEO] to come a few days early to mingle a bit, have lunch with everybody, and be more visible. A few days later, our all-staff meeting was the best we've had in months. The employees *loved* him. They ate him up!"

"Then, why don't they keep doing it that way?" asked Max, somewhat confused.

"They just don't get it," Sarah replied. "They blow it by not showing up again for over a month. It's 'snapshot leadership.' They pose for a few pictures, so to speak, and act like we should be grateful."

## WHO ARE OUR LEADERS?

About a month later, Christine expressed growing concerns about the virtual executives to Max. "Who are our leaders? Nobody knows them. How are they supposed to lead us if we don't even know who they are and they're not here? I mean, who's ever heard of virtual executives anyway? They're taking this whole dot-com thing a little too far."

"I don't see the logic in it either," agreed Max.

Most employees and in-house executives questioned the legitimacy of the virtual executives' membership in the organization and their leadership positions. These virtual executives had no prior relationships with anybody at Zi-Learn's main office in Front Range City and were not hired through members' existing relationships. Employees regarded them as unproven outsiders who lacked the credentials to make the solid decisions.

During a visit by virtual executives, Steve, the CEO, called an all-staff meeting. He announced from the lighted stage of a small auditorium the hiring of yet another top-level virtual executive. Bryan, a high-performing employee, raised his hand during a pause and voiced the frustration felt by many others seated around him, "Could you tell me about the *selection process* you used to make that decision? I hadn't heard that we were hiring for that position."

Steve seemed a bit rattled by the employee's strong tone and replied slowly and cautiously. "Well [pause] he was available and [pause] we had an opening. So [pause] I think we were lucky to get him." His explanation was received with a disapproving silence.

"I'll tell you what happened, Max," exclaimed Christine in the office the next day. "He basically hired his drinking buddy who got laid off when his last company went out of business. 'We're lucky to get him?' Yeah, right. No one even believes the CEO or the other virtual execs. I mean, the first thing out of people's mouths yesterday was, 'Boy I'm lightheaded from all the smoke they blew in there.'"

## NO SENSE OF MUTUAL OBLIGATION

Despite their limited interactions or perhaps because of them, stories about the virtual executives rubbing people wrong began to surface.

"Just the other day," Max reported, "Sean [a virtual executive] walked past my desk and joked, 'Yep, I'll be signing up for some training any day now, Max.' He doesn't even really know who I am. He had to look at my name tag."

"I know what you mean," replied Christine, "He just makes these disrespectful comments, laughs, and motors by without breaking his stride. He acts like he's joking, but what's funny about that? It's demeaning!"

Employees, in turn, antagonized virtual executives whenever they could. Max attended a presentation where employees hammered Greg, a virtual executive, with questions about selecting a company slogan or tagline. Greg stated in his introductory remarks that he would be happy to take questions at the end of his presentation. Employees, however, did not wait until the end.

"So, it looks like we're going with the second tagline listed here, 'Education that transforms,'" Greg said about halfway through his presentation as he pointed at the phrase on the screen.

"How do you test a slogan or tagline?" asked Christine, interrupting Greg's presentation.

"Uh, yesterday we had a couple of focus groups. . . . Most of the people who it has been run past prefer the tagline 'education that transforms,'" Greg replied calmly as he tried to continue his presentation.

Before Greg could proceed, Peter asked, "Who are the people in the focus groups?"

"Uh, they were folks here." Greg shuffled through some papers on the table in front of him. "Gosh, I can't remember who was in there," he mumbled, seeming more flustered by the multiple questions.

In a condescending tone of voice, Juan continued the questioning. "Would that tagline then be run by nurses or other people out there once internally you've decided? CEO's of hospitals? Potential clients? Others? Who?"

"Yeah," replied Greg with a forced smile. "We're going to keep asking. That's why I'm saying that tagline is not *necessarily* it. The decision hasn't been officially made yet." Greg laughed nervously, perhaps to defuse the noticeable tension in the room.

Bryan, however, maintained a serious expression and tone and kept the pressure on. "I'm curious as to the choice for 'transform.' It just seems ambivalent! I mean transform to *what*?" Bryan looked around the room to stir up support for his criticism. "I'm wondering if anybody agrees?"

Max could feel the tension in the room rise with each exchange. He thought to himself, "This is getting a little out of hand. Employees never cross-examine the in-house executives like this."

Greg responded more forcefully this time. "Well, the executive team hopes that individuals are going to be transformed by taking our courses and because of that, organizations are going to be transformed."

"Transformed to *what*?" Bryan repeated sharply with his hands in the air.

"Something better," responded Greg tersely.

"That's the ambiguous part of it. It's not necessarily better or positive," said Peter, jumping in to support Bryan's objection.

Greg remained silent for a moment to stay calm but Bryan kept questioning him. "Yeah. Transform? What does that mean?" Bryan held his hand up to indicate the size of a small toy. "I visualize little Transformers," said Bryan with a laugh. A few other employees laughed along.

Greg, the virtual executive, however, was not laughing. He ignored the employees' comments, forwarded to the next slide, turned toward the screen, and resumed his presentation as if nothing had happened.

The employees' hostility toward Greg and other virtual executives was obvious. Neither the employees nor the virtual executives demonstrated any sense of obligation to each other to work in a spirit of cooperation.

"They don't give us the time of day. Why should we listen to them?" commented Bryan later.

## "THEY HAVE NO BUY-IN AT ALL"

In the coming months, Max noticed that employees' satisfaction and productivity were dropping fast.

"We used to work so hard here," said Christine. "Lately, people are coming in late, taking two-hour lunches, and leaving early. Who cares? Why should we listen to them? There's no respect or trust for our supposed leaders. People here are looking for work at other places and I'm *seriously* considering it, too."

Even worse, Max noticed more infighting between and among employees. This type of interdepartmental conflict had not been a problem in the past. Now, it was a prominent part of employees' experiences. It seemed to Max, however, that the main topic of conversation at Zi-Learn was the in-house members' frustration with the virtual executives.

Late one Friday afternoon, Max popped into Bryan and Peter's sixth-floor window office and heard an all-too-common conversation. Peter was in a near tirade, but he was preaching to the choir.

"So she [a virtual executive] said to me, 'Let's sit down here and analyze some of your work.' I thought, 'Who on earth *are* you? Are you part of *my company*? Are you somebody that I am supposed to *salute to?*' " asked Peter.

"And, so when these meetings occasionally do take place, they become adversarial," Bryan empathized.

"Well, it was more like *bewilderment*," said Peter. "They have no buy-in at all. They started out and mismanaged things and they're so incredibly out of touch. They are so manifestly *wrong* in the many decisions they've made. Well, that directly influences *my* life and the way that I do *my* job."

"You know, they're not here," Bryan responded. "We don't see them in the office. We don't have any contact. We don't look them in the eyes on a daily basis."

Peter and Bryan went on and on. As Max listened, he looked out the window down on the trendy café across the street and remembered his conversation with Sarah just six months before. He wondered, "How did this problem with the virtual executives get so out of control? Could anything be done to fix it?"

## CHAPTER 10

# Knowledge Is Power

## Melinda M. Villagran and Mary Hoffman

Katie Morris* hit the key to send an instant message to her mom. "Just wanted to let you know I am settled in and start work tomorrow. I am so excited that I found a job where I can use my tech skills and help protect the environment."

The next day Katie was set to begin her new position at Green Solutions–one of the most innovative companies in the country. The company marketed technology for use in environmental engineering projects. Katie's position would enable her to assist in the creation of communication plans for Third World nations that were trying to ensure a supply of pure, potable water and to protect their wetlands and other natural habitats.

Katie's interests in the environment and in technology began when she was a child. Growing up, she had often taken walks and spent time watching the herons and egrets that shared the wetland near her home. In college, she especially enjoyed working in an online learning team, something the recruiter had told her was common practice at Green Solutions.

After graduating at the top of her class, she felt Green Solutions was a great place for an environmentally conscious, tech-savvy professional. She knew preserving wetlands would be a meaningful way for her to use her interest in communication technology.

At her interview, Katie had asked about the hardware and software used by the company. The recruiter had assured her, "Oh, we are state of the art in that area. I mean, how could we sell technology if we weren't on top of it ourselves?" He presented an image of Green Solutions as a thoroughly modern company with excellent profits over the last several years.

---

*This case has been developed based on real organization(s) and real organizational experiences. Names, facts, and situations have been changed to protect the privacy of individuals and organizations.

On her first day at her new job, Katie was introduced to Ned Benson. Ned was the Director of Communication Projects and her new supervisor. Ned shook Katie's hand and said, "I'm so glad you have joined our team."

As Ned introduced Katie to her new colleagues, she was surprised by how many people said, "Oh, you're so lucky to work with Ned. If you do everything, just like he does, you'll do great." She was further impressed as she listened to Ned talk about the types of projects he had been part of for Green Solutions. He had been with the company for 20 years, during which time he had built relationships with countless corporate executives, engineers, and government agencies. He had helped solve real environmental problems all over the world.

Clearly, Ned had earned his title and position in the company. He spent years marketing corporate products and building coalitions among groups to tackle environmental issues. Even though they were just getting acquainted, Katie already respected Ned. She admired his rapport with many of his colleagues and his ability to speak with people at all levels of the company.

In the first few days of her training, Katie tediously filled out forms, memorized training manuals, and completed screening tests. During training, she noted many areas where her technological experience could improve company operations. She decided to send Ned an email outlining her ideas:

To: Ned.Benson@GreenSol.org
From: Katie.Morris@GreenSol.org
Subject: Tech Ideas

Ned: I have some really great ideas for how we can improve orientation. I thought you would want to hear them. I can create an interactive website for new employees so they can do their training at home. I can either create the website using html or use whatever web editor you work with. We would need a couple of portables with remote access to LAN. We might also need to expand server capability. I would be happy to spearhead this project if it is something you are interested in. Love working here. ☺ KM

Katie had spent a lot of time thinking about this project, and she was disappointed when she never heard from Ned. She was eager to contribute to the company, and when her initial training was completed, she was ready to begin the work she had been trained to do.

Gradually, after a couple of weeks in her position, Katie realized that although Green Solutions used technology in their external products for clients, a fairly large portion of the staff had little or no expertise with the most basic office technology applications. At meetings, Katie saw lots of people with weekly planners, but almost nobody had a smartphone except her. She was shocked when a coworker asked her to fax something because he did not know how to use the fax machine. She was especially surprised at the number of people who did not appear to even use their computers very often.

It had been weeks since she had sent her idea to Ned, and still she had heard nothing. It dawned on her that maybe he hadn't responded to her email because he rarely used his computer. Indeed, he had an assistant who handled most correspondence through dictation and surface mail. One afternoon, Katie mentioned to Ned that she had sent him a project update as an attachment.

"What was it attached to?" Ned asked. "I haven't seen anything like that in my box."

Katie couldn't believe what she was hearing. She said, "I sent it to your email."

"Oh, that!" Ned joked, adding, "You know, I really prefer the personal touch that a printed letter offers."

Katie thought, "Wow, is Ned ever lucky to have Donovan. Otherwise, nothing technological would get done in his office."

Donovan Adler was Ned's assistant. Although Donovan had been at Green Solutions nearly as long as Ned, he was excited about learning new technology, and he regularly attended workshops and training seminars outside the office. One day he told Katie, "In all the years I have been working with Ned, I have come to the conclusion that although he is great with people, he is totally dependent on me when it comes to technology."

Donovan knew virtually everything about computer software and hardware, fax machines, data retrieval systems, and telephone and video conferencing. Donovan's expertise had the effect of making Ned look good inside and outside the company. In fact, few people perceived a problem with Ned's lack of computer knowledge. It seemed that few people even knew about Ned's technophobia.

Donovan was so capable that he was promoted to become the internal information systems specialist for the entire company shortly after Katie arrived at Green Solutions. Donovan left Katie's office to move to New York, and Ned hired a new assistant who had significantly less experience than Donovan with office systems. At Donovan's going-away party, Katie told him with a wink, "I know who really runs this place, and we're gonna miss him."

Donovan answered, "Call me if you need me. I'll be as much help as I can from New York."

Katie spent the next three months settling into her job, but she became increasingly frustrated and concerned about the leadership of the office after Donovan's departure. Then Green Solutions named a new vice president, Leigh Peyton. One of the first things Ms. Peyton did was to hold a team meeting via teleconference of all employees. During the meeting, Ms. Peyton announced her intent to "make Green Solutions as technologically efficient on the inside as it is on the outside."

In a confidential memo sent to the president of Green Solutions following the teleconference, Ms. Peyton noted, "While many of our executives excel in knowledge and expertise that is important to the attainment of company goals, they are hindering corporate functioning by their lack of knowledge about office technology. Among other initiatives, we will move immediately to institute virtual teams so that the appropriate personnel can collaborate on a regular basis."

A company-wide email appeared the next week:

To: Employees@GreenSol.org
From: Leigh Peyton <peyton@GreenSol.org>
Subject: Tech Updates

In keeping with our new commitment to make green Solutions as technologically efficient on the inside as it is on the outside, we announce the following initiatives:

- In the next 90 days all employees must complete the email proficiency test located on the corporate website.
- Smartphones have been purchased for all employees. All Smartphones must be synched during work hours so that employees receive corporate data in a timely manner. Smartphones will also be used for all scheduling and calendar maintenance.
- All computers are to use the same software systems for easy transfer of information. Data retrieval systems will be enacted to ensure accountability of all internal office information.
- Those without necessary skills should complete a copy of the needs assessment to let headquarters know what types of training will be necessary.

We are serious about these changes—failure to comply in a timely manner may lead to disciplinary action or dismissal of noncompliant employees.

Katie was excited, but she worried about how Ned would handle the changes. Knowing that Ned probably didn't get the email, she printed out a copy of it and took it to Ned's office. "I know you're busy," she said, "so I thought you might want a copy of this email."

As Ned read it, his face got red, and he sputtered, "Smartphones? Data retrieval? Needs assessment?—I'll tell them what I need—the only thing I need is to be allowed to do my job the way I've always done it. Maybe we don't need better machines to run this office, maybe we need better people."

Katie realized that she would have to help Ned transition to the new system. She thought a first step was to show him how to log on to a website that offered basic computer information and instruction.

Ned was reluctant to admit his shortcomings, but as he looked at the website Katie recommended, he realized that he didn't even know where to begin–even the language was unfamiliar. To him, trying to go online to learn about computers was frustrating, confusing, and a waste of his valuable time. He resigned himself to getting help, but he was not sure if he had the skills, or the desire, to make the transition to using technology.

Katie was surprised to be invited to participate in a teleconference with Ms. Peyton the next week. Ms. Peyton explained that, after viewing the needs assessment data, she realized there were lots of people in the organization who needed technological training. To supplement the formal training to come, Green Solutions enlisted the help of Katie and others at the meeting to aid in the transition.

Katie realized that this was an opportunity for her to take a leadership role to ensure compliance with the new policy. Finally, she would be able to use her experience with virtual teams, since she would be training people from several different Green Solutions locations. She was anxicus about her new responsibilities but excited to have the opportunity. She decided to share her concerns with Donovan, since he had offered to help:

To: Donovan.Adler@GreenSol.org
From: Katie.Morris@GreenSol.org
Subject: Help!

Donovan: I guess you know that Ned is going to have to change his attitude about computers. Can you believe they put me in charge of training all these people who have been here forever? I just got here—I can't be a leader. It is unbelievable to me that I am now more knowledgeable about some aspects of Green Solutions than the Director of Communication Projects! It seems like the balance of power has shifted here with this new policy. How am I going to coerce Ned into joining us in the 21st century? I am afraid if he doesn't do this, his job could be in jeopardy—and I think the organization really needs him. Any ideas for how I can supervise my supervisor during this change?
Hope things are going well in NYC. Thanks, KM.

CHAPTER 11

# The Emails in the Clinic Initial Services Department

Heather L. Walter

Peter* sighed as he watched Steve leave for the night. As the Director of the City Mental Health Clinic, Peter had many concerns. Steve had been working as head of the City Mental Health Clinic's Initial Services Department for three years now. When Steve was hired, Peter wanted to give him a great deal of autonomy to manage his department. Now Peter wondered if he should intervene.

The Initial Services Department was the first point of contact for any potential Mental Health Clinic patients. Patients could be referred to the clinic by a physician, a teacher, or social worker, or could call on their own if they believed they needed mental health services. Initial Services was where patient needs were assessed, files were started, backgrounds checked, and courses of action determined. The Initial Services Department was made up of a team of workers with different specialties: a psychologist (Val), two social workers (Beth and Jim), three clerical workers (Dot, Dave, and Rose), and a secretary (Cindy), all working for Steve, the team manager and head. Steve had a dual degree in psychology and organizational communication. Dot was the newest member of the team, having recently transferred to Initial Services from another clinic department.

Although the Initial Services Department was originally designed to have all members work together as a team to take new patients through the initial processes of receiving mental health care at the clinic, an informal hierarchy had developed based on degree and position. As a result, Val was considered the senior member of the staff, Beth and Jim the junior members of the staff, and the clerical workers and secretary were viewed by Steve as support staff.

When Steve first took over the department, it was alive with energy and productivity. Initial Services prided themselves on being a group of people who really

---

*The case is based upon an actual organization and real organizational experiences. Names, facts, and situations have been changed to protect the privacy of individuals and the organization.

loved what they did. The team climate had been a way to get input from all members. Over time the energy had transformed into friction with staff literally yelling at each other. On several occasions Dot had broken down in tears. When Peter first heard of the problems in the Initial Services Department, he hoped Steve would be able to manage the situation. Recently, however, the yelling and crying had given way to utter silence. Communication was limited to covert discussions purposely leaving individuals out of the loop. Resolution efforts had ceased to be face to face and were now a series of long, sometimes accusatory emails.

The disagreements began shortly after Dot joined the team. Clinic rumor had it that she wasn't the easiest person to get along with, but Steve needed the help and, quite frankly, upper administration didn't leave him much choice but to accept Dot into the department. Dot had been working for the clinic for 26 years, considerably longer than anyone else in the Initial Services Department. Over the years, Dot had been transferred several times, but her record did not mention the reasons for the transfers. On several occasions, Dot could be heard telling whoever would listen that she couldn't wait until she hit her 30-year mark so that she could retire with full benefits.

Dot and Steve did not work well together, and quickly the members of the department started to take sides. Val and Beth, who worked closely with Steve, supported their boss. Rose and Cindy were critical of how Steve treated Dot. Rose frequently started arguments on Dot's behalf. Jim and Dave seemed to want to stay out of the conflict, but often found themselves embroiled in the disagreements.

Recently, Steve submitted Dot's yearly performance appraisal, commenting that Dot was not motivated and did as little as possible to get by each day. Steve wrote that Dot met the basic expectations he had set forth for his department, but was not a team player.

When reviewing the performance evaluation, Peter recalled that three months earlier Steve had asked Peter to facilitate a meeting with Val, Beth, and Dot to discuss the conflict issues that had been erupting on a regular basis. As the date drew near for everyone to meet, Dot had asked that they cancel the meeting, claiming it wasn't going to make a difference anyway. On the date of the meeting, Peter remembered that Dot had called in sick causing Steve to cancel the discussion.

Today, both Steve and Dot had stopped by Peter's office. Both had left him with a copy of the same email exchange. Both believed that the email clearly determined they were right, with the other causing the problems. As Peter read the emails he wondered what in the world he could do to help return this department to the energetic and productive place it once had been. Should he go against Steve's wishes and give Dot the transfer she wanted? Should he support Steve as his direct report? Did he have enough information to make a decision? Was there something else he could do?

Email 1
To: Steve
From: Dot
Date: January 12

Steven,

I am writing this because I felt you wanted me to communicate my concerns, and I am moving on that opportunity.

With all due respect, you and I truly speak a different language and seem to have irreconcilable difference–in points of view, beliefs, truth, and ideas.

I "feel" I am always being "attacked" for my ideas, for my beliefs, for my opinion, which more likely than not challenges yours. You have a way then of twisting the situation, thus declining the responsibility of a leader for how your folks feel in your department. Yes, our feelings are our own. However, as a leader, if you have unhappy crying people in your department, you have a problem. According to you, whoever has the problem, it's their problem and if they don't like your answer then they should find employment elsewhere. I really wish you would be willing to do what you can to make me a valuable and valued employee of YOUR department, or at least grant me a transfer to another department so that you can get rid of me.

I would like to bring up a situation that occurred about 8 months ago where you allowed Val to speak to Rose and I in such derogatory ways that it sent me to the bathroom in tears. Rather than trying to remedy the situation, you made it clear that you agreed with Val by not getting involved. I am just as much a member of this department as Val, but I have never been made so feel so. I am not in your clique, never have been. There is a huge difference between Val and me. Val's work is who she IS, not WHAT she does. My work is what I DO, not WHO I am. Neither of us is wrong for our belief in work. Is my work ethics any less than hers because I don't define myself by my work? I believe that you hold her in much higher esteem than me because of her work philosophy, since it more or less matches your own work ethic. I can't compete with that. It really is like a competition here. I'm always the loser, always. It's tough always being the loser, being left out, being talked about behind your back. It's a difficult place to be.

Another issue of concern I'd like to reiterate is of the raises for the past two years. Instead of telling me ahead of time that I would not be getting the 4% raise and why, I had to hear through the grapevine that raises were done and I would be getting nothing and Val would be getting more than the rest of the team. Then, to add insult to injury, I find out that you sent Peter a memo indicating that Rose and Val wrote the majority of the evaluation of my performance that resulted in my lack of a raise.

I am still bothered by the recent false accusation that you, Val, and Beth made, claiming that I yelled at a patient, a patient who has sent a letter clearly indicating that I never treated her badly. I am owed an apology; it would be appreciated and appropriate. A patient would never have been treated in the manner I have been treated. Why is it that you care more about the external (patient) customer, than you do about your own internal (employee) customer? It is very sad, very painful, very hurtful working in a place where my coworkers and leader neither respect nor like me. I feel you have a large responsibility in this situation, and I don't feel you are willing to accept that responsibility.

Your latest email spoke of life being too short not to be happy, and how we are responsible for our own happiness. I agree with you. I would like your help in making this a happier place for me. It is up to you to decide if I'm worthy of your help or not. I'd like to be treated and given the same opportunities that others are given. I'm talking about being made to feel valuable and valued. If you don't feel I am a worthy, deserving employee for this department, then I ask that you use your clout in this organization to find me another position here. I would imagine the sooner the better.

This email is a year's worth of raw, hurtful, painful, difficult, at time resentful and angry, honest speaking here. It is really up to you what you decide to do with it.

Dot

Email 2
To: Dot
From: Steve
Date: January 14

Dot,

I am not concerned about whether we agree on points of view, beliefs, truths and/or ideas...in fact, we can agree to disagree, but for work's production for which I alone will be held accountable by the company's management as the head of this department, then it is the obligation of every department employee to follow my example and lead...and on this point, there is no negotiation.

As for being responsible for every unhappy person in my department, you have set an expectation that is impossible to achieve. It is not possible to have a place where everyone is happy all the time, if this is what you are suggesting then we are not on the same planet, and never will be. My philosophy is that people should fix their own problems and when they cannot or will not then I must assume the role of mediator. You have painted an impossible picture and, all the while, avoiding your own responsibility in the current state of affairs.

If you want to be a valued employee, then make yourself indispensable. But that is not likely to happen. You have rightly identified the very characteristics I embrace in many of your coworkers (these being the most prized in my opinion) and have cast these as being negative attributes. People who are fully committed to their careers understand and accept the fact that there are, on occasion, personal sacrifices associated with supporting team goals and objectives. I have concluded that you and I are never going to be on the same page in this regard. Remember, clinic staff are here to meet the director's standard and not the reverse.

There are many examples of exemplary employees around you. There are people who come to the office each day "excited" about the work we do...excited about learning new things and genuinely eager in becoming more integrated into the department's mission. Our patients love and respect these individuals. There are people who give 100 percent every day, and frankly, I take considerable offense that individuals of this sort I describe are somehow less than noble because they have committed fully to our endeavors. They serve us all as role models and should

*continued*

*continued*

be emulated, not ridiculed. So to answer your question on whether your work ethic is less than theirs, yes it is!!

You mention your concern with the distribution of raises, let me reiterate that several years ago Clinic policies changed from giving across the board raises in favor of a merit pay system. As a result, no one is guaranteed any raise whatsoever. Being present 40 hours a week does not qualify as merit-worthy performance. I don't know how you missed this point, but to think otherwise is a denial of what is real. A merit pool of X percent is just a pot of money that gets divided amongst those who have worked the hardest and contributed the most during the evaluation period...it does not guarantee that anyone will get an equal share or ANY share of the pot.

If you want to be a winner, then I suggest you behave like one. If you want to be perceived as a valuable employee, then behave like one. Stop behaving like a victim. Take responsibility for your workplace relationships. I cannot understand how you apparently conclude that the situation you find yourself confronting all happened without you having a role and responsibility in the outcome. The separation you experience from your colleagues and the creation of the situation you seemingly rail against has occurred with your direct involvement. Frankly, take responsibility and ownership for what has happened, and until you do there will be no progress in this regard. If you want to make the situation different, then make it so for yourself. It is up to you, not up to me.

As for finding you another employment opportunity, that is not my responsibility, it is yours. I suggest you make the most of the opportunity that is before you and be willing to accept responsibility for its outcome.

Your closing statement infers that it is up to me to decide how to deal with your hurt feelings. I have decided what I am going to do...you will be held accountable for the quality of your work; the quantity of your work; your knowledge of the work to be done; your ability to problem solve and take initiative; your communication skills; your dependability; and, your cooperation...meaning, in part, your attitudes towards coworkers and your attitude towards me. These have always been the expectations and will remain so for as long as you are a member of this department.

My questions to you are simply these: When are you going to accept responsibility for your work relationships? What are you going to do to make the situation better? After all, Dot, if not you, who? In not now, when?

Peter shook his head as he finished reading the emails for the third time. Clearly there were a multitude of difficult issues. And these emails were just an example of the adversarial relationships here. He could see many of Steve's points, but Dot was being singled out. Putting her on the defensive was not working for the department as a whole. Was it time to get involved? What was the best course of action?

CHAPTER 12

# Finding a Home for Communications Technologies

## Craig R. Scott, Laurie K. Lewis,

## Jennifer D. Davis, and Scott C. D'Urso

As Derek,* Monica, and Trevor thought back on the last two days, they were clearly pleased. They had just finished several training and orientation sessions with a group of nonprofit leaders and local government officials about the use of multiple new communication technologies. These individuals worked for different organizations, but all of them focused to some extent on providing various services to the homeless in the community. They also represented organizations that often lacked key communication tools that could greatly assist them in their work, which was part of the reason Derek, Monica, and Trevor were so enthusiastic about the opportunity to bring various communication technologies to these homeless service providers.

Even getting to this point had not been easy. The three project consultants had been working with this set of organizations for several months before the key members began to realize they were serious about a project to provide them with these technologies. As Monica had remarked to Derek, "I think they thought we'd swoop in, be overwhelmed with the challenges these providers face, and then quietly leave." These consultants were convinced that the community's homeless service providers were in great need of new communication technologies, and when many of the agencies learned they would be eligible to receive high-speed Internet services, computing equipment they could keep, and free training and technical support, their interest perked. Attending the orientation and training was a condition for getting the equipment, and it also provided a chance to learn how to use some of the software and hardware provided. Though both the homeless service providers and consultants seemed pleased with the project at the training, none of

*This case has been developed based on real organization(s) and real organizational experiences. Names, facts, and situations have been changed to protect the privacy of individuals and organizations.

them could have predicted the ways in which the technology would, and would not, be used in this community of service providers.

## ADDRESSING REAL PROBLEMS

Derek had some experience working with organizations serving the homeless and knew the seriousness of the homelessness problem. Recent research done by the National Law Center on Homelessness and Poverty estimated 3.5 million homeless people in this country in the mid-2000s, with the Partnership for the Homeless noting that the number of homeless is rising annually. Monica and Derek had seen other estimates in a newspaper survey indicating that 1 of every 400 Americans experienced homelessness. In the specific midsized metropolitan city where the project consultants lived, the average daily estimate of homeless persons was 4,000. The fastest-growing population of homeless was families (43 percent of the homeless population in this area on any given day); additionally, unaccompanied youth accounted for 7 percent of the total homeless population.

With her expertise as a trainer and consultant in interorganizational dynamics, Monica was very sensitive to the specific organizations involved. The homeless service providers ranged from food pantries and soup kitchens to shelters for immigrants and victims of domestic violence. They included organizations providing low-cost housing and legal aid to those assisting with education and basic health services. The individual work of these organizations in the community included helping homeless kids stay in school; helping homeless families navigate the system to secure affordable housing and achieve job training; counseling homeless victims of domestic violence and protecting them from threatening behavior of abusers; helping abandoned and abused teens to redirect their lives and complete the GED; helping mentally ill homeless persons to gain access to appropriate health care; providing safe and appropriate shelter and transitional housing for those who were seeking to recover from crisis and obtain permanent affordable housing; and providing the most basic of life's needs: showers, laundry, lockers, phone access, food, clothes, diapers, and dental care.

Clearly no single service provider could address all the needs alone, and thus a patchwork of service provision existed—sometimes with minimal awareness of other agencies and offices. Furthermore, the environment of dwindling financial resources had created a scarcity-induced competitiveness among many providers, evidenced by some mutual protectiveness about sources of funding. Additionally, several disagreements existed in terms of philosophy of service delivery, desire to participate in advocacy efforts, beliefs about how to target the overall mission of the community of providers, and degree of desire to work independently versus collectively on matters related to homelessness. The only formal connection among the provider organizations was the Task Force on Homelessness (TFH), which worked as an organizing and planning body.

## SECURING TECHNOLOGY

Monica and Derek believed this community of service providers could benefit from better tools for coordination, collaboration, and communication. Monica and Derek perceived an opportunity to help with the situation by drawing on their past experiences. They secured external grant funding and community support to launch a project to help the organizations work together more effectively through the use of various communications technologies. They hoped to fill the gaps in the continuum of care that moves homeless persons through a series of steps from crisis to eventual stability and self-sufficiency. Each of the approximately 25 nonprofit and government organizations involved was equipped with the appropriate infrastructure (e.g., high-speed Internet connections, powerful desktop computers, collaborative software) and provided with training and ongoing technical support. Trevor was hired as the technical support person, and he helped conduct the training that introduced the users to an instant messaging tool, file-sharing programs, and a customized website he created for them. The homeless service providers also had access to an online electronic meeting tool for decision making, planning, and surveys. Additionally, an email list was made available to anyone associated with the homeless provider network in the community.

## LITTLE ROOM FOR SOME TECHNOLOGIES

Despite Trevor's thorough training, some technologies clearly never caught on. The instant messaging tool that automatically launched rarely saw any activity. Follow-up surveys with community members reported no use of the file sharing. Derek even convinced an electronic meeting software vendor to provide the group with free access to its expensive tools. Even after several pitches to the group members about how they might best use the tools, they did so only one time—and that was just for an online survey they did to help with the preparation of a grant. As one agency head explained to Trevor, "Life is about who shows up. People are just not ready for the disconnect technology creates. We are in a high-touch business. A lot of what we do is consensus work; not a lot of formal voting."

Trevor and Derek were frustrated. As the homeless service coordinator for the city explained to Monica,

> "Among providers, people in homeless services are the least apt to jump into new technology, because we are so used to working with people who don't have access to a lot of technology, that everything we do is so paper and pencil or here's a phone number, you know, just call them or actually just go over and visit them, you know. It is much less computer-oriented work that we do. And part of it is, again, because our clients don't have access to that kind of thing, so we don't get in the habit of really using this either."

The project website for this provider community was launched in the spring right around the time of the training; nevertheless, many organizational members reported difficulties in accessing and using the site. So, Monica and Derek decided to start over, and the site was redone as an MSN Groups site later that year, with periodic upgrades over the following months/years. The new homeless service provider website included a list of the providers, contact information for each, a community calendar, a bulletin board, and a document-posting site. Derek was able to get communication and journalism students at a local university to write online *spotlight* articles over the course of the project. These articles focused on specific provider organizations, special projects, programs, and key personnel working with homeless in the community. Articles and pictures were posted to the website as a way to both lure members to the site and then to educate them about other organizations once they arrived.

The spotlight articles did seem to capture interest, and there were spikes in hits to the website after announcements about each new spotlight article. A director of one of the organizations felt the spotlight articles "brought a personal touch to the organization or the person they were interviewing." However, other aspects of the website were rarely used, and those who did use them did so less often over the course of the project. One agency director indicated that she didn't visit the website "unless there is a spotlight that comes out that I want to read. Then I have gone and read the article, but I haven't used the [rest of the] website." In addition, some people posted to the calendar tool but when only a few did this there was less incentive for others to do the same. A similar situation existed with the discussion/bulletin board on the site. Even efforts to get community members to update their contact information were generally unsuccessful amid competing client demands. As one of the nonprofit directors confessed to the consultants, "Let me just say that I used to use the calendar, and I never got any response from anything I posted, so I felt that no one else was using it, so I just stopped using it. That was it. I don't know if it was a fair thing, I used it for about eight months in the beginning, and I don't know if people use the calendar now or not." Within three years, the TFH, in conjunction with a larger body overseeing social concerns in the community, decided to develop its own website. Although the TFH did copy over the spotlight articles to the new site, no other part of the website was incorporated into the new one, and the initial project website for the community eventually was abandoned.

## FINDING A HOME ON THE EMAIL LIST

Derek and Trevor launched a community email list in April as a means for individuals within the community of homeless service providers or others interested in receiving information about that community's activities to post and receive messages. The list was unmoderated but open to subscribers only. Initially the list was configured so that all replies went back to everyone on the list as a way to facilitate community awareness; but after a series of unintended personal replies went back to all subscribers, community members requested that replies only go back to the sender (replies to all would still go back to the entire list). Despite Derek's concern that this might discourage online discussion (thus resulting in the tool not being used in certain desirable ways), this change was made in July, with no other major changes made to the list configuration afterward. Unlike the other technologies provided, email list usage grew. Even though the list was started with approximately 60 individuals whom the city homeless coordinator had as part of a set of relevant email addresses she would use to communicate announcements, it eventually grew to twice that size—incorporating a much wider range of organizations and concerned individuals in the process. Over the course of the project there was a clear growth in the number of posts: 234 in the first year, 314 in the second year, and 438 in the third year.

Despite all the energy the consultants had put into state-of-the-art equipment, sophisticated software, and collaboration tools, it was the simple list that served this community best. Email list users confirmed in feedback surveys and discussion that this was the single most effective means they had for disseminating and collecting information from other homeless service providers. As one nonprofit coordinator told Monica, "I find the listserv to be pretty helpful because I am constantly in the loop about things." Even the city's homeless service coordinator who initially expressed reservations about the usefulness of these tools for this group admitted, "I did get a lot of feedback from a lot of people that they really appreciated the things that I sent to the list and it helped them keep at least somewhat abreast of things that they wouldn't ordinarily seek out." Another told the consultants that when people asked about how to learn more about homelessness in this community, he would tell them "If you want information, get on the list."

Derek noticed that most users were not submitting to the list, but were actually lurking. In none of the three years were there more posters than lurkers. Although some in the community expressed concern about this, Monica and Derek assured them that this form of use is not necessarily problematic and may even be construed as a beneficial form of use. As Trevor noted, "there may be real benefit that not all 100+ subscribes were regularly posting to the list!"

Unexpectedly, the email list also took on substantial symbolic value among the homeless service providers as membership on the list began to demarcate this otherwise dispersed and ill-defined community of professionals and organizations. You were part of this community if you were on the list and not part of it if you were not. As a result, the list also created a stronger and clearer sense of community among these organizations serving the homeless. As two individuals in smaller nonprofit organizations told Monica, "People are more connected. There is probably much more understanding of what is happening on a macro level. Before, people operated more in their silos. The listserv has brought people together" and "The list provides more cohesion to our community of service providers."

## TAKE-HOMES AND LESSONS LEARNED

As their project with the homeless service providers officially ended, Monica, Derek, and Trevor had mixed reactions. In one sense, much of what they had tried to do failed. Several key technologies they thought should have been useful never caught on in this community. Some aspects of the website were barely utilized and ultimately abandoned. The computers provided were only sometimes utilized for communicating with other providers. However, the group also felt there were successes. The exposure to high-speed Internet made a real difference for those otherwise without it (and when the project ended, most organizations found a way to continue this use despite limited operating budgets). The spotlight articles were valued and were included in the new TFH website. Most important was the email list. Though it did not often generate elaborate discussion of key issues, it did serve as an information and solicitation tool that was highly valued by community members; furthermore, it served to redefine who this community was. Thus, the consultants arranged for Kayla, who operated several email lists in the community, to manage this one even after the remainder of the project ended. As one provider posted to the email list at the project's end, "Thanks to you for all your work with the task force over the years—especially helping us to get a little more computer savvy and utilize at least the listserv."

At one point Derek admitted, "I initially thought our project was about train-ing people to use technology and then expecting them to comply. It turned out to be about providing opportunities for people, seeing what worked for them in their situation, and then learning from that." The consultants already knew that some-times technology helps solve problems and sometimes it does not—but what they discovered was that sometimes people's work can be so demanding that it often prevents them from ever utilizing anything but the most basic tools (which can be learned quickly without interfering with one's direct work with clients).

Perhaps the most important lessons were not really about technology at all.

# Teamwork and Group Processes

## CHAPTER 13

# Reorganizing Human Resources at ASP Software

### Donald L. Anderson

Nathan Miller's* phone buzzed on his desk in his home office. "Hi, Nathan? This is Susan McNulty, from ASP Software. I'm the vice president of human resources here. I got your name from Joan Orman at Kendall Consulting."

Nathan smiled. Joan had been a talented coworker during his time at Kendall several years ago. He had since received many referrals from her for his growing organizational development practice. "Of course–what can I do for you?" Nathan inquired. ASP Software was a familiar company to Nathan. It was a large employer in the area, a high-tech organization in a community without many technology companies. ASP Software built software products for *Fortune 500* companies, employing about 750 software engineers in product development, and 500 sales executives. Including the other support functions needed to make the company run (marketing, HR, finance, and so on), it employed almost 1,500 people in the region.

"Well, we're reorganizing our human resources department here at ASP Software, and I was asking Joan whether she knew of anyone who might be able to help us with a teambuilding exercise, and your name came up. Do you think you might be able to do that for us?"

"Well," Nathan paused. "I might be able to help you with some ideas–team-building could be a possibility, or there are other initiatives we could work on as well. Can you tell me a little about what you're trying to do there at ASP Software? Perhaps give me some of the context?"

"Sure," Susan said. "We're changing our model from a functional model to a full client management services model. Of course, that model requires a lot of teamwork, and we've also had a small reduction in staff, so..." She paused for emphasis.

---

*The case is based upon an actual organization and real organizational experiences. Names, facts, and situations have been changed to protect the privacy of individuals and the organization.

Nathan listened. He wasn't sure what a "full client management services model" meant, but it was clearly important to Susan.

Susan continued. "So, with this new focus on teams, it seemed important to our change team that we conduct a teambuilding activity. I was hoping that maybe we could meet in person and I could describe our model and we could talk about how you might be able to help us? Say, Tuesday at 2:30?"

"That sounds fine. I know right where your headquarters are located. Should I stop in the lobby and ask for you?" Nathan asked.

"That's fine. I'll see you then."

\*\*\*

"I'm so glad you could make it. It's nice to meet you in person." Susan welcomed Nathan to ASP Software headquarters, a four-story building located just outside downtown. The building was a standard glass-and-steel box, with a shiny chrome ASP Software logo featured prominently in the marble-floored lobby. The lobby was a busy place as employees and visitors were constantly coming and going. Nathan wore a visitor's badge and had been waiting in the lobby until Susan came down to greet him.

On the fourth floor, they sat down in a conference room. It was a large, mahogany table, surrounded by 12 leather chairs. On the wall Nathan noticed a cherry wood-framed print of mountain climbers. At the bottom read "Teamwork: Giving a helping hand makes all the difference." Another showed a kayaker paddling down a river, with the text "Goals: Effort is nothing without a vision." Also in the room were a videoconferencing unit and a recessed screen that appeared via remote control. Track lighting provided spotlights on the framed prints.

"Thanks for inviting me. It sounds like you have an interesting and challenging change underway," Nathan said.

"Oh, yes, I think so. I'm really pleased that the management team has adopted this new structure. I think it will improve our productivity and reputation as an HR team," Susan replied.

"So you said that you're changing models? Can you tell me what that means?"

"Sure." She handed Nathan an organizational chart.

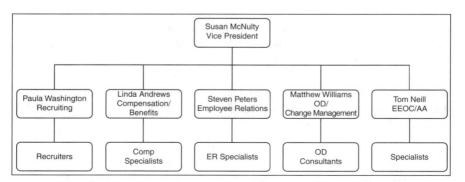

**Figure 13.1** ASP Human Resources Department (old model)

"This chart shows how we are currently organized, by HR function. I have five managers on my team, and each has a separate function. Paula is in charge of our recruiting function, and she supervises all of our talent acquisition work. She has five recruiters working for her. Her recruiters work with managers to open jobs, they search for candidates, conduct preliminary interviews, and process job offers. Linda has compensation, benefits, and rewards. That includes stock grants, executive compensation, and job leveling, plus any other compensation studies that our executive team requests. Linda currently has two compensation specialists reporting to her. Steven Peters has eight employee relations specialists–they do most of the day-to-day work with the management teams they support, to help them conduct performance reviews, and to deal with employee complaints and problems. Matthew is our organizational development and change management expert, and he has four OD consultants working for him. They work on various projects but generally advise the management teams they work with, facilitate meetings, and develop and conduct training. Finally, Tom has our EEOC responsibilities, including legal reporting and compliance, but also investigations of complaints such as harassment or mistreatment of employees. He has three investigation specialists who do data analysis and reporting."

"That sounds like a common organizational structure for a human resources department, in my experience," Nathan said. "What prompted a change?"

"Well," Susan started, "our internal client managers–the internal 'customers' of our department–haven't been very happy with the service they've been receiving from the HR department. One of the company's biggest challenges is recruiting–we have about 200 new positions a year to recruit. Combining those jobs with positions that we need to fill as a result of turnover means that each of our recruiters is handling two dozen positions at any given time. That has led to some frustration from the ASP Software management team. A manager will need to hire someone, and he'll have to call one person in Paula's organization to get the position opened, then deal with a person on Linda's team to figure out what the compensation level should be, and neither of those people is the person that the manager typically works with on employee relations issues from Steven's team. That can cause some problems on its own, but what really has frustrated them is that the next time he has to hire someone, he'll have to call Paula again, and might be assigned a different recruiter. It's a trend that we see in many companies today–our managers are looking for one person to call to handle all of their HR services. And we really need to open positions, interview candidates, and get job offers out much more quickly than we are today. It's a tight market for the best people."

Susan continued. "At the same time, most of the management team really isn't involved with the strategic aspects of the business, designing HR programs that make the most sense with where the business is going. In the software industry, we must move very quickly, and we're constantly looking for new talent and examining different ways to compensate them to maximize loyalty, retention, and productivity. I've been involved with our corporate strategic direction, but the rest of the HR team has been oriented toward the day-to-day activities instead of the bigger picture, so they're not adding as much value as they could."

"That sounds like a common complaint," Nathan said. "What kinds of changes are you going to make?"

"Here's the new organizational chart." Susan handed Nathan another sheet.

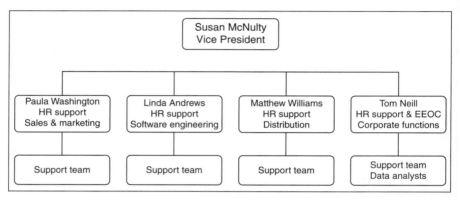

**Figure 13.2**  ASP Human Resources Department (new model)

"In this new model, we've organized teams to serve the various internal departments that run the ASP Software business—we call them our internal customers. So for example, Paula will now support only the sales and marketing team, and she will be supported by a team that will consist of four team members, called 'generalists,' who will all support various assigned members of the management team in sales and marketing. The advantage is that Paula will now be the central point of contact for our VP of sales and marketing, and she will be much more involved in developing and understanding sales and marketing strategy, so that our human resources strategies—compensation, hiring, change management—will all be aligned with the sales strategy. Linda will do the same thing with Software Engineering. Matthew will support our Distribution function. In this way, we'll be much more client-focused, and we will be much more strategic and responsive to the business. Once a new employee is hired, that person will work with one HR generalist throughout his or her career at ASP Software, in career planning, compensation, etc. I also asked Tom to keep the EEOC function with two data analysts, since that was his expertise and it didn't make sense to combine with the other functions. But he'll also take on a support role for all corporate functions, like finance and legal."

"Has this been announced formally?" Nathan asked.

"Mostly. We had our first meeting last week. We told them that some changes were coming, and most people were aware of it generally but not the specifics. Today we had the second meeting where I published the chart with the names in the positions."

Nathan noticed that the new organizational chart contained fewer boxes. "You had mentioned a staffing reduction?" he asked.

"You're paying attention," Susan said. "At the same time as we discussed this model, we determined that our expenses were about 10 percent more than we could afford, so we had to reduce our total headcount by four positions. Those will come from several areas, including two employee relations specialists, one EEOC data analyst, and one recruiter."

Nathan did the math quickly in his head. There was one position unaccounted for. "I only get 22 people when you used to have 27. Am I missing one position?"

"Good observation," Susan smiled. "I haven't published it yet or announced it because I still need to formalize it, but I've asked Steven Peters to take on the role of director of HR operations. The four members of the management team will all report directly to Steven, and he will be responsible for the day-to-day operations of the HR organization. My role will change slightly, since I've been asked by our CEO, David Kaufman, to take on several additional responsibilities and to assist him with special customer calls. While I will have the same title, I won't have time to sort out the daily problems, so I've invited Steven to take on this new responsibility. It's a good development opportunity for him, and it saves me time. We have another meeting with the whole organization on Monday, and I'll share Steven's new role with them at that time."

"Do you have a sense for how people feel about this change generally? Both on the management team and among the support teams?" Nathan asked.

"On the management team I think there's a bit of relief, since they knew I was going to reduce it by one position, and the four that are left are settling into their new roles. They know that they have jobs, although they don't know yet about Steven's promotion. Among the generalists, I think there's a range of opinions. There is a lot of anxiety about the staffing reduction, and I'm not sure that people have gotten over that yet. The old teams were pretty tight, and I think that some people are looking forward to their new roles while others are wondering about their new team members or their new manager. Some of them, particularly the ones that used to be recruiters, are looking forward to expanded roles that will give them more access to their client managers. Others, such as the employee relations specialists, are not looking forward to the recruiting responsibility."

"Have the employee relations specialists ever done recruiting before?" Nathan inquired.

"One or two used to do that in a previous company. But most of them haven't, so they will probably need some training initially. I'm willing to let them have that time to adjust and learn."

"Anything else? Who else might be especially happy or unhappy with this change?" Nathan probed.

"Among the employee relations specialists, Steven was a very popular manager. Matthew has had a couple of run-ins with one of the ER specialists we have assigned to his group–that relationship has been contentious in the past, but it was the only spot to put that one individual, so we had to deal with it. I think Matthew will be very professional about it," Susan added.

"Tell me about the relationship that Steven has had with his peers," Nathan requested.

"Steven has been very popular as a team member and as a leader in his own group, there's no question. I don't think there are any issues there," Susan shook her head. "But it will be a slight change to those who don't know him well, like the recruiters or the compensation specialists. It might be hard for his former team members to relate to him in a different way. But Steven is popular and he projects a very pleasant charisma, so I know he'll quickly take over the leadership position."

"What measures of success are you looking for?"

"We've always measured the effectiveness of our recruiters in several ways: number of qualified candidates presented to management, and in cycle time of open position to acceptance of offer. We'll continue to measure our generalists in that way, which I think makes some of them a bit anxious since they're not used to recruiting. Right now it takes us about 77 days to open a position, find candidates, interview them, and get a job offer out. I'm looking for our generalists to move twice as quickly as that. That means each generalist will have a quota of jobs to fill and will be measured on time to fill those positions. But generally I'm looking for more satisfied internal clients and fewer complaints. We should also be able to do more with less since each person will have direct responsibility for their internal clients–they won't need to go from team to team to get the job done."

"How about for my work–are there any specific outcomes you're looking for?" Nathan wondered.

"Not exactly–I'm looking for your guidance about how to proceed. What we need to do is to get beyond this change as quickly as possible so that we're starting to show real results to our internal client managers. I think people are still pretty upset about losing some of their coworkers, and the rumors have been running rampant for the past several weeks. We stopped some of that with the meeting last week and this week, by sharing our plans and showing them the organizational chart. But we've lost a lot of time in getting to this point and now we need to move quickly to get people into their new teams and to start recruiting immediately," Susan stressed.

"You had mentioned initially that you were looking for a teambuilding activity?" Nathan asked, remembering their phone conversation.

"Yes. With these new teams, only a few of them have worked together before closely. This will require a new kind of coordination among the team members–instead of doing their own thing and managing their own projects, they'll be part of a team to support each business function. They'll still have their own responsibilities, but they will need to share information, determine a strategy and direction, and take on new and unfamiliar responsibilities. I'm thinking that some kind of teambuilding activity would be really helpful to them–they could get to know each other better, perhaps in a social setting. The other thing I was thinking since we talked on the phone is giving personality tests like the Myers-Briggs or another assessment, so that people could examine each other's working style? I just don't know where to start."

The conversation began to die down, and Susan posed the final question: "So after all of that, do you think you can help us?"

"I think there are a couple of things that come to mind that could help make this transition smoother," Nathan said. "Why don't I put together a proposal for how I think things could proceed, and we can take it from there?"

"I would really appreciate that. You come highly recommended and I appreciate your insights and guidance," Susan said. "I look forward to reading your proposal."

## CHAPTER 14

# Teaming Up for Change

## Maryanne Wanca-Thibault and Adelina Gomez

In 1995, during a weekly staff meeting, Lieutenant Jack Whitson,* a police detective with the Castle Springs Police Department, addressed his concerns and frustrations to the others present. "I am very frustrated. As the city grows, the number of domestic violence cases in our community continues to increase. Nothing we do seems to reduce our caseload numbers."

He continued, "We go by the book; we respond to calls and take the necessary information from both parties, and then we determine if the case merits charging one or both parties involved. But then it's out of our hands until the violence happens again. There has to be a better way."

Janet Garcia, the deputy district attorney, agreed. "Our court cases are so backlogged that by the time we reach the court date, the victim often decides to drop the charges."

Sue Mackenzie, the domestic violence victim's advocate, added, "My frustration is in trying to provide the victims with support services to keep them safe while the perpetrators are trying to get them to drop the charges. Usually, they end up right back in the same abusive relationship."

Frustrated with the high volume of domestic violence cases and a bureaucracy in which professionals from across many units did not routinely or formally share information, these three individuals determined that it was time to take action and change the status quo.

As the meeting continued, they began to discuss a possible approach to the domestic violence issue–an approach that had not been tried before. Jack envisioned a collaborative team approach to the problem. "It's obvious," he said, "that we can do a better job of working together and sharing information about our cases. We just have to put the mechanism for it in place."

---

*This case has been developed based on real organization(s) and real organizational experiences. Names, facts, and situations have been changed to protect the privacy of individuals and organizations.

Jack, Janet, and Sue all knew that it would be a challenge to change the attitudes and values of groups who traditionally had worked on the same side, but not always together or with the same information.

Sue countered, "I agree that we have our work cut out for us, but if we are able to convince our colleagues to reorganize into a more efficient and holistic method of dealing with victims and perpetrators, we might get the support we need. Let's face it, we spend so much time trying to handle all of the calls we receive that we really can't focus on things like containment, education, and protection of the victims and their families. A collaborative approach would provide a central source for dealing with all of the issues related to domestic violence."

Janet said, "I agree. It would be great if the new model could better incorporate community policing. But I hesitate to add that, since you know how resistant the old-timers have been to that."

Jack responded, "I wish we had a system where we would regularly rotate police, judicial, and social service personnel through the team. When they leave the team they could go back to their home agencies with a new perspective on working collaboratively. Of course, that means we will have to provide ongoing training for individuals. We haven't traditionally used a collaborative approach in law enforcement. We tend to work independently of social services and the justice system when it comes to handling domestic violence. From my experience, other agencies work in about the same way. Everybody does their thing, independent of others in the system who also work with domestic violence."

"Yes, I agree," said Janet. "Simply putting a collaborative team in place won't accomplish what we want it to. We are going to have to learn how to collaborate, if we plan to make this work."

## CREATING DVERT

It took many more meetings and a great deal more discussion, but in 1996, funded by a federal grant from the Department of Justice and with support from members of local law enforcement agencies, the judicial system, and social services agencies, DVERT (Domestic Violence Enhanced Response Team) was created.

The objective of the DVERT team was to identify and work with individuals who pose a significant risk to their past or present partners because of acts or threats of domestic violence. Under DVERT, a number of community agencies would become real partners and combine forces to identify suspects who fit the profile of abusers. If the DVERT team determined that the level of violence necessitated intervention, the team added the case to their load, meaning that both victim and perpetrator were subject to follow-up meetings with the team.

## THE STAKEHOLDERS

Detective Jack Whitson, the DVERT program manager, sat in his office behind closed doors and replayed the events of the morning's yearly board meeting in his head. "This is 2006," he thought. "We've successfully operated DVERT for 10 years. We've certainly had our ups and downs, and there has been plenty of change during that time. But our future's at stake. We are really going to have to pull together to make some decisions and it's not going to be easy." He knew that frustration was running high among a number of the DVERT board members, and he was going to have to address their concerns in the afternoon session.

Jack was a pragmatic man. He was known to face challenges head-on, and creating and managing a multidisciplinary program like DVERT had certainly tested his leadership skills. But for Jack it always came back to the program's mission: "to work in partnership with community agencies to enhance the safety of victims of domestic violence and their children, while ensuring appropriate containment of offenders." In his mind, regardless of any other differences the agencies had, this was a value they all shared.

The 14-member advisory board of directors (Figure 14.1) was somewhat unique. Each member represented a community agency or group with a vested interest in domestic violence containment and prevention. In addition to the clients, these community members were key stakeholders in the organization. Depending on their expertise, agencies were responsible for negotiating and providing their expertise, manpower, and other resource support to DVERT.

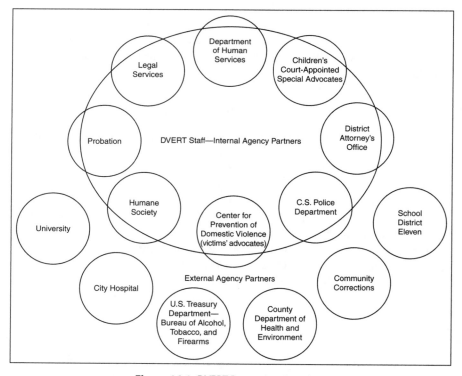

**Figure 14.1** DVERT Partnering Agenices

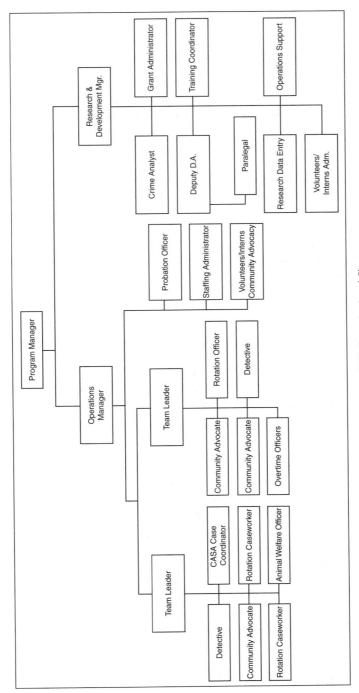

**Figure 14.2** DVERT's Organizational Chart

The eight internal partnering agencies provided permanent and rotational manpower in the form of victim advocates, police officers, court-appointed children's advocates, a district attorney, and animal advocates (since animal abuse is often cyclical and a precursor to human abuse), who actually worked on a daily basis with full-time DVERT staff. The six remaining external agencies acted as consultants and provided expertise and support to the DVERT staff. Generally, the external agencies had more limited interaction with the full-time staff, although a number of them were involved in weekly staffing meetings, where caseload decisions were made. However, all representatives of the board met at least once a year to discuss their ongoing roles and contributions to the program. The diversity of the agencies represented allowed DVERT to address the variety of concerns associated with the containment and prevention of domestic violence. Jack saw the challenge as making certain that each agency maintained its commitment to DVERT's organizational mission and values. This was tough, given that each agency representative also felt allegiance to other people and projects.

DVERT's structural form was different from most public sector organizations that rely on traditional hierarchical designs. In this case, the organization was characterized as a flat organization composed of teams with defined accountabilities and responsibilities (Figure 14.2). There were two full-time managers under Jack's direction. The first managed operational issues regarding caseload. Under this manager were two full-time team leaders who, along with their multidisciplinary teams, assessed and investigated the domestic violence cases brought to DVERT. The second manager handled research and development issues (i.e., training, grants, crime analysis) for the organization. In this high participation environment, decision making was always considered a collaborative process involving all of the appropriate stakeholders.

In the early days of the program there had been many turf battles. It was bound to happen. Most of these groups had rarely collaborated with each other in the past and now found it challenging to share office space, let alone ideas and decision making. It was not unusual for someone from human services to complain that "we don't even share the same language" when speaking of other team members. In particular, many of the rotational staff found that in order to do their jobs, they had to develop a better understanding of what other agencies around them were doing. That resulted in a great deal of negotiation and adjustment on everyone's part. Subsequently, there was an ongoing perception among many of the staff and partners that the program was always evolving.

An unwritten credo among staff was that the one thing you could expect at DVERT was change. This situation was difficult for many of the staff, who had worked in organizations where standards and policies were firmly in place. In those first several years the program lost a number of full-time staff who had a hard time dealing with the change and collaborative decision making. Moreover, many people who had volunteered for a rotation at DVERT left after their three-month commitment, disillusioned with the process. However, in the past two years the membership at DVERT had stabilized, and some members had asked to stay on for more than a single rotation. Some rotational staff had even moved into permanent positions.

Coming from a law enforcement background, even Jack could clearly see how the diversity of organizational values affected DVERT's climate. In his leadership role he often found it a challenge to help the group manage change and to work through the differences that arose. But from his perspective, that diversity and the ability to quickly adapt to the external and internal environment, if channeled correctly, was the underlying strength of this collaborative approach toward domestic violence.

From Whitson's perspective he thought now that the program was moving into its sixth year, they had moved beyond that stage of *muscle flexing* and were working together more effectively. However, it was clear from this morning's discussion that a number of partners were looking to make some changes. While he encouraged planned change as a strategic management tool, he also realized the importance of maintaining continuity when things worked well. In Jack's mind the question was whether these changes were right for DVERT at this time.

## THE ISSUES

During the morning session of the board meeting, Jack had been prepared for questions from disgruntled members. He started by reviewing the issues that would likely emerge. He summarized, "Our first issue is centered on increasing financial support for DVERT."

Kirby Jones, the humane society representative, interjected, "I thought all the funding that we would need would be covered by the federal grant."

"Much of it is," Jack responded, "but we still need to consider other options for ongoing funding. Our grants are getting smaller every year."

Sue Mackenzie, the domestic violence victim's advocate, interrupted, "VAWA or Violence Against Women Association is a potential funding source."

Janet Garcia, the deputy district attorney, added, "We also need to identify other grant sources to help sustain DVERT. We have been extremely fortunate to have had significant monetary support to maintain the program."

"Yes," said Jack, "and let's not forget the rotation staff, which some partners are providing on an ongoing basis, as well as the furniture, office space, and supplies that are donated. Those are critical operating resources." Several members nodded in acknowledgment.

At this point, Jack interrupted the discussion to explain that there were still two key issues left to discuss. "We can't forget the most important issues here," he said. "We touched on funding. The second issue is growth of the program, meaning the expansion of cases that the program can comfortably handle. The third issue is whether or not to expand the partner base."

Elliott Richards, a board representative from the probation department, interrupted. "I'm not convinced that we are informed enough to act on any of these

issues. First, our decreasing budget already affects the level of services we can provide for our clients. How will we be able to increase services without increasing
the budget?"

One of the major arguments among the partners was the issue of quality versus quantity. Many felt that it was the role of DVERT to handle only the most serious and ultimately lethal domestic violence cases, whereas other members felt that
DVERT should not distinguish between the levels of lethality and should strive to
serve as many victims as possible.

Elliott continued, "Moreover, the current economic climate makes the development of the program tenuous, at best. And the way I see it, we will have to really
struggle to increase funding without increasing the number of partners we currently have on the board. It's obvious we have to add new partners."

Jack tried to remain neutral at this point and declined to respond to Elliott's
comment, but he knew that there was political pressure from some local leaders
and politicians for DVERT to address the entire gamut of domestic violence issues.
There was a growing perception in the community that domestic violence was out
of control and better methods of containment and prevention should be made
available. Jack was very familiar with the argument and had recently had a number of discussions with the police chief, the mayor, and several state and federal
legislators about the direction in which the program was headed. Yet, while there
was pressure to grow, there had been no additional promise of community or state
funding in the near future to help defray the costs of the program.

Jack knew that a number of the smaller organizational partners were beginning to worry about their continued participation in DVERT. They, too, had experienced budget cutbacks. In many ways, the cutbacks were harder to absorb in
these smaller agencies. Despite these worries, these were also the groups who were
adamant about maintaining the quality of the program.

The larger community and state agencies that partnered with DVERT saw the
issue from another perspective. Many of these partners (e.g., human services, district attorney's office, Center for the Prevention of Domestic Violence) were feeling
political pressure and felt that the response should be to serve the broadest client
base possible. They believed that taking on more cases and perhaps not spending
as much time on any particular case would be advantageous in two ways. First, it
would expose more clients to DVERT. Second, that exposure would translate into
higher visibility and provide a strong argument for increased funding sources.

While there was disagreement on how the first two issues should be handled,
there was almost total agreement on the third. The partners were all lobbying for
adding more external agencies to the advisory board as a means of maintaining,
if not increasing, current funding levels. Over the years, Jack and his staff had
grappled with the appropriate size for the advisory board. As the group leader,
he knew the inherent difficulties of working with a large group. It had not been
easy to create a culture for this team, which already represented 14 agencies. He
was fairly adamant that adding new partners during a time when the group was
already divided on significant issues would be problematic. However, adding

partners just to increase funding was a disaster waiting to happen, he thought. In the past, Jack had successfully argued his position against adding partners. But, based on this current discussion, it was becoming clear that maintaining his stance against adding new members would be more difficult in light of the other issues the group was facing. Based on the board's discussion, Jack knew he would have to carefully consider the possibilities, and he struggled with what he would say in the afternoon session.

But for now, Jack needed to get back to the team's lunch meeting. Not wanting to waste time, he had invited two consultants to present some of the findings of their communication audit of DVERT. Specifically, Jack has asked them to focus on their findings about leadership and the team's communication effectiveness. Given the decisions that were before them, he hoped they would hear something that would help the group make these decisions about DVERT's future.

## THE CONSULTANTS' FINDINGS

On the way to the luncheon meeting, Janet and Elliott talked about what they thought the study would reveal. Janet said, "I've been concerned about what to expect from the study. On one hand, the DVERT program would not have survived as long as it has without Jack's leadership and guidance. He is the guiding force that has propelled the program and driven the rest of us to work diligently. On the other hand, my informal conversations with others suggest that he spends too much time micromanaging the group. It's almost as if he believes that without him overseeing everything, the program will fail."

Elliott agreed. "I know what you mean. He is an extraordinary manager, but I was honest on the survey in my evaluation of his leadership style, good and bad; I hope others were too. I wonder how he'll react to the consultants' presentation?"

The consultants' presentation confirmed what many of the partners had known all along. One of the strengths of the DVERT program was the group's leadership. In her report, one of the consultants indicated that Jack had been described by others as a "charismatic leader," a "visionary," "goal-oriented," "someone who promotes collaboration and emphasizes success," and an "individual who is committed to serving clients and the community." Jack was also seen as someone who motivated others to perform to their highest abilities. One write-in comment went so far as to identify Jack as the ideal representative for the program. It was true. Jack had gained national recognition for DVERT, due largely to his ability to obtain funding, create a sense of trust among the organizational representatives, and surround himself with high-caliber people.

Ironically, these qualities also created the greatest concerns for some of the partners. As the consultants continued their report to the group, they acknowledged that while the group's leadership was a source of strength for the program, it was also a source of frustration for some of the team members. One of the consultants reported, "Some of the partners felt that performance expectations were too high, and the small number of staff made it tough to handle the expected workload. Others expressed concerns that team members were always expected to be open and insightful while being poised for continual change. There was also the belief that there was too much micromanaging, which resulted in too much attention to day-to-day details and too little attention to the big picture."

The board members continued to listen intently as the consultants presented their findings on DVERT's communication effectiveness. One of the consultants said, "I can tell you that this organization really has some positive perceptions about its communication. That's not to say that there aren't some issues that need to be worked on. The next six slides underscore our key findings."

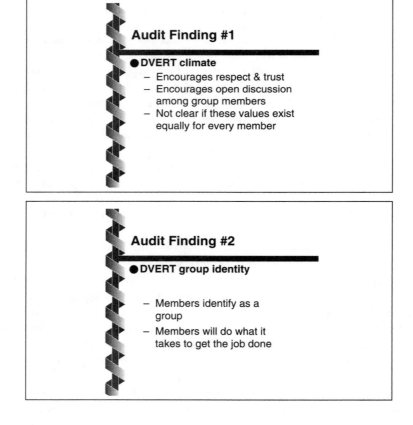

**Audit Finding #1**

● **DVERT climate**
- Encourages respect & trust
- Encourages open discussion among group members
- Not clear if these values exist equally for every member

**Audit Finding #2**

● **DVERT group identity**

- Members identify as a group
- Members will do what it takes to get the job done

## Audit Finding #3

● **Members' perceptions**

- Members see themselves and their coworkers as highly skilled and capable
- Members feel like they are making a difference

## Audit Finding #4

● **Views on collaboration**

- Group works collaboratively, rather than cooperatively
- Members desire more input from staff in decision making
- Members believe constructive feedback from management is lacking

## Audit Finding #5

● **One-on-one communication**

- Most frequently used channel
- Does not guarantee all members receive necessary information
- More timely information needed

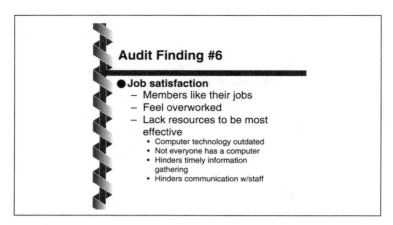

At the end of the presentation, board members asked a few general questions and thanked the consultants for their efforts. Shortly thereafter Jack and the partners reconvened for the afternoon session. Jack opened the meeting by asking the group, "Now we have some insight into the communication in this organization. So how do you propose that we proceed? What is best for the team?"

## CHAPTER 15

# Lessons Learned

## MJ Helgerson

The staff meeting was nearing conclusion, much to everyone's relief, but with open agenda items still remaining. A few of the attendees were engaged in a drive to make a decision about a communication strategy for the factory. Leon*, the manufacturing shift manager, was firmly entrenched in keeping information restricted from the organization. "Why create more churn than necessary? The technicians get so derailed by news updates that they lose focus," he challenged Dante, one of the engineering managers. Dante was losing his patience, but he kept his response deliberate: "Because we told them to trust us, and we owe them an update. This is the fair process we've agreed to. There's more to lose by changing the strategy now and nothing to gain." Donna, the operations manager, sided with Dante. "We've had this discussion before," she reminded the entire group gently, "and we've seen what happens when there's a lack of information flow to the org. Rumors start to fly, and technicians start making up their own versions of reality. I agree with Dante; we need to implement this strategy."

Both Jolene, the business manager, and Parker, an engineering manager, glanced at each other and then at Chris, the factory manager, for any type of guidance. Chris, just returned from being OOP (out of plant), was clearly engaged, not in the meeting, but in answering an email message. Not getting any direction from Chris, Parker and Jolene remained silent. Amanda, the quality manager, just seemed to fidget in her seat, not making direct eye contact with anyone.

The meeting clock was ticking down, and the facilitator, David, Chris' TA (technical assistant), brought the group back together. "Looks like we have some strong disagreement on the direction to take," he concluded. "I'll put this topic back on the agenda for next week. How about we form a subteam to work through the pros and cons of this strategy and come back next week with a recommendation

---

*This case has been developed based on real organization(s) and real organizational experiences. Names, facts, and situations have been changed to protect the privacy of individuals and organizations.

109

for the leadership team. Who wants to take this AR [action required]?" A few hands went up, David wrote the names down, and the meeting ended.

Donna was absolutely confounded. She walked out of the team meeting wondering just what had happened, *again*! A key decision was not made, and only a few fearless individuals were willing to even attempt a discussion of the central issues. "What a pitifully sad group we are," she thought with sheer exasperation. Although her peers were truly some of the most experienced engineers she'd ever worked with, she was disappointed and more than a little irritated. "How can they be so brilliant technically and so blind to the impact they're having on the team and each other? Were they afraid of making some kind of CLM [career limiting move] in front of their boss? Weren't the leaders of the organization supposed to be the risk takers and make the tough decisions?" Donna shook her head and wondered why the team members seemed so reticent to display that risk-taking behavior in this team specifically. She concluded, "If we can't handle a tough discussion behind closed doors after all our years together as a team, then we can't represent a united front to the organization. At the end of the day, we still cannot reach full agreement and achieve everyone's commitment." She was angry at herself and at the team for reaching this level of dysfunctional behavior. Something had to change and sooner rather than later.

Although her experience with teams was extensive under all kinds of circumstances (including life-threatening crises while in the military), Donna was stymied as to how best help this leadership team. She was so proud to be a member of this elite group but simultaneously mystified by its actions. Donna challenged herself: "If you have such intolerance for this type of behavior, then take action and do something about it. See a problem, solve a problem. You can do this! After all, you've solved tougher team issues than this before." Donna knew she was too close to the situation to have a neutral perspective. "I need to approach this like any other problem to be solved: Determine the core issues and the current reality, assess the gap to an ideal state, and then consider alternatives to close the gap. I know that I can deliver some fairly decent problem-solving recommendations to share with my boss, Chris." Donna loved her employer and current job—she could not stand idly by and watch any individual or team fail. And she knew, after all the time she'd invested with the group, that this team was capable of so much more than just treading water. What was it going to take to make a change?

## THE ENVIRONMENT

Donna's employer, Silicon Valley Operations (SVO), is a major player in the semiconductor industry, with over $37 billion in net revenue. The company's longlasting financial success after 30 years in the industry and its enviable record as a world-renowned corporate citizen are testimony to its being a dominant player in the global economy.

The culture is strong and powerfully evident in each employee's everyday work life. These demonstrations include their own short-hand version of techno-speak that is nothing but a series of acronyms that baffles the untrained listener (and sometimes even each other) and an array of other displays and practices that speaks to high efficiency, ever-rising expectations, and demanding results orientation. *Results orientation* is just one of the defined set of values, conveniently provided each year as an easily worn badge with the corporate calendar on the reverse side. *Taking risks* is another corporate value, the one that seemes the most contrary to the geek mentality of minimizing risks. Other values include *quality*, *trust*, *empowerment*, and *fun*. SVO's corporate logo is just as ubiquitous. Employees wear a variety of clothing emblazoned with this symbol: T-shirts, jackets, lanyards, ball caps, and sweatshirts. Also prominent is the use of other logo-bearing merchandise such as an assortment of lunch bags, coffee mugs, pens, and calculators, conveniently available for purchase from an on-site or online store.

Not surprisingly, the company's overwhelming success and staying power reside in its ability to attract and keep "the best of the best" employees: Gifted engineers worldwide compete for internships and employment with this firm. Just including a stint of employment with SVO on a résumé is worth the investment of hard work and often intense pressure, opening doors to other employers and opportunities.

Most employees of SVO know how to be successful with and on teams. In fact, very few units within the company can survive without the contributions of dynamic and dedicated teams tackling tough issues and solving complex problems. Teams and teamwork are part of this company's DNA. The company even offers a series of training classes addressing team development, team management, and virtual team leadership.

The site where Donna works is a sizable manufacturing hub, one of the largest within the company. The factory runs 24–7, 365 days a year, staffed by over 1,200 employees in a variety of roles, including technicians, engineers, and managers. This factory became famous within the manufacturing annals of the company by beating all production expectations, setting new benchmarks in quality achievement, maintaining all safety standards, and becoming the most cost-efficient factory throughout the entire corporation. The employees here had many reasons to be proud of what they accomplished in the six years of their factory's existence. And this is what truly stumped Donna. "How could this factory achieve all these milestones and boast all these achievements when the leaders of the organization can't even begin to disagree on a topic before someone shuts down and withdraws from the discussion? It just doesn't make sense to me."

## The Leadership Team

The leadership team charter is simple: The team sets factory direction and bears overall responsibility for all aspects of the factory, including planning, policies, and resource management. Membership is comprised of the factory manager and technical department managers. Managers of supporting departments such as Finance and Human Resources were also included in the team membership.

Most of the individual members were long-term employees of the corporation, 14 years and longer, many starting out as fresh college grads with the ink still drying on their engineering degrees. They transferred from factory to factory, advancing both their technical knowledge and leadership skills as they rose through the ranks to achieve departmental manager status.

Most of these managers were male, a trait typical of the semiconductor industry. There were only four women on this team of 15; one of these managers was Korean. Overall, the leadership team composition received high marks for diversity when compared with the composition of other technical teams throughout the corporation. The women also happened to be the newest members of the team. Although several members of the team changed during the factory's life, the majority of the leadership team enjoyed relative stability and worked together from three to five years. This stability was a unique characteristic of this leadership team.

Donna worked directly for Chris, the team leader. Chris, short for Christina, joined the factory as an assistant factory manager and quickly became factory manager when the incumbent was selected to lead a spin-off organization. She immersed herself in the new role, volunteering to lead a variety of high-level teams and task forces to better represent her factory's needs and perspectives. Chris earned her reputation as a driven, high-endurance leader with a passion for mentoring other women.

Chris was devoted to continuous improvement of her own leadership and management skills. She maintained a reading list of management books and articles, both classics and new releases. Chris was well aware of her shortcomings and tendencies, reinforced by the anonymous feedback she received from the team semannually. When times got tough, and the pressure was on, Chris' first reaction was to become a directive and tactical manager. This was truly her default style and one in which she felt very comfortable and in control. Only through self-control, discipline, and practice could she maintain her strategic perspective on the issues and allow her team to dive into the details and tactics of the problem.

## Decision Making

Chris and her team determined the direction of the factory, designing discussion and work sessions to agree on goals and indicators of success, strategic objectives, and communication tactics. One of the hallmarks of these sessions was that everyone wanted to weigh in on whatever topic was on the table. Some of these discussions really felt as if every person needed to voice his or her opinion, even if the opinion was no more than a "me, too" form of agreement. These conversations typically looked like this coming from different meeting attendees: "I agree with Jolene [or Parker or Dante...]. Me, too. Me, three. Ditto. No disagreement here." Donna witnessed the visible frustration of individuals as the discussions dragged on and on. Donna observed that "we seem to always achieve strong agreement on the what of the issue but never the how."

A second hallmark of their meetings caused even greater agitation. On any given issue, who really was the decision maker? Was it Chris as the overall factory manager, or was it the individual who brought the issue to the team? Was Leon, the manufacturing shift manager, the decision maker for all manufacturing issues, or was consensus by the team required to determine factory-wide resolutions? The team struggled with this lack of clarity.

The leadership cohort conducted semiannual strategic sessions to work on team building and long-term goals and to have some fun as well. The members engaged in learning about their individual conflict management styles and how their strengths contributed to the collective capability of the entire team. Donna reflected that after all these events and time spent together, "shouldn't we be a high-performing team by now, instead of feeling like we're just forming?"

Notably absent from all these strategic sessions were genuine dissent and conflict. There might be disagreements, such as the one that occurred between Leon and Dante at the last meeting, but never an occurrence of a passionate argument over any issue. There were no challenges to Chris' direction, no visibly apparent power struggles between members, nothing at all to signal any chafing between the team members. This is why Donna felt the team wasn't going anywhere productive. Everyone was still so polite to each other. Donna once voiced this observation to the team and found other members agreeing with her, but that didn't change the team members' engagement with each other or their performance. There was a general reluctance to engage, period. Donna concluded that the idea of holding peers accountable in front of each other and their own manager was just too distasteful and too risky. There was just one instance when the quality manager, Amanda, took intense pressure from the team by backing away from a committed factory goal. She never openly disagreed with the team but shared her commitment to a *lower* goal at an open factory meeting. The department managers were visibly taken aback by her actions and apparent betrayal; the consternation showed in their facial expressions. But, again, this topic did not arise at the team meeting. Donna surmised, "I bet Amanda is taking heat for this—an open disregard for what the team agreed upon for factory goals." Donna never saw what occurred with Amanda and her peers from the leadership team. At the next factory meeting, all the managers rallied around the lower factory goals that Amanda espoused just a week ago, just as if this was a group consensus and planned factory target.

Interestingly, Chris also did not push individuals and the team collectively to force conflict. Instead, when decisions needed to be made, Chris would, for the most part, assume the decision-maker role. In her absence, the team members struggled to agree and typically didn't, simply waiting for Chris to return. When time allowed, one or two team members would volunteer to form a subteam and return to the team with recommendations or act as a proxy for the cohort and make the final decision. The team would commit to abide by the process, but without fail one or more individuals would form a splinter coalition and go off to lobby Chris, pleading their case about changing the decision. Chris seemed to tolerate this behavior, apparently concerned enough about the validity of their arguments and always trying to do what was right for the factory. Eventually the leaders of these coalitions, a select group of managers, came to be seen as Chris' favorites, or the *chosen ones* of the team. This group included both Leon and Dante, Jolene the business manager, and Parker, an engineering manager. Chris extended her patronage to these individuals repeatedly for high-visibility or high-impact projects, trusting that they would deliver the results she sought. This, of course, left the rest of the team members wondering when they would get the same opportunity to excel, when Chris would allow them to prove their capabilities and competence. But these insiders, once selected, were never unselected by Chris. Donna didn't know if any of the excluded managers discussed the issue with Chris or not; this topic, like so many other sensitive issues, never saw the light of day at a team meeting.

After reflecting on her experiences with the team, Donna thought she finally understood the problems. She also decided that she was prepared to make some recommendations to help the team become more effective. Here's what she proposed.

## CHAPTER 16

# Taking Charge

### Joann Keyton

### JUNE 13

"Hi, everyone. Let's get started. As you know, I'm Bob Reynolds*, innovation strategist, here at New Ideas. I think I've had a chance to talk to each of you. If not—then welcome. As your email stated, you have been selected to be part of a team. More than just a team, really. But, nevertheless, a team charged with developing a strategic innovation plan for New Ideas. I know that you don't all know one another. So, let's get started—sorry, I've already said that."

The 12 people at the table carefully shifted their eyes to look at each other. Jess wondered, "Does anyone else know what is going on?"

Staring at Jess, Bob said, "Jess, let's start with you."

"I'm Jess—from the Kansas City office. Nice to meet you."

After a moment's silence, Ron introduced himself. But before the next person could go on, Bob interrupted. "Ron? I don't have a Ron on my list."

"That's right. I'm Ron Evanston from the Omaha office. Geraldo couldn't make it, so I came in his place."

"Right. OK. Well, nice to meet you and have you here. Next."

"Hello, everyone. I'm Bryan from Louisville."

"OK, I'm next. I'm Bert from Little Rock. I didn't know New Ideas had so many innovation specialists," Bert exclaimed.

Again everyone carefully looked at one another. "Well, you see," Bob hesitated before explaining, "everyone at the table isn't an innovation specialist. But we are all here to develop an innovation strategic plan. Right?"

Several people at the table nodded in agreement; others looked cautiously around. Some fiddled with their pens and pads of papers. One of the team members reached forward for a box lunch.

---

*This case has been developed based on real organization(s) and real organizational experiences. Names, fact, and situations have been changed to protect the privacy of individuals and organizations.

Wondering if she should just go ahead with the introductions, Lydia stopped but then continued. "I'm Lydia Rothrock from Tulsa. I manage the financial operations there. Nice to be here. I've not been to the home office before."

Jumping in, Bob said, "That's right. Most of you haven't been here. As an *ideas* company, we've put a premium on working virtually. But we are glad to have you here now in St. Louis. Recently I was at a management conference where I learned that taking risks works better when team members know one another, really know one another. That's why you're here in St. Louis. We're going to have three 90-minute meetings over the next 90 days. It's called a *hot team*. You'll fly in; work in the team; and then fly home—so you don't miss much time out of the office or away from your families. Who's next to introduce themselves?"

At the end of 75 minutes, the 12 team members had introduced themselves. Only one member, Mario Barnetti, did not attend. Everyone had a box lunch, and Bob had handed out a guide for developing innovative ideas. Lydia glanced at her watch, noticing how much time had been wasted with Bob's frequent interruptions. Glancing at the guide, she wondered how they would use the little time they had left.

"OK, now, I'm the team leader because I called the team together. But we need a shepherd," Bob said looking around the table.

The silence around the table was broken by a few chuckles.

"A shepherd?" asked Bert. "What's a shepherd?" Several others burst out laughing.

Someone else chimed in, "A hot team with a shepherd?"

When the group became quiet again, Bob, with a very patient tone, explained that a shepherd was a team member who kept all the notes, contacted team members between sessions, and compiled all team documents. "In those ways," he explained, "this team member *shepherds* the team through its processes to its outcomes. It's another thing I learned at the management conference."

Wanting to blurt out, but knowing better than to do so, Lydia thought to herself, "Aren't those the responsibilities of the team leader?" And shouldn't a secretary be doing those tasks?" Lydia took one more look around the table and painfully reminded herself that she was the only female. To move the meeting along so she could get on her flight, she offered, "I'll be the shepherd." As the others applauded, she thought to herself, I'm the only woman; they would label me with those tasks anyway. But as the applause subsided, Lydia became angry with herself. "Why did I do that?"

Bob congratulated Lydia and handed out a plan of work. It looked more like a concept plan with columns for ideas and their outcomes, resources, timelines, budgets, and champions. "OK, great start. Our next meeting will be July 7. Lunch meeting, like today. ninety minutes. We've got only two more meetings to develop and refine our ideas. Lydia, get a hold of everyone before we meet next, and let's get the ideas rolling."

## JULY 7

Bob walked into the room and glanced at Lydia. He took the position at the head of the long table and asked her to sit next to him. Others found a seat, and the meeting began. "Let's call roll, Lydia."

"Jess? Ron?" Lydia waited to get a signal from each person.

"Not Ron today. I'm Geraldo from Omaha. Ron took my place at the last meeting."

Lydia smiled and acknowledged Geraldo. She continued, "Ryan? Bert?" But Bert wasn't there. "Does anyone know about Bert?"

Walking in and talking at the same time, Jayson said, "I'm Bert. Not really. But I'm Bert today. He couldn't make it. He always takes the two weeks around the Fourth of July as his vacation. So I'm here instead."

Silence.

"Sorry, I'm Jayson from Little Rock, where I manage the sales staff."

Under someone's breath, "Great—sales replacing innovation."

Bob welcomed Jayson, and Lydia continued calling the roll. When she finished Bob turned to Lydia and asked, "So, where did you get since the last meeting? How many ideas do we have to talk about?"

Lydia bit her lip and then started to talk. "Well, we didn't get very far. Some of the team were on vacation. And we have two new members here today. And two members who were here last time but not this time. But I did collect three ideas. I've got them on this PowerPoint."

While Lydia brought the slide up, Bob smiled. Everyone else looked at the slide. Knowing the time pressure of their 90-minute meeting, Lydia broke the silence. "What other ideas can we add?"

Geraldo said, "I don't understand any of these. Does anyone else?" Some team members mumbled; others looked away.

Seeing that Bob wasn't going to facilitate the meeting, Lydia began. "OK, let's start from the beginning. As a team we're supposed to identify and develop innovation ideas for New Ideas. We are charged with creating innovative ideas about the services we provide—or could provide. I realize, of course, that each office has somewhat a different specialty in service provision and that we have different functional expertise around the table. Ideally, we should be able to draw upon those differences and collaborate."

No one talked.

"OK," thought Lydia. "Now what do I do?" She looked at Bob, who was still smiling. But she didn't know him well enough to tell if the smile was one of pleasure or disgust. Without knowing what else to do, she just kept talking. "OK, here's our concept plan. For each idea, we need to identify outcomes, resources, timelines, budgets, and champions. I've created a chart." She put up the next slide. "Let's work through the first one."

| Innovation Idea | Desired Outcome | Resources Needed | Timeline | Budget Required | Champion(s) | Other |
|---|---|---|---|---|---|---|
| 1. Integrate existing staffed and web-based services for cross-selling | | | | | | |
| 2. Design 12- and 24-month-based upgrades for each software service | | | | | | |
| 3. Identify ways to move professional software services to mobile devices | | | | | | |
| 4. | | | | | | |
| 5. | | | | | | |
| 6. | | | | | | |
| 7. | | | | | | |
| 8. | | | | | | |
| 9. | | | | | | |

**Figure 16.1** Concept Plan Chart

Remembering something someone once told her, Lydia remained silent. It killed her to do this, but she agreed to be the shepherd, not to *be* the team. Finally Peter spoke up. "Here's how I see it...." Within 60 minutes the team had filled in all of the columns of the concept plan for the three existing ideas and had generated four more ideas.

Having just a few minutes left and knowing that everyone except Bob had a plane to catch, Lydia complimented the team members on their collaboration and identified what needed to be accomplished before their next meeting in August. "Maybe this hot team concept was valid," she thought.

Interrupting her thinking, she heard Gene. "Lydia—can we change the August meeting date—it conflicts with our summer scheduling." Several others agreed that Gene had a good point; many had travel plans, both professional and personal, for August. After a short discussion, the team members agreed to meet on September 10, just three days short of their 90-day goal.

Lydia protested but could see she was not building the steam needed to persuade the team members differently. Perhaps the longer period between meetings was needed. But it did concern her that they would meet September 10 and have to turn in their final ideas with completed concept plans three days later. Before she could protest further, Bob stood up and called the meeting to an end with "See you in September."

## BETWEEN JULY AND SEPTEMBER

It was clear to Lydia that Bob was expecting her to facilitate and manage the team's ideas. She talked to her boss and was released from other tasks so she'd have more time to concentrate on this project. She scheduled a biweekly web-based conference. Attendance wasn't perfect, but she didn't expect it to be. It was the summer—people had time off scheduled. Subteams formed to complete the concept plans for the ideas for which work remained. Another subteam formed outside of the conference calls and generated another five ideas. Lydia frequently emailed back and forth individually with team members.

In preparation for the September 10 meeting, Lydia sent an email reminding the team members about their meeting date and what was left to be accomplished. She heard back from nine of the members. Sean and Jess indicated that they wouldn't be traveling to St. Louis, and they didn't explain why they were unavailable. Geraldo emailed that Ron would once again be taking his place. Likewise, Bert indicated that Jayson would permanently replace him on the team. Bryan, Blake, Peter, and Gene confirmed their attendance. Louis emailed to say he'd be there, but the airline schedule had changed, so he would be late to the meeting. Lydia did not receive any notice from Arnie and Mario.

| | June 13 | July 7 | September 10 likely attendance |
|---|---|---|---|
| Bob Reynolds St. Louis | x | x | |
| Jess Danforth Kansas City | x | x | Not available |
| Geraldo Mendoza Omaha | Ron Evanston took his place | x | Ron Evanston will take his place |
| Bryan McGee Louisville | x | x | x |
| Bert Campbell Little Rock | x | Jayson Schneider took his place | Jayson Schneider will take his place |
| Lydia Rothrock Tulsa | x | x | x |
| Arnie Guthridge Chicago | x | x | ? |
| Blake Purcell Columbus | x | x | x |
| Peter Sampson Minneapolis | x | x | x |
| Gene Davis Birmingham | x | x | x |
| Louis Robinson Denver | x | x | x |
| Sean Thomson Dallas | x | x | Not available |
| Mario Barnetti Amarillo | | x | ? |

**Figure 16.2** Meeting Schedule and Attendance

## SEPTEMBER 9

Not wanting to risk missing any part of the meeting due to a delayed flight, Lydia flew to St. Louis the night before. That gave her time to accomplish two things. First, she wanted to review her plans and preparations for the meeting. Second, she wanted to meet privately with Bob before the meeting began.

# Decision Making and Problem Solving

## CHAPTER 17

# How Much Does Passion Count?

## Stuart L. Esrock, Joy L. Hart, and Greg B. Leichty

Mike Kuntz* stared at the ceiling and desperately tried to gather his thoughts. The decision that he and his colleagues were about to make would have widespread repercussions. Not only had his group accepted the resignation of its executive director, but they had also worked hard to try to fill the vacuum of leadership triggered by that event.

Kuntz was the chair of the steering committee for Kentucky ACTION, the Alliance to Control Tobacco in our Neighborhoods. His group was about to decide how to handle a change of leadership in the midst of the largest and most important campaign in ACTION's history–a statewide initiative to raise the cigarette excise tax for the first time in over three decades. Kuntz and the ACTION steering committee had tried to move quickly. But not, it turns out, without hesitation.

### TOBACCO AND KENTUCKY ACTION

The roots of Kentucky ACTION laid in a youth tobacco education program created in the 1980s by the American Cancer Society, the American Heart Association, and the American Lung Association. In 1994, ACTION was formally chartered to increase public awareness about the dangers of tobacco. Under the stewardship of its founder and first executive director, LynnCarol Birgmann, the group had become a well-respected voice for tobacco control in Kentucky, as well as across the nation.

Beyond acting as a clearinghouse for tobacco and health matters, ACTION had become an important player in tobacco policy and legislative initiatives. Birgmann, Kuntz, and other members of their anti-tobacco coalition had successfully lobbied the Kentucky legislature to devote money from the historic Master

---

*Kentucky ACTION and participant names in this case study are real and have been used with permission.

Settlement Agreement with tobacco companies to fund smoking prevention and cessation programs. Moving forward beyond that matter, ACTION was in the midst of a landmark campaign that was heretofore unheard of, at least in a state like Kentucky.

Unlike most states where tobacco was highly regulated, in Kentucky growing tobacco and even its use were encouraged. Kentucky had the highest adult smoking rate in the nation and ranked second among all states in tobacco production with more than 47,000 tobacco farms. Many of Kentucky's small farms relied on tobacco sales for a significant portion of their income and, perhaps for that reason alone, tobacco had an almost mythical connotation in the state. Tobacco also had deep cultural significance, as it was associated with families gathering to work the fields and share meals during the planting and harvesting seasons.

It was in the midst of this unlikely landscape that ACTION was leading the charge for one of the Holy Grails of tobacco control–an increase in the state's cigarette excise tax. The Kentucky cigarette tax had not been raised for more than 30 years and, at 3 cents per pack, it was the lowest in the nation. Birgmann, Kuntz, and their colleagues believed that the tax should be hiked dramatically, without delay, to help lower the state's abysmally high smoking and illness rates.

Because so many Kentuckians smoked, the state had among the nation's highest rates of cancer, emphysema, and heart disease. Tax-hike advocates had solid evidence that basic laws of economics could work to improve these tragic problems; the higher the price of goods (e.g., cigarettes), the lower the consumption. Indeed, research from other states clearly indicated that any significant increase in the price of cigarettes, either from taxation or manufacturers, resulted in a decline in smoking.

Tax-hike proponents also argued that the proposal should be enacted because the state of Kentucky had basic economic realities it had to face. To combat tobacco-related illnesses such as lung cancer and heart disease, the state was spending more than $1 billion each year. Accordingly, many proponents viewed the tax hike as a way to increase revenues to help offset the extraordinary health care costs that were bankrupting the Kentucky treasury.

But Birgmann was perhaps most passionate about tobacco issues (and the excise tax proposals) because of the havoc cigarettes were wreaking upon the state's children. And it was not just the tragedy of children whose parents had died or were seriously ill as a result of smoking-related illnesses. She, Kuntz, and others in the tobacco-control movement were well aware of studies that indicated youth smoking was much more likely in a state like Kentucky where tobacco is culturally accepted, many adults smoke, and tobacco is grown. As a consequence, Kentucky was at or near the top in youth smoking rates among all age groups. Sadly, one-third of the people who begin smoking before age 18 end up dying prematurely.

For tobacco-control advocates in Kentucky, an excise tax increase was important because it would signal that the state was finally getting serious about addressing the problem of youth tobacco use. Indeed, excise tax hikes in other states clearly demonstrated that cigarette price increases were particularly effective in lowering tobacco consumption among youth. ACTION had received a multi-million dollar grant to build statewide public support for an increase in the cigarette excise tax. And, in the first wave of the campaign, the group stressed that the excise tax hike was the best means to protect Kentucky's children from the dangers of tobacco. Birgmann, Kuntz, and other advocates had appeared on television and radio programs around the state, arguing the case. The issue also had been prominently featured on newspaper front pages and in editorial columns, with the youth angle notably featured.

Momentum was building and discussion levels were reaching a new high. Birgmann, Kuntz, and other leaders of the group were united in their belief that merely placing the issue on the public agenda in Kentucky was a significant move forward. ACTION had succeeded in the initial effort, but the group had to build on its success if it was going to generate enough public support to pass an excise-tax increase in the state's legislature.

## LOOKING FOR LEADERSHIP

Just as the group prepared to take center stage in promoting the first cigarette excise-tax increase in Kentucky in three decades, Kuntz and the ACTION steering committee were startled to hear the news from Birgmann: The group's founder and spiritual center was leaving for a more lucrative position with another non-profit group.

LynnCarol Birgmann had 10-plus years of knowledge and experience with tobacco-control issues, and she was spiritually and emotionally connected to the matter. She had fervently argued against Big Tobacco and the scourge of cigarettes before men and women, adults and children, journalists and doctors, school and church groups, federal and state lawmakers, and on and on. Her enthusiastic, emotional, and often fiery rhetorical style had moved many people across the state to volunteer to work on a variety of tobacco-control issues. Birgmann had been at the center of a small cadre of activists that had fought many battles for tobacco control in what was often a hostile environment. But, just when ACTION needed her to guide the culmination of a highly charged campaign, Birgmann made a difficult decision to advance her career.

Kuntz, and indeed the entire steering committee, firmly believed their campaign was bigger than one person or personality. Still, he knew his group had a challenging assignment to find a new leader. Kuntz said, "There was no doubt in anyone's mind that LynnCarol had provided vital start-up leadership for Kentucky ACTION through the history of the organization and for the excise-tax campaign. She had a vision and a heart, if you will, that just fit the job."

The problem of finding a new ACTION executive director was exacerbated by timing. ACTION was midway through a three-year grant funding the excise-tax campaign and the state legislative session was quickly approaching. Kuntz said, "There could have been a better time. We were definitely in the middle of it. There was a pressing feeling that we needed to get someone into place before the legislature reconvened."

However, Kuntz said the steering committee also viewed the search as an opportunity to find an executive director who could bring new perspectives and skills to the position. Kuntz noted, "We believed we could find someone who could really take us in another direction in an even more unified fashion. We wanted a strong executive director to implement the plan without our (the steering committee's) daily involvement. We felt in our hearts that we wanted to relinquish a lot of control, but not guidance. We wanted to help set the plan with the executive director but we wanted that executive director to be a strong leader, one we knew could coordinate, direct, lead, and manage our staff. That person had to implement the plan and we had to have 100% confidence that they could do that."

Given the large grant funding the excise-tax campaign, another key characteristic that ACTION sought in candidates was a track record of fiscal responsibility. According to Kuntz, "Budget management was just crucial. The director had to be able to control budgets, review financial reports, and understand our financial situation and be able to make adjustments as needed."

The steering committee wrote a job description, placed ads, and informed key contacts within their network of tobacco-control activists about the job opening. A pool of applicants surfaced, with candidates from a variety of backgrounds in both the public and private sectors. The steering committee did an initial screening and selected several applicants to interview. Going into the interviews, Kuntz was hopeful, but he and the other committee members ended up disappointed. "The communication backgrounds of the selected candidates were strong. They had done marketing campaigns and had media experience, that sort of thing, which is obviously an important part for us. But they were lacking on the budget management side. That was the biggest missing link for most of them and that was something we just had to have."

Under ideal circumstances, the ACTION steering committee would have faced a difficult task in trying to find someone to replace Birgmann's knowledge about, and passion for, tobacco issues. Given the lack of qualified candidates in the first pool of applicants, the search took on an air of urgency. Kuntz and his committee simply did not have the luxury of lengthy and careful deliberations. "We were overly optimistic that, one, we could find someone quickly and, two, we were going to be able to find this ideal candidate. It was a learning experience for me that there probably isn't any ideal candidate for any position and that really good quality people are hard to find. This search was very exhausting and so the panic did not set in at the get-go, but the panic most definitely came."

The start of the Kentucky state legislative session was imminent, so Kuntz decided to move quickly to re-open the search in a last effort to find qualified candidates. If this second effort failed, the campaign would have to be managed via a patchwork system involving steering committee members, at least through the key legislative period.

Several new prospects emerged and the committee moved swiftly to conduct interviews. Kuntz said it soon became apparent that there was only one possible candidate for the position among this pool. Once again, though, there was discussion within the committee about whether the right person had been found.

## THE LEADING CANDIDATE EMERGES

When they looked at Carol Roberts, Kuntz and the Kentucky ACTION steering committee found a capable public-health professional. Roberts had been serving as a Regional Cancer Control Director for the American Cancer Society. She had energy and organizational and administrative skills, as well as a background in promotion and public relations. She was looking for a change so that she could manage a public-health campaign and ACTION's battle to raise the cigarette excise tax seemed like a good fit.

Kuntz said several aspects of Roberts' candidacy reassured his group. "She was a public-health professional. Right there you've got a connection. I did know her and I knew that she had experience through [the American] Cancer [Society], and I had served on a board with her once before and she seemed knowledgeable enough on public health." As a public-health professional, Roberts knew what it was like to advocate for such issues, usually within the confines of limited budgets. Educating the public about disease prevention and control could be a thankless task that required a selfless individual who was often willing to work for far less money than counterparts in the private sector.

Furthermore, Kuntz said that Roberts matched one important job criterion much better than the other candidates. "She had a strength as a leader on financial issues. She was able to show us that on paper and she was knowledgeable when she spoke. She knew about grants and funding and how to administer those kinds of things. In her past work she had done a good deal of budget management, so we felt strongly that she would do a good job in that regard in administering our grant."

Roberts understood the dynamics of communication in advocacy organizations. This experience was important because the ACTION executive director had to maintain strong ties with allied groups like the Lung Association and the Cancer Society. Further, she also had navigated the bureaucracy of a large organization like the American Cancer Society (ACS), the grant administrator for ACTION's funding. According to Kuntz, "Carol knew how the ACS system worked, and the fact that she would be working all those budgets, all the check requests, all those things and would be able to hit the ground running on the business side of things was extremely important to a steering committee that didn't, and couldn't, mess with that stuff."

Roberts' background in public relations and campaign communication was an added plus. ACTION possessed only a modest budget (relatively speaking) to publicize its case for the excise-tax increase. And, ACTION needed to convince the news media to carry its message. Though other members of the ACTION steering committee and staff had experience in framing messages and utilizing the media to communicate with the public, the fact that Roberts also had this background enhanced her candidacy. She was a good speaker as well, which was an added bonus.

There were some questions about Roberts that lingered, however, even after a couple of interviews. Kuntz said the steering committee had concerns about the kind of leadership Roberts would provide for her staff and a network of volunteers across the state. "There were questions about, can you manage these people? In the interview she really worked hard to convince us. I went in with apprehension and it took a while for me to become convinced that she would give us the kind of coordination and management that we wanted."

It was also unclear how much Roberts really knew about tobacco-related issues like excise-tax increases. Activists who were immersed in the tobacco-control movement acquired a wealth of knowledge about related scientific, health, agricultural, economic, legislative, legal, and business matters. The voluminous data, studies, opinions, and legal cases were sometimes difficult to decipher. The trail of material dated back more than 50 years to the first public health studies on the dangers of tobacco. Kuntz said, "I think we probably get numb to the fact that we do this kind of thing every day and have done it for years. I've been in it for nine-plus years. The truth of the matter is that it's not difficult to become a master of a subject when you work on it every day for a long period of time. Sometimes there is a tendency to discount how much information and how many layers there are in this cause."

Nonetheless, Kuntz believed that Roberts had at least some specific limitations related to their campaign. "Carol was not an expert, but because she was from ACS, she had some tobacco-control experience. She had some tobacco knowledge in terms of very basic stuff about the dangers and risks. But she did not know tobacco-control policy really at all."

Although Kuntz recognized that Roberts needed to be brought up to speed on tobacco-control matters, he felt this shortcoming could be surmounted. He and his committee believed that Roberts was an intelligent and motivated individual who would work hard to learn what she needed to know. Kuntz said, "I know people who have come into this with absolutely no tobacco knowledge. The knowledge will come because it is so well-documented and because there are great resources available that you can use to become educated." Kuntz also pointed out to the committee that Roberts would be surrounded by a cast of experts who would quickly compensate for her short-term lack of knowledge. "We decided she would not have to know all of the intricacies of all this stuff. She could take her time learning it. She could rely on the steering committee, the staff, and other supporting agencies. They know this stuff inside out." He further rationalized that if Roberts was hired, they would shield her from media interviews until she got up to speed. Educating her about tobacco-control matters would take some time, but Kuntz said the steering committee believed she would be able to manage this process because of the considerable knowledge and talent she could draw upon.

## PASSION AND COMMITMENT

The other issue the committee had to confront about Roberts was less tangible and more difficult to assess. According to Kuntz, all of the steering committee members had a deep passion for tobacco-related issues. Whether it was due to experience with respiratory illness like asthma, a loss of a loved one to cancer, or other factors, all of them had a seemingly personal connection to tobacco-related issues that resonated when they talked with reporters and editors, lawmakers, volunteers, and others. Kuntz, himself, was so emotionally attached to the issue that on at least one occasion during a televised program, his anger at a tax opponent's attacks exploded as he blurted out, "What rock did you crawl out from under?"

Kuntz and the ACTION committee speculated about Roberts and her level of attachment to the issue. Inevitably, they compared her to LynnCarol Birgmann, who lived and breathed the cause. Kuntz said, "Not only was LynnCarol as passionate as anybody I've ever met on this issue, she remains that way today. That was the biggest, most apparent difference between her and Roberts. LynnCarol was passionate, not only about the excise tax, but about every aspect of tobacco control. We wondered whether for Carol, it was just a job. Would she say, 'This town hall meeting about smoking, is it part of my performance evaluation? Is that a part of my job, part of my benchmarks? If not, I'm going to yoga.' We were not sure."

On a campaign issue like the excise tax, proponents in a state like Kentucky needed a high level of commitment to deal with the glacial pace of change. Even after a 30-year wait, the issue had taken a while to establish in the newspapers and on nightly television broadcasts. Optimists like Kuntz and the other ACTION partners celebrated even small victories like introduction of the first bills in the Kentucky House that proposed an excise-tax hike. Without a heart-felt attachment to the issue, Kuntz believed that passage of controversial legislation, like a cigarette tax hike in Kentucky, simply would not become a reality. "There are only two ways to affect public policy from the legislative side, and that's money or people power. To me, the passion is what brings the people power. I think in our issue, without passion, the cause is dead on arrival. I think it is imperative that a person has deep, deep passion. I just don't think there is any other way around it. If you are not passionate and it doesn't radiate from you, you are not going to excite your partners and get the public involved. And this is an emotional issue. People die and lives are ruined by tobacco. And that's the way we win at the legislature, by making it emotional. I don't think that passion can be faked. You can't pretend it nine to five. I think people see right through that."

Gauging passion was tricky, though. Kuntz said, "Because we are passionate about the cause, it's a given that we were going to try to hear the candidate say something that says they are vested in the issue. Maybe it was something like, 'my mother died from lung cancer.' Or, 'my favorite uncle had emphysema and suffered and died and this is something I believe in.' Those types of things tell me this is a person who understands that this is all about human life and that is important to us. So we were listening for that."

However, passion isn't necessarily something that a person has or doesn't have; it is also something that can be acquired. Indeed, many tobacco-control partisans have not lost a loved one due to tobacco. So beyond personal stories involving tobacco, Kuntz said he looked for other clues that would suggest attachment to the issue. "The candidate should have some knowledge about tobacco-control issues, proving that they have enough passion to get involved. Or they should be on our mailing list or should be a member of the lung, heart, or cancer groups. But truthfully, I'm extremely passionate about the issue and I was none of those things when I first came to the Lung Association."

Because the core of the excise-tax campaign message had been tied to emotion (pulling on the heartstrings with the idea of protecting the state's children) and not necessarily to logic, this trait was perhaps even more magnified. And Kuntz said he wasn't sure if Roberts would inspire the public in this regard. "When you heard LynnCarol talk about tobacco, it dripped of passion. To us, when Carol talked about the topic, it just sounded more logical."

Passion was, however, only one element within the larger context of what was needed in a new executive director. Kuntz and the committee also looked inward and analyzed ACTION's resources, its standing, and where it needed to go next. This introspection led the group to an increasing comfort with Roberts. They believed that she had the ability to get more interested in the matter and would, as Kuntz calls it, "get fired up" about the excise tax. Becoming more invested in the issue, in Kuntz's mind, was a natural progression of working in tobacco control. "You become infected with this and you start to do it in your off-time and in the evenings and on the weekends. It's not just reading books and articles. There are always events and meetings, and activities to go to, to support. This is an issue that you get infected with, even if you don't come into it with that passion. I'm an optimist. I always think that people love life and they are passionate about human beings around them. I just assume they are going to get hungry and excited."

The characteristic of passion was also, quite possibly, not as vital as it might have been previously. Although tobacco-control advocates and ACTION at one time were fighting such an uphill battle that everyone needed to be 100% emotionally invested to persist through resistance and setbacks, the group had made significant recent inroads. The most difficult part of the journey was behind, so passion, although important, no longer seemed a fundamental prerequisite for survival. In addition, ACTION already had a large number of passionate speakers at its disposal to talk with reporters, lawmakers, volunteers, and other groups.

Furthermore, Kuntz acknowledged that the campaign message was broadening and as a result, concerns about Roberts' zeal for tobacco-control were possibly not significant enough to remove her from serious consideration. Although the campaign had initially focused on portraying an excise-tax increase as a means to protect children, the campaign was by this time also communicating the beneficial economic impacts that would come from a tax increase (i.e., reduced health costs and more income for important state programs). Kuntz said, "We could not discount the logic behind the money, behind the revenue, behind the health-care costs that are associated with tobacco. We have to talk about those because, number one, keep in mind that more than two-thirds of our state doesn't smoke but they are still paying those costs. So for those folks it's a logical reason, because it involves their pocketbooks." In that respect, Roberts, regardless of passion, was qualified.

## TO HIRE NOW, OR NOT TO HIRE NOW?

The time had come for Kuntz and the ACTION steering committee to make a decision. The start of the state legislative session was nearing. ACTION needed to move forward with developing the message for its fall campaign to encourage citizens to contact their state lawmakers in support of an excise-tax increase. Meetings needed to be arranged with newspaper editors across the state to generate support. PR materials needed to be drafted to background reporters on the latest developments and tax increases passed in other states. Volunteers had to be rallied to promote grassroots informational meetings in communities throughout Kentucky. Kuntz and his committee needed to determine whether to hire Roberts as their executive director.

Kuntz said, "The ideal candidate should have been dripping with passion. They most definitely should have had a solid background in tobacco control. We needed someone who could manage a budget. And, we needed a leader who could implement our plan and manage and supervise staff, a lot of staff." Kuntz and Kentucky ACTION had found many positive qualities, but not the ideal package, in Carol Roberts.

Seated around a conference table, Kuntz and the steering committee members discussed what to do. Should they postpone the search? Should they leave the executive director position unfilled and try to manage the campaign through the end of the grant period in a different manner? Should they offer the position to Carol Roberts, despite some concerns? Would Roberts' many skills overcome her possible lack of issue-related passion?

After a lengthy meeting, the door to the conference room opened. One by one, the steering committee members filed out and as Mike Kuntz emerged last, his secretary called out to him, "I'm glad you are finally done. Carol Roberts is holding for your 11:00 A.M. call on line two."

## CHAPTER 18

# Permission to Walk

## Michael W. Kramer

Dennis James* enjoyed looking out the windows of his office for United Computers, Electronics, and Telecommunications Corporation (UCETC) at its international headquarters. His office was in Pearson Hall, the oldest building on the company's campus, which was named after the organization's founder. UCETC started out as Midwest Telegraph and Telephone Company in the 1920s. The eight original buildings had been extensively remodeled over the years, but the exteriors still retained their charm. Together these eight buildings on UCETC's campus were affectionately known as the "Quad." Everyone who worked for UCETC knew stories about the founder, Jake Pearson, and the Quad.

The Quad was the only part of UCETC's campus with large oak trees and an open grassy area. Most of the rest of the campus had been built in the last 20 years as the company grew by expanding its markets, acquiring other smaller companies, and expanding beyond its core telecommunication business into computers, sound equipment, and other electronic components. The rest of the campus looked more like a warehouse district with only an occasional tree or grassy spot squeezed in between buildings and streets. The entire sales division was located in buildings around the Quad because its picturesque setting made such a positive impression on business clients who visited the headquarters. The sales division avoided showing clients the rest of the campus if they could.

Dennis had been in this office since he had been promoted to Head of Telecommunication Sales in the Midwest Region of UCETC two years ago. He was pleased with the promotion and the potential for future advancement. He took his responsibilities seriously and had attended as many executive training sessions as possible. At one of the recent workshops he attended, executives were encouraged to take the initiative to increase the human touch of the organization. Since the company

---

*The case is based upon an actual organization and real organizational experiences. Names, facts, and situations have been changed to protect the privacy of individuals and the organization.

had increased in size dramatically over the last two decades, many employees with longer tenure felt like the organization was becoming very impersonal. Calling the headquarters a campus was not enough to change that perception. They missed the feeling that they were part of a family business that valued each employee, rather than feeling like they were just a number in a large corporation. Dennis agreed that the company was less personal than when he first was hired.

Unfortunate circumstances in his division gave Dennis an opportunity to try to bring back some of that personal touch. The former vice president of telecommunication sales, Marsha Applebaum, had retired early when she was diagnosed with multiple sclerosis. She was undergoing the available treatments, but the long-term prognosis was poor since there is no cure. UCETC had an excellent medical plan that covered all the direct medical costs, but not the incidental costs associated with extended treatments and necessary lifestyle adjustments. People at headquarters and out in the field had been asking if they could do anything to help. Dennis had decided that organizing a fundraiser for Marsha was the right thing to do, and it might bring back some of that personal touch people missed.

He contacted Karen in the human resource division to see what they could do. Following the lead of various nonprofit fundraising organizations, they decided to organize "24 Hours on the Quad." The idea was that current employees in the sales division at the headquarters would take turns walking on the Quad for 24 hours over two days. Then other employees at headquarters, sales staff in the field, and even former employees would be asked to make donations for each hour of walking. Dennis and Karen worked on the solicitation letter and prepared the mailing. With Karen's help and with permission from the vice president of human resources, they were able to put together a mailing list of over 3,000 current and past employees of the sales division, as well as employees of other divisions who had worked with or known Marsha. This was unusual cooperation because names and addresses of past employees were not normally released, but because of the uniqueness of the situation, it was decided that doing this one time would be a good idea.

As he was about to mail out the letters of appeal, one of his long-time sales staff supervisors, John Snellen, mentioned, "We may need to get permission to do this on the Quad. You should probably contact Mark Johnson in facilities management to make sure it's okay."

Dennis was surprised that no one in the human resources division had mentioned getting approval for the event, but to be safe he called Mark immediately. He introduced himself and explained the plan. "We will only have two or three people walking most of the time so it won't really disturb anything. It will just be from 7 A.M. to 7 P.M. for two days. We'll just be walking around the Quad."

A bit concerned, Mark asked, "Will you be on the sidewalks or on the grass?"

"We'll be on the sidewalks. It won't really be that noticeable. But someone on my sales staff mentioned that we probably should contact you."

Mark replied, "That seems rather harmless. I can't think of any reason not to approve it. But could you do me a favor? There's a facility use request form available online. Could you fill that out so that we have a record of the activity?"

Dennis agreed to the request, hung up, and immediately went online and filled out the request. Because the form was for facilities-use requests and designed primarily to make sure meeting rooms were not overbooked, it only had buildings on it, nothing for outdoor spaces like the Quad. Doing the best he could with the somewhat inappropriate form, Dennis marked his own building, Pearson Hall, as the location of the event since that would be the headquarters for the event, described the walk on the Quad, and completed the request.

The automated system promptly forwarded his request to the building coordinator for Pearson Hall, Dennis's administrative assistant, Janice Vogel. Janice approved the request immediately, and an email stating her approval was automatically sent to Dennis. The email included a statement that the activity was not officially approved until it appeared on the schedule of activities. Dennis joked with Janice and the other staff members about the silly bureaucratic requirements, considering that Janice was given the authority to approve the activity.

With five weeks left until the event, planning proceeded smoothly. The solicitation letters were sent out and donations started to arrive. Dennis and Janice were impressed with people's generosity. Many sent cards or notes to give to Marsha as well. A number of retired folks volunteered to walk the Quad to support the effort. It was turning into a remarkable effort.

After brainstorming at a weekly meeting, the event increased in size. A barbeque to celebrate the final lap of the walk was organized. They would invite Marsha to be present if she could and present her with a check of the donations up to that point. A spouse of an associate in the department who had a talk radio show agreed to broadcast from the steps of Pearson Hall on the morning of the walk to solicit funds for the National Multiple Sclerosis Society on behalf of Marsha. Dennis also asked a number of other top executives to support the fundraising by participating in the walk. He really didn't think any of them would participate, but thought that making them aware of the activity would be good publicity for the sales division. After all, his division was putting some of that personal touch back into the company as they had encouraged. That should please them. To his surprise, all three executives he asked–the CEO, the CFO, and the President of the Board–all agreed to participate and included checks in their responses. He was quite pleased with the way the event was turning out.

Three weeks after receiving approval of the activity, Dennis was shocked when he received the following email:

From: ROOMRESERVATION
To: James, Dennis; Vogel, Janice;
Subject: Req ID: D0101225 – Temporary Use of Facilities Request

This request has not been approved by my supervisor, Mark Johnson. This event would be better accommodated by the facilities at the Employee Health Center—please contact Bob Schmidt at the Employee Health Center to make arrangements for this area.

Sandy Chase
Assistant Facilities Manager

As he was reading the email, Janice entered his office and spoke in amazement.

"Did you get the email I just got? Can you believe it? I already approved this three weeks ago."

"It's just ridiculous, but I'm sure once I inform Sandy that Mark Johnson already approved it, everything will be fine." With that, Dennis sent the following email:

> From: James, Dennis
> To: ROOMRESERVATION
> Subject: Req ID: D0101225 – Temporary Use of Facilities Request
>
> Sandy Chase,
> I already did contact Mark Johnson about this. He approved the idea, but said that we needed to submit a form. So we did submit it. Because the Sales Division is located on the Quad, moving the walk to the Employee Health Center would not be appropriate.

Thinking the problem was solved with Sandy's supervisor already having approved the event, Dennis went back to work only to be surprised by another email the next day.

> From: Johnson, Mark
> To: ROOMRESERVATION
> Subject: Req ID: D0101225 – Temporary Use of Facilities Request
>
> Dennis,
> I do remember us discussing this event and advising you to submit the online request. I regret that you perceived our discussion as an approval of use of the Quad for this event. I could not have issued approval over the phone, because as I told you, these requests are routed through several offices for approval. As Sandy indicated, we do not believe that the Quad is an appropriate location for this activity. We would suggest that the Employee Health Center is a better location for the activity, albeit perhaps not as convenient for your department. Please let me know if you have any questions.
>
> Mark Johnson
> Facilities Management

Dennis was in a state of disbelief. The Employee Health Center was a brand new exercise facility with an artificial surface and no trees, way on the other side of the UCETC campus. It was located between a couple of warehouses. Most days, more people walked around the Quad on their lunch hours rather than around the Health Center because it was a more pleasant environment and closer to their offices. In addition, most of the retired sales people would never have even heard of it. It had no connection to the division and none to Marsha. It would be absurd to walk there. Beginning to be concerned by Mark's inflexibility, Dennis dashed off another email:

From: James, Dennis
To: Johnson, Mark
Subject: Req ID: D0101225 – Temporary Use of Facilities Request

Mark,
I am surprised by the trouble this seems to be causing.
There will be two or three people walking around the Quad at a time during this event. I do not see how this creates any problems. When I spoke to you, you agreed that it did not cause any trouble.
This is not a matter of inconvenience. It's a matter of connection. We are located on the Quad. Asking this to be moved to the Employee Health Center would be like asking the engineering division to move their St. Patrick's Day celebrations, which create a great deal of disruption comparatively, to the Employee Health Center.
Our walk will be far less disruptive and should be approved.

Dennis James
Head of Sales, Midwest Division

The next day Mark called Dennis. He began by apologizing for giving the impression that the activity was approved. Then he reiterated: "We need to protect the integrity of the Quad. Because of that, we think that you should move the walk to the Employee Health Center, which is much more suited for exercise."

"This is not about exercise. This is about fundraising for a member of the sales division who is suffering from multiple sclerosis," Dennis argued. "Marsha worked on the Quad and we are located on the Quad. It makes no sense for us to walk all the way across campus to the Employee Health Center. Besides, there are only going to be two or three people walking at a time. How is that disruptive to the integrity of the Quad?"

"If we approve this activity, then others will also want to do things on the Quad. We have to protect it from such problems."

"What about all the activities that the engineering division does throughout the year on the Quad? They are far more disruptive than our event will be. They test their new outdoor sound equipment and we all get to listen to the feedback. They do all kinds of things every year to celebrate St. Patrick's Day, the patron saint of engineers. They cook out and have loud music. Last year they added one of those inflatable jumping houses for their kids. This all goes on while we're trying to conduct business."

"On a campus this large," Mark explained, "there are always some activities that occur without our permission. Some of them we would not allow if we knew about them."

"So what you are telling me is that if I hadn't asked for permission, I could have just gone ahead with this. You're punishing me for asking."

"Don't take it that way. We just think it would be better on the Employee Health Center."

Dennis became adamant. "This needs to be on the Quad. CFO Mary Brewer has agreed to walk for us, on the Quad. CEO John Gerhardt has agreed to walk for us, on the Quad. And President of the Board Charles Taylor has agreed to walk for us, on the Quad. You need to approve this."

"There's a meeting in a few minutes where I'll talk about this with the Vice President of Facilities Management."

"You mean Carl Powell?"

"No, he's only involved in the production plant. It's Larry Kempf, in charge of all building facilities. I'll get back to you this afternoon after the meeting." With that, Mark ended the conversation.

After the call, Dennis was certain that he would not mention the radio broadcast or the barbeque to Mark even though they already had a food permit for it from the city's Health and Safety Division. It would obviously only make approval that much harder if not impossible. If they had trouble getting approval for walking on the Quad, who knows what might happen if he mentioned the other activities. The other activities would simply occur without the building facilities managers knowing about them.

Dennis expected a phone call within the hour. He thought that after he named three top executives who were Mark's superiors in the chain of command and repeated "on the Quad" three times, it would be easy for Mark to make the correct choice. He thought a little about what he might say when Mark approved the walk. He could say, "You've made the right choice," but that might seem a little condescending. Perhaps he should just say "thank you" and hang up before he said anything he might regret.

Then for the first time, he began to wonder what he should say if Mark insisted they still move the walk to the Employee Health Center. All of the appeal letters had already gone out and money was coming in. If Mark did not give approval, should he appeal to one of the top executives to override the decision, or would it be better to just go ahead without permission and hope that nothing happened? Dennis became increasingly anxious as the day went along. As he was preparing to go home, he had still not heard anything. He was about to turn off his computer when he received this email:

From: Johnson, Mark
To: James, Dennis
Subject: Req ID: D0101225 – Temporary Use of Facilities Request

Dennis,
I apologize for not getting back with you earlier in the day. This issue is still being discussed in the Facilities Management Division and I'll be following up early next week.

Mark Johnson
Facilities Management

Dennis was fuming. The event was next week and here he was waiting for approval from some petty, no-name bureaucrat he had never heard of before and who didn't seem to understand that this project had support from all kinds of people higher up in the organization. What was Mark's problem? What was his issue that was preventing him from approving this walk?

Driving home that evening, Dennis thought about another potential problem. If Mark turned down the walk and he appealed to someone higher up the chain of command or went ahead with the walk without permission and Mark found out, it was possible that this would create problems for the division when they made routine requests for meeting rooms and for other special events. It was possible that Mark would be uncooperative in the future, making it that much harder for Dennis to do his job as division head.

Friday evening happened to be the UCETC Annual Awards Dinner, where people were recognized for years of service to UCETC and other awards for service to the organization or to the community. Dennis attended because his staff member, John Snellen, was receiving one of the service awards for his work with the local Big Brothers and Big Sisters organization. As they sat at the table he told John about the situation. John agreed that it was ridiculous. He commented: "You know, I don't even know if they can prevent you from walking on the Quad. It's practically a public space. Anyone who wants to can walk on it."

"Maybe you're right."

"What could they do? Arrest you for trespassing? You're an employee."

"That's a good point," mused Dennis. "Maybe I don't need their permission. I certainly will never ask for it if we do something like this again."

Then John asked a troubling question: "Now, would Mark have anything to say about your potential promotion to head of U.S. sales? I mean, he's not part of the decision, is he?"

"Oh, no. He's just part of the facilities management group. He has nothing to do with promotions in the sales division."

Dennis said that with confidence, but then thought about how this might limit his options. Because of Marsha's retirement, there were new opportunities for advancement. He was being considered for Director of U.S. Telecommunication Sales. He would have liked to be considered for the job under different circumstance, but he was still hoping it would happen. He understood that the Board would be making a decision in the next monthly meeting.

Could this create a problem for him? If Mark refused to approve the event, Dennis might have to appeal to one of the executives who did have some say in his promotion, to have them fix a rather petty problem. Would they remember that he wasted their time when they considered promoting him? Would it help his case since he was showing initiative and putting some personal touch into the organization? Or if he went ahead without Mark's permission and they found out, would they be concerned about his willingness to be a team player and follow the organizational rules? What had started out as a simple fundraising idea to help out a former colleague was turning into a nightmare that might impact his division and his promotion.

As the dinner broke up, Dennis found himself next to CEO John Gerhardt. He took advantage of the opportunity. "I just want to thank you for agreeing to support our effort to raise money for Marsha Applebaum by walking in our '24 Hours on the Quad' this week. We really appreciate it and your generous donation, too."

"I'm glad to do it. It's such as shame what happened to her. It's the least I can do. Besides, it will be good to get out of the office for a while. The exercise will do me good."

"Well, I'm trying to put some of the personal touch back into the organization that we maybe have lost over the last few years."

"That's terrific, Dennis. I thank you for your initiative and leadership in this area."

As he was walking back to his car, Dennis ran into Rose McNichols, the Head of East Coast Telecommunication Sales. He vented one more time about his situation with Mark Johnson. Rose empathized with him. She added: "Larry Kempf and facilities management are the main roadblock in our system. Because he has oversight of all the facilities he puts the brakes on any good idea. A few years ago we were going to do a great community outreach program. We were going to support local scouting programs by having a festival on the Quad. He claimed it would be a potential liability situation and got the whole thing cancelled."

"What's his point?" Dennis asked.

"I don't know if it's because he's a lawyer or just likes to wield power, but everyone gets frustrated with him from time to time," Rose added.

"Why doesn't somebody do something about it? Surely Gerhardt or someone could put a stop to it." Then Dennis asked, "What would you do if you were me and didn't get permission to walk?"

Rose thought for a minute. "The rebel in me says go ahead and do it without permission and let the chips fall where they will. Of course, the administrator in me says follow the rules. Hopefully you won't have to make that call. Good luck."

---

From: James, Dennis
To: Johnson, Mark
Subject: Req ID: D0101225 – Temporary Use of Facilities Request

John,
FYI—
At the UCETC Annual Community Awards Ceremony Friday evening I spoke to CEO John Gerhardt. I thanked him for agreeing to walk in our 24 hours on the Quad this week and for his generous donation. I mentioned that we were trying to increase the personal touch of the division. He thanked me for my leadership and mentioned that he had been saying good things about the division to the Board.

Dennis

After that, Dennis thought that he would give email one more try. Perhaps Mark just needed one more nudge to make the right decision. He sent the email over the weekend so it would be waiting in the inbox first thing Monday morning.

Dennis waited all day Monday for a reply. Nothing came. Tuesday morning came and went and there was still no message from Mark. The walk on the Quad started Thursday. If approval did not come, what would he do? And even if approval came, should he make top administrators aware of the roadblock in the system or let it go?

CHAPTER 19

# For the Good of Many

## Nancy M. Schullery and Melissa Gibson Hancox

A delay in orders compels the layoff of the company's most productive manu-facturing team–or does it? Company founder and CEO Howard Crane* has an innovative solution for this crisis that can benefit the organization, the employ-ees, and the community. But can he and his management team make it work? So far, the solution has triggered only more organizational crisis.

### THE CRISIS

"What do you mean they don't want to go, Anne?"

Howard Crane, my boss, the founder and CEO of Wister Manufacturing, fought to control the drop of his jaw. As I struggled to find words to answer him, he tiredly sank into his desk chair. It had been a long two days. As director of human resources and training at Wister, I was in the thick of our second internal organizational crisis in less than 48 hours. Wister, a 50-person auto parts manu-facturing company, was facing an unforeseen downtime in orders that threatened the jobs of 19 employees. Many of these particular employees were the least senior of our assembly workers, but had set a model for productivity. They had finished their latest assembly job *one whole month* ahead of schedule, a record in the com-pany. However, we had hit a schedule delay: Our largest customer had just pushed back its next order for an additional two months, so now we were faced with up to 90 days downtime, instead of the 30 days we had expected. The delay created a crisis for our small company, which had no other major orders right now and expected none in the near term. Laying off the employees seemed like the only option, until–just yesterday–we devised an innovative solution. However, all too

---

*This case has been developed based on real organization(s) and real organizational experi-ences. Names, facts, and situations have been changed to protect the privacy of individuals and organizations.

soon Jason Loomis, chief financial officer, and I found that the employees didn't want any part of our proposed solution.

## THE MONDAY MORNING BLUES

My Monday morning had started like any other, but little did I know that I'd soon be facing the worst organizational crisis in my six years at Wister. Bleary-eyed, I stumbled into my office at 8:10 A.M. only to hear the bad news. My assistant confirmed that the 19 member employee team would not have any work for the next 90 days. My boss, Howard, called 15 minutes later to schedule an emergency meeting.

"Anne, this is big. We have to sit down and figure something out. I need to see you and Jason in the conference room now!"

Howard tried to smile as he nervously passed around the box of jelly doughnuts he had picked up on the way to the office, and we began to discuss the situation. We all knew we needed a win-win solution to this organizational crisis. Also, we all wanted a systematic way to manage this crisis and effectively respond to this challenge. How ever, we all came in with slightly different perspectives and agendas.

From my vantage point in HR, I looked at the problem from a human capital perspective. This team of employees was the most productive team at Wister Manufacturing, despite many obstacles. Many in the group spoke English as a second language and came from diverse backgrounds (African American, Caucasian, Hispanic/Latino, and Vietnamese). They had worked together only a year at Wister Yet, they had finished the latest job in record time by becoming familiar with one another's strengths and tapping each worker's unique talents. It seemed unthinkable that the best workers in the company would be forced out of their jobs because of their own success. The irony pained me: the apparent *reward* was so out of step with their efforts.

Further complicating the issue from a human resources perspective was the fact that Big Falls, the small midwestern community where the company was located, boasted a 3.2% unemployment rate, typical of the prosperous economy shown in that region of the state. I know we ran a big risk if these employees were laid off: sending a negative message to other employees that the company didn't value productivity. Without a solution we would likely lose these productive workers to competitive manufacturers. As a small company, we couldn't afford to just throw away the accumulated training our company had invested in its employees. And, as their company trainer, I had to admit that this group was exceptional. It had been slow going initially, due to the language barriers, but the nonnative English speakers were particularly motivated to prove themselves. In all my six years at Wister, this group of employees stood out for how quickly they caught on to their new jobs and how tirelessly they worked. Maybe many of them tried harder because they were single parents–sole support of themselves and three or four kids, in some cases.

Jason's perspective was different. Middle-aged and squarely built, Jason was a product of this predominantly Dutch community and had worked with Howard for nearly 15 years. He was well aware of the difficult times the company had gone through and knew Howard would want a solution that considered the workers' needs, but he had to be practical. After all, company profits were his stock in trade. As the CFO, Jason tended to favor what we all knew to be the obvious solution—downsize, lay off these employees for 90 days until orders picked up. Layoffs of the least senior employees were typical in the auto industry and worked well with the schedule of our largest customer, Jobson & Jobson, a car seat manufacturer. Jason's boss, however, had a slightly different view.

Howard's perspective was based on 26 years of industry experience. He was well aware that layoffs were typical in small to medium-sized companies like his, but the typical outcome had no appeal. Howard had witnessed tremendous downsizing of the auto parts industry, starting 20 years ago with layoffs of over a million employees in the 1980s alone, as the industry shed hierarchy and streamlined operations. A total of 90,000 jobs had been forever lost in the $200 billion auto parts industry, and hundreds of firms the same size as Howard's had gone belly-up. Howard had never expressed a desire for early retirement, much less bankruptcy, I thought.

I roused myself from my thoughts just in time to catch Howard recapping why he wanted to avoid a layoff: the group's productivity, the risk of losing the employees permanently to competitors, the motivation the employees had shown, and his history of taking care of this company's workers. The typical solution, to lay off or downsize the employees, did not appeal to me and especially not to Howard. He had built a successful company from a small family operation and felt proud of the strong organizational culture he had helped create. I knew that he read a lot to keep up with the industry, but it was Howard's nature that brought an extra ingredient.

Howard took great pride in having helped shape a culture in which employees were valued and respected. He and Nora, his wife of 28 years, and his entire family showed the employees their appreciation every Thanksgiving. Nora, an excellent cook, fixed the traditional turkey dinner and all the trimmings. For the last 23 years, Nora and their children had spent several days before the holiday preparing the appetizers, vegetable casseroles, and desserts. At Christmas time, everyone had the week off, and employees never worked on their birthdays. He prided himself on his willingness to listen to employee ideas (which had brought the company increased profits) and concerns (which he saw as showing respect for and developing trust with his employees). Indeed, Howard had always been one of those rare bosses who defied the typical *Dilbert* cartoon image of a contemporary manager.

## THE BEST LAID PLANS

Faced with the unwelcome situation of high inventory and no major orders, Howard believed that he had come up with a clever way out of Wister's crisis. In a time when management had been accused of losing confidence, and even doubted its ability to create instead of cut, Howard's idea showed true leadership. As Jason and I waited with anticipation, Howard said, "You know, I think this is an opportunity to respond to our changing work environment, to maybe even transform the way we think about working here."

Jason asked, "What do you mean, transform?"

Howard didn't answer. Instead, he abruptly quit pacing and said, "I was just wondering what on earth we're going to do, and I thought, 'Hey, that's it!'" Then, turning to Jason, he asked, "Can we do this?"

Jason seemed to know what Howard meant. Howard was asking if the company could afford to pay the 19 employees for the next three months, even if the employee team assembled nothing. Jason didn't look happy, but he answered, "We could for a while," his voice lingering on that last word.

Howard pressed: "A while?"

"Well, yeah, three or four months, probably, assuming all our other orders are on schedule," Jason responded.

Turning to me, Howard finally explained his idea. "I'm thinking we'll pay our most productive team over the next three months, but instead of working here, the employees will spend their workday time at nonprofit organizations in the community, we'll loan them our workers. You know, being socially responsible," he said.

I nodded. "We talked about this in the graduate class I'm taking. Corporate social responsibility is a big thing now—but I haven't heard of anyone loaning labor to nonprofits. This sounds like a win-win solution all the way round."

"My favorite part of this," Howard continued, "is that we can demonstrate we're a family." Howard had to agree when Jason raised another important consideration.

"And it will keep our best workers on the payroll and out of the clutches of our competitors." We all nodded as Jason continued. "You know, we have a chance here to send a solid goodwill message to the entire Big Falls area, since we'll be providing paychecks for these folks while they're making improvements around the community. We can only guesstimate the value of that kind of thing."

As the implications sunk in, I saw another advantage. "This way the workers will keep their health insurance for their kids and stay off unemployment." Last but certainly not least, paying the employees to work at nonprofits would allow employee relationships to continue, not only with each other but with us, and with Wister, as committed employees. We sat grinning at each other, impressed with ourselves and the solution.

Finally, Howard asked (without really expecting an answer), "How can I do anything else? A layoff would betray employee trust, after these workers have struggled so hard to contribute and succeed." Howard concluded the meeting with the comment, "OK, we're agreed. Let the nonprofits know we have people for them—and let me know the plan."

## AN UNSEEN HURDLE

As Jason and I returned to our offices, I was bursting with enthusiasm. "This is the most exciting program we've done since I've been here. Let's split the list and get started on those calls."

Jason agreed. "Yeah, let's get this thing solved so we can get back to work."

Jason and I began contacting a list of 18 local community organizations. Soon I heard his voice coming from down the quiet hall. "Well, if you can't do it, you can't do it. We want the solution to be a good one for everybody. Right. Thanks for your frankness. Bye."

Soon, Jason's discouraged face appeared at my door. "All I'm getting is, 'Thanks, but no thanks.' How 'bout you?"

I had to admit my luck was the same. Although most nonprofit organizations vie for volunteers and every one of the 18 organizations reacted positively to the program in concept, none were prepared to take on 19 volunteers for 40 hours per week for three months. Bob Dillard, director of the local United Way, pointed out the reality of nonprofit labor: "It takes a lot to organize volunteers and see productive results from their work. We would have to make sure that this was a mutually beneficial process so your employees wouldn't get abused and we wouldn't get abused." Most of our community contacts, recognizing the same problem, reluctantly declined to participate.

However, after what seemed like endless phone calls, by 3:00 P.M. we eventually identified eight community sites that agreed to participate. The local Habitat for Humanity, YWCA, and YMCA offered to provide the majority of assignments for the employees. At Habitat for Humanity, employees could work for three days a week and then choose another nonprofit agency on the list for their remaining two days. Now that enough nonprofit sites were secured, it was time to inform the employees of the solution. I proudly drafted a memo to employees announcing the plan and asked Monica, Howard's secretary, to see that the 19 employees received it when they came to work Tuesday morning. Monica also agreed to post an announcement on the bulletin board in the employee lounge. Jason and I left the building with a sense of smug satisfaction for the great plan we had organized and set in motion, all in one day.

## TUESDAY MORNING—REALITY CHECK

When I strolled into work this morning, I immediately sensed the tension. Employees glared sideways at me from corners, whispering as I passed. I realized that they had read the *loaned labor* memos, and it wasn't long before their reaction became clear: "No way!" I was shocked and taken aback by the variety and intensity of the negative comments.

As word spread, a line formed outside my office door, and the stream of employees with complaints seemed continuous and unending. Just when I thought the complaints were over, Carlos Toscano, a 15-month employee, leaned against my office door and said, "What they should do is give us a bonus for sticking with this place. We don't get paid enough to begin with."

Phan Doc, another worker, chimed in, "I don't see why we have to go out there and work like that. I could be getting unemployment."

As they walked away, I found myself seething with anger. "How could they even think about a bonus? Don't they realize they're lucky to have jobs?"

I was muttering to myself as Kalena Johnson, a 10-year employee, plopped down in my visitor's chair and said, "Look, my car pool comes to Wister. I don't have no car to be driving all over the county to work for these other people."

"I'll work on it, Kalena. We're still trying to iron out the wrinkles," I said, now only half convinced myself. As soon as she had left, I grabbed the phone and dialed Jason's extension. "I can't take this anymore. Let's have lunch and discuss this. Meet you at Big Mack's Diner at 11:30."

## TUESDAY AFTERNOON—FIGURING IT OUT

As I slid into the booth at Big Mack's, I could see the look of despair on Jason's face. Our waitress turned over my coffee cup and splashed it full of java as my words, rapid-fire, spilled out to Jason. "You're not going to believe this. The employees think our brilliant solution sucks!"

"Tell me about it," said Jason. "This morning Luisa Sanchez came to my office saying that she can't work in the community because the nonprofits don't open until nine in the morning and she's used to working 7:00 A.M. to 3:00 P.M. She has her entire schedule built around when her kids get on and off the school bus. She says she can't afford to disrupt her family like that."

I shared with Jason the problems I had heard; then we sat munching our sandwiches and pondering what we were now facing. A major implementation challenge had surfaced: conflicts with personal schedules and transportation. The nonprofits often didn't start operations until two or three hours after our plant opened. Luisa Sanchez's experience was typical of the single mothers among our employees: The employees had each gone to substantial effort to find effective child care providers and arrange transportation to day care as needed before or after school. Understandably enough, they were reluctant to disrupt their inter-woven schedules.

And the children were not the only ones with transportation problems. Many employees had no way to get to the designated nonprofit destinations. Most did not own cars and relied on a limited city bus system or neighborhood car pools to get to Wister's plant. Taxicabs in the small community were rare and expensive. To Jason and me, the once-attractive solution now loomed as another huge problem. So our second internal crisis had arrived. If that were the only problem.

Behind the facade of schedule complaints, we could see the reluctance of many employees to leave their known environment, where they were part of a successful manufacturing team, and go out on their own to an unfamiliar setting to do unspecified work. At the nonprofits, they didn't know what they might be asked to do: anything from putting up plasterboard, to installing a sink for a new home, to dealing with mounds of paperwork in the nonprofit offices. And, as one employee reported, "I don't know anything about building a house!"

On top of the logistical challenges and fears of unspecified, changeable work responsibilities was another concern. The employees were confused. They had never heard of or seen a company bestowing such an unusual solution as the loaned labor program. Instead of getting the gratitude we expected, we were finding that employees were suspicious, alarmed, and concerned about the impact on their personal and work lives. In school I had studied the ways in which employee resistance to change can be a normal part of organizational functioning, but now I was seeing it up close, and it was hard not to take it personally. The employees' comments forced our attention to more subtle issues that would need resolution, beginning with employees' suspicions of the program and including the employees' substantial resistance to change, a resistance often based on lack of trust.

Organizational change naturally elicits fear and uncertainty on the part of employees. In this case, the problem was compounded with the repeated layoffs and job losses in the industry, which had conditioned workers to expect similar treatment in this, now comparable, situation. Despite the benevolent nature of Howard's proposal and his intentions, employees were upset and confused by the lack of explanation accompanying the announcement. In my haste to get the word out, I had committed the same sin most other organizations do while in the thick of change—limited communication. And now it seemed that we were going to pay for it.

Back at the office, Jason and I continued to field mostly negative comments from workers, many of whom came looking for further explanation about the plan. By late in the afternoon, I found Jason in the employee lounge and said, "We've got to get the word out, and the first person who needs to know is Howard. He has to explain why we're doing this, or the rumors will take on a life of their own." Without an explanation in their brief announcements, workers couldn't believe the loaned labor solution was real or that it would actually be implemented. Employees wanted their information from the top; they needed to understand the changes better, and Howard needed their commitment. "Oh, why didn't I word that memo differently," I thought, as Jason and I gathered our forces to tell the boss. "After all, I'm supposed to know something about communicating crisis information to employees." Aloud, I said, "Jason, didn't Howard say something about leaving early tonight?" We hurried down the hall to his office and found the door open; Howard was packing his briefcase as he always did before going home.

## TO BE OR NOT TO BE?

When he heard our news, Howard's mouth seemed stuck, wide-open. He appeared dumbfounded by the unexpected problems with his presumed win-win solution. "Wh…wh…what are you saying?" he stammered. "I feel as though I've been stabbed in the back!"

I tried to explain. "We need to look at this again. The employees are worried about several things. One, how they're going to get to these other work sites; two, what they're going to do when they get there; and three, what's going to happen to their kids while their parents are working all over the county."

Jason chimed in, "It all sounded great when we talked about it, but the problem is that there've been so many layoffs in the industry—and a lot of those jobs have just gone away. Our people think we're gonna do the same thing, and before that happens we're putting them in some sort of twisted routine that's gonna turn their lives upside down before they *really* get laid off. They're not willing to go through the hassle."

Howard was quiet, listening as we explained. Finally, he spoke slowly, as if forming the thoughts while he spoke. "Well, maybe we should just forget the whole idea. I thought we had come up with something worthwhile. I really thought the employees would see the same vision I see, that this solution could be good for so many. Maybe we should just forget the whole idea and lay off those 19 employees for the 90 days. It sure would be easier. Or..." he paused, reflecting, "maybe we should try to convince our reluctant employees?" Then, a bit hurt, he mused, "...or I could just order them to go to the nonprofits and let the chips fall where they may. After all, if they don't believe that we have their best interests at heart, maybe we're wasting our time," he rationalized.

Howard's disappointment was clear. He's not just worried about losing employees, I thought. He really did hate to see them, and us, miss this opportunity to do some long-term good. By having our employees work in the same community that had been so good to Wister over the years, we could give back so much. If we could only pull this off, it would be a truly unique solution and absolutely transform what had been a crisis into a wide-ranging benefit.

"Howard," I said quietly, "you can still do something about this. Do you remember that article in *Harvard Business Review* that I gave you to read last month? The one that talked about transformational leaders? You know, leaders who get their organizations pumped up about their vision—whatever it happened to be."

"Yes, that rings a bell. Transformational leadership, yes," Howard mused, growing quiet as he realized the challenge that awaited. "Somehow, I'll have to help them figure a way to get there."

I couldn't help but think that, given the current employee mood, Howard had his work cut out for him.

Jason looked at the two of us quizzically. "How're you gonna do that?" he asked.

Howard seemed to be thinking aloud as he replied, "I remember reading that the real movers and shakers out there make such things happen by enlisting their followers in achieving a vision. Whatever noble cause the leaders have chosen, somehow they manage to spell out a way to actually make it happen. They get their employees to follow."

Jason and I exchanged discreet glances. Clearly, Howard would have to be very eloquent to enlist *these* followers, even when the noble cause was helping out at nonprofit organizations.

Howard grew more excited as he continued. "I'm convinced that once the employees actually get out there and work with the nonprofits, they'll feel good about doing their part."

Then Howard's jaw set as it often did when he felt strongly about something and he continued, quickly outlining the issues. "How can we communicate the potential solution to the employees? And how can we make loaned labor work for them? Will they trust us?" Then, hardly able to restrain his delight at his strategic brainstorm, he confided to us, "You know, there's no way to demonstrate respect for the employees like empowering them to help solve the challenges that they've raised."

Surprised, Jason blurted, "But they expect answers from us!"

I nodded, noting, "This plan has a challenge around every corner, it seems. Maybe we all need a little time to think about it."

Howard glanced at the clock; it was almost 4:15 P.M. He had promised Nora that he would attend their daughter Jessica's school play tonight. "Let's sleep on it," he said. Howard hurriedly closed his briefcase and left for home. Jason and I looked at each other, shrugged in unison, and wondered how Wister's crisis would ever be resolved.

# CHAPTER 20

# A Matter of Perspective

## Paaige K. Turner and Robert L. Krizek

The Metropolitan Medical Group,* or MMG, is the practice arm of a private university's medical school. This was the first time that MMG experienced significant revenue loss, which interestingly followed three years of declining levels of patient satisfaction. Perhaps even more interesting, the onset of the decline in patient satisfaction coincided with the divestiture of the hospital to a national health care conglomerate. While a major component of the MMG's mission has always been to provide a clinical environment for medical interns and residents, it had become increasingly clear that this mission would be in jeopardy if MMG could not cover its costs. The administration of MMG, which in the past had relied on reactive cost-cutting measures to address decreases in revenue, decided that a more proactive strategy needed to be devised if they were going to halt this trend in declining revenues.

The thinking on the part of the administration was that declining patient satisfaction and revenue loss were inextricably linked. As part of a larger project to address these two related issues, Mike Taslow, the CEO of MMG, hired Betty McDaniel as the director of patient care. This was a new position for the MMG. In their initial interview, Mike told Betty that he wanted patients to have a *seamless experience* at MMG. "Patients should expect the same procedures, the same treatment from our staff, and the same efficiency from all the various departments of the MMG," Mike explained.

When he offered Betty the job, Mike challenged her to first assess the problems surrounding reduced patient satisfaction and then solve them, always keeping in mind his vision of a seamless experience. Betty, in accepting the position, agreed to present her ideas for improving patient satisfaction in three months.

---

*This case has been developed based on real organization(s) and real organizational experiences. Names, facts, and situations have been changed to protect the privacy of individuals and organizations.

She was confident that the three-month time frame would be enough for her to develop a preliminary plan of action.

Prior to accepting this position, Betty had spent nine years as part of the practice management team at an affluent suburban medical center owned and operated by a competing regional health care system. Although Betty had considerable experience dealing with issues of patient satisfaction, she had never operated in an environment that included a medical school or in one that drew a substantial number of its patients from an urban population. Consequently, during her first few weeks on the job, Betty set out to gather information about the organization and the various factors that were affecting patient satisfaction.

## UNDERSTANDING THE ISSUES

Betty quickly learned that there were many issues at a teaching facility with which she never had to deal at the suburban medical center. For example, since they were associated with a medical school, MMG doctors not only saw patients, they also taught classes and supervised medical students. These multiple and conflicting roles reduced the number of days and hours that doctors were actually available to see patients. Also, in order to facilitate learning, residents were sometimes present when the physicians saw the patients; other times they were not. Patients never seemed to know what to expect or even who was a *real* doctor and who wasn't. In addition, since the administration divided the practice according to academic departments (i.e., surgery, internal medicine), different department heads oversaw each area within MMG without the coordination of an overall practice manager.

Finally, Betty learned that while its midtown location made MMG easily accessible to a large urban population, the flight of many white-collar, middle-class professionals to the suburbs resulted in a patient population that was primarily lower-income individuals and families, often without health insurance. In addition to their medical issues, these individuals often had other concerns that could affect their satisfaction with their visits to the MMG. For example, many of these individuals had limited health coverage and even those with health insurance frequently had to take time off from their hourly jobs to visit the doctor. Betty, like many of the newer hires at MMG, had not worked with a clientele with these types of concerns.

During this time, while she was getting the lay of the land, Betty decided to observe actual interactions between the MMG staff and their patients to see how they could be potentially influencing patient satisfaction. She sat in the waiting area watching people arrive for their appointments and checking in with the intake desk. She listened to their conversations with one another and took notes discreetly.

## THE OFFICE VISIT

It was a Wednesday afternoon about 2:15 as Betty walked past the waiting area for internal medicine. The two dozen or so brown and gold cloth chairs were about

75% filled with patients and family members. As she passed, Betty noticed that a 40-something woman and the intake nurse, Carolyn, were having some difficulty in confirming an appointment. Being relatively new and not knowing proper protocol in these matters, Betty elected to stand back and simply observe.

"Are you sure your appointment is today, Ms. Dillard? I can't seem to locate your name. You wouldn't happen to have your appointment card with you, would you?"

Ms. Dillard searched her billfold and then her purse, dumping its contents onto the narrow counter in front of Carolyn's window. A few pieces of paper and some change fell to the carpeted floor. "I can't seem to find it. I'm sorry, but I'm sure my appointment was for today at 2:30. I hope this doesn't cause a problem–I have to get back to work soon."

Carolyn seemed sympathetic. "I'm sure we'll get this cleared up," she said. "Just have a seat and I'll check to see if maybe your appointment was made with another department. Did you talk to us or to central scheduling?"

"I don't remember, but I'm sure it was for today."

From her position Betty could hear Carolyn on the phone saying, "She's very nice. Could you check and see if she has an appointment in your department?"

After a few minutes, maybe 10, Jacqueline, a receptionist from acute care, entered the waiting room and escorted Ms. Dillard over to acute care and sat her down in that waiting area. Betty could overhear Jacqueline saying calmly, "We're sorry for the confusion. I'm sure we'll get it straightened out." Jacqueline excused herself and went back to her office to check on the appointment.

A short time later Ms. Dillard and Jacqueline returned to Carolyn's intake window, and after a brief three-way conversation Ms. Dillard, somewhat jokingly, turned to another waiting patient and said, "I don't want to have to get ugly today." As Betty was taking notes, she wrote down that the patient had been there for over 30 minutes and it was still unclear if she had an appointment and if she would be able to see her doctor.

Carolyn slid her window shut, and Ms. Dillard began talking to other patients around her. Each of the waiting patients took a turn telling their MMG horror stories. At some point Ms. Dillard said rather loudly, "I'm wondering what they're talking about back there. Just get me in to my appointment. I took time off work today and had my sister give me a ride just so I could be here."

Just then Carolyn slid the window open once more to call Ms. Dillard over. "Again I apologize for the confusion. We're trying to figure out what happened. I should have an answer in a few more minutes."

"This is a big problem. I'm not going to deal with this anymore!" Ms. Dillard said to anyone who would listen. "I don't need a doctor I can't get to see. If she doesn't see me today, I'll…" In the middle of her speech, Ms. Dillard was called to the window.

Betty was tempted to intervene, to go over and offer her help. But she didn't, wanting to see how the intake receptionist would handle the patient.

Carolyn shook her head and said, "I'm afraid there is some confusion. Your doctor works with residents today; she doesn't see patients except those scheduled as patients of her residents."

"So what can be done? I took off from work today and my sister gave me a ride. I wouldn't have done this if someone hadn't scheduled me an appointment."

Carolyn continued. "Again I apologize for the confusion. Let me give you a couple of options. The doctor is in clinic with her residents, and as I said she doesn't see her own patients when she's with her residents. Clinic is finished at five o'clock and she can see you then."

Betty wrote in her notes that it had been almost an hour at this point.

"I can't wait until then. I have to get back to work. Let me talk to the doctor," Ms. Dillard pleaded. "Last time she fit me in when you said there were no appointments."

"We could schedule you for another day," Carolyn offered.

"Can I get another doctor? Is there another doctor I can see? She seems real good, but if I can't see her...." Ms. Dillard turned to another patient, one of her complaint group. "I had to wait to see her the first time I came here. Now this for my second visit."

"Again I apologize for your inconvenience."

"I've had a lot of problems with this place. Today I left work to get here. I guess I'll have to find another doctor. Or maybe I can go to the nurse where I work. I think they let us see her sometimes, even when it's not work related. Maybe she can recommend a doctor for me to see."

She grabbed her purse and stormed off, looking for her sister.

The next day at lunch Betty discovered from Joyce, one of Carolyn's intake associates, that Ms. Dillard actually had an appointment scheduled for the same time and date the following month. "It was her fault," said Joyce. "We weren't wrong here. It wasn't our mistake." Betty also discovered that Carolyn hadn't informed her immediate supervisor about the incident. She wondered if there was a mechanism in place for reporting these types of patient issues.

## MAKING SENSE OF IT ALL: FROM THE PATIENT'S PERSPECTIVE

Betty's experience with issues of patient satisfaction and her basic instincts told her that assessing and solving MMG's problems would be more difficult than she first thought. But she had told Mike Taslow that she would have an initial plan at the three-month mark, which now was only six weeks away. She decided that her best strategy at this point would be to hold some one-on-one conversations with patients to hear what they had to say directly, and decided that she would begin interviewing patients the next day.

Getting off the elevator on the second floor, Betty identified a woman who she presumed to be a patient, as her wrist was bandaged, and introduced herself.

"Hello, my name is Betty McDaniel. I'm the director of patient care. I'm trying to improve patient care here at MMG and would like to get your opinion on how we are doing."

Startled by the abrupt introduction, it wasn't clear if the woman would agree to respond to Betty's introduction. Finally, she said, "My name is Miriam."

"Miriam, if you wouldn't mind, why don't we sit over here so that you can be more comfortable and we won't be in the way," Betty offered as she motioned toward some chairs in an adjacent waiting area. "Please tell me, how did you happen to get started coming to the MMG?"

"I work only a few blocks away and going to MMG would be convenient. I just never took the time to come over here. But everyone I talk to always says how wonderful the doctors are at MMG, and I wasn't that happy with my own doctor. I just didn't take the time to switch. But then I hurt my wrist and my boss, of all people, suggested that I come here to see them. She had hurt her wrist playing sports–tennis–and said how great her doctor was."

"So you started coming here because of our doctors' reputations?"

"Yes, but you folks have some problems. The first time I called to make an appointment I had to push about 10 different buttons on the phone just to talk with someone. When I finally spoke with someone, I was told that I would have to wait four to six weeks to see a doctor. But since I had heard such good things, I decided to go ahead and wait even though my wrist hurt now. They told me about acute care, but what they told me didn't make sense. Then about a week or two before my appointment I got a letter saying that my appointment had been moved, but they moved it to a time when I work. I called the nurse and she checked with the doctor. They managed to fit me in at a better time. I thought that was really nice of her and, of course, the doctor. I remember thinking that I understood a little better why people spoke so highly of the doctors at the MMG."

Betty asked her to continue, to tell her more specifics about her experiences when she arrived at the MMG.

"Well, I went upstairs to sign in but had to go back downstairs to register. No one told me to register downstairs, not even the receptionist in the lobby. I was on time for my appointment, 1:15 I think, but going downstairs took some time and I got back up to my doctor's a little late. The waiting room was OK, a little crowded, but I've seen worse. They had some magazines set out, but nothing I was interested in.

"Anyway, after signing in I waited in the waiting room for about 15 minutes and finally asked how much longer. The woman didn't even look up from what she was doing. She just told me that the doctor was with other patients and she would see me as soon as possible. I just wish I would have known how long that would be. I mean, I was afraid to go to the bathroom. While I was there waiting, this guy sitting next to me told me that on clinic days you could sign in early and they would see you first.

"At about 1:45 or 1:50 a nurse took me into the exam room, I sat for another 45 minutes–just the exam table and me. No books, no nothing! It felt like they had forgotten about me. Eventually, a doctor came in, at least I thought she was a doctor and she asked me a bunch of questions and then told me that my doctor would be there in a little bit. I thought she was my doctor, but she wasn't. I'm not sure who she was. After 10 minutes or so another doctor came in and asked all the same questions. She also asked a lot about my work and what I do all day. She was really nice and figured out that I had, and still have, some inflammation in my wrist. She suggested that I get an X-ray to be sure that was all. I could tell she really cared about me and wanted me to get better. She told me that I needed an order to take to their X-ray department and that the woman at the intake window would make it for me. From the woman's response I guessed that this was something she normally didn't do.

"When I got back to work I was complaining about the cost of parking and my boss asked why I didn't get my parking ticket validated. You know why–no one told me! I don't have money to throw away. I don't know. I really like my doctor, but..." Miriam paused as if waiting for Betty to respond.

"How would you rate your satisfaction with your visit to MMG?"

"On a scale of 1 to 10 I'd give it about an 8. The doctor was a 10, the appointment process was close to zero, and the rest was about average, maybe a 5 or 6."

A day or two later Betty talked with Roz, a patient at the MMG for the past three years.

"I never understand how you schedule appointment times. The doctors are always late, at least 20 or 30 minutes, or even an hour behind on most days. And waiting for me–you know, a single mom–is difficult. I have to bring my kids with me, since I don't have any day care. That's tough. Especially if the appointment is around lunchtime, when my kids get really hungry. The first couple of times I came here I looked for a lunchroom or something to get them a snack, but there were signs everywhere saying that there was no food or drink allowed. I don't know what that was about, since I can always smell food cooking in the back, like popcorn or chicken or something. Now I sneak in a couple of snacks, you know what I mean, just in case the kids get hungry."

"Please continue. These are the kinds of things I need to hear," Betty said to encourage Roz to tell her more.

"And then some departments, I don't remember the names, have a few toys for the kids in the waiting areas, but others don't. Don't they think people have kids?"

"Is there anything else beside the appointment times that you don't understand?" Betty questioned.

"Well, there's referral. One woman I talked to when I was in the waiting room one day called it referral hell! She was right. I needed a referral to see some specialist and when I went to the referral office, the office on the first floor, and knocked, no one answered. I mean I could hear them in there. Then, as I was waiting for the elevator, someone came out and I asked him about getting a referral. They told me that I had to call the office. So I went into the registration office and called, but no one answered. I called back when I got home and then once I did get through they told me I needed something from my insurance, but when I called my insurance they told me I needed a referral number. It's all too complicated."

At that point Betty jumped in and said, "Well, it's my job to make this all a little less complicated. Please tell me, how would your rate your satisfaction with the MMG?"

"If you mean with my doctor, I guess about a 7. He's getting better with me, but at times he just doesn't listen to me. If you mean everything else, I've got to be honest: I wouldn't rate it that good. The phone system makes me mad because I can't talk to anyone and every department, every doctor, seems to have a different set of rules. And don't get me started telling you about how I got lost trying to find another part of MMG over on the other side of the hospital. You probably don't want me to go there."

## MAKING SENSE OF IT ALL: FROM THE STAFF'S PERSPECTIVE

Although Betty felt she had a fairly good idea of what problems looked like from the perspective of the employees of MMG, she decided to sit down with a number of them and hear what they had to say. She hoped that they might provide her with some ideas for developing her plan. Now she had only three more weeks to finalize her plan to present to Mike.

"Jennifer, I want to thank you for taking some time to talk with me. As you know, I've been charged with the task of improving patient satisfaction and I would like your help. Any thoughts?"

Jennifer, a department coordinator, started right in. "I know that we have to do something. Our patient satisfaction ratings are falling. We do these recall phone surveys from our list of recent patients, and we can see that our numbers keep slipping. Actually, we don't need our patients to tell us we're slipping; all we have to do is look at our bottom line. We lost a lot of money this past year."

Betty asked her what she thought was the problem.

"What I think patients want and what we need to give them is this seamless experience that administration has talked about. Gee, I'd like a seamless experience when I see my doctor here. But that's easier said than done. I think we first need to educate our patients about how we do things here," Jennifer explained.

"Can you tell me why you think we need to start there?" Betty asked.

"I mean, some people show up and expect us to see them without an appointment or even if their health insurance doesn't cover our office. One of the biggest problems we have is walk-ins late in the day and no-shows. I think people see us as a free clinic, and they can just come when they please or just not show up for an appointment if it's not convenient. Sometimes we have to move their appointments because the doctors have an emergency or need to teach a class. But sometimes our patients tell us little white lies that create problems for us. I mean, they will say that they can't get off work or something, but if they could get off for the first appointment, why not the next? It isn't everyone, just some people. I know

I probably shouldn't say this, but I really wouldn't be upset if those individuals left. They tend to see us as a drop-in clinic rather than a medical practice. We need to somehow explain to them the difference. We need to educate these people so they understand what we are, how we operate, or things will never be seamless."

"What would help, specifically, to improve patient satisfaction?"

"What would really help me do my job would be access to an electronic medical record system. Sometimes I have to go to two or three different departments to find someone's file, and that takes a lot of my time. And I have to do it. If I send the intake nurse, then there isn't anyone to greet patients as they arrive.

"There's another problem," Jennifer continued. "People don't understand how what they're doing affects other departments. We have no communication between departments. If I need to solve a problem, I just go to a friend in the department and have them fix it. And then patients need to understand that we aren't always in control of what happens. We have only one person working referrals, and in order to get referrals they need to be on the phone calling insurance companies and doctors' offices. So if they are on the phone trying to get referrals, they can't answer the phone, let alone answer the door. One thing that we are really proud of is the fact that our patients don't wait very long before we get them into an exam room. Usually they are only in the waiting room 10 to 20 minutes. Patients need to understand that we have ways of doing things so that we can ensure they get quality health care."

Betty talked with a department head, Dr. Penev, that day as well.

"Our employees and staff do a wonderful job, but we are overcrowded. We have multiple staff members in one office, and you can never find a place to sit down in the waiting area. Sure, we have our problems, they kind of percolate up. I mean, my secretary will get a call from a patient that there is a problem and I get on the phone with them. Usually we can fix it with a quick call. For example, a quick call can get an appointment set up or a report forwarded. But I also talk to a lot of people in the halls and on the phone who really like and appreciate their doctors and the rest of our staff. Sure, I get satisfaction reports from MMG and sometimes the numbers drop, but I know that my patients are satisfied.

"We provide world-class health care," he boasted. "Our doctors have national reputations. We can provide almost every service right here within MMG. Yeah, you may have to go to a different building and I know that it can be difficult, but we take care of our patients and our students. We just need more room."

At the three-month deadline, Betty scheduled a meeting with Mike Taslow. As they sat down, the first thing Mike asked was, "Okay, why aren't the patients satisfied?"

CHAPTER 21

# The Expert Facilitator

## Mary E. Vielhaber

"**M**arlene,* what do you think about having an external consultant facilitate our strategic planning session?" asked Mitch Johnson, the vice president of finance for the Midwest Energy Company. Mitch posed this question as he and Marlene Lewis, the director for banking relations, met to discuss the upcoming departmental strategic planning session.

"That sounds like a great idea to me, Mitch. You and I want to be actively involved in the discussion rather than leading it, so it probably would be better to have a facilitator help us."

Deregulation of the electrical utility industry had led to new competitive pressures for all electrical utility companies. Both Mitch and Marlene knew that the energy companies that would survive in this new environment had to meet customer demands by cutting costs and providing reliable, safe energy. Mitch and Marlene also knew that the finance department had to make changes in how it managed the company's cash and pension investments. Marlene, in particular, was keenly aware that there would be considerable resistance. Some employees always seemed to cling to the old ways of doing business.

"There's a consultant I know named Tom Davison," said Mitch. "I think he would do a good job for us. Last summer, he worked with the top-level executives at our teambuilding retreat. I am not sure if he does facilitation, but I'll check with him."

Several days later, Mitch mentioned to Marlene that he had hired Tom Davison to facilitate the strategic planning session. "I told Tom that the goal for the departmental strategic planning session was to come up with a strategic plan that could move the department forward in the new deregulated environment.

---

*This case has been developed based on real organization(s) and real organizational experiences. Names, facts, and situations have been changed to protect the privacy of individuals and organizations.

I asked Tom to meet with a smaller committee to prepare for the session. Then I asked Bill Edwards, the director of risk management, and Susan Maher, the director of pension investment, and four of our top financial analysts to work with Tom to prepare for the departmental session."

## THE STRATEGIC PLANNING SESSION

As members of the finance department came into the conference room on the day scheduled for the strategic planning session, Marlene noticed the room and the refreshments were all set. There were six round tables with six chairs at each table. Marlene greeted Tom. "Hi, Tom. I'm Marlene Lewis. Is everything ready for today?" As Tom looked around the room, he replied, "I think so."

Tom continued, "I met several times with the six people who were on the preparation committee, but I wasn't able to schedule much time with Mitch. Clearly, he is one busy guy. We talked by phone yesterday, and he seems fine with the agenda I developed for today."

Just then, Mitch walked in and greeted Tom. Marlene excused herself as Tom and Mitch chatted with each other.

By 9:10 A.M., most people had arrived and sat down. The seating was typical. The financial analysts sat together; the directors were at another table; the assistant directors were at another table; the administrative assistants were at a table in the back of the room; and the last two tables had a mix of the people who arrived late. Marlene sat with the directors and waited for things to get started.

As Marlene sat down, she noticed at each place there was a small wireless keypad the size of a television remote control. The keypads would allow each person to register individual responses of strongly agree, agree, neutral, disagree, or strongly disagree. Marlene assumed that Tom planned to gauge their reactions to ideas with these feedback mechanisms. Next to each wireless keypad, there was a cardboard tent that had a number corresponding to the number on the keypad.

Prior to the meeting, everyone had received an email with the starting time (9:00 A.M. sharp!) and the ending time (4:00 P.M.). The notice said that this meeting was to develop the strategic plan that would guide the department for the next three to five years. Since there was no written agenda, Marlene was really not sure how the day would be spent.

Finally, at about 9:20 A.M., Mitch Johnson began the session with some opening remarks. "I want to thank everyone for coming. This is a very important meeting for the finance department. We are going to begin a strategic planning process today that will culminate in a three-to five-year strategic plan for the department. I want each of you to contribute your thoughts and ideas openly today. The contributions of each member of the staff are valuable.

"Prior to today's session, a committee from the department met and they generated some ideas about our mission, vision, goals, strategies, and action plans. Our goal today is to build on those ideas and to reach some common understanding as a department about where we are going and how we plan to get there.

"This plan is important because with all of the change that is going on in our company and our industry, we don't want to be over a barrel and have to dig our way out of a hole."

Marlene chuckled to herself as she thought about the way Mitch mixed metaphors. Mitch continued, "To help us reach consensus today, I have asked Tom Davison to facilitate our session. Tom has his own consulting business, and I have seen his work. Last summer Tom ran an outdoor teambuilding session for our executive team." Then, turning to Tom, he said, "Tom, are you still doing those ropes courses?"

Tom nodded and said, "Yes. Those are still quite popular for teambuilding. For those of you who are not familiar with ropes courses, they are experiential training courses that are held outdoors. Typically, a variety of team exercises are used that require all of the team members to tackle some physical challenge like climbing over a wall or crossing over a fast-running stream on a narrow plank. The goal is to develop trust and confidence in each other as you take on outdoor challenges as a team. The thought is that the trust and confidence will then be transferred to working together on business issues."

After a brief pause, Tom began the session by thanking Mitch and then said, "To start today's session, I would like each of you to get up, walk around, and introduce yourself to two people you don't know."

The group laughed. We know each other all too well, Marlene thought. We meet quarterly as a group, and there have been no new hires in the last two years. Hesitant, but willing to respond to Tom's request, Marlene introduced herself to Susan Maher, sitting next to her, even though she knew Susan well after working with her for seven years. In fact, Susan and Marlene were both on Mitch's executive team, so they met together every week for several hours. Following her lead, others got up and shook hands with colleagues, imitating what Marlene had modeled. Anyone listening to these *introductions* would have noticed that people were faking it. Yet people played along and pretended to enjoy meeting colleagues they already were quite familiar with. Meanwhile, Tom did not seem to notice that his icebreaker wasn't accomplishing much at all.

As people shook hands, Marlene heard the song "Celebration," a popular tune from the early eighties playing in the background. Obviously, Tom chose some very upbeat but dated music to get the day started. Marlene also noticed that Mitch must have slipped out of the room when the introductions started. Mitch wasn't someone who could fake an introduction just to be polite. He probably thought he could take a quick break, check his phone messages, and get back before the real discussions began.

## GETTING DOWN TO BUSINESS

When it became clear that everyone had exhausted the introductions, Tom continued. "Well, now that you have had an opportunity to meet some new people, I would like to get started. Today we have a lot to cover. We will be developing our mission, vision, goals, strategies, and action plans for the next three to five years. I know this may sound like a lot, but I have some technology here that will allow us to move more quickly through these topics. My job is to help you find the most expedient way to reach consensus."

Taking a wireless keypad in his hand and holding it up for everyone to see, Tom continued, "At each of your places, you will find a wireless keypad for voting. This mechanism will allow you to vote anonymously on ideas today. After you vote, the totals will be displayed on this large screen in the front of the room. To test this out, please answer the two questions that you can see on the screen up front with strongly agree, agree, neutral, disagree, or strongly disagree."

> Question 1: If I was independently wealthy and I did not need to work for a living, I would still work.
>
> Question 2: If I was independently wealthy and I did not need to work for a living, I would still work for *this* company.
>     Strongly agree—agree—neutral—disagree—strongly disagree

"Now let's look at the results."

Marlene was not surprised. A large majority (65%) agreed that they would still work even if they were independently wealthy. However, an even larger majority (75%) disagreed that they would work for this company. Marlene knew that recent rumors about a reorganization had made most people concerned about whether their jobs were secure. There were also rumors of a merger with another, larger energy company. These rumors were especially troublesome, since people were speculating that the larger company would keep their own finance department and Marlene and her colleagues would be replaced.

Tom briefly commented on the results from the voting. When he asked for questions, the participants looked around nervously. No one asked a question or offered a comment about the results. Moving on, Tom explained that the group would continue to use the wireless keypads to determine team consensus on a variety of issues.

As Marlene thought about the rumors, and her colleagues' obvious reaction to them, Tom put a mission statement on the screen. He explained, "This mission statement was drafted by a few of your colleagues in the department." Since most of the people in the room were seeing the mission statement for the first time, they carefully read the words on the screen.

Tom continued, "Now, I want you to vote on this statement. Again, choose one of the following responses: strongly agree, agree, neutral, disagree, or strongly disagree."

Ralph, a supervisor in the cashier's office, raised his hand and asked, "Tom, can we discuss this statement before we vote?"

Tom quickly replied, "No, I just want you to vote so we can see if we have consensus."

Ralph frowned and looked around the room to others for support. No one said anything, so he continued. "That doesn't make sense to me. How can we vote when we have not talked about this mission statement at all? I'm not even sure what the statement means."

Tom looked away from Ralph and directed his attention back to the group. "After we have tallied the votes, we can discuss the statement. Will everyone please vote now?"

When the results appeared on the screen, it was clear that just over half of the participants either agreed or strongly agreed with the mission statement. Tom summed up the results by saying, "Just over 50% of you either strongly agree or agree with the draft of the mission statement. You will also notice that another 20% are neutral. While this is not a strong consensus, the results show that most people agree with the mission statement proposed."

Without asking for questions or comments, Tom moved on. Next, he put up a vision statement and asked the participants to vote. This seemed really odd to Marlene, and she suspected others were uncomfortable as well. How can we decide our vision when we have not all bought into the mission statement? Marlene decided that she would abstain from voting. She looked around and saw confusion on some of the faces. In fact, many of the individuals at the meeting seemed to be preoccupied with something else. Some were attending to their PDAs, and some were looking over papers they had brought with them.

Tom looked at his computer screen and announced firmly, "It looks like not everyone has voted. Please vote now."

There was a brief pause, followed by another request to vote on the vision. When it didn't look like people were responding, Tom turned to his laptop computer and pushed a key. As he turned back to the audience, the numbers of the keypads that had not been used appeared on the large screen in the front of the room. Since the numbers on the tent cards at each person's place were also large, most people could glance around the table and see who had not voted. Marlene's number was there. And so was Ralph's number.

Tom again announced, "These five people have not voted. Will each of you vote now?"

An undercurrent of whispering became obvious. Finally Ralph stood up and said, "I object, Tom. You said that this voting would be anonymous. Why are you singling us out? I honestly feel that I cannot vote on a vision statement until I have had an opportunity to talk the mission statement over with colleagues."

Marlene looked around the room and wondered why Mitch still had not returned to the room. She wondered if anyone else, including Tom, had noticed his absence.

Tom again looked away from Ralph and explained to the group, "This is not a final vote. I just want everyone to let us know how they are feeling."

"I would be glad to tell you how I am feeling, but you said we can't discuss the mission statement yet," Ralph interrupted.

Tom turned to the group and asked, "How many of you would like to stop and discuss the mission statement?"

Hands went up. Marlene thought it looked like more than half the people there had their hands up. She did notice, however, that all of the committee members who had worked with Tom to prepare for the session did not raise their hands.

"It looks like the majority are happy with the voting," Tom concluded.

Not to be deterred, Ralph continued, "It looked pretty even to me. Maybe we should count hands."

Again, Tom seemed to ignore Ralph as he turned to the group and asked, "Do you want to continue?"

Marlene could see by Ralph's expression that he was angry as he continued. "I thought my contribution was supposed to be valued. Where is Mitch? What are we doing here?"

Marlene sighed. This meeting would be a disaster if Tom did not take control immediately. Just then, Mitch walked back into the room.

Tom turned to Mitch and said, "Mitch, we seem to have some disagreement about the process you and I discussed for today. I planned for the group to vote on the draft statements for the mission, vision, goals, strategies, and action plans. Then I thought we would discuss them and vote again. I want them to vote to find out how many people agree. If we all agree, there is no need to discuss the statements. What do you want to do, Mitch?"

Clearly, Mitch had little idea of the controversy that was brewing as he answered, "Tom, you are the facilitator, you decide."

Before Tom could say another word, Ralph and two other people who had not voted and whose numbers had appeared on the screen got up and walked out of the room.

Marlene wondered what she should do. She knew that Ralph and others, including herself, were frustrated by the process, not necessarily the ideas. What could she say to help Tom understand that he needed to stop and resolve this misunderstanding before the group could continue with a productive discussion of strategic planning?

CHAPTER 22

# Corporate Social Responsibility Versus Greenwashing

Astrid Sheil and Heather Gearhart

B ecker Dairy is a giant in the dairy industry. A family company, Becker Dairy was founded in 1918 and is known for its high-quality products, which include milk, ice cream, butter, and cream cheese. It also operates one of the largest dairy farms in the United States, with a herd of more than 25,000 cows and has separate manufacturing facilities for each product line.

Sarah Fairchild was recently hired as Becker Dairy's public relations special-ist. It is her first job out of college, where she was a standout in PRSSA, the Public Relations Student Society of America. Sarah is joining a diverse marketing team at Becker Dairy. Structured as an in-house agency, the marketing team—comprised of designers, advertising/media buying experts, and public relations profession-als—is responsible for preparing in-depth recommendations and executing major integrated marketing campaigns for the company.

During her interview, Becker Dairy's director of marketing particularly impressed Sarah. Alice Markham has been with Becker Dairy for more than 20 years. She worked her way up from being a public relations specialist to managing the entire marketing team—no small feat in this privately owned patriarchal busi-ness. On Sarah's first day, Alice took the time to introduce Sarah to the corporate culture at Becker Dairy. "You remind me a lot of myself," Alice told Sarah. "You have a great future here—just remember who you work for and that you serve at the pleasure of the CEO."

Sarah nodded as she thought about Geoffrey Becker, the fourth-generation Becker leading the business. Geoff Becker had a reputation in the industry for being no-nonsense and a hardball negotiator with vendors and suppliers. With a pedigree that included an undergraduate degree in finance from Princeton and an

---

*This case has been developed based on real organization(s) and real organizational experi-ences. Names, facts, and situations have been changed to protect the privacy of individuals and organizations.

MBA from Wharton School of Business, Geoff Becker was business royalty. His reputation as a tough manager often had a chilling effect on dissent among his direct reports. Word around the water cooler was that it was professional suicide to challenge or question a Geoff Becker decision.

Alice kept her conversation upbeat and practical. "Sarah, you were hired because you are sharp and smart. I expect you to contribute fresh, new ideas," she said. "It's about time we stirred up the cobwebs around here!" Both women laughed.

## GREAT IDEA—LET'S GO GREEN!

Alice opened the meeting by introducing Sarah to all members of the marketing team. Sarah instantly felt at home with these folks. The banter between and among team members was gentle and good-natured. Alice then kicked off the agenda with "Works of the Week." Each team member shared a success from the previous week's assignments and ongoing projects. Sarah thought how lucky she was to be part of such a supportive team.

The meeting progressed to current project updates, next steps, and new business. Here Alice shared news from the executive board that the company had identified a unique opportunity to both reduce the bottom line and enhance the company's perception as a socially responsible company.

Becker Dairy had been losing an average of $2.2 million per year in plastic delivery crate losses. Used to deliver all Becker Dairy products, the crates were being stolen and used for storage both by grocery store customers and consumers who considered the crates to be trash or no longer needed.

"More importantly, we need to be aware of the impact that this has on our environment," continued Alice. "More than 3 million pounds of plastic enter the world every year simply because we have to replace the stolen crates. If we can prevent crate loss, we'll improve our bottom line *and* help the environment. I'm going to need a dedicated team to put together our plan of action, and this is top priority for the e-board [the executive board]."

Sarah eagerly raised her hand to volunteer. As president of her PRSSA chapter in college, Sarah had led the campus initiative to go green with recycling bins in every building and a "Turn Off the Lights!" campaign that reduced energy consumption by 7 percent in its first semester. For her work, Sarah's PRSSA chapter had won a national award.

"Great, Sarah, you can get your feet wet with this one. You'll work with Mark, Jess, and Dave to pull together the formal recommendation. We need a complete campaign highlighting Becker Dairy's green practices. There's been a lot of press about companies doing something to help the environment, and it's time for Becker Dairy to have a piece of that pie. I need a recommendation in one week," concluded Alice.

Sarah left the marketing status meeting bursting with excitement. Mark, Jess, and Dave all agreed to let Sarah lead the initiative. She would conduct the research and shape the strategy while the team prepared marketing materials to support the new direction for Becker Dairy. Sarah knew that she needed to start with powerful research to support the marketing department's loosely formulated strategy of positioning Becker Dairy as a green company.

## IT ISN'T EASY BEING GREEN

Sarah began her research with Lexis-Nexus, a news media database. Using the key terms "Green Corporations," she discovered more than 1,000 articles the past six months. As she began clicking through stories in prominent publications such as *The New York Times, USA Today,* and *Washington Post,* she realized that a large percentage of the stories were focused on disclosing companies guilty of Greenwashing.

Concerned, Sarah Googled "Greenwashing" and found its definition on Wikipedia:

*Greenwashing* is the term applied to companies spending more money on marketing efforts than on their sustainability initiatives. The six deadly sins of Greenwashing include:

- Sin of the hidden trade-off (more energy efficient but hazardous materials)
- Sin of no proof
- Sin of vagueness (claiming 100 percent natural but using hazardous naturally occurring elements)
- Sin of irrelevance (free of already banned substances)
- Sin of fibbing (claiming approval from organizations when it does not exist)
- Sin of lesser of two evils (organic cigarettes)

Sarah also noted that the Federal Trade Commission had recently held hearings on green-marketing claims and eco-labels. In an effort to shut down environmental claims such as Home Depot's "Eco-Options," the FTC had ruled that businesses should not make any *green* claims until standards could be defined and verified.

Sarah went back to her notes and immediately recognized the warning signs of the proposed Becker Dairy campaign. As it was today, the company wanted a complete marketing campaign around one green initiative, the real purpose of which was to save the company money. Thinking ahead, Sarah began imagining the news headline that could follow: "Becker Dairy Denies Allegations of Greenwashing With Its Delivery Crate Recycling Campaign."

With her mind spinning and a headache building, Sarah Googled "Becker Dairy, Responsible" to see if there were any negative stories about the company. Alice had mentioned that the company had tangled with an animal rights group in the past—due to a lack of education, as she put it—but Sarah was completely unprepared for what she found.

Two years ago Becker Dairy had been attacked for a mixed-media campaign about its ice cream. According to what Sarah found online, the campaign was in response to a competing ice cream line's advertisements, which featured children first having difficulty pronouncing the ingredients on one ice cream container and then reading wholesome ingredients like "milk, sugar, and cream" on the advertising company's label.

Becker Dairy responded with an aggressive campaign hyping its ice cream as being "all natural." Campaign imagery featured dancing cows in a green pasture (whereas Becker Dairy cows are actually kept in crowded dirt corrals with shades) and a slow churning of animated ingredients—such as vanilla flowers and sugar—by hand instead of at the high-tech ice cream manufacturing facility. Consumer advocates called the advertisements misleading and demanded that Becker Dairy discontinue the campaign. One animal rights group was so upset by the misleading commercials that it trespassed onto Becker Dairy property and took footage of the dairy cows in the crowded dirt corrals and small holding pens and posted the video along with a voiceover about the company's misleading campaign on YouTube.

Alice entered the room just as Sarah finished viewing the disturbing video on YouTube.

"Doing your homework? I always like to see that," Alice said with a smile. "Let me tell you *our* side of that story. First, these people are absolute radicals and extremely overzealous. They even got to some of our employees—who we then had to fire. These animal activists were just searching for a negative angle and then went crazy with it. Second, we *do* have all-natural ice cream but use a naturally occurring chemical compound to enhance the flavor and extend the product's expiration date. We weren't breaking any laws, and it was a great campaign. You understand."

Sarah noted how the "you understand" was specifically phrased as a statement and not a question. As Alice left the room she said over her shoulder, "I'm looking forward to your presentation. This will really elevate your visibility at Becker Dairy."

## GOING GREEN

Sarah had already put in a 12-hour day when she got home and started working again. She wanted to be sure that her plan for Becker Dairy's green positioning would be seen as more than a branding ploy and that the company could live up to its position as a responsible corporation. In order to do that, her plan would need to avoid the six deadly sins of green washing. She also wanted to focus on recent research that suggested companies should consult publics prior to engaging in corporate social responsibility initiatives in order to assess public expectations.

The findings of the independent study found that in order of importance consumers want a company to be honest and transparent in its communication, produce quality products, and treat its employees fairly. At the bottom of the list was "make a profit." Sarah knew that if saving money were the only reason why Becker Dairy initiated a delivery crate recycling campaign, the public would soon find out and possibly punish the company by boycotting its products.

The next day Sarah contacted the nearby university's School of Sustainability to get its advice and input. The school was thrilled to learn that Becker Dairy was considering green initiatives and put Sarah in touch with a sustainability expert to help the company go green. Additionally, the university agreed to be a partner of Becker Dairy, with its students participating in projects and reviews to help the company become truly sustainable.

Energized, Sarah pulled her team together to review the strategy and discuss possible creative. The focus of the campaign would be an internal initiative to identify an overarching commitment to sustainability that would extend through all facets of the business. The entire initiative would have to be rolled out to employees at company meetings. Buy-in from employees would be a critical part of acceptance and accountability for the sustainability initiative. If it was done well, Becker Dairy would become a case study for dairies across the United States and set the standard for sustainable practices. The delivery crate recycling program would be at the center of it all and the first public program of the sustainability initiative.

With her team working on different mixed-media campaign options, Sarah put together a formal presentation for the executive board, including the cost of the sustainability expert consultant and proposed initiatives at $250,000. Careful not to spend more on the marketing campaign than the green programs, Sarah also budgeted $250,000 to raise awareness of Becker Dairy's efforts.

Sarah couldn't sleep the night before her presentation to the executive board because of her excitement. Alice reviewed a copy of the final proposal and didn't have any changes. Sarah felt as though she had found her place in the world and tomorrow would prove her value to the team.

## THE GREAT GREEN PRESENTATION

"…And that is how Becker Dairy will become known as the industry leader in sustainability," concluded Sarah. She smiled at the executive team members, who all turned in their chairs to look at Geoffrey Becker, president and CEO of Becker Dairy.

"I love it!" he exclaimed. "There's just one problem, not really even a problem as I see it…"

Sarah leaned forward, eager to receive his constructive criticism. She couldn't believe how well today's presentation had gone or what she was hearing—he *loved* it. There wasn't even one problem as he saw it!

"We are doing this to save money and create a branding buzz, but the budget of $500,000 will severely cut into our savings of $2.2 million if the campaign works," Becker explained. "The campaign is great, and I really see the benefits of going this direction. So, I'm not going to cut into the marketing budget. But this sustainability expert…I don't think we need him—especially at $250,000. We're already going to be helping the environment by collecting delivery crates, so we're covered there as I see it. Great work, and I'd like this campaign launched by summer."

It was already spring. Before Sarah could say anything, Geoffrey Becker stood up and left the boardroom. On his way out, he gave Sarah a winning smile and the thumbs-up sign. Everyone else followed suit.

Alice walked over and started offering praise. "I knew you brought something special to the team! Geoffrey never approves anything the first time he sees it. You really did an exceptional job with this!"

Sarah's other team members agreed and were equally excited. This would be the first campaign Dave led the design for, and he was eager to see his concepts transformed into finished ads. Jess didn't even wait to get to her desk before calling media buyers from her cell phone to line up the ad runs, and Mark began outlining the campaign timeline, engaging the web team for a special site dedicated to Becker Dairy sustainability and the like.

Sarah wanted to scream. This was all happening too fast, and didn't anyone else see the major problem here? Geoffrey Becker had approved the campaign but not the substance behind it. There was no campaign without the sustainability expert and his recommendations for helping the company go green. Hadn't these people learned anything from the ice cream campaign two years prior? They were going to get slaughtered.

## THE FINAL GREENWASH

Sarah felt sick at the celebratory lunch. She could barely smile at the toasts made in her honor. Afterwards she sat in her office, popped a couple of aspirin, wishing they were something much stronger, and thought about what to do.

As a public relations professional, she felt it was her job to warn the company about the possible—and probable—backlash. "It's the only ethical thing to do," she thought to herself. "I need to stand behind my initial recommendation and guide Becker Dairy through a successful transition to green practices." Feeling her confidence rise as she mentally reviewed the scholarly research and her own understanding of sustainability, Sarah knocked on Alice's closed office door.

"Ah, there's my favorite new PR specialist! What can I do for you?" Alice asked as Sarah opened the door. "Have a seat. You know, you were really great in today's executive board meeting. I've received a lot of calls complimenting your work and my talent for hiring only the best—what do you say to—"

"I need to talk with you about Geoffrey's feedback. What he's recommending is setting this company up for disaster, and it's my job to warn you about the potential backlash," Sarah interrupted.

Alice looked shocked as Sarah turned red and fidgeted in the plush chair. "Maybe that wasn't the smoothest opening," Sarah thought as Alice confirmed it with a stern, vocal "Excuse me?"

"What I'm saying is true. I conducted extensive research on this, and Becker Dairy will be slammed in the media and by consumers for greenwashing if it doesn't more sustainable practices. By killing the consultant, Geoffrey has killed the campaign and . . ." Sarah trailed off as Alice held up her hand to silence her.

"Sarah, I genuinely appreciate your enthusiasm but will respectfully ask you to remember that you have been on the job less than a month. Geoffrey—or as we like to call him—"*Mr. Becker*," is a genius. He is the fourth generation in his family to run Becker Dairy and has helped it grow each and every year that he's been with the company. You know, there's a reason this organization has been around since 1918. Additionally, I personally have more than 20 years' industry experience, compared to your three weeks. We know what we're doing," Alice chided.

Stunned, Sarah tried to respond but wasn't able to formulate the words.

"I'm going to close this door and pretend that this conversation never took place. You really did do good work. Try to stay focused on the positives and work toward making this campaign a success," Alice concluded while showing Sarah the door. Her smooth demeanor and smile had returned.

Sarah stood outside Alice's office in disbelief. Had that just happened? Sarah felt betrayed. She had come to Alice in good faith and had been summarily dismissed! Angrily Sarah thought, "Wait a minute here...I'm the responsible employee warning Alice that this campaign is sure to fail if it is just about delivery crate recycling, and she treats me like I don't know what I am talking about!" Sarah knew that Alice would not even mention this to Geoffrey Becker. Sarah was torn. Should she go over her boss' head and tell Geoffrey Becker her concerns? She knew that would be a risky thing to do—it would give Alice grounds to fire her immediately. But if the campaign goes forward without real substance behind it, "It's going to fail," she said out loud to no one in particular. Becker Dairy was an incredible opportunity for her. Would simply executing the marketing campaign as Alice ordered really compromise her values? She wondered. As president of PRSSA in college, she had championed the campaign to turn her campus green. Her drive and commitment had helped the chapter win a national award for the best college initiative. Sustainability was her passion, but Becker Dairy was her employer. What would happen if the crate recycling campaign were labeled as "greenwashing" by the media and the public? It wasn't her decision—she would be just following orders—but would she be the scapegoat for an expensive marketing campaign that was sure to fail?

Sarah knew she was between a rock and a hard place. It was going to be a long night...

# The Individual and the Organization

## CHAPTER 23

# Bob's Dilemma

## Erika L. Kirby

It was Monday morning, and after hitting the snooze button for the third and last time, 32-year-old Bob Anthony* awoke thinking of the issue that had plagued him for weeks.

"Lee is due in two months. I really should make my request for paternity leave by Friday if I want to stay at home with her once the girls are born. How much leave should I ask for? How should I bring it up? Should I just talk to the boss or should I tell the coworkers on my team as well?"

Until recently, Bob had never considered taking off the full six weeks at partial pay allowed for paternity leave at his workplace, Audits, Inc. In his mind, he was thinking something more like three days to a week. But last month in the obstetrician's office, looking at an ultrasound that showed twin girls, Lee somewhat nervously said to him, "Once they are born, I really think I would be more comfortable if you were home for an extended period, at least until we got situated as a family. I can't imagine nursing and caring for two children at once as a first-time mom!"

Bob rolled over and looked at Lee as she slept, wrapped around a body pillow to support her expanding belly. A few days after the ultrasound and news of the twins, Lee went to her supervisor at Clark Corporation, where she was a consultant. She asked for eight weeks of maternity leave instead of six, and her request was granted without question. But Bob had been putting off asking for his leave from Audits, Inc., where he was an accountant, since that day of the ultrasound.

"How are people going to react? For that matter, how would I react if another guy wanted six weeks off to stay home with newborn babies?" Bob continually wondered. Over the course of the past month, he had been thinking about prior conversations about work and family and seeking some opinions from people he respected about what they would do in his situation.

---

*This case has been developed based on real organization(s) and real organizational experiences. Names, facts, and situations have been changed to protect the privacy of individuals and organizations.

## ASSESSING THE ORGANIZATIONAL
## AND SOCIETAL ENVIRONMENT

Before he talked to his supervisor or the coworkers on his team about the issue, Bob wanted to find out exactly what his options were. He reviewed the employee handbook and read about the Family Medical Leave Act, a law instituted in 1993 mandating that, as a full-time employee, he be allowed to take up to 12 weeks of unpaid leave in a year. But the provisions at his company were more generous–the handbook actually outlined a paternity leave policy in which he could take up to six weeks *with* partial pay. It did make Bob more comfortable that both federal law and company policy were on his side. But still he wondered, "If it really is acceptable policy to take paternity leave at Audits, why doesn't anyone ever do it?"

In fact, from the limited research Bob had done since trying to decide how much leave to take, he discovered that most men rarely take advantage of the full amount of paternity leave afforded to them–not just at Audits, but at any organization. A recent article in the paper reported that only around 3% of fathers took more than a week off after the birth of a child, so his request was not a typical one. Accordingly, Bob was worried about the reactions he would get about taking six weeks of paternity leave from other people besides his coworkers. In particular, he was worried about his father's reaction. When he had asked him for advice about how much leave to request, Jim Anthony had replied, "I don't know why you are even considering staying home. Your job is to go out and earn money for the family so that Lee can stay home with the twins...who knows, maybe you can even convince Lee to stay at home until the girls are in school–home is where she belongs." Bob remembered being taught about men as breadwinners in a gender class in college, and he was surprised at how tempted he was to follow this traditional pattern.

Bob also felt deeply anxious about how his career success would be affected by taking six weeks of paternity leave. His job as an accountant at Audits required him to travel to different locations for the audits. He did this along with a group of colleagues–typically, in a team of five. Since their work was team-based, each person had a discrete part of the audit to cover, so if someone was sick or on leave, it affected the others, who had to increase their workload to make up for the absent person. In the past this had caused resentment. Bob recalled his own reaction when Mike was gone for three days while his son played in the state basketball tournament. "I was angry that I had to do his work, and that was for only a few days. I wondered why his family was more important than getting his work done. Now I am going to ask for six weeks? I just don't see how." Bob reflected how, when he was *not* an expectant father, he often found himself venting with other colleagues about work-family policies, complaining that "other people get benefits that we don't." Bob was now almost ashamed of his previous attitude. "My, how your views can change when the shoe is on the other foot," he thought to himself.

Some of the work family benefits that Bob remembered complaining about included six weeks of paternity leave, 12 weeks of maternity leave, flexible scheduling, and part-time work. Because of these policies, Audits was touted as an award-winning, family-friendly company. But the inner workings of Audits often told a different story. Bob remembered an especially ironic moment when he was reading the quarterly newsletter and saw an article about the importance of "making time for family and making time to play" on the same page as a list of deadlines by which audits must be completed. Now that Bob really thought about it, people he considered serious workers did not take advantage of these policies.

In fact, most of the people who were acknowledged as ideal workers at Audits were certainly not the type of person he expected would ever take advantage of paternity leave–or any other family-friendly policy, for that matter. In fact, many of these people worked more than 12 hours a day and almost had to be forced to take vacation. As word had it, the real "gunners" at Audits often worked weekends, occasionally sent emails at three in the morning, and stayed out at an audit (and thus away from their families) for as long as six weeks. Bob was not sure how convincing an example that set for making time for family.

The emphasis on dedication to the company reminded him of a long-circulating company story. Several times, Bob had heard that a well-respected vice president had told an expectant father (who wanted to make sure he was scheduled close to home around the birth of his child), "Audits, Inc., should not have to be concerned with people's family lives. If we meant for our employees to have children, we would issue them, just like the army." With all these mixed messages, Bob wondered, "What will happen to my career if I ask for six weeks of leave?"

Bob decided to talk to Beth, a 35-year-old married colleague who was one of his closest female friends. He felt safe talking to her because she was not on his auditing team, so she could keep his confidence, and she had taken 12 weeks of maternity leave the previous year, just recently returning on a part-time schedule.

"Beth, I wanted to ask you something. Lee really wants me to stay home for the full six weeks of paternity leave after the twins are born, but I'm not sure how people will react. Based on your experience with maternity leave, what do you think?"

Bob was not encouraged by the long pause Beth took. Then she responded. "Well, Bob, I think you may be in a rough position to get support for taking much paternity leave here at Audits. To be honest, I think my team resented my leave when I was home with Collin. Don't get me wrong, no one talked to me directly and said, 'Gee, I resent the fact that you were on maternity leave,' but I sensed that people felt that way. People don't understand that when I had those weeks off, I needed them. I didn't sit there and play cards or go shopping every day, you know what I mean? I'm afraid that you may face even more of that stigma, Bob, because there is *no* biological reason that you even need leave. You are not the one who is going to be nursing babies or recovering from childbirth, even though I am sure Lee will need and appreciate your help. Right or wrong, parental leave is still seen as very different for women than for men."

Since Beth had worked at Audits three years longer, Bob flat-out asked, "Why don't any fathers ever take the amount of paternity leave that is allowed here?"

Beth got a very serious look on her face and replied, "Through the grapevine I have heard of situations where men have communicated that they wanted to take paternity leave and have not gotten receptive feedback. Either not gotten it approved at all, or certainly not received what they had asked for." She added, "One of my former coworkers, Jake, wanted to take an extended paternity leave, and everybody laughed. They thought it was funny. Jake left for a place with a more family-friendly environment. I hate to be the bearer of bad news, but don't expect anyone to lay out a red carpet for you here."

## ASSESSING SUPERVISOR AND COWORKER REACTIONS

Bob appreciated Beth's perspective on how paternity leave was viewed in the organization as a whole. Yet he was most concerned with how his own supervisor and coworkers on his team would react, because those were the people he worked with every day. If there was resentment about his leave, that is where he would feel it. Anticipating their reaction, Bob reflected on conversations about work and family practices and policies he had heard over the years working at Audits.

Bob thought about Steve, his supervisor of five years, and what his response might be to a request for six weeks of paternity leave. Steve was 56 and married, with two adult children. Bob knew that Steve struggled with how to manage a staff that had varied work and family needs. He remembered having a discussion about scheduling travel around employees' differing marital and child-rearing responsibilities. Steve had said, "From my standpoint, it can be a problem. Married with young child. Single guy. Somebody has to travel. Who is it? The hardest thing for me has always been being fair because I can't necessarily be consistent." Steve had mentioned this philosophy several times–being fair if not consistent.

Although Steve had always kept Bob and his team informed of the family-friendly benefits that were available, he had never really encouraged their use. Instead, Steve was always pushing deadlines: "We've got to have this audit done by this date to get started on the next one." There was such an emphasis on time constraints and deadlines at Audits that people rarely took time off unless it was an emergency. Bob remembered his performance appraisal meeting nine months ago, where he was teasing Steve about all the long hours he was putting in. Steve got somewhat serious and replied, "Well, as you move up and get more years of service, you also get more leave as a benefit–but the irony is that you're less likely to be able to actually miss work and take the time to utilize your vacation hours."

Bob cringed as he remembered his comment at the time. "If that is what it takes, I'm ready to make sacrifices and put in all the necessary hours to keep moving up at Audits." Now he thought. "How hypocritical will I look in asking for this leave? What happened to my dedication? How would Steve react?"

Then Bob thought about his fellow accountants. Since they all worked as a team, Bob really felt a sense of peer pressure. If he took these weeks off, he would be putting everyone else in a bad spot. He was apprehensive that asking for this special treatment would require the other auditors to do more, and he wondered,

"Why does my taking advantage of the paternity leave I deserve, and am allowed by company policy, have to be to their detriment? Isn't there something wrong with this system?" Bob knew that if his coworkers thought he was not pulling his weight, their consequent behaviors and attitudes could punish him.

Mike, 46, was married with three teenagers, and he would occasionally take time off–but only when important events, such as the state basketball tournament, warranted it. Bob remembered Mike being away from town on the birthdays of his children several times, and Mike always had the same calm reaction: "It's the structure of the job. If you want to move up, you keep quiet about family needs unless it is really important." When people would express resentment that work-family policies were unfair, Mike would always talk about the policies in terms of use versus abuse. He would say, "There is nothing wrong with these policies. The problem is when people try to take advantage of them and use them too much. When people are always gone because their kids are sick or whatever, then there is a problem."

Bob wondered, "Will Mike think I am using or abusing the policy by taking six weeks off?" He wasn't sure.

Judy, a 38-year-old single mother, was another coworker on Bob's team. Judy was outwardly supportive of the work-family programs and policies available at Audits. She always said, "I wish more people would take advantage of them, so this organization would truly practice being family-friendly rather than just having the policies on paper." Of those who denigrated the policies, Judy remarked, "All these people are going to have needs later on; whether they are married or not, whether they have kids or not, they are going to have needs eventually–isn't it nice that these policies exist to help balance those needs?"

Judy occasionally took time off to spend with her son, but since it was not typical to regularly use family-friendly benefits at Audits, even she did not do this very often. As she had commented once to Bob, "I am a single mother supporting a child. If I use the benefits, it might make me seem less dedicated, which could impact how my performance is appraised. I can't afford to lose this job, so in the long run, it probably is better for Josh for me not to take a lot of leave to spend more time with him. How ironic, huh?"

From these conversations, Bob felt that Judy would support his request 100%.

Manuel, a 29-year-old single male accountant, was Bob's closest friend on the team. About a year earlier, when both Mike and Judy were gone on the same day, Manuel had commented to Bob, "It isn't fair that they get more time off because their kids are sick or have special events. Why can't I get that same amount of time off? I think we are discriminated against because we don't have children."

Bob recalled replying, "Yeah, it has worked out very well for them. Unfortunately it has increased the workload for us."

Manuel joked that the two of them should become members of the Childfree Network, an organization he read about that believes many family-friendly policies are discriminatory and should be eliminated to provide equal treatment. Bob sensed that even though they were good friends, Manuel might be vocal about having to take on his work if Bob was granted an extended paternity leave. He could hear Manuel now: "You know, it just doesn't quite seem fair that just because you now have two babies, you get to take an extra 30 days off. It doesn't benefit the rest of us. What am I getting in return for that?" Although he hoped for the best, Bob was quite certain that he would get a negative reaction from Manuel.

The last accountant on his audit team was Jessica, a 24-year-old woman who had recently graduated from college, was engaged, and still had an ideal view of the world. Bob remembered Jessica saying, "What is all the fuss about these work-family policies anyway? If the company has them, you can use them–duh. No one will look at you differently because they are part of company policy." Although her communication indicated that Jessica would probably be supportive, Bob was not so sure how long her idealism would last once she started covering his work.

As Bob got out of bed, he continued to wrestle with his thoughts. "I love Lee and my baby girls with all my heart, but given the environment at Audits, I might be committing career suicide if I do what Lee wants and ask for six weeks of paternity leave. How much leave should I ask for, and when do I ask for it? Should I run it by my team first, since they are the ones affected, or should I start with Steve?"

Bob hoped a hot shower would bring him some clarity–he did not have much time left to decide.

## CHAPTER 24

# Working Without Papers

## Shawn D. Long

On Sunday, the *Daily News** reported the incident on its front page. It read, in part:

> Shouting "Go home!" at the brown-skinned drivers passing by, about 75 protesters gathered along Main Street in this Jackson County town on Saturday to blame immigrants for the area's high unemployment and crowded schools. The two-hour rally drew worried blue-collar workers, immigration opponents, and admitted white racists alarmed at the influx of Mexicans. Together, they stood near the town's Confederate monument and hoisted signs: "No Illegals. No Unemployment." "It's Our Borders, Stupid!" and "Now Swim Back."

The article acknowledged the existing tension between Latino immigrant workers and native-born Americans in this southern community. The picture above the article showed protesters, anxious and angry about the growing Latino population, carrying signs and yelling at vehicles with Latino drivers and passengers.

The article was especially troublesome to Javier, a Honduran construction supervisor, who was carpooling to work on Monday morning with Bob Jones, another line supervisor at Three Sources Construction, located in a neighboring town.

### JAVIER AND BOB

From all accounts, Javier and Bob were good friends. They lived in the same neighborhood, took their kids to the same park, and often carpooled back and forth to work. When Bob was laid off from his manufacturing job at Pales Manufacturing three years earlier, Javier had recommended that Bob apply at Three Sources Construction. There was an opening, and Javier knew Bob would be perfect for the job. Javier had even put in a good word with Jack Hart, the owner of Three

---

*This case has been developed based on real organization(s) and real organizational experiences. Names, facts, and situations have been changed to protect the privacy of individuals and organizations.

179

Sources Construction. Bob applied and eventually got a job working on the line, with Javier's recommendation. Within a year, Bob was promoted to a line supervisor with Javier. Bob was primarily in charge of supervising the crew of American workers, whereas Javier was responsible for the crew of Latino workers.

## THE TENSION

Although Javier had been pleased that he could help out his friend Bob, Javier was amazed at Bob's quick promotion. His amazement really reflected his disappointment in how Three Sources had treated him and other immigrant workers in regard to promotion and compensation. Javier was the first Latino worker to become a supervisor at Three Sources Construction, and it had taken him eight years to get the position. He had often applied for and asked about becoming a line supervisor, but he was repeatedly told he needed more experience and more time to build trust with the other line workers.

Although Javier had not been the first Latino to apply for a supervisory job, he was the first to land one. Many felt that his promotion was due in large part to the company's need for someone who could speak fluent Spanish, someone who could relate to the 70% of line workers who were Latino and who spoke very little or no English themselves. Nevertheless, Javier, his family, and the other Latino workers were thrilled when he finally got the nod.

## THE COMPANY

Three Sources Construction, a small construction company in a county neighboring Jackson County, had a great reputation for producing quality work on schedule and below budget. Three Sources often served as a subcontractor for much larger construction companies, companies that appreciated the consistent effort and attention to detail that it provided.

However, among its immigrant workers, Three Sources had a less than favorable reputation. While it was always willing to hire workers without papers, it also consistently discriminated, harassed, and exploited Latino workers who were not legal. This side of Three Sources was hidden from the public view, including the prime contractors, but was well-known among immigrant workers. When Cortez and Roberto were in the process of showing John, a newly hired worker, how to put on a harness, Cortez warned John, "They treat you like a lower class. They take advantage of people who don't speak English."

Roberto piped up, "Maybe, maybe not. What happens is that the people don't speak English, so they get tossed to the side."

Cortez warned John especially about Joe, a Three Sources manager and the foreman on this site.

"Joe treats Latinos worse. There are a lot of things that we don't know, and he gets mad at us. He doesn't get mad at the Americans. Just us. Because we are not from this country."

## MONDAY MORNING AT THREE SOURCES

That day there was tension in the air at Three Sources. Many of the American workers had read the article in the *Daily News* before they arrived at work. Someone had placed the article on a workbench, in plain view of everyone, including the Latino workers, and several workers were uneasy about it.

Joe, the site foreman, walked toward Bob, his face scowling. "Bob, did you see the front page of the newspaper?"

"I did," Bob responded.

"What did you think about it?"

Bob replied in a rather disinterested tone, "It's a free country. Anybody can say what they want to." Then Bob quickly changed the subject. "Have our new drills arrived yet?"

"Not yet. I'll let you know when they arrive."

"Thanks a lot, Joe. I'll talk to you later." Bob quickly walked away from what could have been a very long and uncomfortable conversation with Joe.

The Latino workers were working steadily, with little conversation among themselves. It was clear that the workers were much more involved in their work than usual. They had been forewarned by Luis, an English-speaking Mexican, who had told them on their way from the worker pickup station in Jackson, "Everybody just work hard and stay to yourself. There are a lot of angry Americans around here, and we just need to stay low for a while."

Luis had worked in transportation for Three Sources for two years. One of his jobs was to pick up workers who did not have transportation at designated sites in the early morning hours. Luis was usually the first Three Sources contact many of the Latino workers had, and he was a valued and respected resource for the immigrant workers. He would often tell the workers what was going on at the site and what Joe's mood was for the day. Because he had been one of the drivers taunted at Saturday's protest, Luis was very tense this particular morning.

On the drive to work, one of the workers asked Luis why the Americans hate them so much. Luis explained, "Saturday's protest is part of a growing backlash against Latinos in the United States and in this state. My daughter is in fifth grade. She told me she learned in school last week that our Latino population has grown by 58% nationally and 394% in this state since 1990. We have 95,076 Latinos living here. Her teacher told her this huge increase in immigrants from Mexico and Central America was because people like us want to get jobs in construction and hotels and restaurants. In landscaping. And in manufacturing and agriculture."

"Pretty smart girl you got there, Luis," Ron replied.

"You better believe it." Luis grinned.

Luis went on to say, "Many employers have rewarded these workers for their strong work ethic. Others, like Three Sources, have taken advantage of this vulnerable workforce. They deny us the basic benefits of work guaranteed by state and federal labor laws. They abuse the basic right of workers to be paid for work they perform."

Luis and the immigrant workers were particularly familiar with these abuses because, over the last couple of weeks, they had not received their pay.

## ISSUES AT THREE SOURCES

Indeed, a common complaint among the immigrant workers at Three Sources was the company's failure to pay them for work performed. Jack Webster, Three Sources' owner, and Joe, the site foreman, would often ask Javier to tell the workers that the construction company had yet to be paid by the general contractor, so they were unable to pay their employees; they promised to pay them when Three Sources got paid. At the same time, many of the American workers under Bob's supervision never appeared to complain about not being compensated on time.

As Cortez explained to John, "We are illegal. We don't have papers. We came here to work, but the work that we do here does not benefit us much. It benefits Jack more than us workers." Cortez warned John about another problem. "John, I want you to know that those who have papers around here are paid more than the ones who don't have papers. Documented workers earn a little more money."

This kind of conversation was common among the Latino workers. It appeared to be part of their training process.

## CONFLICTED JAVIER

Javier suspected the American workers were being paid while his Latino workers were not. Occasionally, Javier would ask Bob about this issue.

"Bob, how are your men handling Jack's news about not being paid again this week?"

Bob would always quickly change the subject to something else to avoid Javier's question, so most times Javier would just drop the topic and move on.

## JAVIER'S TENSION AT WORK

Because most of the Latino workers could not speak English, Javier was a great resource for Three Sources, the workers, and the owner. Many of the Latino employees looked up to Javier because he treated them with respect and would often hire their family members and friends who needed a job but had no papers. The workers appreciated that Javier would hire immigrants without papers, but some also felt he did not stand up to Jack and Joe about issues affecting the Latino workers. José, a line worker, often said, "Javier is a racist because he thinks the workers should do everything. He wants to show off to the bosses. The Latinos who have papers, especially Javier, treat those who don't have papers very badly. Sometimes they don't even pay you."

José's work partner, Rocky, always mumbled, "Javier treats us worse than the gringos do. For good or bad, we came here to work, we have to work, whatever it is."

Javier felt this characterization was unfair, and he would often speak to Bob about this dilemma.

"It is a no-win situation for me. I work hard to get my people jobs because I know how hard it is to support a family, and then it seems as though they all turn on me at once. Sometimes people, even your own people, are just ungrateful and can be your worst enemies. I'm just trying to do my job."

On the other hand, Javier was genuinely concerned about Three Sources' treatment of workers and the off-colored comments and jokes made about the Latino workers by the Americans in managerial positions, especially Joe. Although Javier was often tempted to say something about the offensive comments, he felt that if he spoke up, he would alienate himself from everyone. Even worse, he would possibly be replaced for not being a team player or one of the boys. He knew how hard he had worked to get where he was. Making waves was not an option!

## MONDAY AFTERNOON AT THREE SOURCES

José and several other men on Javier's crew met with Javier after lunch to discuss their lack of payment over the last couple of weeks.

"Javier, you told us on Friday that we would get our money on Monday. We have worked hard for you and the gringos have been paid. Where is our money?"

"Look, José, I understand your concern, but Jack told me he has not been paid from the general contractor. My hands are tied," Javier replied.

"You are a racist sellout, Javier," José retorted. "You and your gringo buddy Bob make sure his men are paid, while we work for free! You are no better than the Americans who treat us bad."

Javier quickly replied, "José, I am going to walk away now and let you and the boys cool off before you say anything else that will hurt you and your family."

"Javier, we need our money by tomorrow!" yelled José as Javier left.

Javier was angry and upset at José, and more so at Jack for putting him in this position. Javier's mind was racing. "Where was Jack? How come Joe could not provide any answers? Why weren't the Americans complaining as well?"

Construction resumed as usual, but there were obvious tensions in the air. Javier's men were not speaking to him. They only mumbled things when he walked by. The American workers were disturbed by the tension the article had brought to Three Sources and kept to themselves. When Javier walked by the American workers, they would suddenly stop talking and turn their backs to him.

## QUITTING TIME

At 4:45 P.M., it was time for everyone to get off. Javier hated to leave the pay situation the way it was, but he had no more answers to provide his crew. Jack still had not shown up at the site.

"Joe, will Jack be in tomorrow?"

"Your guess is as good as mine, Javier."

"Is there anything that you can do for me?" asked Javier.

Joe's only response was, "Check with Jack!"

## THE END OF THE DAY

After work, Javier and Bob were on their way home. Javier was outwardly frustrated. The first few minutes of the drive were deafeningly silent. Then Javier broke the silence.

"Where the hell was Jack today?" complained Javier.

"I think he was at the other site today," replied Bob, adding, "Today was sure one hell of a day."

Javier was silent. Glancing at Bob's hand, he saw a copy of the newspaper. This made Javier even angrier.

"Why the hell are you holding on to that piece of shit? I am getting it from all sides—my own people, your crew, and even you!"

Bob quickly cut Javier off. "Look, Javier, I was taking this paper off-site. I was going to throw it away before any of the wise guys at work decided to hang it up somewhere. Why are you busting my chops, man? You need a drink, my friend. My treat! Let's go to Blues Tavern."

## THE BLUES TAVERN REVELATION

Once inside Blues Tavern, a favorite watering hole of Javier and Bob and other construction workers in the area, Javier quickly apologized.

"Bob, I'm so sorry for blowing up at you. You know that I didn't mean what I said. You and I are friends, and a lot has happened over the last few days. You know our men are pissed at Jack and everyone else about not being paid two weeks in a row. On top of that, Jack is nowhere to be found. José and his buddies are ganging up on me about their money. And then at work all I hear from your crew is mumbling about that damn article. You can cut the tension with a knife, and I feel like I'm going to be the one stabbed with it. I am stuck in the middle. My own people hate me and are losing respect for me, and the gringos, I mean the Americans, in this damn community hate me because I am just trying to support my family like anyone else. I am sick and tired of this."

Javier paused for a minute and then asked, "Bob, how are your men handling not being paid?"

Bob cautiously took a drink of his beer and began to stare deep into his glass. "Javier, I have something to tell you. Please don't be angry at me or my men, but my crew received their pay on time!"

Bob took another drink as silence fell upon both men. Then Bob continued, "Joe told me and my guys not to tell you. He felt as long as you got your money, things would be okay. You know, Javier, Joe and Jack really like you. They are thinking about promoting you to the foreman's position at the other site next summer."

Sitting silently, Javier showed no emotion.

"Javier, I'm sorry, man. Please don't say anything, man. Jack would probably fire me if they found out I told you. I'm not like those rednecks protesting in Jackson." Bob paused briefly. "Do you want another beer?"

Javier shook his head no and said, "I need to get home for dinner."

"Are you okay, Javier?"

"I'm fine. Maria is making her delicious enchilada casserole tonight," Javier said with a slight grin.

## INSIDE JAVIER

Neither friend mentioned the Blues Tavern conversation in the car. "What else is Maria cooking tonight?" asked Bob.

"I think she may be baking a pie. She was rolling out dough last night. At least that's what I am hoping for."

Javier and Bob both laughed at Javier's dinner prospects as Javier pulled into Bob's driveway to drop him off. "Javier, see if Maria would put a slice of that pie in your lunch for me tomorrow."

"I sure will... maybe a little casserole, too?" asked Javier.

"You are the man, Javier. I'll see you in the morning. I'll bring the coffee."

Javier drove off and continued to reflect on his and Bob's conversation. His thoughts about Three Sources were confirmed. He knew he was in a vulnerable position. He loved his job and the opportunity that Three Sources gave him, and he felt an obligation to the company for giving him a chance, regardless of how long the company had taken to promote him. But he also felt a responsibility to the Latino workers and community to expose the blatant exploitation. Javier was struggling with the question "What should I do now?"

Javier knew most of the workers lacked knowledge about their rights as employees and they depended on him to see that they were treated fairly, even though other immigrant workers, like José, mistrusted Javier, considering him "Jack's Latino puppet." They often called Javier a racist to his own people because he didn't complain about them not being paid or their being put in dangerous work assignments. Javier did not want their criticisms to come true.

Javier recognized the serious implications involved in trying to improve the situation for his crew. If he became a whistle-blower, his opportunity to work again in construction and possibly in this area was in jeopardy. If be kept quiet, he would be promoted and eventually be able to make changes at Three Sources from a more powerful position, possibly this new foreman's position.

## AT HOME

Javier pulled into his driveway and walked into the house. Maria greeted her husband with a big smile and a kiss.

"Good evening, honey. The casserole is almost done, and I am getting ready to put your favorite peach pie in the oven."

Javier did not respond.

Noticing Javier's apparent depressed state, Maria turned to him. "What's wrong, honey?"

Javier started to explain....

CHAPTER 25

# Corporate Counseling

## Steven K. May

Elaine Jenkins* had just left another one-hour counseling session with her therapist, Marta, with a greater sense of well-being, satisfaction, and security. To her surprise, counseling seemed to help her, if only as a way to express some of her work- and family-related frustrations. In particular, counseling helped her cope with her anxieties about her job security as well as frustration with a new management team at her company, GeneSel, a large U.S. pharmaceutical firm. The new management team was the result of a merger between Genetair and Techsel, her original employer. The organizational change had taken its toll, both on employee morale overall and on her own sense of job security specifically. Her original employer, Techsel, producer of technical solutions for drug development and delivery, had been acquired nine months ago in a hostile takeover by Genetair, a British pharmaceutical company. The new CEO, however, dismissed claims that it was an acquisition. Instead, he called it a merger of equals, describing it as an "opportunity for GeneSel to develop integrative solutions that will provide greater economies of scale through reductions in force." In the end, though, Elaine felt that a new CEO, a new management team, and downsizing nearly 25% of Techsel's employees were clear indications that this was an acquisition, not a merger. Her most recent discussion with Marta had clarified how much the downsizing of many of her coworkers and friends at Techsel had affected her.

She was so comforted by her most recent session, though, that she let out an audible sigh of relief as she left Marta's dimly lit yet cozy office, looking around to make sure that nobody had noticed. Elaine never really expected to have such a favorable response to counseling sessions, particularly since it was only her third meeting with Marta. It would certainly have embarrassed her if the two other patients in the waiting room had noticed such a public show of emotion from

---

*This case has been developed based on real organization(s) and real organizational experiences. Names, facts, and situations have been changed to protect the privacy of individuals and organizations.

her. She tried to keep such feelings to herself, if at all possible. Although she didn't recognize either of the patients, she still wondered whether they knew her. Deep down, she questioned whether going to a corporate counselor to discuss her feelings about the downsizing was such a good idea. GeneSel's Employee Assistance Program (EAP) touted the company-sponsored counseling program as an effective means of "integrating the needs of employer and employee to produce happier, more productive workers." Yet, even with the progress she made in the sessions, she still had her doubts.

## COUNSELING RESERVATIONS

Thirty years old, college-educated, and very successful as a research associate at GeneSel, Elaine never thought that she would ever see a therapist for any problems. Even when her husband, Alan, suggested that they go to marital counseling because of stress-producing conflicts six months ago, she suggested that it would be a last resort, a sign of failure, to her.

"I just don't see the use of counseling. We should be able to work through our own problems without the help of anyone else."

Although he did not press the issue too far, for fear of increasing her resistance to the idea, Alan still tried to convince her. "But if it helps, why would you not want to try it?"

"Because to me it would mean that we had a bad marriage. That we had failed. That we had made a mistake and couldn't handle things on our own."

"So many people benefit from it, though, and I think that we do need the help. We're both struggling. The downsizing has taken a toll. We're not alone in that."

"Yes, Alan, but I still feel uneasy about it. In my head, I know it might help, but deep down I worry about trusting some stranger with my innermost fears and concerns."

Raised in a small rural town in the Midwest, Elaine had learned over the years that airing one's dirty laundry in public was not a good idea. It wasn't necessarily productive and, at worst, it could lead to gossip that was hard to dispel. At the time, she certainly didn't feel like talking about the downsizing, as Alan had frequently suggested to her. She thought it was more of a work related topic than a personal one. So when she emerged from Marta's office, she still retained some mixed feelings about going to a counselor. She had a lingering feeling, an intuition, that it wasn't necessarily a smart thing to do, even if Marta's office was off-site, away from GeneSel. Part of Elaine's feeling came from the fact that she had been asked to meet with a counselor by her supervisor, Jackson Sunderlund. Although she trusted and respected Jackson, counseling still had not been her idea. She felt pushed, maybe even coerced, into going. Yet, it seemed to be helping.

Elaine had first considered counseling, somewhat reluctantly, at the suggestion of a coworker, Kathryn. Kathryn had praised her own therapist, to whom she was referred by the EAP at GeneSel. She had also reassured Elaine that it was safe to go to a company-sponsored counselor.

"It's not that bad. You don't have to worry about it. They are required to keep their sessions confidential. Plus, the cost is much more reasonable. Because you'll be going through the company, you'll get a group rate discount."

Elaine, however, was not convinced. "It's not the money that worries me. We can afford it, if necessary. It's more about the fact that it is company-sponsored. It feels a bit like Big Brother to me."

"No, it's not like that at all. They walk you through all the conditions and legal issues involved in going. The EAP counselors follow a strict professional code of ethics, just like any other therapists."

Although Kathryn's comments were somewhat reassuring, Elaine still had questions.

"But it doesn't seem exactly the same to me."

"Why?"

"Well, for one thing, it's unclear to me who the counselor is working for. Who is the client–me or the company?"

Kathryn had not necessarily thought of the EAP in these terms but responded confidently. "Elaine, I think you're being a bit paranoid about this. So many people I know have been helped by our EAP. It seems that the EAP works for both."

"Yes, maybe. But, in the end, as long as GeneSel is paying the bills, the counselor is ultimately working for them, not me."

"Elaine, loosen up. It's just like going to any other therapist. Just cheaper."

## LEARNING ABOUT THE EAP

Elaine's concerns had not been resolved even as the company began to further publicize its EAP. Maybe she had just never noticed it before, but now that she was considering counseling, the company's EAP seemed to be publicized everywhere. It was touted in the company newsletter, in company-wide emails, in brochures, and even in an occasional poster. To her, it seemed that the EAP was a way for GeneSel to address some of its rising health care costs, particularly since some of its workforce was aging.

As a part of the health care industry, employees at her company were all too aware of issues related to cost and access to health care. It was Elaine's job, in fact, to work on a project team to bring a new AIDS drug from research and development to delivery to the public. It was an expensive proposition and one that would take years–possibly without success. As a research associate on the AIDS drug development team, Elaine was responsible for analyzing and evaluating physicians' willingness to use the drug during development by including their patients in clinical trials sponsored by the company. Her three years as a pharmaceutical sales representative had prepared her well for her role as a research associate, a position she had held for the last four years. So GeneSel's effort to be more proactive about the physical and psychological well-being of employees seemed like a laudable goal to her. It fit with her own mind-set, as well as the company's core values.

In fact, one of the EAP brochures she had picked up in the HR office, out of curiosity, described it as a "win-win" situation for both GeneSel and its employees. According to the brochure, the EAP offered "affordable, accessible, and excellent professional services to employees, with the opportunity to be both more productive and satisfied at GeneSel."

Intrigued yet still skeptical, Elaine had read further. The brochure described the many services available to employees. These included counseling services for stress and anxiety, drug and alcohol problems, relational problems, debt, death and grieving, sexual dysfunction, and depression, among others. They even offered conflict resolution sessions for coworkers who needed on-the-job disputes settled. In addition to these services, the EAP also offered an array of medical services. The brochure explained how EAP professionals would be available to conduct a variety of tests and screenings for high blood pressure, body fat, high cholesterol, breast cancer, and migraines. Apparently, the weight loss workshops presented by the EAP had been particularly popular–and successful–at many other companies around the country. They also offered weekly specials which, according to the brochure, included services like free eye and hearing exams.

While reading the brochure, Elaine remembered how the new CEO had touted the company's new Wellness First program the last few months. He readily admitted that it would help the company reduce some of its health care costs, but he also explained how the program was the first step in a longer process for GeneSel to be included among *Fortune* magazine's 100 Best Places to Work. His plans included an expanded, modernized gym facility, an on-site day care center, and eventually the purchase of land surrounding GeneSel's offices to create a park-like campus with a lake, hiking trails, and bike paths. It all seemed a bit idealistic to Elaine, but it did give her hope about the future of the company. If this was his vision of the future, she liked it.

## A "SUGGESTION" FROM JACKSON

Several days after reading the EAP brochure, Elaine was called in to her supervisor's office. Jackson Sunderlund, the project manager for her AIDS drug development team, was one of the few employees within Elaine's division that she knew well from her earlier employer, Techsel. He was known as a savvy yet supportive manager who had high aspirations. Only 36, Jackson seemed to be on the fast track to division manager, according to most of Elaine's former coworkers at Techsel. He was direct and demanding, but he also stood by his employees and listened to their input. As a result, he was known for leading highly motivated, cohesive teams.

Elaine trusted Jackson and had begun to view him as a mentor in the months following the acquisition. He had offered to help her find another job, but he had also encouraged her to stay. He told Elaine she had great potential in the company, but that it would take some time for former Techsel employees to be noticed and rewarded with the transition to a new management team. Jackson was a veteran of several mergers and acquisitions. As a result, he expected that the next few months would be difficult but that, eventually, things would get better.

The meeting began simply enough, as Jackson explained that he viewed the future direction of the company as very encouraging.

"Things look very good right now. We're on track with several new drugs that will go to market in the next two years, with FDA approval, and the stock has rebounded."

"That's very reassuring, Jackson. I'm glad to hear that."

"What we really need to talk about now, though, is your performance in the last few months."

Elaine had not expected the meeting to take this turn. Her performance appraisal was not scheduled for another three months. Jackson was always very meticulous about describing the process and preparing her for the appraisal meeting. This was not his typical manner. It was too sudden.

"So, why now? Can't this wait until our regularly scheduled appraisal meeting?"

"Well, Elaine, things are changing rapidly right now. I've been asked to do immediate evaluations of all members of my teams and submit a summary report of our expected progress for the upcoming quarter."

Elaine had been around long enough to know this wasn't good news. Jackson's more reserved, serious tone didn't help, either.

"The management team is interested in an across-the- board assessment of all personnel, myself included. Nobody is exempt."

"So, what does this mean?"

Jackson explained with some very unexpected news, that GeneSel's recent progress had been noticed by a number of larger pharmaceutical companies looking to expand their market shares. Elaine knew that the industry was increasingly competitive and was prone to consolidations, but she thought she had survived the worst when Genetair had acquired Techsel. Another acquisition? That seemed too disruptive. The even more disturbing news, though, came toward the end of their meeting, as Jackson explained how Elaine should proceed during the period of uncertainty about the merger. She listened intently.

"Elaine, you've done excellent work for me. There is no doubt about that. You have consistently met your specs and standards. Your past sales work with physicians gives you a great rapport with them that you have developed even further since you've been with us. However, since the acquisition, things have begun to slide a bit."

"I don't disagree that I have been stressed about the transition. I lost a lot of good friends. Isn't that natural, though, to have some downtime, when your work dips a bit? I hope that you can trust that things will improve, based on your experience with me."

"I can, but my superiors can't necessarily."

"What's that supposed to mean, Jackson?"

"It means that, right now, there is much greater scrutiny of everyone's performance. What's more, the management team is concerned about any employees who may struggle with possible changes or, worse, resist them."

"But you know that's not me."

"I do, Elaine, but they don't."

"So, what do I do?"

Choosing his words slowly and carefully, Jackson suggested that Elaine meet with one of GeneSel's EAP counselors. He told her that, according to the new management team, Elaine had been identified as a "troubled worker." Jackson told her not to be alarmed by the label, that it merely meant she was having some difficulty with the transition that was affecting her performance. Elaine admitted to herself that this was true. But she was reluctant to see a counselor.

"I don't see what going to a counselor will have to do with my work performance. It's true that I feel hurt and betrayed by the downsizing, but that's my personal business."

"Well, not exactly. It's my responsibility to ensure the positive performance of my teams and, if I feel that personal problems are affecting performance, it is my obligation to the company to consider counseling as an alternative."

"Jackson, you're serious?"

"I am."

"Is this you speaking or the new company?"

"Both."

"So, are you saying that I am required to go to the company's EAP counselor?"

"Elaine, I am saying that as your supervisor–and your friend–I strongly suggest that you make an appointment as soon as possible."

As she left the room, shaken and stunned, Jackson told her, "Be sure to let me know when you've made the appointment and I'll make a note of it."

In the next week, Elaine's work suffered even more. It was hard to focus on the work at hand, knowing that rumors of another merger–and another downsizing–might be near. Worse, she felt like her personal connection with Jackson was gone. Their interactions during the next week were brief and awkward. Although she was not fully against the idea of counseling anymore, she wanted to go on her own terms, on her own time.

Elaine thought it might be time to do some additional digging about EAPs. By looking at several websites–some sponsored by the EAP profession and some sponsored by unions–she learned some interesting things. First, she learned that apparently EAP professionals took their code of ethics very seriously. For example, most websites spoke specifically about the need for patient confidentiality. On the other hand, she also found several legal cases in which employee information from counseling sessions had been used to fire or reassign employees. It was relatively rare and it was done in more extreme situations. But it did seem to happen. She even learned that some companies were beginning to fine employees who did not meet certain health standards. The EAP profession reasoned that this was appropriate, since the employees who incur greater health care costs should shoulder a greater portion of that financial burden.

Elaine became even more ambivalent about EAP counseling and so she made a quick call to one of her neighbors, who was a lawyer. He reminded her that the U.S. Constitution does not, in fact, guarantee an employee's privacy rights from intrusion by one's employer. Those rights are usually dependent on state statutes and he wasn't sure about their state, North Carolina. However, he was aware of several high-profile cases in which email messages and website use by employees had been subpoenaed. The standard was based on whether the employees' communication or Web use was in the business interest of the company–or if it occurred with or on company facilities.

## COUNSELING PROGRESS

Finally, after a week of soul-searching and uneasiness on her job, Elaine decided to schedule an appointment with one of GeneSel's EAP counselors, Marta Melendez. She called Jackson, as requested, and he thanked her, as if she had done him a favor. Given her ambivalence about going to Marta in the first place, Flaine was somewhat surprised by how comfortable she felt with her, even from their first meeting. It was a straightforward, easy meeting. Marta acknowledged that she understood Elaine's hesitation to meet with her. She also reassured Elaine that she was there to help her talk about whatever concerned her, whether work- or family-related. Marta also explained that their sessions were voluntary and that all conversations would be kept confidential, although she needed to tape- record the sessions to best assist her.

At the end of the first weekly meeting, Marta informed Elaine that she would need to stop by the HR department and complete a few items. The first was a legal disclosure statement. It stated that if the counselor were to notice problems that might put the company at risk, they could be notified. HR explained to Elaine that this was common practice, particularly since many companies were increasingly concerned about employee violence. It was a means to protect themselves and other employees. At the HR department, they also asked Elaine to take a couple of personality tests, the Myers-Briggs˚ and the MMPI, the Minnesota Multiphasic Personality Inventory.˚ Elaine knew this was now a common practice for new employees of GeneSel, but she had never been required to take one at Techsel. The request seemed harmless enough, though, and she was even a bit curious about her Myers-Briggs type, since some of her coworkers seemed to refer to the types in work-related conversations.

The second session was also fairly easy. Marta just asked her a series of basic questions about her background and, eventually, about her feelings at work. These were deemed background questions to provide Marta with a frame of reference for their work together. Slowly, but still somewhat reluctantly, Elaine was coming around. Marta seemed to be on her side and she felt comfortable talking to her. The nicest part was that, unlike her husband, Alan, Marta did not seem to evaluate her in any way. Elaine was free to say what she pleased, to confess any anxieties and insecurities, without fear that Marta would judge her.

By the third session, Elaine was beginning to feel like she was gaining new insights about herself. For the first time since the acquisition and subsequent downsizing, she was able to talk freely and openly about how it had affected her. She had been holding in so much anger, hurt, and frustration about how it had been handled. Elaine became aware of how very alone and betrayed she felt at work, and she began to realize how much it was affecting her marriage, too. It was a very emotional session, with Elaine breaking down in tears several times during the hour.

She left Marta's office that day feeling drained but with a greater sense of comfort. The counseling session was definitely cathartic. She wondered how the rest would go.

Her only reservation was related to Marta's last-minute reminder that she would be providing Jackson with an update on her progress on a monthly basis. She had forgotten that Jackson had mentioned this fact, if only briefly, in their initial meeting. Because of the initial shock of that meeting with Jackson, she couldn't remember exactly what he had said to her.

Aside from that minor concern, though, the next four sessions with Marta went quite well. Elaine was able to be more assertive about some of her frustrations with the new company, its management team, and some of its policies. She even felt like the sessions gave her some insights into how her work was affecting her marriage. That felt like real progress.

## ORGANIZATIONAL REDUNDANCY

On the morning of her eighth counseling session with Marta, Jackson called Elaine into his office once more. It was only 9 A.M., still early by Jackson's standards. He rarely met with anyone until after he had his coffee and checked his overnight voice mail messages, so his request to meet with her first thing in the morning seemed unusual. In fact, it was. As she entered his all-too-familiar office, she immediately noticed a striking difference. Standing behind Jackson was an unfamiliar man, whom Jackson did not introduce. The man's stiff stance gave him an eerily ominous appearance.

"Elaine, sit down."

"What's up. What's going on? Who is this?"

"I'll explain in a minute. But first, I have to give you some bad news. I am very, very sorry to tell you that you have been let go. We are, in fact, being bought out and we need to streamline our operations. An assessment team has determined that your job is redundant."

"Redundant?"

"Yes, that is the word they used."

"This is absurd."

"Elaine, I know that it may feel that way, but it is true. You have no idea how difficult this is for me. Maybe the hardest thing I've ever done."

"Well, how do you think I feel?"

"Later, maybe we can talk about this further, but right now I have to ask you to leave with this man now. This is Jermaine. He will escort you to the outplacement office that the company has set up to process your transition."

"Process my transition?"

Jackson looked away and averted his eyes as Jermaine gently offered to help Elaine out of her seat and out the door. Before she left, though, Elaine turned and glanced at Jackson one more time. He stared blankly out his office window and it dawned on Elaine how old, how ragged, how tired he looked.

## TRANSITIONING OUT

Jermaine slowly led Elaine out of Jackson's office, down the elevator, and through the glass doors that were dwarfed by the building's atrium. He led her across the lawn and into the company's small, antiquated gym. Once inside, the scope of the situation at GeneSel came into clearer focus. There in the gym were at least 10 cubicles that had been set up on the basketball floor. She could see inside them just enough to realize that they were nearly all full, with pairs of people. Jermaine led her to the nearest cubicle, asked her to sit, and provided a fuller explanation.

"My name is Jermaine, and I will be working with you this morning on your transition. I understand that this is a stressful time for you, but I have some important items to discuss with you and some documents for you to sign."

Elaine met with Jermaine only for about 15 or 20 minutes, but it seemed so much longer, like she was in a slow-motion replay. Much of the conversation was a blur. Jermaine told her that the company would provide a severance package, and would offer her out-placement services to find another job, if she wished. In order to receive the package, he told her to sign a couple of documents. He also asked her to confirm her signature on a noncompete agreement that she had first signed as a new employee at Techsel. It seemed so long ago now. She told him that it was, in fact, her signature.

Jermaine said, "Elaine, you know this means that you cannot accept a job with a competitor in the industry within a 500-mile radius for the next two years?"

Elaine nodded her head.

"And I also need to inform you that, after this morning, it is unlawful for you to enter the GeneSel grounds or building again. You can have an hour to pack up your office. I'd discourage you from talking to any of your coworkers. It's usually easier that way for everyone."

Suddenly, she now understood why her coworkers at Techsel had left so abruptly without much conversation or, in some cases, even good-byes.

In their short meeting, Jermaine gave only a few details about the downsizing and, at the time, she didn't even feel like asking. She just wanted to get out of there as fast as possible, call Alan, and meet him at home. She strode back to GeneSel's main building, took the stairs instead of the elevator, and entered her small office packed with books, binders, and personal keepsakes. She sat down for a moment, took a deep breath, gathered herself a bit, and glanced at her calendar. It read: "3 P.M.–Marta two-month anniversary of counseling."

## A LINGERING QUESTION

At that moment, it struck her. She vaguely remembered a brief segment of her conversation with Jermaine. In the midst of some of the legalistic chatter about noncompete clauses and placement services he had said, "I understand you've expressed some serious reservations about the management team." Where would he get that information? She had disclosed those concerns to only a couple of people. With a bolt of energy, she quickly rose from her chair, left her office, and began her way down the hallway. Where should she go first, she thought to herself. To Marta? Jackson? The HR office?

CHAPTER 26

# Managing Multiple Roles

## Caryn E. Medved and Julie Apker

My coworkers told me I was crazy to request an alternative work schedule at the same time my employer, Mount Adams Hospital of Cleveland,* announced a merger with crosstown rival St. Mary's Hospital. The merger was promoted to employees as a marriage of equals–a joining of forces that naturally played upon the strengths of both health care facilities. As manager of internal communications for Mount Adams Hospital, I was well aware of the organization's growing economic woes and its need to solve its financial problems in order to remain competitive in the cutthroat health care marketplace.

Many Mount Adams employees had their doubts. They wondered how the consolidation would affect their job security, supervisory relationships, job tasks, and work autonomy. Officials from both organizations assured workers that the transition to the new "Consolidated Care Hospital" would be seamless and smooth. In fact, I was the one who wrote the new CEO's speech promising employees that their work lives would not be disrupted and urging them to conduct business as usual. Back then, I believed what I wrote. Today, I say to myself, "Marcus Hernandez, things have certainly changed in the past few months. What will the future bring?"

While issues related to the merger were beginning to be sorted out, a lot was also happening in my personal life that prompted me to request a change in my work schedule. I had been divorced from my wife for about three months, and although the visitation agreement for our 8-year-old twin daughters, Kate and Maggie, seemed okay initially, I quickly realized that seeing them every other weekend was not much time together. So with the approval of Tameka Anderson, the director of organizational development and my immediate supervisor, I changed my traditional 9 A.M.–5 P.M. work hours to 7 A.M.–3 P.M. on Mondays

---

*This case has been developed based on real organization(s) and real organizational experiences. Names, facts, and situations have been changed to protect the privacy of individuals and organizations.

and Wednesdays. Sure, I had to skip lunch on those days, but my new schedule also allowed me to pick up my girls after school and spend time with them two afternoons a week. I could also squeeze in my responsibilities as vice president of the local Public Relations Society of American (PRSA) chapter and as chair of the hospital's United Way campaign. It seemed like the perfect solution to managing my hectic life.

Now, four months later, I don't question my decision to spend more time with my daughters, but I do wonder about my commitment to Consolidated Care Hospital. It's almost 10 A.M. and I have already been at work for three hours. I have drunk more cups of coffee than I care to remember and I'm still tired. In a few minutes, I have a follow-up meeting with Tameka to review how my new schedule is working and discuss future plans for internal communications in the newly merged organization. What I haven't told her is that there is one additional item for the meeting's agenda: my doubts about remaining here as an employee.

While waiting to meet with Tameka, I reflect on the events of the past four months, wondering how things could change so much in such a short time. How did I get from being employee of the month to dreading going to work each day? I still love many aspects of my job, but why do I feel so emotionally exhausted? When did I start to resent coworkers with less-demanding jobs or no children? Why do I often feel that I haven't accomplished anything at work, even though I work on weekends and longer hours on Tuesdays, Thursdays, and Fridays? How can I recapture my old enthusiasm for work? Or do I even want to? At least I can pinpoint when my quality of work life began to diminish–it happened shortly after my first meeting with Tameka to propose changing my work schedule and, at the same time, learn about my new job duties at Consolidated Care.

## A NEW, MORE CHALLENGING ROLE

Four months ago, on the day before my initial meeting with Tameka, Mount Adams CEO Helen Wilder had just announced to employees that the proposed merger with St. Mary's Hospital was a *go*. Members of the organizational development staff had quickly assembled to discuss implications and changes in internal communication resulting from the merger. Tameka led the staff meeting with her usual efficient and no-nonsense style. At age 35, Tameka had assumed leadership of the department after serving in a similar position at a major health insurance company. She knew the marketplace and was well connected with its key players. I'll be the first to admit I wasn't thrilled that someone from the *enemy* (insurance people) was joining our organization, but I will also be the first to say that Tameka is an outstanding boss. She's a straight talker, not the kind of person to hold back her opinions. In our relationship, I have always known where I stand with her and that my work is supported 100%.

Tameka concluded the meeting by briefly addressing the new roles to be assumed by various members of the department. I was surprised to hear my name mentioned and see my coworkers' heads whip around the small, crowded conference room to watch my reaction to Tameka's final comment.

"I will be visiting with each one of you this week to talk about your new roles. Marcus, I'd like you to codirect the merger transition team from the standpoint of internal communications. You'll work with Lorie Lockart, the public relations director from St. Mary's. We can iron out the details of your new assignment later, but I know that you will direct the dissemination of all merger-related information to both hospitals via their respective intranets. You will also oversee plans to integrate the two intranets as we finalize the merger. Are you up for the challenge?"

"Sure, ummm . . . okay," I responded. I tried to appear confident, but inside my stomach churned with uncertainty. Would I be able to balance these new job duties along with my existing work responsibilities? I was still determined to spend more time with my kids, even though my job appeared to be changing.

The next day I met with Tameka to learn about my new work responsibilities and pitch my idea for a new work schedule. I thought about the various internal communication challenges that lay ahead for the transition team as I walked down the hallway toward her office for our appointment. Cautiously knocking on her door, I also wondered how receptive she would be to my proposal to work a more family-friendly schedule during this time of transition.

"Please come in and have a seat, Marcus," said Tameka. "You seemed a little hesitant yesterday when I asked you to codirect the transition team. What's on your mind? Be honest. We've always had a good working relationship, and I am confident that you will do a great job codirecting the transition team."

I took a deep breath and said, "Tameka, I'm so glad you feel comfortable putting me in that position. I'm very excited about it! Of course, I have many questions about how this role will be defined. First, though, there is one issue that I'd like to talk to you about.

"As you know, it has been an adjustment for me to be a part-time father now that Sophie and I are divorced. Tameka, I miss seeing my daughters. I need to find a way to be with them more during the week. So I guess, as we move through this transition, I'd like to talk to you about ways that I can manage my schedule so I can spend some time with them without jeopardizing my work commitments. I have an idea to discuss with you, but maybe this isn't the time."

As always, Tameka got right to the point. She responded, "Marcus, you know we have a lot to talk about with the folks at St. Mary's, and I'm going to need you 110% for the next few months. The quality of your work in the past makes me believe that you are the best staff member to codirect the transition team. I wouldn't assign this job to anybody else in the department. What are you proposing?"

"Can we do some sort of an alternative work schedule? I've heard that Jan in accounts payable is doing something like this. She works four 10-hour days and takes Fridays off," I said. "In my case, I'd like to leave work at 3 P.M. on Mondays and Wednesdays so I can pick up my daughters from school. I would start work at 7 A.M. on those days and work through my lunch hour. I am happy to work longer on Tuesdays, Thursdays, and Fridays and come in on weekends when Kate and Maggie aren't visiting me."

"So you would still work at least 40 hours per week and be flexible to put in extra time when needed?" asked Tameka. "I'm counting on you not only to develop and maintain our new intranet site, but also to assess employee communication needs about the merger. We need to raise worker awareness of the benefits of the merger and reduce their fears about downsizing, job restructuring, and pay cuts. It will also give us an opportunity to get a pulse on overall employee quality of work life."

I answered quickly. "I am committed to making this schedule work and not reducing my productivity. I think that my plans will allow me to balance my job and family responsibilities more successfully. We may even be sending a positive message to other employees who are wondering how this merger will affect their quality of work life."

"I trust your ability to make this work, Marcus, so I will agree to these arrangements on a trial basis," said Tameka. "Let's try it out for four months and we will meet again to evaluate your performance. You can start the new hours next week, but make sure to contact Lorie Lockart, your partner at St. Mary's, about your new schedule."

## THE ROAD TO BURNOUT

I was pleased that my meeting with Tameka had gone so smoothly. It was great to know that I was a valued employee. As I walked back to my desk, I thought, "It looks like having it all—successful career, being an involved father, United Way campaign chairperson, and PRSA officer—is within reach!" I was feeling so good that I decided to email Lorie Lockart and get the ball rolling on the transition team.

To: Lorie Lockart
From: Marcus Hernandez
Cc: Tameka Anderson
Subject: Transition Team

Lorie: Tameka Anderson asked me to contact you to coordinate our codirector responsibilities for the Consolidated Care Hospital transition team. Tameka said that you would supervise information dissemination about the merger via company publications and all external communications with the public. For now, I am assigned to manage communications to employees via our respective organizational intranets. Eventually, I will also direct the creation and ongoing development of our joint intranet site. Tameka has also requested that we survey employees about the merger and quality of work life issues as we begin our communication efforts.

Before I propose a meeting, I need to mention that beginning next Monday, my hours will be 7 A.M. to 3 P.M. on Mondays and Wednesdays and 9 A.M. to 5 P.M.

on Tuesdays, Thursdays, and Fridays. Tameka and I have agreed to implement this schedule on a four-month trial basis. While these changes will not affect my work responsibilities, I wanted to make you aware of them for future reference as we schedule our joint activities.

Would you be able to meet next Wednesday at 9 A.M. to begin discussions about the transition team and our assessment of employees' quality of work life? I can meet you at St. Mary's if that is most convenient for you. Please email me as soon as possible. I look forward to meeting with you to discuss our plans.

Thank you. Marcus

---

To: Marcus Hernandez
From: Lorie Lockart
Cc: Tameka Anderson
Subject: Transition Team

Marcus: A meeting next week at 9 A.M. in my office works for me. I spoke with Tameka last week about the division of labor that you discussed in your email. I think the duties are clearly assigned, but we will need to work closely together to make sure that our internal and external organizational messages are consistent.

Tameka reinforced the importance of conducing a survey immediately to assess employees' perceptions and attitude about their work lives, particularly in regard to the merger. St. Mary's employees completed a quality of work life (QWL) survey about five years ago that we can modify and update by adding items about the merger. In addition, I know our human resources staff is interested in learning more about employees' stress and burnout as well as how workers balance their job and family responsibilities. The HR director just mentioned to me the need to create schedules for employees (as in your case) that are more flexible for them to meet personal and professional obligations. Particularly with the shortage of nurses, we need a competitive edge for recruiting RNs.

Your new hours don't pose a problem for me, and I don't see any complications with them regarding the transition team. I am a part-time graduate student at City University, and my night courses this term require that I leave work at 4:30 P.M. on Tuesdays and Thursdays. Still, there are many hours that we can both meet face-to-face, and emails and telephone calls can help us communicate.

I'll see you next week. Lorie.

---

Lorie and I met as planned to talk about the size, scope, and structure of the transition team. Our personalities clicked immediately, and soon we were discussing the team's first major responsibility–developing, distributing, and analyzing the QWL survey.

"This first project is really critical to the credibility of the transition team," I said. "It seems to me that we should divide up the assignments as equally as possible and enlist some help from our support staff."

"I couldn't agree more," Lorie replied. "I'm happy to be the contact person for the human resources departments at Mount Adams and St. Mary's. I have a good relationship with the St. Mary's HR unit already, and this project will help me establish a similar one with the Mount Adams HR staff. I know that they will want a lot of input in refining existing survey items and developing new questions that assess employees' opinions about stress, burnout, and work and family balance."

"That's fine with me. For my part, I will write survey items that specifically address workers' perceptions of their quality of work life as it relates to the merger and pilot test those items with employees. What do you think of each of us individually coordinating the distribution and collection of the surveys at our respective hospitals?"

"It makes good sense to me," said Lorie. "We know the key players in both of our organizations and it will be easier to manage the survey distribution system as a result. Soon we are going to be busier than before the merger, with our new transition tasks, regular job duties, and respective work schedules. We need to take every opportunity we have to streamline survey operations."

I left that first meeting with Lorie believing that I could handle the increased workload successfully, and at first I was able to easily manage my new transition team duties with my existing work responsibilities. It helped that Lorie and I had similar collaborative communication styles and we were able to work interdependently on our assigned tasks. Despite our multiple work and family obligations, telephone calls and emails allowed us to update each other on our progress, troubleshoot problems, and plan the next steps of the QWL survey process. Over time, our roles evolved and we both took on survey-related duties that we hadn't anticipated earlier. For example, Lorie began to be the main contact person to answer questions about the survey from other departments and coordinate the transition team's creation. I supervised personnel assisting with the survey and planned for survey data analysis. Even with these additional tasks, I felt that I was handling my work and family roles fairly well. I also enjoyed spending more time with Kate and Maggie as a result of my new work schedule. Sure, I had to work longer hours and come in on weekends, but now I was able to watch their after-school soccer games and help them with their homework. Admittedly, I hadn't spent much time on my PRSA responsibilities in the last few months and our company donations to the annual United Way campaign were down somewhat from the amount we contributed last year, but overall I felt that I was doing well.

## JOB PRESSURE ESCALATES

However, about six weeks into the QWL survey project, things at work heated up significantly. Countless technical problems arose as we integrated the two hospitals' intranet sites. It also became my job to put out the daily fires that occurred because of personality clashes between internal communications' staff members in both organizations. In addition, fears about job security in the merged hospital led frontline employees working at the patient bedside to leave in droves for jobs with other health care facilities. Thus, our department scrambled to develop messages to attract new employees to fill vacant openings and encourage current workers to remain. Morale kept dropping as new crises emerged. About this same time, I began to suffer from anxiety attacks not unlike the ones I experienced during stressful times in graduate school.

Just two months after the merger was announced, I felt that I was always behind in my work and hadn't accomplished anything. My new job duties forced me to come in early and work late most Tuesdays, Thursdays, and Fridays. I also worked every weekend that Kate and Maggie stayed with their mom. Even on the weekends the kids visited me, I had work assignments to complete after they went to bed. I stopped going to the gym and routinely canceled or avoided social events. I was angry with my coworkers, who had less work to do and fewer family obligations. One day, as I was walking down the hall, I overhead Emily and Jack, two colleagues whom I considered to be close friends, discussing my recent meltdown at our staff meeting, when I had discovered that the launch date for the Consolidated Care Hospital intranet needed to be delayed again.

"I couldn't believe Marcus' behavior yesterday at the meeting," remarked Emily in hushed tones. "All that yelling and finger-pointing at people who had nothing to do with our technical problems. All of us–including Marcus–knew that the launch date would have to be postponed. I was surprised at his lack of professionalism. What's wrong with him lately?"

"That incident was just the tip of the iceberg for me," said Jack. "I'm sick and tired of being snapped at by him when I walk into his office to ask a simple question or remind him to do something that is supposed to be *his* job. Marcus used to have an open-door policy, but now his door is shut most of the time. He doesn't even treat me like a colleague anymore, much less a friend. He told me the other day to stop whining about the merger like all of his other employees! I'm ready to start looking for another job."

I stormed into their conversation and announced, "Well, I wouldn't mind looking for another job myself because I'm sick and tired of you two complaining all of the time! You try having my job!"

Mad and embarrassed by my outburst, I turned around and quickly left. I went to the cafeteria, got a cup of coffee, and tried to calm down. Managing others used to be one of my greatest strengths, but now, after hearing Emily's and Jack's comments, I realized I wasn't even getting *that* part of my job right. I shouldn't have yelled at them. I knew that I had to get back to being my old self somehow. I hoped that could happen once the QWL project was completed, but I also feared that my workload would only increase as the merger moved forward.

The QWL project was a bright spot in my job even though it increased my workload substantially. Three months after our first planning meeting, Lorie and I arranged to visit face-to-face to proofread the survey one last time and review its distribution and collection procedures. We had promised Tameka the survey would be mailed no later than the following week, even though I was scheduled to be at an out-of-town conference during this time period. Tameka was anxious to

get its results and plan the next stage of internal communications. The survey findings were critical to what merger information would be communicated to employees and how this information would be disseminated, along with what training
interventions would be designed to facilitate the transition.

## A WORK-FAMILY ROLE CONFLICT ARISES

Lorie and I deliberately set the meeting to finalize the survey for Friday at 3 P.M.
Neither of us needed to leave work early for family or school obligations that afternoon. We planned to work until the job was done. We were both looking forward
to finishing up the survey and getting on with our other job duties. Then, just after
lunch, my former wife unexpectedly called on her cell phone from the Chicago
airport.

"Marcus, this is Sophie. I have a huge favor to ask you. I missed my flight and
now I'm stranded at the airport in Chicago. I won't be able to pick up Kate and
Maggie. The next flight I can get won't get me home until late tonight. Could you
meet the girls at school and bring them to your place until I get home?"

"Sophie, I have an important meeting this afternoon that I scheduled weeks
ago. Can't you try another airline?"

"I've already tried that and all of the flights are booked solid. Why can't you
reschedule your meeting? You always tell me that your daughters are the most
important parts of your life."

"Being a father to Kate and Maggie is the most important thing in my life! But
I can't reschedule the meeting because I'll be in San Diego next week for the PRSA
annual conference. You know that. Can't you find someone else? How about your
mother?"

"Mom is out of town with her boyfriend. I've called several other people, but
no one can help me on such short notice. Marcus, it's up to you."

"Okay, Sophie, okay. I'll do it. I'll be at the girls' school at 3:30 P.M., but this
is not the best time for you to have missed your flight. Why can't you ever be on
time?"

After hanging up with Sophie, I dialed Lorie's office telephone number and
left the following voice mail:

> Lorie, this is Marcus. I have to cancel our meeting about the QWL survey because
> Sophie had an emergency and can't pick up Kate and Maggie from school. I know we
> had been planning on finishing things up for the survey, but there is no one else to
> drive the girls home and stay with them until Sophie returns late tonight. I fly out in
> the morning, but I hate to leave you with the final details. Let me know what I can do
> via email from San Diego. I'm so sorry for the inconvenience.

When Lorie checked her voice mail, she was irritated that I had canceled
our meeting on such short notice and left her with the responsibility of finalizing
the survey. "Surely," Lorie thought, "Marcus could have made arrangements for
another person to get his children from school. Or he could have brought them to

the meeting. Now I have to deal with the last-minute details of the survey in order to meet Tameka's deadline."

As Lorie tackled fine-tuning the survey on her own, I brought my daughters home from school, made them dinner, and packed for my trip until Sophie arrived. I tried calling Lorie at home after doing some last-minute errands late that night, but she didn't answer the phone. I finally fell into bed at midnight. As I was drifting off to sleep, I promised myself I'd call Lorie first thing on Monday to check in on the survey. To be honest, I was so tired from rushing between my work and home responsibilities that I didn't even want to go to this conference anymore. I just wanted to sleep for a week with no interruptions. No coworkers. No kids. No ex-wife. Nobody.

Thankfully, Lorie and I were able to iron out the survey details over the phone while I was at the conference. Lorie gained the necessary approval from administrators, and her assistant made the final corrections to the survey. Despite the extra help, Lorie still was forced to skip class the week that I was away to ensure that the survey was completed and distributed by Tameka's target date. I felt so guilty that Lorie had to take on the extra stress that when I returned from my trip, I plunged directly into the QWL project. Even though my flight arrived at 9 P.M., I went directly to the office from the airport to begin analyzing the survey data.

About a week after my return from the conference, I felt completely burned out and used up by my job. My resentment toward my coworkers increased and I refused to socialize with most of them. My daily interactions with others became even more defensive than in the past. I knew things were at a crisis point when I called in sick one Monday simply because I couldn't face going in to the office. Suddenly, changing jobs and even switching careers were attractive alternatives. I had to talk to Tameka about my future at the hospital, but I didn't know what to say or do.

## STRATEGIZING INTERNAL COMMUNICATIONS

All these thoughts were going through my mind when Lorie and I sat down with Tameka the next month to review a few key findings from the quality of work life survey. The results were particularly interesting to me because it appeared that, as in my own experience, other employees were also struggling with stress due to work and family role conflict.

"The survey yielded a number of interesting findings that will help us develop communication strategies to enhance employees' quality of work life and ease the merger's transition period," Lorie said to Tameka. "I will highlight a few key results, and Marcus will outline our recommendations for internal communication strategies."

Lorie continued, "First, employees appear to understand why the merger was needed, but not necessarily if and how their jobs have been changed by the merger. This finding suggests that workers are experiencing uncertainty about their roles during this time of change.

### Consolidated Care Quality of Work Life Survey Executive Summary

Consolidated Care employees were recently surveyed to better understand their attitudes and opinions on issues related to the recent organizational merger, job stress and burnout, and work/family balance. This summary reflects responses from all full-time personnel.

**Perceptions of the Organizational Merger**

| The merger was necessary to maintain our financial stability. | | Since the merger, I clearly understand any changes in my job duties. | |
| --- | --- | --- | --- |
| Strongly agree | 55% | Strongly agree | 10% |
| Agree | 5% | Agree | 5% |
| Neutral | 10% | Neutral | 20% |
| Disagree | 25% | Disagree | 35% |
| Strongly Disagree | 5% | Strongly Disagree | 30% |

**Job Stress and Burnout**

| I often feel emotionally exhausted at the end of the workday. | | I often feel overwhelmed by the amount of work I need to accomplish each day. | |
| --- | --- | --- | --- |
| Strongly agree | 65% | Strongly agree | 45% |
| Agree | 20% | Agree | 35% |
| Neutral | 5% | Neutral | 10% |
| Disagree | 5% | Disagree | 5% |
| Strongly Disagree | 5% | Strongly Disagree | 5% |

**Work and Family Management**

| My supervisor is supportive when family emergencies arise. | | The stress from my job often negatively spills over into my personal life. | |
| --- | --- | --- | --- |
| Strongly agree | 20% | Strongly agree | 45% |
| Agree | 45% | Agree | 30% |
| Neutral | 15% | Neutral | 15% |
| Disagree | 10% | Disagree | 5% |
| Strongly Disagree | 10% | Strongly Disagree | 5% |

Second, the majority of employees reported experiencing job stress and burnout, particularly in the areas of work overload and emotional exhaustion. Finally, although employees believed that supervisors supported balancing work and family issues, the negative spillover from work-related stressors into workers' personal lives was high. Marcus?"

"Huh, what?" I asked. Rats! I had been caught daydreaming. "Sorry, Lorie and I had to work late last night finalizing our report for you, Tameka. I'm a little tired. Anyway, based on these findings, we propose several strategies to increase and enhance employee communication about the merger and managing stress and burnout."

I handed Tameka our recommendations.

Tameka reviewed our recommendations and asked a few probing questions. At the end of her queries, she smiled and remarked, "I am really pleased with your work. Let's move forward with these suggestions. I've got to get to another

**Consolidated Care Quality of Work Life Survey**
**Employee Assessment Recommendations**

1. Design a managerial training program on counseling employees about the merger's impact on their job responsibilities. Invite managers to bring along a key employee from their departments to these sessions.

2. Include ongoing sections in the employee newsletter and on the Intranet that discuss merger-related issues. Topics would include job security, role restructuring, and answering general questions about the merger. The newsletter would also encourage employees to seek out their supervisors to discuss the effects of the merger.

3. Design a special component of the intranet that provides employees with information about job burnout—particularly as it relates to work and family stressors—as well as resources to help employees cope with these issues (e.g., related websites, practical tips and strategies, informal brown bag lunches to share information, etc.).

4. Create and disseminate an internal memo to supervisors that summarizes information about the hospital's work and family policies and strategies. This document would provide managers with organizational resources to which they could refer employees who need counseling, social support, job restructuring, etc.

5. Develop a task force made up of employees at all organizational levels to investigate and address QWL issues.

meeting, so I'm going to let you two figure out how to get this done. Thanks for your hard work. Keep me updated on your progress."

Just as she was leaving the conference room, Tameka turned to me and added, "Marcus, we need to schedule that follow-up meeting to discuss how your schedule's been working out lately and a few other things. Call my office this week and set up an appointment." With that, she left us to figure out the details.

Lorie and I just sat at the small conference table for a minute, not talking, exhausted.

Then Lorie said wearily to me, "I'm glad she liked all of the recommendations, but now we need to actually do them!"

Although we laughed and relaxed for a minute, I couldn't stop the feeling of dread as I anticipated more long hours and weekends at work. Summer was coming up soon, and my girls would be out of school. How would I balance my workload and parenting responsibilities now? My stomach was in knots and I could feel a migraine coming on.

"I'm beginning to think we're crazy!" I told Lorie.

"Come on. Come on. Look at the bright side," Lorie replied encouragingly. "Tameka supported our ideas and we have complete autonomy to get our recommendations implemented. We just need to divide and conquer like before."

I still had my doubts, but after another hour of discussion, Lorie and I developed and delegated our assignments. The training program was assigned to one of the training specialists in the human resources department. Lorie agreed to work on recommendations two and four, and I took on implementing the intranet recommendation and facilitating the quality of work life committee. However, despite my close relationship with Lorie, I didn't tell her how uncertain I was about my future at the hospital. Would I let her down by leaving?

Later that day, I set up a meeting with Tameka for Friday at 10 A.M. to review my work schedule. I knew that I was at the end of my rope and it was time to make a choice to stay or leave. I just was so confused about what the right decision would be.

## A DIFFICULT DECISION

The next week was busy, and Friday came fast. I spent much of my time designing the job stress and burnout section of the intranet. I asked a number of employees to write weekly columns about how they managed work and family roles to post on the site. I also added hyperlinks to a number of useful websites.

Suddenly, I stopped reflecting on the troubles and triumphs of the last four months and looked at the clock. Now we were back to where we started this story! It was 9:55 A.M. and I needed to get to my meeting with Tameka. I remembered my optimism of just a few months ago about balancing the two most important things in my life—my kids and my career. I still loved many aspects of my job: the autonomy, creativity, work relationships like the ones with Lorie and Tameka. But now, I also felt like a burned-out mess who couldn't do anything right. I had already written my resignation letter to give to Tameka during our meeting if necessary. As I knocked on Tameka's door and heard her say, "Come on in, Marcus," I checked inside my jacket pocket to make sure the letter was still there. It still was.

CHAPTER 27

# No Laughing Matter

## Linda B. Dickmeyer and Scott G. Dickmeyer

Dante* was a confident 22-year-old who welcomed a challenge. He was used to getting what he wanted due to his competitive nature. During his senior year of college, he received an assignment to select an organization and analyze its culture. He researched Bedrock Communication (BC), a mid-size PR firm in the same city as his university. Dante was impressed with how selective the company was in its hiring practices, which included several interviews, tests, and meetings. Creativity and skills were essential in the interview process, but a fit with the Bedrock "family" was crucial for a job offer. At the completion of his cultural analysis, Dante became convinced his first job would be with BC. Following the presentation of his report to BC officials, Dante continued contacts with the company and asked for an interview. His persistence paid off when he was offered an interview. Dante was articulate, prepared, and charming. He thought it was a good sign when he was invited to speak with Stan, the CEO, Emmett, the Senior Vice President, and other executives following his fourth interview.

The executives spoke highly of his qualifications, especially his ability to analyze consumer data, a unique strength for a new college graduate. They also liked his energy and sense of humor. However, he was warned that his confidence may be perceived as arrogance. Stan and Emmett wanted assurance that he was a team player. Dante acknowledged that at times he was misunderstood due to self-assurance, but convinced them that he would work hard to be a team player. He was thrilled when they offered him an entry-level position.

Dante's new position involved uncovering unique and unrecognized needs of potential clients. After thoroughly researching an industry, he used existing consumer data and collected new consumer data through surveys and focus groups. He was required to be inventive, identifying what set one company apart from

*The case is based upon an actual organization and real organizational experiences. Names, facts, and situations have been changed to protect the privacy of individuals and the organization.

another. The Creative Team used his research to develop PR campaigns, which were ultimately reported to the executives and hopefully implemented. Although his work was done independently, he was officially a member of the Creative Team. He would spend much of his time on the Internet and in libraries and was grateful that his college coursework prepared him for such in-depth examinations of existing documents.

His first assignment was to work with consumer data previously collected for a major pharmaceutical company. Dante was disappointed that he had to take over someone else's project, but assumed he was being tested before he received his own accounts. The company wanted to introduce a nationwide campaign for a "male-enhancement" drug, but was concerned how consumers would respond. Dante felt the data suggested a conservative campaign. The Creative Team used his analysis in their proposal and the pharmaceutical company executives agreed. Dante felt like a king when he heard the news, pleased that his first analysis held so much weight. Unfortunately, the campaign was not as successful as hoped and ran for less than a month. Stan indicated that was not surprising with a new product. Secretly, Dante assumed the data were flawed.

Dante's job was challenging and at times tedious. However, it allowed him to get to know people from every part of the company. He liked his coworkers and looked forward to going to the office each day. The climate of Bedrock was similar to what his college cultural-analysis study had indicated. There was support for employees at all levels. An added bonus was that people worked hard but played harder. He felt like one of the gang and that people cared about him as a person, not just an employee.

For example, Emmett took him to lunch at one of the newest restaurants in the city during his first week. Dante expected he would have to sit and listen to the Vice President explain "the way things are around here." Instead, Dante did almost all of the talking as Emmett used this opportunity to listen and get to know him. When Dante's girlfriend ended their relationship, his supervisor Connie and the rest of the Creative Team took him out on the town. They listened to him vent about his ex's "cracked comments" like "you're not funny anymore, you're just mean." They agreed with his assessment that she was just jealous of his new job.

The relationships extended beyond the office–there was a Bedrock co-ed softball team in the summer and a bowling team in the fall. Nobody seemed to care that Dante rarely bowled above a 70; in fact, it gave them good-natured fodder during the many Happy Hours. Dante loved these outings where he told jokes and elaborate stories that often put him at the center of attention. He proudly wore his logo-emblazoned jacket and answered amiably to his new nickname, Sparky.

It was during an office party to celebrate Dante's positive six-month review that he first heard about the legendary Bedrock Christmas party. Dante thought the party sounded like standard fare–an open bar, a catered dinner, a dance, and an end-of-the-year awards ceremony. Although Dante didn't expect to win an award this early in his career, he did pay close attention when he heard about a unique Bedrock tradition–the Christmas Roast. According to his teammates, the roast was hilarious as long as you had "thick enough skin" to handle it. Typically, people from across the company performed humorous skits and standup comedy acts. Executives, including Stan, were known to say a few words of their own. Dante was warned that the Creative Team often took the heaviest hits because it was easy to make fun of their work.

"Think about it," said Edwardo, who had been at Bedrock for five years. "How do you crack funny jokes about our friends in legal or accounting? And executives just aren't funny!"

Dante nodded in agreement as Zack and Amy, from legal and accounting respectively, threw popcorn at Edwardo. Privately, Dante thought he was up to the challenge of poking fun at every department. The Christmas Roast became his new challenge, and he planned his speech every chance he could get.

Dante was in a festive mood as he arrived at the Christmas party. He was impressed with the live band and the large table of appetizers. He met Edwardo at the bar and ordered a martini.

"I thought you were a beer man," Edwardo said.

"Not when someone is paying for my drinks! As the guy here paying student loans, I have to take advantage," replied Dante.

"Just don't get stupid. You know we lost our last 'Sparky' because of too much booze," said Edwardo, smiling.

Dante had heard references to employees who didn't really "fit," but this story didn't ring a bell. He found himself annoyed that his nickname was being used in reference to someone else.

"Yeah? Well, don't worry about me, dude. I'm a big boy you know," said Dante.

After three martinis, Dante was ready to eat, filling his plate with freshly carved turkey, ham, and prime rib. After dinner, he ordered his favorite micro-brew from the bar and settled into his seat for the Christmas Roast. He was not disappointed. Dante and the rest of the company laughed hysterically as the show unfolded. Stan the CEO targeted the VPs with his act and the VPs went after the managers in a hilarious skit. Dante and the rest of his coworkers were slammed for nearly 15 minutes by their management team. Dante found himself thinking about responses to all these jabs and became more and more convinced that his act would be the most entertaining.

As Connie and other team leaders walked off to applause and cheers, Dante practically ran to the stage. His heart felt like a jackhammer in his chest as he stepped up to the microphone. He wasn't sure if it was the excitement from being on stage or the anticipation of what he was about to do. He started his act with a series of one-liners about Stan and Connie, including an impersonation of Con-nie's cackling laugh. He moved to cracks about his colleagues' unique sense of fashion. Dante continued with gusto although he was confused. He knew his stuff was funny, but he wasn't hearing much laughter. This type of ribbing was typical in the employee lounge at work. Why weren't his coworkers laughing now? They usually loved his impersonations of "Stan the Man." Maybe he just wasn't funny enough yet. Dante spotted Emmett looking slightly amused at the bar. But even Emmett stopped laughing when Dante made a crack about the Creative Team's "impotence in pitching the male-enhancement account."

Dante felt a hand on his shoulder. It was Stan, who smiled warmly at him while taking the microphone. "Let's give Dante a hand, and hey, Emmett! Get this guy a glass of Christmas cheer," Stan said. Dante walked off stage amidst polite applause. He felt embarrassed for reasons he did not understand. No one noticed when Dante slipped out the side door.

*** 

The next morning Dante woke up with a nagging feeling that went far beyond too much Christmas cheer. Then he remembered his not-so-well received act from the night before. Still struggling to understand what happened, Dante launched into his Saturday morning routine that included a cup of espresso and reading newspapers at his neighborhood coffee house. After reading three different sports sections, he opened up his laptop to check his email. He was surprised to find messages from Stan, Connie, and Emmett. "This can't be good…" he thought as he anxiously opened the email from Stan. The subject line, "What happened to you?" did not prepare him for the note that followed:

> Dante—
> Where did you go last night? We could have used your singing talent! Connie went onstage for a song and could have used a partner.
> I'm writing to tell you some good news. You missed the awards ceremony so I hope I am the first to congratulate you for receiving the New Employee of the Year Award. You are truly deserving of this honor.
> Stop by my office Monday so we can talk.
>
> Stan "the Man"

Dante tried to make sense of Stan's message. He was surprised to hear about the award and wanted to bask in the honor, yet he was confused that there was no mention about his failed comedy act. He opened the emails from Connie and Emmett, and both congratulated him about the award. He tried to read into their references to the party messages, but could see no evidence that he did anything wrong the night before. Maybe the only thing he did wrong was to leave the party early. Maybe he was really funny. Maybe he did deserve the New Employee of the Year Award. He started to feel pride, and his reaction to the award diminished his embarrassment. Of course it was OK to make mistakes at Bedrock. After all, that is what he had been told from day one at the company. He wondered how his coworkers responded to his honor and assumed their congratulations would come at work Monday.

Dante drained his cup and packed up his laptop. He decided he would spend the rest of the weekend relaxing instead of going to the office. He usually went in on Saturday afternoons and Sunday mornings. This weekend would be spent on the couch. He had every right to relax. After all, he was the New Employee of the Year! He tried calling Zach and Amy for dinner that night, leaving messages on their cell phones. Strange they didn't call back, he thought. He rented a couple movies instead and called his parents to share the news about his honor at work.

Dante went into work early on Monday morning. He was relaxed, refreshed, and ready to show everyone why he deserved to be an award-winning employee. On the drive in he wondered how he would be received–would he hear congrats and get slaps on the back, or would people be teasing him for his failed standup act and missing the award ceremony? He was prepared for both, but got neither.

In fact, when Dante got to the office, he got nothing. No one paid any special attention to him at all. When he said "good morning" to Jan in customer service, she said, "Oh, good morning, Dante," but nothing else.

He saw Edwardo in the employee lounge and tried to strike up a conversation about a current project. Edwardo mumbled, "Uh, I haven't looked at the data. Check with me later in the week," as he started to walk away.

"Wait! This is important–where are you at with it?" asked Dante.

"Oh, Mr. Backstabber getting all huffy now! I'll let you know when I have something to say," said Edwardo, leaving the room.

Dante had no idea how to respond. Backstabber? Confused, Dante headed off to his cube to get to work on his latest project, theme parks. He knew the project was assigned to him as a way to develop his creativity. Cornering the market on innovative theme park strategies was wide open and Dante was being challenged to think outside the box. Secretly he was hoping for a trip to Orlando to gather consumer data.

The morning passed quickly and Dante almost worked through lunch. "That's funny," he thought when he noticed the time. Usually on Mondays his friends met at noon to catch up on their weekend activities. Maybe he missed the plans while he was meeting with Stan. Stan enthusiastically presented him with a plaque and a pretty decent-sized check! Dante had planned to pick up the tab for lunch, but found himself at the vending machine contemplating burritos. Just then Connie came into the break room.

"Stop! Step away from the vending machine.... OK, let's go out for some *real* lunch and celebrate Mr. Employee of the Year," Connie said.

"Sounds good! Where is everyone else from the team?" asked Dante.

"Who cares? You're the one that makes *me* look good right now," she joked.

"Yeah, well, someone needs to pick up the slack around here," Dante smiled.

Dante and Connie caught up on the weekend and strategized about projects over their extended lunch. Upon returning to work, Dante checked his voicemail and was surprised to get a message telling him about an exciting position available in a rival company. He had heard of "headhunters," who were hired to find successful employees and encourage them to "move up" with another organization. "Wow," thought Dante, "I'm on someone's radar screen. That's cool." Although Dante was flattered by the call, he couldn't imagine leaving Bedrock. He strode to the employee lounge to put his leftover pasta in the refrigerator. Although he heard voices and laughter coming from the lounge, the room got quiet when he walked in. Edwardo, Becky, and Theresa, members of the Creative Team, started to move from the room.

"Hey, guys. What's up?" asked Dante.

"Not much, Dante. Just work," said Becky, slipping past him to go out the door.

"Theresa, can we chat about your ideas with cell phones?" he asked, desperate for acknowledgment.

"Um, Edwardo hasn't looked at your data yet, so no," she responded.

"Yeah, that's on my list," said Edwardo, exiting with Theresa. Dante watched them walk down the hall, their heads together in a quiet whisper.

The rest of the week unfolded in a strangely uneventful way. While management acknowledged Dante's award, his coworkers seemed oblivious to it. Nobody mentioned it at work, at Happy Hour, at bowling…in fact, in all these situations, Dante felt a little ignored. He was happy to receive a congratulatory balloon bouquet from Connie and the rest of his coworkers, but hurt that his friends simply signed the card, with the only personal message written by Connie herself. He was not part of the lunch crowd until late in the week, when the Creative Team invited him as they were leaving the building. Instead of following the traditional policy of "no shop talk" over lunch, he found himself defending his cell phone consumer data. Apparently, Edwardo had gotten around to the data but didn't talk about the work until this lunch. Dante hardly got a chance to take a bite between stabbing questions about his work. Was he falling down on the job or had the Creative Team's expectations changed? And who were they to question his work? Dante was confused.

Confusion moved to frustration on a Friday afternoon in early February when he was called into Emmett's office for his next review. Prior to this, his reviews came from Connie, which were always positive. However, she prepared him for Emmett's meeting with "Don't be surprised if the big guy makes you squirm." Emmett began with what Dante perceived as a backhanded compliment.

"Well, your reviews from Connie are fantastic. I've never seen a new employee pick things up so quickly. While others were trying to get traction, you were fighting for pole position in the Daytona 500! But it looks like you've hit a speed bump, champ. What happened? Can't handle the pressure of being new employee of the year?"

"I can handle the pressure just fine, thank you," Dante claimed. "What I can't handle is the Creative Team slowing down my progress. They still refuse to move forward with the cell phone campaign and that has backed everything up. I want to get moving on the theme park project, but can't until we get the phone thing to the exec team."

"From what I hear," Emmett said, "they are concerned about the accuracy of your consumer data and the phone 'thing' is too big to rush to the exec team," said Emmett, sounding a bit edgy.

"Yeah, but Creative has never questioned my analysis before; why now?"

"Think about it, Dante," Emmett went on, "They took the hit for you on the male-enhancement project and you threw it in their face at the Christmas Roast."

"What?" Dante said defensively, "I didn't come up with that pathetic pitch; they can't blame me for that one."

"Slow down, Sparky," said Emmett. "Everyone gave you a pass on that account because it was your first one and you were working with data collected by someone else. But your analysis was the basis of their whole approach, and as you just said, it was a pathetic pitch. But more importantly, you need to remember that at Bedrock we work as a team, and at the expense of sounding cliché, there is no "I" in team."

Emmett's tone had changed. Dante remembered the stories about Emmett taking cocky employees down a rung during this review. Was that happening here? Legend had it that once Emmett was fired up, there was no stopping him. The advice Dante heard was strap on your emotional seat belt and shut up. But Dante was never good about taking advice, especially when he saw an opening for humor.

"Yeah," Dante said, smiling, "but if you switch the letters in team you find the word 'me.'"

"You think this is some sort of joke?" Splotches of red were appearing on Emmett's face. "This company does not work on some sort of star system. It's about teamwork and caring more about assists, or helping others succeed, than about your own production. We deal in results at BC and our results come from team production. I don't know what to call the last quarter's work in research, but I know it would be hard to call it results. Makes me wonder if maybe the rumors I'm hearing about you are true, that you are only looking out for yourself, that you consider yourself a free agent. If you want to be a member of the Bedrock team, than that attitude better change–and fast!" Emmett stopped, took a deep breath, and tried to calm down.

"Look," he said, "I want you to succeed. You're a good kid, Dante, a smart kid. Apparently the team had confidence in you when they put you up for the award. We were looking at Tracy in Graphics until we read your nomination. From what Edwardo tells me, every member of the Creative Team was involved in nominating you. I know you have talent and believe you can be a real player in this game, but I have to tell you, I'm worried. I hope you use this weekend to really think things over and come to work on Monday ready to make a fresh start."

Dante did not know what to say. His head was swimming with emotions. He felt confused, angry, surprised, flattered, and embarrassed.

As he left Emmett's office, Dante looked at his watch and thought about heading for the bar. It was late in the afternoon and he could not imagine getting any real work done now. Not after all the things he just heard from Emmett. He went over the past weeks in his head. Something changed, but he didn't know what. He thought about stopping in Stan's office, but what would he say? Was he different, or was everyone else? What did he have to complain about? He just couldn't explain....

As he passed the lounge he heard other employees laughing and deciding where to go for happy hour. Suddenly he didn't feel very thirsty. He returned to his desk and checked messages. An email from Zach turning down Dante's offer to go out for steaks Saturday ("Sorry, man, just too busy"); a request from Connie to meet early Monday morning ("to re-evaluate the theme park project"); and another call from a headhunter (he wrote down the number). "Yeah," he thought, grabbing his jacket, "I have some serious thinking to do this weekend."

## CHAPTER 28

# Not on My Sabbath

## Joy Koesten

It was late in the day. I was tired and more than ready to begin a well-deserved five-day vacation. After months of stress and strain in a job that should have been a piece of cake, I was looking forward to the time off. As I closed down my computer and cleared off my desk to leave, Gloria* came into my office. She was dressed to go out in the cold and from the looks of it she was in as much of a hurry as I was to get out of here.

"Hi, Joan," Gloria greeted. "Are you wrapping it up for today?"

"Yeah, I'm finished." I looked up from my chair and leaned back. "Just cleaning up a few things before I go. I'll be gone until Wednesday; everything should be under control until then."

"Great! Here is a copy of your new job description. I know you and Sue have been working on all the changes pretty intensely. On top of everything else that's been going on here I'm sure you'll be ready to finalize this piece at least." Gloria handed me the document with a smile. "Have a great time while you're away!" she said as she fled out the door into the cold evening air.

Gloria's easy manner had always fascinated me. She had started out as a social worker for the Jewish Civic & Counseling Services 14 years ago and had taken the position of executive director only a couple of years before I arrived. The nonprofit Jewish agency provided resettlement, counseling, and elder care services to people of all faiths who lived in the midsize metropolitan area. I had grown to admire the casual but dedicated way that she approached problems within the Agency, but I had to wonder today if she was even aware of all the conflict that had been brewing during the last few months between Sue and me. I thought Gloria must have been at least somewhat aware of our mounting conflict. When I had received my pay raise during my annual review last month, a $500 bonus had been included in

---

*This case has been developed based on real organization(s) and real organizational experiences. Names, facts, and situations have been changed to protect the privacy of individuals and organizations.

the envelope. When I thanked Gloria she told me that the board had voted unanimously to give it to me. She also asked that I not tell Sue about it. When I questioned her as to why, Gloria's comment was, "It will only aggravate the situation."

Sue had been with the Agency for five years. After two failed marriages and only a high school education, she had worked her way up to her current position as development director from an entry position of receptionist. As development director, Sue was responsible for working with the Board of Directors to raise money for the Agency. When Sue had hired me she only had a sketchy outline of what she wanted to accomplish in terms of marketing and development, the rest had been up to me to define and implement. Delighted with my degree in marketing and experience in business education, Sue and I had few problems in the beginning as we worked to reconstruct the Agency's marketing efforts. By the end of my first year, however, I was producing results far beyond Sue's ability and Gloria's expectations. Now, every time I requested more information from Sue, she was reluctant to offer much assistance. Lately, with every successful project I completed, Sue would publicly shower me with kudos at the staff meetings, but behind closed doors offer only icy cold comments that she called "constructive criticism" in hopes that my "attitude" would improve concerning her supervision.

I looked at my watch and then at the document Gloria had given me. The cover memo read:

> Joan:
> Attached is a copy of your newly revised job description. This has been reviewed and revised by our supervisor at least twice with your input into the process. A copy of your job description will now be placed in the Agency personnel manual. If you have any questions, please talk with your supervisor.
>
> Gloria

Simple enough, I thought. Sue and I had reviewed this over and over. We had worked very hard to define my job in precise detail and with every meeting the scope of my responsibilities was more defined. Every time I explained what I did, Sue would make a note of it and rewrite the job description for continued discussion.

Even though my body told me it was time to go home, I leaned back in my chair and began glancing through the three-page document. It summarized in detail what Sue and I had agreed would be my duties as her development assistant. In essence, the document confirmed that I would be responsible for evaluating the marketing needs of the professional staff, and then design and implement a marketing plan to increase exposure of the professional staff throughout the community. In addition, I would design program evaluation questionnaires to collect feedback from the community concerning events and programming that the Agency sponsored; and I would be responsible for tabulating, analyzing, and reporting the results of that research to the Board so they could make decisions about future Agency events and programming. Sue and I also had agreed I would be responsible for designing and producing all promotional brochures and flyers, Agency newsletters, and visual aid materials used in presentations for professional staff. I would also be responsible for coordinating the annual meeting for the Agency, including developing all the materials and promotion related to the event. My fatigue set in deeper as I read through the litany of duties for this "assistant" position. Even so, I felt satisfied that my contribution to the Agency was becoming more focused on marketing as my skills had become more recognized. Everything looked familiar until I read the last paragraph.

> Job requires driving, public speaking, listening and writing skills, telephone communication skills, ability to enter data on a computer, occasional lifting, familiarity with word processing, spreadsheets, and the Internet, knowledge of and ability to relate to Jewish traditions. **Must be available to work evenings and weekends when needed.**

I stopped and sat upright in my chair. The last sentence was new to me. The issue of working weekends had not been discussed over the past few weeks as we had worked on these revisions. I had been with the Agency over a year and had been asked to work on Saturday only once during the time. At the time, being the new kid on the block, I didn't feel comfortable saying I couldn't work, so I didn't object. But after the event was completed, I told Sue that my family had made it a practice to attend synagogue on Saturdays and requested that other arrangements be made. We agreed that the non-Jewish staff could work on Saturdays and I would work on Sundays.

The subject had never come up again. However, over the course of the year, Sue and I had engaged in many discussions concerning my religious observance. As a convert, I felt a particular need to bring newly learned rituals into my home. Sue, who was a Jew by birth, did not. These discussions had become more uncomfortable in the past few months, I thought.

I dug through my file and took out my old job description. No, there was nothing there about working Saturdays. What was going on here? Sue had left hours ago and had never mentioned any of this to me. This had to be a mistake, I thought, as I glanced at my watch again. It was late and I was exhausted, but I knew I had to at least alert Sue to the fact that we would need to discuss this issue when I returned from vacation, so I turned my computer back on and wrote her a memo.

After printing the memo, I placed it in a sealed envelope with Sue's name on it and put it in her box. She would find it on Monday and we would talk when I returned on Wednesday. Weary, I went home.

When I returned on Wednesday I found no response to my memo. I assumed that the subject would be discussed sometime during the day at Sue's request. Sue and Gloria worked behind closed doors all day. While this was not altogether uncommon, it made me uneasy. When the day drew to a close and Sue had not yet emerged to discuss this issue with me, I knew something was wrong. Just as I was getting ready to leave Sue entered my office and handed me another memo.

MEMO
To: Sue Arnold
From: Joan Kissinger
Date: February 22, 2005
Subject: Job Description & Job Requirements

I have reviewed my new job description and believe it outlines very well my responsibilities as Development Assistant. I do however need clarification on the job requirement, specifically the section that states: "Must be available to work evenings and weekends when needed."

While I am always available, with adequate lead time, to work an occasional evening and/or on Sundays, I am not available on Saturdays. As I have indicated to you before, this is my Sabbath and I use the day for spending time with my family and going to services. I hope that this will not be a problem, but felt I needed to clarify my parameters concerning this job requirement before it was put on permanent file. This was not one of my job requirements when I accepted my current position.

I will be happy to discuss this with you upon my return from vacation, but felt it necessary to voice my concern before any time lapsed.

"This is to address the issue of working on Saturdays," she said in a cold and condescending voice. "If you have any further questions, I suggest you take it up with Gloria." Sue turned without waiting for a response and left for the day. I looked down at the memo from Sue and began to read. Sue had typed the memo in all caps; she and Gloria had both signed at the bottom, with Sue's signature on top.

MEMO
To: Joan Kissinger
From: Sue Arnold
Date: February 28, 2005
Subject: Job Description & Job Requirements

THIS LETTER IS IN RESPONSE TO YOUR MEMO DATED FEBRUARY 25, 2005, REGARDING YOUR JOB REQUIREMENTS.

THE JOB REQUIREMENT REGARDING AVAILABILITY ON EVENING AND WEEK-ENDS IS CONTAINED WITHIN THE NEW JOB DESCRIPTION/REQUIREMENTS OF EVERY PROFESSIONAL STAFF MEMBER AND MOST OF THE CLERICAL STAFF. YOU WERE MADE AWARE OF THE NEED FOR FLEXIBILITY BEFORE YOU ACCEPTED YOUR EMPLOYMENT AT THE AGENCY AND YOU HAVE ALREADY PARTICIPATED IN EVENTS THAT OCCURRED ON SATURDAY AND DID NOT EXPRESS AT THE TIME THAT IT WAS A PROBLEM.

WE ARE CERTAINLY AWARE THAT SATURDAY IS NOT ONLY YOUR SABBATH, BUT THE SABBATH FOR MANY OF THE EMPLOYEES OF THE JEW CIVIC AND COUNSELING SERVICES. AS A SECTARIAN AGENCY WE CERTAINLY RESPECT THE RIGHT OF ALL EMPLOYEES TO OBSERVE THE SABBATH AND ANY OTHER PERSONAL RELIGIOUS

OBSERVANCES. WE TRY NOT TO PARTICIPATE IN EVENTS THAT REQUIRE STAFF TO WORK ON THE SABBATH. HOWEVER, ON RARE OCCASIONS WE MAY ALL BE ASKED TO ATTEND OR ASSIST WITH AN IMPORTANT AGENCY PROGRAM THAT OCCURS ON A SATURDAY. UNLESS AN EMPLOYEE IS SHOMER SHABBOS, WE DO NOT FEEL THAT IT IS UNREASONABLE TO ASK FOR PARTICIPATION AT AGENCY EVENTS, ON RARE OCCASIONS, THAT OCCUR ON SATURDAY.

OUR GOAL IS TO DEVELOP A TEAM OF AGENCY EMPLOYEES WHO WORK TOGETHER AND DO WHAT IT TAKES TO GET THE JOB DONE. WE APPRECIATE YOUR FINE WORK AND HOPE THAT THIS ISSUE WILL NOT BECOME A PROBLEM. IF YOU HAVE ANY FURTHER QUESTIONS REGARDING THIS MATTER, GLORIA WILL BE HAPPY TO DISCUSS IT WITH YOU.

Sue Arnold
Gloria Davis

Just as I finished digesting the words, Gloria walked by with two of the counselors on their way to a manager's meeting. I jumped up and went into the hallway.

"Gloria, I assume you know about this memo," I asked quietly, but candidly.

"Yes, Sue and I had a long discussion about this today," Gloria replied in a somewhat guarded tone of voice.

"Gloria, this issue is not resolved. I feel very uncomfortable about how this has transpired, but Sue won't even address the issue with me face to face. Can we meet tomorrow to discuss what's going on?" I pleaded.

"Sure Joan, you know how Sue gets sometimes. How does 9:00 sound? I'm sure we can come to an understanding." Gloria smiled as she resumed her gait with the others.

"Thanks, Gloria. I'll see you then." Gloria went on to her meeting and I went back to my desk, thinking I had an ally in Gloria–she had always been the voice of reason before.

When I met with Gloria the following day, she confirmed the stance she and Sue had taken in the written memo. Gloria told me that although she would never ask any employee to do something she wouldn't do, she felt she could not make any exceptions with this policy. She explained that she had never been made aware that working on Saturdays was an issue for me until yesterday, when Sue wrote her response to my memo. Gloria said that she wished that I had brought the issue to her attention sooner, before the document was completed. As it stood now, if I were asked to work on a Saturday and no one else was available, I would have no alternative but to perform that job or be dismissed. Ironically, Gloria ended our meeting by telling me she was trying to "build a team" and that I needed to be a team player.

CHAPTER 29

# The Aggrieved Mediator

## Christine E. Cooper

When Gail Newsome* heard of her supervisor's intent to leave, she was saddened by the loss of a valuable colleague but excited by the possibility of moving into the role of student programs manager. She had begun working in the student activities area of Barkersville College five years earlier as an intern and had quickly moved into a full-time position as student activities coordinator. Her background in concert promotion and passion for student development served her well as she brought more than 300 programs, speakers, and entertainers to campus. Student workers responded well to her enthusiasm and personal management style. She was open and easygoing, always willing to help students and fellow employees. Over the years she participated in student success initiatives, was president of the staff council, and provided conflict resolution training on campus and in the community. Personally, she was pursuing a graduate degree in communication and in the final stages of designing thesis work that explored student success strategies and initiatives on the Barkersville campus.

### THE SEARCH

That spring Gail was heavily involved in negotiating a variety of possible events for the campus community and exploring best practices and current research on ways to improve student success on college campuses. She confidently submitted her application for the student programs manager position and enjoyed going through the interview process. She was one of two candidates in the final stages of the recruitment process. One day her supervisor, Cynthia Douglass, asked her to lunch and proceeded to tell her that the other candidate had been offered the position. As Gail was adjusting to this information, her supervisor continued by

---

*This case has been developed based on real organization(s) and real organizational experiences. Names, facts, and situations have been changed to protect the privacy of individuals and organizations.

clarifying that the candidate had turned down the offer and that she was declaring a failed search. Gail was shocked. Her performance appraisals had been very positive, and she felt ready after five years to move to the next level in the department. She felt somewhat encouraged when Cynthia asked her to temporarily take on a portion of the program manager's position until it could be filled.

Despite her disappointment, Gail decided to take on these responsibilities plus several other high-profile activities to enhance her experience and highlight her abilities before the next recruitment was posted. When the position reopened, Gail's supervisor encouraged her to reapply. Once again she entered the process hopeful of a successful outcome. Once again she was not offered the job. Confused and saddened by this result, she decided to resign from her current position.

## THE GRIEVANCE

After much deliberation, Gail decided to file a formal complaint with the Human Resources Department and grieve the result of the search process. She requested the hiring file from HR and was in disbelief when she discovered that Cynthia Douglass, the supervisor who had encouraged her to reapply, had formally petitioned Human Resources to have her file removed from consideration in the second recruitment. As Gail explored the file in detail, she discovered what seemed to be clear discrepancies during the first recruitment between the feedback in her performance evaluations as an employee and the reasons given by Cynthia for removing Gail from the offer list. Gail knew that there were differences in the way that she and Cynthia managed people and processes, but she always felt that their styles complimented one another. Gail also felt that some of the statements in the file seemed to contradict the information provided by the hiring committee regarding the two candidates' experience levels and interview scores. The hiring committee seemed to have viewed her favorably.

When the HR counselor completed his investigation, he sent the report to Gail indicating that the hiring authority had acted within her rights and followed college policy. At the conclusion of the report, the counselor stated, "Please contact me if you have any further questions." Wondering why she had not been interviewed in the process of the investigation, Gail responded with a 16-page email of specific questions based on information from the documents in the hiring file. A series of communications went back and forth with various personnel in the chain of command who address hiring and grievance processes at the college.

As a trained mediator and someone who believes in the power of the conflict resolution process, Gail was deeply disappointed and indignant at the lack of response to her questions. Because of her strong connections to students and staff across campus, there were great interest and concern in the outcome of this hiring process and the resulting review. Gail was at a loss for where to go next. The position had been filled; that would not change. She simply wanted recognition from the college that treatment of staff did not always follow stated values. She wanted to affect change for others in the future. Gail had an idea. She would try making the college community aware of the events of this failed search and hope that open communication could eventually lead to honest review of current practices and positive changes in organizational procedure and culture.

## THE PUBLIC FORUM—ONE LAST CAMPUS EVENT

The events calendar on the college's website showed the following information.

---

"Failed Search?" presentation by Gail Newsome
Wednesday, November 28, 7:00 P.M. Student Union Stateroom
Sponsored by: The College Coalition for Peace and Justice and the Department of Communication

In April, Gail Newsome submitted her application for the Student Union's vacant student programs manager position. Her supervisors had called Newsome a "programming powerhouse" and a "campus resource for events" who "brought a fresh perspective of event management, activity promotion, and just a general enthusiastic attitude to the Student Union and the college." Despite these positive performance reviews, five years of success as the student activities coordinator, and the recommendation of the members of the hiring committee, her application for the Student Union's student programs manager job was eliminated from consideration during the final phase of the hiring process. What happened? During this presentation, Newsome will take you on a bizarre, unpredictable, and sometimes hilarious ride through a hiring process that resulted in a failed search. Admission is free.

---

Prior to this announcement, students, administrative staff, and faculty all had ethical choices to make regarding the potential consequences of such an event on the college's campus and its stakeholders. When sponsorship was requested, several student groups jumped on board. When the event request was made to the activities office, one staff member had to consider whether she would suffer any negative response for moving the activity forward and, if so, whether that was more important than giving voice to a friend who was hurting and an issue that seemed to highlight an organizational problem. Administration had to decide whether it would impact the campus climate more favorably to allow or prevent this open forum and how the event might influence the ongoing issues with Newsome's grievance. Faculty in Gail's home department knew to varying degrees about her struggles over the past six months. When asked to sponsor this public campus event, all faculty members expressed a desire to support Gail; however, it wasn't obvious to everyone what to do. The request came through Gail's faculty adviser in an email to the rest of the faculty in the department. The decision was then made through a series of email exchanges. A junior faculty member responded first:

"I feel for Gail in this situation and am personally very disturbed by the choices and motivations that the situation suggests are present within the college system. I applaud Gail for wanting to continue the conversation and am amazed at her ability to present her thoughts professionally. I'm not sure I fully understand Gail's strategy with this event but believe her to be approaching a lack of response to her questions in a creative way in order to raise awareness of such situations and force some response. I, too, would like to show Gail support.

   With that said, I am awaiting response from our senior faculty on having the department named as a sponsor. I have no idea if that choice can be seen as a show of support for open communication within the organization or will instead be seen as taking sides and thus have political implications for the department with the dean or with the college overall. I am aware of politics in organizations but don't feel that I have adequate knowledge or experience in this organization to know what to do."

## THE EVENT

The back of the room was lined with tables, each displaying many of the events and programs Gail had coordinated at the college. It was impressive. The room was set up to accommodate about 100 people. As the room began to fill with students, faculty, and staff, it became apparent that more chairs were needed. Before Gail spoke more than 200 were in attendance.

Gail's desire to see positive change guided her approach to planning and facilitating an evening where her greatest disappointment was outlined for anyone who chose to come. She desperately wanted to understand what had happened to her and thought that if she outlined what she knew of the events, others might provide insight. She began with gratitude toward the many people she had worked alongside and the college whose mission had been a driving force for her during the last five years. She outlined several conflict management principles and set a positive tone for the evening.

She presented the Human Resources Department's mission statement, outlined the job description for the student programs manager, the timeline for the two searches, and the reasons given for removing her from the offer list in the first search and from consideration in the second search, and then questioned those statements based on comments in the hiring file and in her personal performance appraisals. At times some in the audience laughed at the decision makers or booed the actions taken toward Gail. When she opened for others to comment at the end, some relayed other circumstances in which they felt the college's treatment of staff was not in line with Human Resources' mission statement and questioned what else could be done. Many showed great support for Gail and all she had done at the college.

In closing Gail noted that the interaction they were having sounded a lot like "break-up talk." She said, "I hope we both find something better. As for me, I have a new exciting job that taps into my other great passion in life." She then reemphasized that "we came together tonight because we care about the college and higher education. We want to prevent this stuff from happening in the future. Not in spite of this but because of this I will be an even better advocate for Barkersville College."

## EPILOGUE

Even after all of this, Gail Newsome received no more explanation for the failed search. Gail thought there might be one more avenue to explore with college personnel that could illuminate what had happened. She met for three hours with the director of human resources. When asked what resolution she was looking for, Gail stated that she wanted people held accountable by the college for their actions, particularly if any laws were violated. The director agreed to have the hiring process reviewed and the HR counselor's review assessed. Following review, the director's response addressed only the specific questions Gail had raised in an earlier memo to the HR counselor and then concluded generally that the hiring authority showed no impropriety, no inconsistency, and no improper motivation in her decision making.

Having lost out on her dream job and feeling she had failed in all her attempts to discover what had happened, Gail was left with only questions: How should professional development work among college staff? Had there been any attempt at succession planning in her circumstance? How are employees made aware of performance areas that need development? When supervisors give performance appraisals, are the evaluations honest and employees simply disregard anything that might be considered negative; or is the appraisal more positive than deserved because it is easier to deliver, leaving the employee with unwarranted hope? Are the values professed by an organization and the organizational values evidenced in everyday activity ever the same? When they don't run parallel, how can you voice this so that it can be heard? If the recommendations of a hiring committee are not binding or are easily disregarded, why do organizations have them?

## CHAPTER 30

# An Officer First and a Nurse Second

## Colleen Arendt

Lieutenant Megan Davis walked out of the major's office not sure what to do next. "I can't believe Captain Walker tried to blame me for what happened last night. He broke the rules when he left the hospital in the middle of his shift; he's the incompetent one. He's the one that doesn't belong anywhere near an ER; I don't care if he does outrank me." Megan's face was red with anger, and her heart was still pounding as she walked right out of the major's office, out of the army hospital, and to her parked car. Suddenly the straightforward rank system and the whole army seemed much more bureaucratic and complicated than it ever had in her previous two years as a military nurse and certainly much more strategic and contradictory than her nursing classes had led her to believe.

After earning a nursing degree in college, where she had participated in ROTC, or Reserve Officer Training Corps, Lieutenant Davis was now an active duty military nurse, living and working at Fort Alpha, an army post in the western United States. Megan has been working in the ER since arriving at Fort Alpha two years ago.

As a first lieutenant with two years' experience in the ER, Megan is often the charge nurse, which means she is in charge of the other nurses. So far her experiences as a military nurse have been challenging and exciting, especially when working the night shift. She loves being in the military, too. Megan loves the soldiering aspect of her job; she loves doing field exercises and is proud of her sharpshooting ability. Growing up Megan thrived on structure, and so it was no surprise to anyone in her family that she loves the strict military hierarchy. For Megan, the rules are numerous but easy to follow: You listen to people who outrank you; you stay in the chain of command. However, Megan's ability to "respect the rank" has been tested the past few weeks after a new staff nurse joined the floor. Joe Walker

---

*This case has been developed based on real organization(s) and real organizational experiences. Names, facts, and situations have been changed to protect the privacy of individuals and organizations.

is a captain, which means he is one rank higher than Megan. Though they both work as staff nurses, as a captain, he should have been left in charge over Megan. However, because Joe had zero experience working in the volatile and unpredictable ER, whenever Megan and Joe worked together, Megan was always in charge. However, there were times when Megan was not working when Joe was put in charge. This worried Megan enough to keep her up at night.

Megan often complained about Joe to her husband, Chad, who is also in the military, saying, "Well, Captain Walker's working again today. When my shift ended this morning, I told him like I always do, 'If there is a code, do not handle it yourself. Call in other nurses from other floors.' I'm not kidding, Chad. This guy is totally incompetent and has absolutely no sense of urgency. I would not wish my worst enemy to be in his care."

Megan is upset that someone so inexperienced could be placed in the ER, but she knows Joe got the position because of his rank. Still, this fact of military life does not sit well with her sense of duty to her patients. However, Megan has to tread lightly when disagreeing with Joe because he outranks her. The relationship between Megan and Joe had grown tenuous throughout the last few weeks, with disagreements occurring more and more frequently.

## A BREACH OF PROTOCOL

During their shift last night, the situation between Megan and Joe finally had come to a head. Last night, as usual, he had been working rather slowly and not getting a lot of work done. As Megan later told her husband, "You know, Captain Walker was just being his usual useless self." Last night, though, Joe claimed that he was sick. Megan believed that he was ill, but she was upset over his behavior. He was sitting around at desks and at the nurses' stations with his head down, trying to gain sympathy, which was not becoming an officer. He was so useless that finally Megan walked up to him and said, "You know, maybe you should just go home" and then continued walking.

And with that, Captain Walker walked out of the hospital in the middle of his shift. He just left! He stood up, got his things, and walked out of the hospital. Joe was not dismissed properly by the doctors, per protocol; he just left. Absolutely no one knew he walked out of the hospital, including Megan, who had assumed he would have followed the chain of command and gone through the proper channels, which include notifying everyone that you are leaving and passing your patients to another nurse. People were looking all over the hospital for him and paged him repeatedly on the loudspeaker. They were understaffed that night as it was, and no one knew where the missing ER nurse went! Megan told her husband, "Thank God someone else had the narcotics key for once. If he would have left without handing it over, we would not have had any access to the drugs for patients! I'd say 'thank God' we didn't have to call a code that night, but he's useless during codes anyway."

Eventually people figured out that Joe must have gone home. Megan was angry, but she left work that morning confident that someone would take steps to reprimand Captain Walker and relocate him to another department in the hospital. Megan was sure she would return for another shift that night and learn that Joe was gone.

Megan said to her husband later, "I still can't believe he just walked out of the hospital! I thought for sure he would be kicked out of the ER."

## "WHAT? YOU'RE YELLING AT ME?"

However, that morning Megan got a phone call telling her to come to the hospital. That meant Megan had to put back on her uniform and head to the hospital, even though she had just returned from working a 12-hour night shift.

She was called into a meeting with Captain Walker and the head nurse, a major. Megan was caught offguard when the captain blamed her for dismissing him. Megan was furious.

"I did not dismiss you! How could I do that? You outrank me!" Megan challenged.

"Well, you are always in charge whenever we work together," Joe countered.

"Yes, I have more experience, but you are a captain, and I'm a lieutenant. You outrank me!"

"Lieutenant Davis told me to go home." Captain Walker insisted to the head nurse.

"Yes," Megan interjected, "but even if I was the captain and you were the lieutenant, you would have to get dismissed by someone ranked much higher than a captain nurse! Everyone knows the protocol. You go to sick hall and get looked at by a doctor. Everyone knows that!" Megan stopped herself from saying more and was afraid she had already said too much. For once Megan was not sure how to handle herself. Should she be a lieutenant and keep her mouth shut and accept part of the blame for a captain's confusion? Could she speak out as the more experienced ER nurse? Of course, if Megan had her choice she would stand up for her patients and say what was really on her mind—that Captain Walker did not belong in the ER—that every night he works patients' lives are at risk—that she has nightmares about him working in the ER. If Megan actually said all of those things, the major might interpret Megan's statements as questioning his judgment in placing Joe in the ER, or he might yell and punish Megan for speaking out against a ranking officer. Conflicted, Megan decided to continue speaking, this time focusing on the captain's breach of protocol.

"Sir, if I may. Even if Captain Walker thought I had dismissed him, he still left the ER without informing anyone he was leaving. He did not brief anyone on the status of his patients, and he did not ensure that anyone would be looking after them. He should have known better as a nurse. As an officer, he should not have been moping around the hospital, slouching over the nurses' station with his head down. And as an officer, he should have known the proper protocol for calling in sick. I have a hard time believing Captain Walker forgot he outranks me last night."

After arguing back and forth for a few more minutes, Megan was dismissed from the major's office while Captain Walker remained in the room. Megan was furious that she was being yelled at by someone who was such an incompetent ER nurse. Megan wished she had not been blindsided so she could have figured out ahead of time what would have been appropriate to say and in front of whom. Had she just said too much? There was certainly more that Megan wanted to say. She wanted to tell everyone how Captain Walker was not only a bad ER nurse but also a poor excuse for an officer. Megan wished she could have told everyone how he had frozen when a convulsing child had been brought into the ER. Instead of rushing in to help her, Joe had not wanted to handle the situation. Megan had pushed him to the side as she had run to the child's side.

Later, while holding back rage and trying to remember the captain outranked her, Megan approached Joe and said, "Listen. Number one: You are a captain. Number two: You are a nurse. What happened earlier can never happen again. You cannot wear your emotions on your sleeve!" Megan thought that reminding him that he was an officer in the United States military would knock some sense into him. Even if he did not like the situation, as an officer, he should have overcome his emotions and gotten the job done.

## THE "REAL DEAL ARMY"

Megan was now driving back home to sleep for a few hours before her night shift started at 7 P.M. She knew she needed her sleep, but she was too riled up. She contemplated calling one of her old ROTC friends she had visited with a few months ago.

Earlier that fall there had been an ROTC reunion at her university. Dozens of ROTC nurses came to the reunion, many of whom were still in the military. Other nurses were much older and had retired from the military after 20 or 30 years of service. At the time Megan thought she could see herself as a "lifer," or someone who spends an entire career in the military. Now, after what just happened, she suddenly understood why some of the men and women left after their mandatory four years ended.

As Megan drove home from the hospital for the second time that morning, she remembered that it was great to hear the older nurses talk about life in the military before they were part of the "real deal army," as some of them called it. Megan remembered Samantha, who had been in the military for two and a half years before being taught how to fire a weapon. Megan could not imagine being in the military without a weapon—especially because she used to hang her old firing targets all over her dorm room.

Like Samantha, some of those men and women at the reunion remembered a time when they wore white uniforms to work instead of camouflage and a time when they had rank, but they still felt like an auxiliary part of the military. After they were taught how to be a soldier and starting dressing like the rest of the military, they began ascending to the highest ranks and began taking command of more than just other nurses. It was as if being a soldier gave these officers the credibility to take command and gave them a place in the "real deal army." Megan was glad that she was a military nurse at this point in history because the soldiering part of her job was just as exciting as her nursing role. But Megan wondered as she drove home if this new power and credibility for military nurses had come at a price to their patients.

## "AN OFFICER FIRST AND A NURSE SECOND"

Megan never realized that she really plays two roles. She always says, "I'm an officer first and a nurse second," but it never occurred to her that this was a dual role that could make navigating the military difficult and the rules sometimes contradictory. After all, unlike Samantha and the other older nurses, Megan has never said, "I'm a nurse first and an officer second." Today everyone says, "We're officers first, nurses second." Megan never before thought to question how her duty to the military might contradict her duty to her patients. Megan remembered a conversation at a pub the Friday night of that reunion weekend. Everyone was sharing "war stories" from working in the military hospitals, both in the United States and abroad, but Megan had only positive things to throw into the conversation.

"C'mon, Megan, you mean to tell me it's been nothing but roses for you?" asked Teresa, who had graduated with Megan.

"Yeah, I love it," Megan answered. "I'm thinking I want to sign on for four more."

Teresa looked like she didn't believe Megan, and Megan wondered what stories Teresa had to share.

"Well, it wasn't all bad for me either," said Bert, an older nurse who retired from the army. "I actually miss being a nurse in the military. Being a male nurse isn't as manly when you aren't dressed in camo and carrying a gun," Bert said, laughing. "Plus, the doctors see you as more than just the people who get Cokes for patients. They asked for my opinion so much more than doctors do in the civilian world. I mean, we weren't buddy-buddy, but the power difference was so much less. We were officer-officer, not doctor-nurse. I miss that."

"Right. I was surprised at how tricky the rank thing is," Teresa said, looking at Megan. "They didn't tell us that in our nursing classes! And I remember a few weeks ago, a nurse far outranked a doctor, but the doctor needed to correct the nurse. But the same saying goes for doctors, too: You're an officer first and a doctor second. So you could just see this doctor catch himself and squirm as he tried to think of the most appropriate way to say, 'Yes, ma'am, but—.' Seeing a doctor squirm like that was priceless—I imagine you don't see that in the civie world, Bert."

"No, I suppose we don't." Bert smiled.

Samantha interrupted. "Yes, but Teresa, that is so rare. To have a nurse outrank a doctor is rare. First of all, the higher-ranking nurses are administrators, they aren't even doing patient care anymore, and doctors almost always come in one or two ranks higher—they have to in order to be paid appropriately. No, I'm the total opposite. I thought the doctor thing was so hard."

"Really? Why's that?" Megan asked.

Samantha put down her drink and said, "Well, I know we are supposed to be the patient advocate, and sometimes we nurses are so strong that we're the perfect people to stand up for our patients—especially as we grow in rank. But it totally depends on the individuals working together. I mean, I worked for some absolute jerks. It'd be hard enough in the civilian world to speak up, I mean, no one wants to get chewed out, but when the doctors outrank you, too? It's like having not one, but *two* giant reasons to keep your mouth shut. For a civilian nurse, you may say something and face the repercussions later, but for me it was like, 'Samantha, don't even *think* about saying it.'"

Megan remembered that no one said something for a few moments after Samantha finished. Some agreed and nodded their heads. Others, Megan could tell, did not have that experience but were imagining how tough that would have been to negotiate. Finally Tim, another "lifer," broke the silence, laughing:

"And then there were the patients."

"Oh, God. The poor patients!" Lisa, Bert's wife and a Navy nurse, said. "Even in the hospital those poor guys can't catch their breath!"

"We had the enlisted guys getting trays for the sicker patients, making beds, and mopping floors. And they did it!" Bert reminisced, laughing.

"Well, their rank followed them everywhere just like ours did. We just made it work to our advantage," Tim said.

"Yeah, but don't tell me that as a nurse, you didn't hate to ask—not that we technically 'asked' them. I hated ordering the patients around, but we are always so understaffed. Plus, it's so easy because they can't complain, poor guys," Bert said.

"Except if they were generals," Lisa interjected. "They can complain all they want, but you better hope they don't. Samantha, tell them that story you told me this morning."

"Oh, right! So we had this general, and he got the best, most preferential treatment for the entire time he was there—which was a few months! He eventually passed away. The problem was we didn't know what to do with him. We were so afraid of getting in trouble that we just left him in the room for almost the entire day. No one knew how to deal with a general passing away, and no one was willing to stick their neck out- figuring out the problem," Samantha recalled.

"So it's true what they say—rank stays with you forever!" Tim held his pint in the air and laughed.

"Sometimes I think the patients' commanders took that a little too literally," Lisa chimed in, rolling her eyes as people nodded in agreement.

"We had this patient, poor guy, he was really sick, I mean *deathly* ill, and in storms his commander. And he tells us," Lisa said in her best deep, tough guy voice, 'I want a trapeze put on his bed because he needs to keep his fitness up and so he'll be doing chin-ups.' And the other nurses and I just looked at each other and said to ourselves: 'I don't think so. This guy barely has a blood pressure.' So here we are trying to save this guy's hands, and his commander wants him doing chin-ups! I mean, give me a break."

"Yeah, give me a break and get the hell out of my hospital!" Bert said.

"Ha, like we could ever say that," Lisa said.

"Wait," Megan asked, "I thought the rule was that we get the final say because we're the ones with the expertise. I mean, that's the rule, right?"

"Seriously, Megan?" Samantha asked, "haven't you learned yet that for military nurses there are the rules, and then there are the ways things actually happen? There are the rules for being an officer and rules for being a nurse. Just wait until you have to choose and you feel like you are being split in half."

Pulling into the driveway of her Fort Alpha home that morning, Megan realized she was just learning this lesson. Everyone that day at the reunion had some story; these past few stressful weeks must be Megan's. She realized as she opened her front door that Samantha's metaphor was perfect; for the first time, Megan is split in half. Still she does not want to end up bitter and burned out like Samantha. Megan loves the military and until now has never had a conflict between being a great nurse (and outspoken patient advocate) and being a fine military officer. She would find out later how the situation with Joe was resolved, and she hoped her nurse voice was louder than her pensive, fearful lieutenant voice had been. Soon Lieutenant Megan Davis would see if speaking out didn't come at too high a price.

CHAPTER 31

# Finding the Right Associate

## Leslie Reynard

*The firm of Borbowe, Ralsap and Malkbank is an equal opportunity employer. Borbowe, Ralsap and Malkbank does not discriminate on the basis of race, religion, color, gender, sexual preference, age, height, weight, national origin, or disability.*

### THEY'RE *ALWAYS* HIRING AT BORBOWE, RALSAP AND MALKBANK

Since its founding in the early 1960s, the law firm of Borbowe, Ralsap and Malk-bank* had achieved much success even as it developed a reputation for somewhat ruthless effectiveness. The firm had grown from a six-member practice specializing in incorporation strategies and tax problems for fairly dull midwestern clients to a glamorous global firm with over 200 attorneys practicing in 22 major cities and eight countries. By 2008, the Borbowe firm represented clients throughout the United States and in major cities on four continents.

But despite the firm's success and continuous growth, the turnover among the lowest tier of junior associates in the past decade was becoming apparent and slightly embarrassing. This turnover was even more problematic given that demographic analysis revealed that only about 60% of new hires since 1999 had remained at the firm two years or longer. Furthermore, of this 40% attrition, fully three-quarters of those leaving were female associates. In addition to the costs of constantly searching for and training new lawyers, some in the firm began to fear that these statistics would translate into problems attracting new associate attorneys, not to mention problems with the EEOC.

While some of the women resigning said in their exit interviews that "family matters" were the primary reason for their resignations, the majority of those who

---

*This case has been developed based on real organization(s) and real organizational experiences. Names, facts, and situations have been changed to protect the privacy of individuals and organizations.

even consented to exit interviews were noncommittal, even evasive, about their reasons for leaving. Quite a few were clearly angry but were not willing to discuss it. Some associate attorneys who stayed categorized them as "the PMSers."

Thus, the firm was required to remain in a constant "search mode," running advertising, developing search strategies, conducting interviews, and facilitating training and assimilation of a steady stream of new hires for its junior associate pool. On the bright side, third-year students at area law schools were able to resolve their anxiety about finding a job after graduation because word had gotten around that "They're *always* hiring at Borbowe, Ralsap and Malkbank."

## THE SEARCH COMMITTEE'S PROJECT AND PROCESS

The associate-recruiting procedure had actually become institutionalized into an efficient and cost-effective operation:

Templates were developed by which it was necessary to fill in only three or four blanks to create a "help wanted" ad, area newspapers had granted nice discounts for classified advertising because of the high number of column-inches the firm purchased each quarter, and there were three rotating search committees in place at all times to review the résumés as they came in and to make recruiting visits to nearby law schools.

One of these search committees was made up of three of the firm's female attorneys: Clotilde Philibert (a senior associate who had transferred in from the California office several years earlier and who had been with the firm for total of 12 years), Riva Enyo (a Cypriot woman, also a senior associate, who was an outstanding international law student, wooed into the firm's global law section nearly 20 years before), and Celia Galen (a attorney in her 40s who had been, just out of high school, one of the Borbowe firm's youngest legal secretaries. Celia had then been a paralegal for 18 years as she completed college and law school, taking one or two courses every semester. Earning one of the top scores on the state bar exam two years before, she had been hired into the firm's junior associate ranks).

## CELIA GALEN

When Celia began working for the Borbowe firm, she was the teenage secretary to both the senior partner, Mr. Borbowe, and to the raw young associate he was mentoring, Almer Clay.

Mr. Borbowe found Celia's secretarial work to be expertly done but was even more impressed with her ability to notice the small details in the various documents, to find discrepancies in contracts and briefs, and to synthesize complex cases into a coherent whole. Soon Celia was more Mr. Borbowe's assistant than his secretary.

As pleased as he was with Celia's competence, Borbowe was equally disappointed with Almer Clay's work. Borbowe felt it did not reflect the strong grades that appeared on Almer's transcripts, nor did Almer's character-in-action mirror the glowing references contained in the letters of recommendation he had presented at his interview.

Mr. Borbowe's wife had once been his secretary—as was the case with several of the partners and senior associates of the firm—so Borbowe was certainly no prude, but he'd observed with distaste how grossly familiar and flirtatious Clay was with many of the prettier secretaries. The firm's grapevine was always vibrating with stories about Almer Clay and a broad spectrum of secretaries and receptionists.

Ultimately Borbowe was forced to have a stern talk with Clay about both the poor quality of his work and his randy behavior when Clay was caught in flagrante delicto on the conference room table with a new receptionist on her third day of work.

The receptionist had been terminated, and Celia was charged with the task of being "first reader" in helping Almer research his cases and drafting his legal pleadings. She enthusiastically performed these tasks, finding them interesting and challenging. The work stimulated her to the point that she began taking college courses after work to augment her abilities. By the time Celia accumulated enough hours to be classified a college senior, she had been given the title "paralegal" and assigned to work solely with Mr. Borbowe.

From the day Celia was ordered to "help" him, Almer Clay despised and resented Celia Galen. By the time she was made a paralegal and given a fellowship to finish college and attend law school through the firm's recommendation, Clay's resentment had evolved into a simmering hostility demonstrated in such actions as his pointedly ignoring her whenever a group of employees was together or rolling his eyes at a buddy whenever she made a comment having to do with a case or a client. Celia did her best to tune Almer out.

Both Almer and Celia continued to do well in the Borbowe firm. In the 12 years it took Celia to earn her legal credentials part-time while earning her living as a staff person full-time, Almer Clay was also moving up through the ranks. The same year Celia became an attorney with the firm, Almer became a senior associate and managing partner.

## A Working Lunch

"Hi, everyone," Celia said as she took her place at the round four-top in the middle of Rambert's, a local sports bar that served a great steak sandwich and the strong, sweet drinks preferred by one of the search committee members. "I have the 10 résumés you wanted to take another look at, and we should be able to narrow it down to our top three by the end of lunch."

The committee had begun meeting at Rambert's rather than in the conference room at the office because it made the ongoing résumé review seem more like a social event and less like boring work.

"Now you *know* I prefer to work with men," Clotilde said. "And don't give me that feminist crap, Riva. Women are just bitchy. I always get along better with guys."

Riva rolled her eyes and scowled darkly but kept chewing her tuna melt. She had heard all of this before, and each time she had made it clear that she strongly disagreed. For all the good that did.

"OK, OK, let's move on," Celia diverted attention back to the project at hand. "I put mostly males' vitas in the stack. But I still say that Lorena—that woman you both saw argue the Montague case in court last week—is one of our best bets. She's hard-working—she told me she usually does the work no one else wants to do—*and* she's likely to stay more than two years. When she called yesterday, she was emphatic she's extremely interested in us because of our growing caseload in admiralty law."

"Well. Remember what Almer's friend at the Wright office told him." Clotilde placed her steak sandwich down, careful not to get any of her coleslaw on it. "He told Almer she's very hard to work with. Almer specifically told me when he looked these over he didn't think *that* one would fit in here."

"Did he say *why* Lorena's supposed to be so hard to work with? Were there any specifics, other than she's a smart female who doesn't wear eye make-up?" Riva queried. "Almer's made it quite clear he doesn't find redeeming qualities in women over 40—especially women lawyers! Any woman who won't fall for his line or bring him coffee is 'hard to work with.'"

"Believe me, I know," Celia answered. "And I wouldn't be surprised if that's the basis of his buddy's attitude, too. But what can you do?"

She kept shuffling through her papers so the others wouldn't see the hot color she felt flowing into her cheeks. This attitude of many of the associate partners was getting old—the rule and not the exception—and not just a little disturbing.

"Look at these 30-somethings blackballing a 40-something because 'she wouldn't be a good fit'—even though he has never laid eyes on her or taken a look at her work!" Celia stopped there, realizing she was not making any ground in getting her favorite candidate onto the short list. She dipped her napkin into her water glass and rubbed it on the cover of Lorena's file, trying to remove some greasy thumbprints.

"Anyway. I told you I work better with men, and it looks like you've found some!" Clotilde pulled the cherry and the orange pulp from her drink's garnish with her teeth as she tapped the stack of résumés with her forefinger. "Let's not waste any more time talking about this Lorena person. Almer said they want to see our short list of three at the partners' meeting in the morning, and some good guys have applied."

## The Partners Check Out the Short List

"OK, girls. Let's take a little looky at what you've brought us." Almer reached for the three manila files.

The polished mahogany conference room table was really too large for a meeting of seven people—the three search committee members and the four partners who would determine which of the top three candidates would receive the job offer. But it was the custom that all "official" firm business was carried out in this room, with its heavy maroon draperies, walnut parquet floor, its 24 high-backed chairs upholstered in russet leather, and its walls hung with gilt-framed portraits of the men who had achieved senior partner status since the firm's founding.

"I've told you before, Almer, I haven't been a girl since I was 12, and I'd appreciate it if you didn't refer to me as one." Riva's Mediterranean accent became more pronounced and her voice louder whenever she became angry—which was fairly often in discussions with her fellow senior associates.

Almer and the other men laughed.

"You'd better watch out, Clay, we'll set the Turk on you, and then you'll be sorry!"

"Yeah, watch your mouth, you lout!"

Riva just shook her head and muttered something under her breath in her native tongue while Clotilde thinned her lips tightly together and shook her head slightly, making eye contact with Riva in a warning way. Celia simply acted as if she had not been witness to the exchange and continued to pass around copies of the three résumés that the committee had settled on. Three men.

"Hmmmm. This guy, Jenks, has a lot of litigation experience, both as a plaintiff's attorney and also as a prosecutor. Pretty odd, but a good broad base."

Mitch Malkbank, the most senior partner still active in the firm's business, waved the résumé in the direction of the other men.

"Yeah, but look here. It says his last actual employment was six years ago. What's up with that? And his first employment shows up being in the late 60s—is this guy a retired hippie or what?" he objected.

Celia looked at her notes. "Well, yes...he *is* a retired California civil rights attorney. But he wants to move back here from the West Coast. He said specifically that he wants to deepen his focus and get more hands-on experience in global human rights."

Celia was aware that the partners' comments were just skirting the issue of the man's age and political orientation, but none of these objections was clear enough or overt enough to respond to without seeming too controlling or what the guys sneeringly referred to as *politically correct.*

"Moving on." Almer Clay looked again at the first résumé. "Aban Abd Al'alim? *How* do you say it!? What kind of name *is* that anyway!?"

"It's Egyptian." Celia felt again the familiar anger and frustration at trying to get something accomplished in this group and struggled to keep her feelings to herself.

"Al is from Egypt, but he's been here for nearly 20 years. He was one of my administrative law professors, and he's great. He's very well known for his work in global IPOs and has quite a few international publications. He has really a strong record. He's a good friend of mine—actually, I encouraged him to apply here because I thought it would be doing everyone a favor." At that point Celia began to rethink this.

"What is he—a Mohammedan? Ha ha." Ferd Broley, one of Almer Clay's most reliable henchmen, snickered.

"No, I've met him, and I think he's a Hindu," laughed Almer. "But we're not supposed to talk about that. Let's just say it's about the dress code: no turbans in the court room!" He nearly choked himself trying not to laugh too hard at their joke.

In this vein, the decision makers shared a few off-hand comments, jokes, and asides with each other as they reviewed the three résumés and recommendation letters.

"How old is this Abn-Allah guy anyway? It looks to me like he is too old."

"What!" Celia finally looked up from her paper organizing at this last remark. "That's enough! Just stop the comments. He's younger than I am!"

She looked directly at each partner as she added, "And besides, I really don't think it's a good idea to be so obviously making your hiring decisions on the basis of how old the people are. Or where they're from! Or what kind of religion they believe in. You of all people should know that's not only wrong—it's also illegal!" she exclaimed.

"Oops," Celia thought to herself and immediately checked her emotional response as all eyes turned to her, some with surprise and some with appraisal, doing math behind their eyelids and figuring her age.

"Wow. She's older than I thought!" she could actually *hear* some of the men thinking from the expressions on their faces and what they *didn't* say.

"We don't need that EEOC nonsense in the board room," Celia could see on the faces of several others.

"Well, then....Ok..." Almer Clay peered more closely at Al's dossier. "Then what is his *alien* status? His residency status, I mean—he's not an American, right? Does he have a green card, or is he just here on a visa? Is he a citizen?"

"I believe he's a permanent resident. And his wife Jill is American. From Des Moines," Celia responded.

"*That* could be a problem." Almer Clay put the dossier aside. "We sure don't need any problems with the INS, especially in this day and age. It would be better if he's a citizen. Someone find out and get back to me."

Almer picked up the third file. "Oh, yeah. I think we'd better take a good look at this last one. Jason Mead. I know his mom, Lilly. And his father."

## The Aftermath (the Annual Performance Review)

In the two decades Celia had been with the Borbowe firm, she had seen many things change, but she had seen other things stay very much the same. As the firm grew, there was less socializing with all of the people you worked with and fewer firm picnics and seasonal parties.

Now smaller groups of three and four people might spend time together having lunch or talking at the firm's few "social" functions. There once was a ladies bowling team with attorneys and secretaries. Celia had been with the firm so long that she knew everyone who worked there by name. But her workload at home, at school during the years of study, and at the office in each of her job descriptions left her very little time or energy to develop deeper bonds with anyone at Borbowe. Even so, she had felt accepted and fairly well-liked until she had finished law school and become an attorney with the firm.

When she was in her late 20s and 30s, the men she worked with were very nice and quite friendly to her. Several of the lawyers asked her out to dinner or complimented her work (and, often, her hair or her dress). While the young lawyers, all men in the earlier years of her employment, could frequently be heard making rude, sexually explicit remarks about some of the women who worked there, most seemed respectful of Celia and were friendly, some even flirtatious, married or not. Mr. Borbowe's admiration and respect probably helped in this regard. But as Celia progressed through her schooling, she felt things changing. Of course, it was logical that the flirtatiousness would be directed toward the younger women and less and less toward Celia. That was fine.

"Isn't that what women want—to be taken seriously in their work?" was Celia's attitude.

But where Celia expected the other attorneys to appreciate her hard work and accomplishment as an attorney and act accordingly, instead she increasingly felt almost anger toward her from the men her age who had trod the same path. It certainly felt different—but not better!—to be a 40-something attorney than it had to be a 20-something paralegal!

At first Celia thought she was being paranoid, but one or two of the other women attorneys in the firm made comments that let Celia know they felt the same way. Celia was among those who became aware that certain types of less desirable assignments (drudgery, really, of the sort she had done as a paralegal) and more demanding clients (who seemed to think she *was* a paralegal) were generally given to the most experienced women associates. This sort of work was occasionally given to the two semisenile senior partners, but generally the more interesting, challenging work and the more important, high-status clients were awarded to the younger male associates.

After Celia's comments about the legality of their hiring discussions in the partners' meeting, she thought she was getting a real understanding of the "hostile work environment" she had studied about as an abstract concept in law school. Celia had begun keeping a journal when she was a paralegal and could actually pinpoint in her entries when the increased scrutiny and heightened criticism of her work began. After that search committee meeting Ferd had shared with Celia what he considered excellent advice:

"Celia. Hon. You just need to learn how to go along to get along, like the other girls do."

## The Performance Review

In all of her annual reviews at the firm from the first year of her employment, Celia had been given highest ratings in virtually every area covered. She'd never earned less than an "Outstanding" in any category and received the highest rating, "Excellent," in over 91% of all items reviewed since year one.

In the annual review that took place three weeks after the recruiting conference, Almer Clay advised Celia with serious and sorrowful eyes that, "We have some concerns about your work." He then began detailing in a general way a number of areas in which her performance appeared to have declined.

"Can you give me some specifics or show me some examples of errors I've made or deadlines I've missed?" Celia asked. "I'm so surprised to hear this. But I certainly can and will get back on track."

"It's more your attitude," Clay responded. "You seem kind of bitchy lately. And you're just not taking on as much committee work and fundraising and the other community things we do around here."

He looked up at the ceiling as if searching for one of the pencils he was always flipping up there. "You seem standoffish, for example, and don't mix in enough. You're kind of one of those people who stands around the water cooler and complains."

"Almer, we don't have a water cooler. You have that fizzy water in the green glass bottles delivered once a week, and I don't even drink that." Celia felt acid reflux in her gut even though she hadn't had lunch yet. "And I never complain to my colleagues. Especially since, as you've observed, I *don't* do a lot of socializing here at the office. I just do my work."

She looked at the sheet of paper with her review comments on it; there were simply hashmarks in the boxes for "Satisfactory," "Fair," and "Needs Improvement" without any text in the areas provided for reasons and examples. Her usual "Excellent" areas were empty boxes.

"I would like a written copy of your report and your support for these low marks, and I'd also like a chance to respond to it in writing. I think my work deserves a rating of 'Excellent' again this year or at least a 'Very Good.'" Celia was well aware of the posted procedures for performance reviews, although it was standard practice in the firm to forgo those unless a paper trail was needed...in cases like this.

"I think, based on the criteria you're *supposed* to be using for these evaluations, that my work is far more than 'Satisfactory,' and it is certainly not just 'Fair.'" Celia modulated her voice as she tried not to scream at him or, worse, cry.

"OK. Will do. I guess that's it then."

Almer picked up his phone and dialed his wife. He turned his chair to the window and leaned back as Celia first stood up to say something else but turned and left the room when she saw she was being dismissed. "So...what's for dinner tonight, Sugar-Tits?" Almer asked his wife.

## TO FILE OR NOT TO FILE...AN EEOC COMPLAINT

Celia was not surprised that, after eight weeks, the documents she'd requested were not provided to her. She was somewhat surprised, though, to see that her work assignments were becoming even more routine, detail-oriented, mundane, extremely time-consuming, and demanding than they had been before her performance review. Her workload degenerated in interest quotient and challenge until it was virtually identical to the workload she had carried when she was simply a paralegal without a law degree. And without $47,000 in student loan repayments.

Almer Clay had also begun sending out emails to the entire population of the firm—attorneys, secretaries, paralegals, even the receptionists and the mail boy—that critiqued Celia by name and referred in a derogatory way to certain behaviors and mind-sets that Celia thought were specifically about her.

"Or," she wondered, "am I too thin-skinned? Am I just getting paranoid in my old age?"

When she asked Almer Clay about the documentation she'd requested and asked that he cease and desist making her the focus of the emails he had been sending, he responded, "As managing partner, I am your mentor, and this is what I need to do to help you fit in here."

"I've been fitting in here at least as long as you have, Almer," Celia retorted. "You're being very demeaning to me. And I think it's deliberate. None of the male associates or the two younger women are being given these sorts of low-level work assignments, this heavy a workload, or being criticized publicly."

"You're way too sensitive, Celia," Almer replied in a patronizing tone. "Maybe even paranoid! Just do your work and quit your bitching. You're being treated no differently than anyone else."

At home that night, Celia finally told her husband what had been going on at work and tried to explain why she'd been so down for the past few months.

"It was bad enough when I was treated like a freaking bimbo—pinched and grabbed and talked down to—by some of the guys when I first started there." Celia looked at her face in the mirror, trying to remember how it was she used to look when she attracted that kind of attention from the men at work. "But now...now I'm *old*. It's almost worse in a way *not* to be seen as a sex object. At least they had some use for me then."

Celia brought their tea and coffee cake into the living room and flopped down beside Stefano on the leather sofa. He turned the television down and turned to her, looking worried.

"I don't think it's about your age. *Or* the fact that you're a woman. They're just guys. They're just jerks. Don't worry so much about it," Stef reassured her trying to get her to hold his hand.

"Well, let's not talk about it any more tonight. I have a little work to do on this deposition summary. I promised Riva I would have it for her first thing in the morning."

Celia retrieved her journal from the coffee table and began ruffling through it, counting up the days and months that had passed since *This happened* and *That happened*, making notes of each event and its date, who had been party to each situation, who had been witnesses, what words had been said, what actions had been acted.

Paranoid or not, she knew enough about employment law to realize she was coming up on some filing deadlines, that she had only a certain number of days from dates of occurrence to bring up certain episodes in any EEOC complaint. Celia knew that, either way—whether she decided to file a charge or not—she needed to construct a timeline and get her documentation in order. Maybe the EEOC could tell her whether she was paranoid and thin-skinned or simply aware of a difficult reality.

## CHAPTER 32

# Conflict Around Performance Review

## Elayne J. Shapiro

Pat* worked in an organization in which management was fluid. In one project person X could be manager and person Y employee, but six months later on a different project, they might find the roles reversed.

Pat hired Chris directly out of college. Four of the five interviewers agreed that Chris would be a good hire; one felt strongly that Chris should be eliminated from the hiring pool based on lack of experience. Pat prevailed, and an offer was extended.

The first few months went fairly well, although there were some obvious points of frustration: Chris did not have deep technical skills. This is common for new hires into the group, and this had been addressed. Chris seemed to have more trouble than usual getting up to speed, but Pat found a project that seemed suitable to Chris' skill set.

About the fourth month, however, things started to take a turn for the worse. Chris seemed hostile when Pat addressed performance during weekly status meetings. Chris avoided Pat in the halls.

In the latest project, Pat assigned Chris to work directly with developers. The job required extensive interaction with the programmers on the team and great organizational skills. Chris excelled in both of these areas and in addition was very methodical and effective at solving tricky organizational problems. The assignment required little technical skill, but the developers were pleased except in those instances where Chris needed technical know-how and fell short. It was up to Pat to address this issue. However, the single biggest challenge Pat had with Chris was providing any corrective feedback. Any critical advice, no matter how constructive, resulted in anger, frustration, and even insults from Chris. Pat tried surrounding critical comments with genuine positive ones, but Chris seemed to

---

*This case has been developed based on real organization(s) and real organizational experiences. Names, facts, and situations have been changed to protect the privacy of individuals and organizations.

243

filter those out. Chris developed a number of effective ways to prevent Pat from delivering feedback. Avoidance was common.

Aside from difficulty in providing feedback, Pat learned second hand about decisions Chris had made well after the fact. If Pat said anything, Chris would argue, interrupt midsentence, and vehemently insist that the decision was the right one. Once Chris replied, "Well I don't see *you* doing that." Pat worried Chris was trying to circumvent the chain of command. Sometimes Chris claimed that someone else had given different directions. Finally Chris invoked an accusation of bias: "Other people do this, and it's OK for them, but when I do it, I'm yelled at. You're treating me differently."

Chris was finishing up for the day when Pat sat down in the chair next to the desk. "Chris, I want to congratulate you on the manual you completed last week. It was a beautiful piece of work. I was very impressed that you got it done ahead of schedule. The writing was clear and very accessible to a new user of the product."

"Thanks, Pat. I reworked the language several times to make it comprehensible."

Pat added, "Remember that we are meeting this Thursday to do your performance review."

"Excuse me?" Chris responded edgily. "Usually managers and employees plan a mutually acceptable time for such important matters like performance reviews. You can't just put it on the calendar and expect me to have the paperwork done in time for it."

Pat leaned forward over the desk. "I appreciate your perspective, Chris, but I have a deadline to meet. I've been trying to get hold of you, but you haven't answered my emails. You also haven't answered the messages I've left on your voice mail."

Chris looked down and then away before responding. Pat had been instrumental in Chris getting hired, but Chris did not want to be bound by that obligation. After a pause Chris responded, "You're not exactly easy to get a hold of either. I was talking to Terry the other day, and Terry said—"

Pat interrupted, "What were you talking to Terry for? I'm your direct supervisor. Chris, did you go over my head?"

Chris looked a little embarrassed, "Well, I was having trouble figuring something out on my current project, so I thought I'd find out what Terry's opinion was."

Pat sat back in the chair and wondered about what had happened to the relationship with Chris. Was Chris gunning for the manager position or more?

PAT: "Why didn't you consult with me? You canceled our last meeting regarding your current project. Chris, we have a chain of command for a reason. You are supposed to report to me. If anyone were to seek Terry's opinion, that would be me."

CHRIS: "I just wanted someone to kick ideas around with. You seem to want to micromanage everything."

PAT: "Chris, I am stunned by what you are saying. What do you mean 'micro-managing'? Can you give me some examples? It is my responsibility to see that what leaves our office fits the specs. And furthermore, instead of talking to me you felt that the best way to avoid my micromanaging was to consult with my boss?"

CHRIS: "Pat, you seem to be getting upset."

PAT: "Of course, I'm upset! If sounds like you have been behaving in a very unprofessional way at my expense."

CHRIS: "Perhaps we can talk about this at some other time when you are calmer."

PAT: "I think that's a good idea, Chris. We can discuss this on Thursday along with your performance review."

## CHAPTER 33

# There's a New Sheriff in Town

### Lori J. Joseph

Nicole Gates* was anxiously waiting for the meeting to begin. Even though it was a Monday morning, the room was packed with close to 75% of the 200 on-and off-duty sheriff's deputies as well as administrative and dispatch employees. Alicia Washington had won the election a few months ago—beating her former boss and nemesis by a landslide—and this was her first official day on the job. Not only was she the first African-American to be elected to the top post of Southwest's Sheriff's Department, but also she was, more importantly in this occupation, the first woman. She had run against Sheriff Bates before and lost—and was forced into "retirement" because of it. That this victory was such a runaway served to mitigate that previous humiliation but not the challenges that were before her. They were not insurmountable, but they were deeply rooted and highly divisive.

Former Sheriff Bates had a long tenure with the department—several decades—and was currently awaiting a civil trial on charges of sexual harassment brought against him by several female deputies. The department was fractured along many lines because of that as well as other issues, such as the low number of female deputies with rank and lack of opportunity for female deputies to work the warrant detail and get out of the building into a patrol car. There were those who supported him and were vehement that the sexual harassment charges were trumped up by women who just couldn't hack it. There were others who wished him good riddance but had no stand on the harassment charges. Finally, there were deputies—mostly women—who anxiously awaited the demise of the "good old boys club" and hoped a female sheriff would work toward a fair and equitable workplace. To add to this mix, there were also organizational members across all occupations and sex who questioned the ability of a woman to lead them in this

---

*This case has been developed based on real organization(s) and real organizational experiences. Names, facts, and situations have been changed to protect the privacy of individuals and organizations.

fiercely male-dominated environment—no matter that she had 25 years of experience working the jail and the courts.

As Nicole waited in the conference room, she was thinking of how gendered—yes, and sexist—the occupation of policing is: Only about 10% of peace officers are women. She knew she was entering a male-dominated field, but she really had no idea of the challenges that she would face. The organization that Washington would be taking over was at least 60% white male—the other 40% was labeled "minority," which included black males and all women. From that perspective, Nicole concluded, Southwest's new chief was a double minority. Not to downplay her race—especially in the South—but her being a woman was the most critical obstacle for her to overcome. And even though the treatment by men was sometimes unfair, what was sometimes more difficult to overcome, Nicole thought, was how women treated one another. She didn't know if they tried to ingratiate themselves with male deputies or if they really felt that way about their own sex, but women were 10 times tougher on each other. They commented on each other's moods ("boy, is she PMSing today"), took part in or ignored the sexual jokes by male deputies, even when other women said it made them uncomfortable ("Oh, grow up—it's just a joke"), and they found it difficult to stand up for one another. "Was it the limited opportunity," Nicole wondered, "or the tight space we have to work in that turns us against one another? Well, now that a woman is at the helm, maybe things will finally start to change." With this in mind, she perked up when Sheriff Washington walked into the room. How this woman would navigate the challenges of an intensely political, highly gender-segregated workplace was the question of many—inside and outside of the organization. As Sheriff Washington stepped to the podium to give her welcoming speech, the people in the crowd hushed and gave her their full attention.

"Good morning! I am going to be brief this morning as I realize that many of you must report to your posts. I want to say that I am proud to be your newly elected sheriff. I know there are challenges ahead for all of us, but I assure you that I will serve you, this organization, and the citizens of Southwest to the best of my ability. I promise you that I will take the time to listen to all of your concerns and suggestions as we work together to unite this department and strengthen our organization. My experience as a former deputy gives me unique insight into the challenges you all face on a daily basis. In the coming months you will each be receiving an invitation to meet with me face-to-face to share your thoughts and ideas. Your input is important to me, and I look forward to talking to each one of you. Once again, I am proud to begin serving as your sheriff, and I thank you for your time this morning."

When the sheriff was finished, some stayed to congratulate her, but Nicole had to hurry for shift change. As she walked to the records room she thought about what Sheriff Washington said about the challenges the organization faced and wanting to meet with everyone. "Finally," she reflected, "someone is going to listen to us." Nicole was also excited that Sheriff Washington was not only a woman but also a former sheriff's deputy. "We will finally have someone in a position of power who understands what it's like for women in this organization," she thought. With this hope in her heart, Nicole began to reflect on her four years as a deputy sheriff and what she might share with Sheriff Washington during their meeting. She began thinking about what it was like for her when she joined the department and what it's like now. It was then that she realized how her past expectations were many times different from her actual experience.

When she started as a sheriff's deputy, Nicole couldn't believe how lucky she was—a young, single mom with a high school education earning a starting salary of nearly $31,000 with good benefits—health insurance and a 401K. Her family was so proud of her! Her family members couldn't stop telling people that their daughter was in law enforcement—"protecting the citizens of the city." Nicole still loves how most people look at her when she wears her uniform—such respect— especially for someone in her late 20s. When she sees people look at her like that, she feels a sense of accomplishment and, for a moment, forgets some of the more daunting challenges of the job. But, all in all, Nicole has learned to manage her unmet expectations and roll with the surprises—she wants to make a career of law enforcement. In this way she's different from some of the other female deputies who hate the job but can't quit because the money is too good.

She had been told when she was hired that her responsibilities would include working with inmates, staffing the records room, working court, and possibly serving papers. She knew of female deputies in other cities and counties in the state who patrolled a certain area—making arrests and protecting the public. That opportunity wasn't available to female deputies at Southwest, and some left to become police officers instead. But maybe with a female sheriff those women who want to serve in a different capacity will be given the chance to do so.

Anyway, Nicole's first awakening came after what deputies call "jail school"— her training to ready her to work for the Sheriff's Department. She hadn't realized then that her work world would be confined to one floor of a four-story, mostly windowless, concrete building. The jail could hold about 800 male and female inmates; however, the female population was usually about one-third the size of the male, so for now they were housed on one small floor. To enter this floor, all officers and official visitors had to pass through the Records room—an oblong space, about 12 by 20 feet, that housed three computer work stations and a window counter. This cramped location usually held four female officers who worked 12-hour shifts. Moving to Records from the "floor" was thought of as a promotion, primarily because employees didn't have to work face-to-face with inmates for 12 hours straight. Working with inmates is stressful but sometimes fulfilling work, and most deputies are glad when they are moved to another position. "Except Linda," Nicole thought. "She's been working with inmates for 18 years and loves it—that takes a special kind of person." As much as Nicole felt useful and strong (people joked that they couldn't mess with Nicole anymore) working with inmates, Nicole was glad when she was moved to Records last year.

When she worked in Records, she was responsible for entering and retrieving data on all inmates—male and female. She also had to keep track of which inmates were leaving the jail and why and when they would return. Additionally, she was in charge of who entered and exited this side of the jail. Even though there were three computers, they could not be used to surf the Internet or check personal email. Working in such cramped quarters for such a long time sometimes gave rise to petty disagreements and pitted the women against one another. "It wasn't unusual," Nicole thought, "to begin hating the women you worked with for being so catty and whiny." Nicole thought about how refreshing it was when male deputies stopped by and how she wished she could walk the entire building like they did.

Nicole realized that working in Records and working on the floor each had its own challenges and rewards. Even though the women's jail is confined to one floor and is windowless and a bit depressing, working with the inmates can be gratifying. Often the women who are in jail are there for nonviolent crimes such as writing bad checks or possessing drugs. "Crimes," Nicole thought, "that could be committed by anyone—these women just got caught." When she started on the floor, Nicole felt compassion for many of these women—especially those who seemed so scared. She was determined to maintain a professional demeanor but also to offer comfort and reassurance to the inmates. There were times when she struggled with caring too much for some. It also made her feel good about herself to help others. Nicole really loved seeing inmates succeed after they left jail. She can recall a few women she has seen on the street—employed, sober, and happy to see her. She feels tremendous gratification for any small role she may have played.

On the other hand, no one told her how stressful working with the inmates could be. "I guess I should have known," she thought, "I mean, they did train us how to intervene in fights and subdue inmates." But somehow she just didn't imagine that it would really happen. The first time it did—another officer called to her to help break up a fight between two inmates—she froze. She couldn't believe she had to jump into the middle of an actual physical fight! She finally found her nerve and reacted in time. Thank goodness she did—she'd heard enough talk later about deputies who couldn't pull their weight when things got tough, and she was glad she wouldn't be branded as a coward. Nicole experienced sincere concern when an inmate was inconsolable, having lost her children and preparing to go away for a long time. Lately Nicole feels like the only way to keep doing her job is to harden her heart against the inmates—it's a change she doesn't like seeing in herself.

With these thoughts swirling in her head, Nicole approached the Records room and saw that Trina was working the morning shift. Trina was laughing (and flirting!) with a male deputy, Joe Jones. Nicole began to think about an entirely different set of concerns she wanted to share with Sheriff Washington. "Why is it," she thought, "that some women have to make such fools of themselves in front of men? I love working with male deputies, but why do some women have to make it something sexual? It makes it so hard on the rest of us. And, worse, Joe is definitely not one of those deputies who thinks women have earned the right to wear a badge."

"Hey, Trina. Hey, Joe," Nicole said as she walked into the suffocating 10-by-20-foot room. "How goes it?"

"Hey, Nicole," both Trina and Joe said at the same time.

"So, how was it? Are we on the verge of a great feminist revolution? First a female sheriff and next thing you know the jail will be painted pink and all the captains will be women," smirked Joe.

"And what's wrong with that?" asked Nicole.

"Well, first off, pink is not my favorite color," Joe laughed. "Well, I gotta go," Joe said, smiling and winking at Trina.

"Yes, you do," Trina chuckled as she playfully swatted Joe on the arm.

When he was down the hallway Trina turned to Nicole and asked, "So, really, what was she like as the sheriff?" Trina had been around when Washington was a deputy and had reservations about her becoming the sheriff.

"She seemed excited about taking over, and if she does what she said she will, I think things might get better. Hell, maybe we'll even be allowed on the street." Nicole sighed and went to check the records request box.

"I'll believe that when I see it," dismissed Trina. "Do you really think things will change just because she's a woman?" Trina doesn't really care that Washington is a woman—the last thing she would want anyone to think is that she's one of those feminist types.

"Well, they have to be better than they were when he was sheriff."

"Hey, speak for yourself," Trina shot back. "I had no beef with him; as a matter of fact our two highest-ranking women were promoted under his watch."

"Wow. Two female officers out of how many: 15, 20? Give me a break. Plus, they both have to deal with all the rumors and innuendos about how they got their rank."

"And do you think it will be any different if she promotes a lot of women—same crap, different reasons. It's all politics—always has been, always will be. I make no bones about doing this for the money—do you think if I could make this kind of cash doing something else I wouldn't hand in my notice immediately? Fighting inmates and a bunch of gossipy women—this is not my idea of a great day at work. If they had told me half of what I would be up against when I signed on, I'd probably be working at the mall right now—but it's hard to go back to making 22–23 grand a year after starting at 31. That's why I come here, put in my 12 hours, have a little fun, if I can, and go home."

"Yeah, I noticed you having a little fun when I walked up."

"Yeah, so, I flirt a little. Hell, it passes the time, and I happen to like it when men come around—it gives me break from all the estrogen trapped inside this windowless cube they call an 'office.' So, don't get all high and mighty with me, little Miss Bucking-for-a-Promotion. I've paid my dues—gone several rounds with the inmates, been on the business end of a left hook, served and protected; hell, I've even defended your ass from the gossip mill....So, forgive me if I don't contribute to your vision of the perfect, genderless female officer—if there is even such an animal."

"Look, I'm not trying to start anything with you; I'm just excited about how things might change. Tell me you don't want things to be different. I mean, I remember how stressed you were for months about how male deputies treated you like a second-class citizen. Gosh, remember Jolynn? After she found out what it was really like to work the jail, she dreaded coming to work—cried when those two interviewers were here talking about what it was like on the job. Hell, she's doing hair right now.... And, yes, do I want a promotion? Damn straight. Do I have *hope* about her trying to make this job better for women? Hell, yeah. We work hard here, Trina, and half the time we're fighting each other. I don't care if you flirt with Joe, but I do care about how that makes female officers look to other male officers. Whether you like it or not, people generalize that behavior to all of us, and we already have it hard enough—men thinking we can't do the job, can't handle ourselves in the trenches. Hell, yes, I want to get out of this box and work the streets. But that is never going to happen until the perception that we're just a bunch of jail matrons changes. We need to stand up for each other, and I am hoping, perhaps foolishly, that having a female sheriff will make that a little bit easier. Anyway, she said she wanted to meet with each of us individually to hear our concerns about the job and listen to any suggestions we might have about doing this better."

"Okay, okay. You've made your point!" Trina smirked. "Well, I will be making my list just as soon as Santa is proven...." The phone rang, and Trina answered, "Records. How can I help you?"

Nicole was feeling a little less optimistic now and was amazed at how someone else's attitude could affect her. Well, she wasn't going to let that stop her from hoping that things could change. "I mean, you hear about that all the time—new leaders, new culture," she thought.

During the next few weeks, Nicole found that several deputies—female and male—were anxiously awaiting Sheriff Washington's first actions. So far nothing monumental had happened, but Nicole figured that Washington was just trying to figure out the best course to take. Nicole had heard through the grapevine that the sheriff didn't want to be seen as favoring women. "I mean, she is in a sort of double bind," thought Nicole. But the news did disappoint her a bit. "Well," Nicole decided, "it probably is better for her to wait before doing anything drastic."

Actually, the first thing Sheriff Washington did was to paint the jail pink (Joe got a lot of mileage out of that one). Washington had read that pink has a calming effect on inmates. That didn't sit too well with a lot of deputies, and it had an effect on the way she was viewed ("Female sheriff, pink jail. Ugh."). But she kept her word about setting up meetings to talk to each deputy. Nicole was surprised when she got one of the first appointments, but she was ready. She had her list of five major issues:

**1.** Better organizational and job socialization is needed. Help us to understand what it's really like to work here.

2. The female deputies need help in getting along better—maybe some communication workshops? Possibly have them for men and women to make sure that women aren't seen, once again, as the problem!

3. This is a long shot, but maybe redesign the jail to get us out of this confined space. Maybe that would help us to get along better.

4. More promotions for female deputies (who deserve it, of course!) are needed. Investigate how many females would like to work the warrant detail. Give us more opportunity to attend police school after jail school.

5. Mix us up with the male deputies so they can see we can pull our own weight.

As Nicole walked through the door, Sheriff Washington nodded, "Deputy Gates" and stood to shake her hand.

"Sheriff," answered Nicole with a bit of anxiety but an attitude of determination. She shook the sheriff's hand and took out her notebook.

# CHAPTER 34

# Resisting Disability Epithets

## Carol B. Mills

Krista walked in a few minutes late to a meeting to discuss changes in some insurance regulations.

"I'm sorry I'm late," she said. "My computer was acting retarded, and I couldn't get it to print."

Everyone laughed and told her that it was okay and that the old computers were always a pain. Everyone, that is, but Stacey. Stacey sat quietly and looked down at her pencil. She twirled a paper clip in circles as she tried to gather her thoughts, tried to remember what clever thing she was going to say next time someone used a disability slur.

As she sat there trying to remember, she got angry with herself, and before she knew what was happening, a teammate spoke up, "Stacey, what do you think about this idea?"

She stammered, "I'm sorry, I was thinking about something else."

The meeting continued, and when it was over, Stacey went back to her desk. As she moved her mouse, her screen saver popped up. She immediately grinned at the adorable six-month-old in the cowboy hat looking at her from the monitor. But then she thought, "Again I have failed to stand up for you, Jake. I'm sorry. I'll do better next time."

## STACEY'S LIFE AND CAREER

Stacey and her husband, Jeff, had been college sweethearts and had married two years after graduation. They had wanted to make sure they had a good start to their marriage and their careers before they started a family. Stacey worked in a

---

*This case has been developed based on real organization(s) and real organizational experiences. Names, facts, and situations have been changed to protect the privacy of individuals and organizations.

medium-sized insurance company, Hemitt Life and Auto, and Jeff was moving up the ranks at his consulting firm. Then, right before they turned 30, they decided to have kids.

For nine months, Stacey and Jeff rubbed her belly and anticipated their unborn child. And when Jake was born, they immediately fell in love with his tiny fingers and little baby eyelashes. He looked perfect. He *was* perfect.

As they cuddled the newest member of the family, a geneticist came into the room to tell them the obstetrician who delivered Jake had suspicions that Jake had Down syndrome based on some physical markers. The next few days were a blur for Stacey and Jeff as they looked at their precious baby and tried to figure out how they—how he—could have something so horrible!

As the days and weeks progressed, Stacey and Jeff realized that Down syndrome wasn't so bad after all. In fact, most children with Down syndrome go to school with their typically developing peers, participate in sports and social activities, and grow to lead happy and productive adult lives.

By the time Stacey headed back to work, after eight weeks off, she had learned more than she ever thought she would have needed to about a chromosomal arrangement. She loved her son and was proud to have this new wonder in her life.

When she walked back into work the first day after her maternity leave, people acted a bit awkwardly, asking how Jake was doing and if there was anything they could do to help. A few people offered their apologies, and Stacey reassured them that she was not sorry Jake was born nor that he had Down syndrome.

As she tried to tell them about all the things that kids and adults with Down syndrome were doing, she found herself feeling extra proud of both Jake and herself for coming so far in her own acceptance in such a short time. Within days things at work got back to normal.

## BACK TO NORMAL

Funny thing, though: "Back to normal" seemed different to Stacey now. She wasn't sure if she just missed things before, or if now she was just more sensitive to them.

But as she was walking down the hall, she heard her friend, Dan, say to another friend, "Stop acting like such a freakin' retard."

Stacey stopped in her tracks. She wanted to say something, but she didn't know what or how. She just went to the bathroom and cried.

At home, Stacey talked to her husband, Jeff, a lot about what Dan said.

Jeff said, "Stacey, you know they weren't talking about Jake."

Stacey pushed him and said, "Then who are the retards he was making fun of?"

That gave Jeff pause. And he realized Stacey was right. But, he wondered, "Can we really stop people from using such common terminology?" And he thought, "Is it fair to ask people to stop using such pejoratives just because they might hurt people like my son?" "Heck," he asked Stacey, "it's not like they would use it in front of him, right?"

"Like that matters?!" retorted Stacey. "So, you can use racial slurs as long as you don't use them in front of the group you are offending?"

That got Jeff focused, and he decided Stacey was right—and he would deal with the situations when and if they arose.

Stacey decided to come up with some things to say when the offensive comments were made. She was sure that if she addressed the issue, her colleagues would listen.

Just two days later a coworker said to Stacey, "Some days I hate our clients. They all act like a bunch of retards who can't understand the simplest policy."

Stacey winced but knew this was her chance. She took a deep breath and said, "You know, hearing you call our clients 'retarded' hurts me because my son has an intellectual disability."

Without hesitation her coworker retorted, "Great, now the PC Police are going to keep me from using that word, too? Give me a break! It's just an expression."

He walked off. A few days later he acted like nothing happened, but Stacey was still hurt.

Several more comments were made over the next few months, and some she tried gently to address, and others she let go, knowing that the person didn't really care and thought she was being overly sensitive. A few people she spoke to were genuinely apologetic and said they never realized the implications of what they were saying. And a couple gave her the "toughen up—they are just words" speech.

## THINGS HEAT UP

Over the next few months, Stacey talked to Jeff, her husband, a lot about this issue. These days at his consulting firm, he did not hear many slurs because he decided to address them early on, and people tended to look up to him as a leader in the office. One time at a meeting, a junior executive said that a client acted like a "spaz."

Jeff said, "Really, I didn't know he had cerebral palsy?" The room was silenced.

Another time a buddy of Jeff's called someone "retarded," and Jeff responded with a devilish grin, "Interesting. I didn't know that he had an IQ test recently. You shouldn't be making fun of him for that."

Apparently after that most people considered their words carefully around him. Stacey wished she had that kind of influence!

So, when Krista walked in a late to the meeting that was scheduled to discuss the insurance regulation changes and said, "I'm sorry I'm late. My computer was acting retarded, and I couldn't get it to print," and everyone laughed, Stacey was angry and stunned.

Everyone was in a hurry that day because everyone was leaving for a regional meeting with all of the southeastern offices in the company, so Stacey just let it go. She, as most employees were, was excited about the regional meeting.

They would get to see friends from other offices who were known mainly through email, and they could socialize between sessions with friends who had transferred to other places. The regional meeting was a lot of work, but it was also known company-wide as a great experience for camaraderie, teamwork, and fun.

The meeting was wonderful in many ways. Stacey made new friends and reconnected with old ones. She learned a great deal more about her job and looked forward to some new and exciting changes. The work sessions weren't bad at all, but sometimes the informal sessions and social events left her stewing in her emotions once again.

## THE LETTER

When they all got back to the office after the regional meeting, Stacey had spent a great deal of time composing her ideas and thoughts. She loved her coworkers and her job, but she was feeling increasingly alienated and angry with herself for not being more of a voice for people with intellectual and cognitive disabilities.

Though Jake was still a baby, this issue was one that affected the very way that other people looked at him and his worth as a human being. She began to question why her coworkers, who knew better than to use racist or sexist remarks, would readily target disability.

Stacey composed the letter she wanted to send to her colleagues. She wondered if she should email it to the people just in her office or in her entire division. Should she ask for it to be included in the company *News and Notes*? Or, like some colleagues warned her, should she just toughen up?

What do you think Stacey should do?

> An Open Letter to My Colleagues:
>   On the way home from the regional meeting for Hemitt Life and Auto, I sat on the plane reflecting on the week, the changes occurring in our territories and in our business, and how despite the challenges and changes that lie ahead, most of us embraced the week with an eye on the future and the potential that lies before us.
>   However, I also found my mind wandering to some unsettled feelings I have as a result of comments made during the week and the types of comments I hear quite regularly in my daily routine at this company. To keep this issue focused, I will recount some of the specifics that bothered me.
>   Not less than 50 times this week I have heard coworkers make references to "having to ride the little bus" or ask one another, "where are our helmets since we're on the little bus?" Or, worse yet, "pick me up at my door like they do the retards on the little bus!" Statements like these went on all week long and seemed to get worse as the days progressed, with some of our colleagues even imitating the speech problems or physical handicaps thought to be typical of those with various disabilities.

While said in a joking manner, the statements are direct and derogatory references to the fact that children with disabilities often are transported to and from school, not on the typical school bus, but on a smaller school bus, more appropriate and safer for whatever their special needs happen to be.

In addition, I had to stop counting the number of times I heard people refer to themselves as "just a retard" or say "I'm so retarded" when it came to trying to learn the new material. Though I try to gently remind people when I can that this language is hurtful, often I'm unable to address the comments appropriately and privately.

If you feel "stupid," then say so; but likening yourself to a person with a true disability is insensitive and disrespectful. People with true mental retardation work hard every day to achieve even a portion of the abilities that we take for granted and the opportunities that are afforded to us on a daily basis.

I had hoped that we as people who work with the public day in and day out might be more sensitive to this type of behavior in public. I am sure that I am not the only associate of our company with a child, friend, or relative with special needs.

I also realize that not one person intended to be offensive or hurtful toward me personally. However, as a parent of a child with special needs I am compelled to bring these matters to the forefront so that hopefully it will become a learning experience for everyone involved.

People with disabilities are just that: people first and disabilities second. And I can assure you that not one person with special needs asked for their particular situation. In fact, I believe that most would change it if they could.

As representatives of Hemitt Life and Auto, we have a responsibility to represent ourselves in our work and personal lives in a manner that reflects a profound sensitivity to *all* people of the world, no matter their race, religion, political or cultural differences, sexual orientation, or mental and/or physical disability.

It is my sincere hope that this letter is taken in the manner in which it is intended and that starting tomorrow each and every one of you has an opportunity to get to know a person with special needs. The relationship will enrich your life and theirs and hopefully change your attitude and outlook forever.

Sincerely,
Stacey Smitter

# Organizational Diversity

CHAPTER 35

# Where Does It Hurt?

## Cynthia A. Irizarry

"**S**he said I was incompetent and if I couldn't schedule patients correctly you would fire me!"

"She said *what*?" Dr. Jason Mortensen* asked incredulously.

Sabrina Ramos, the office manager, stood shaking in Dr. Mortensen's office. "Dr. Swenson yelled at me in front of the entire office staff this morning! She said that I was scheduling too many patients for her to see. She asked me a couple of weeks ago to not schedule patients past four o'clock on the weekdays. I tried my best to accommodate her, but I can't turn patients away! The other doctors never seem to mind. You don't mind! Are you going to fire me?"

Dr. Jason Mortensen intently regarded the woman who had been his office manager for the past 15 years. "Of course I'm not going to fire you, Sabrina. I'll speak with Dr. Swenson about this."

As she turned to leave, she put in her final words. "You know, I thought it would be great to work with a female doctor. Now, I don't know what to think."

My thoughts exactly, thought Jason. Ever since Beth Swenson had her baby, it has been one conflict after another. At this rate, she'll never become a partner, even if she was the first and only female physician in his practice.

### DR. MORTENSEN'S PERSPECTIVE

Jason Mortensen was the senior partner of Advanced Women's Health Care Associates, a thriving practice that specialized in obstetrics and gynecological care. The practice was located in a town just outside of Charlotte, North Carolina, one of the fastest growing cities in the nation. Jason had seen the population of his town grow

---

*This case has been developed based on real organization(s) and real organizational experiences. Names, facts, and situations have been changed to protect the privacy of individuals and organizations.

from 5,000 to 50,000 in the past decade, as it slowly became a suburb of Charlotte. As a result, the practice began thriving with the attendant increase of women in the area requiring obstetrical and gynecological care. Jason often described his practice as one of the premier OB/GYN groups in the Piedmont area. Business was so good that they were set to open a separate clinic that would offer routine gynecological care. Advanced Womens Health Care Associates could then concentrate solely on surgery and obstetrics.

The influx of new patients also increased the hiring of new personnel. To date, the practice employed four doctors and was looking to hire a fifth. As senior partner and founder, Jason Mortensen was responsible for all final decisions made in the practice. The next senior partner was Dr. Dwight Solomon, who had been with the practice for 25 years. The most recent partner was Dr. Richard Worthy, who had joined seven years ago. The latest hire and potential partner was Dr. Beth Swenson, who started working at the practice one year ago.

## It Seemed Like a Good Idea

Jason was reluctant to hire a woman. The issue had nothing to do with competency. He thought that women physicians were just as skilled as their male colleagues. However, Jason had always felt that women didn't make for good partners in a profitable practice. If a woman physician wanted to have a family, she would request more time off and other changes to her work schedule. Jason also figured once he bent the rules for one physician, he would have to bend the rules for all the physicians in the practice.

Yet, Jason also realized that many patients these days prefer to have a woman as a physician. Moreover, he didn't want their competitors to be the first to hire a woman. To Jason, it was simply a matter of good business sense to hire a highly competent woman physician. As he thought back, he remembered that Beth had seemed an excellent choice. She was fresh out of medical residency, and she came highly recommended. Her mentors at the medical school praised her work ethic and her ability to relate to patients. She consistently scored in the top 10% of her national board exams. She also was a winner of the Golden Stethoscope, for excellence in intern training. She wasn't perfect, of course. She still needed more surgical experience. But that was common for most new physicians straight out of residency programs. Jason was confident that she would learn from his guidance and instruction.

Beth also seemed committed to working in this town. Her father-in-law had founded one of the most established and lucrative dental practices in the community. Her mother-in-law owned a public relations agency. Moreover, Beth's husband would soon be joining the pediatric clinic down the street when he finished his medical residency. Because of her family connections, Beth would bring in good business, Jason surmised.

But Jason's worst fears were realized when Beth volunteered in her interview that she looked forward to having children and raising a family. Beth assured them that pregnancy wouldn't pose a problem with her work schedule. Besides, wouldn't a female physician who was also a mother understand obstetrical patients better?

Hiring Beth was one of the toughest decisions the partners ever made concerning the practice. While Jason would make the final decision about any hire, Richard and Dwight's opinions were still instrumental in the hiring process. Both Richard and Dwight seemed to concur that Beth was the best candidate they had interviewed. If they didn't hire her now, she would most certainly join one of their competitors. Yet, it was Richard's comment that ultimately swayed Jason's opinion about hiring Beth.

"After considering all of our criteria for a new hire, we would want a skilled surgeon and physician who is also a woman who does not want to get married and have children and is also willing to relocate to a suburb in the South," Richard stated.

"Gentlemen, I think we're going to be waiting a long time to find that person–even if she would be the ideal candidate. Beth is the best person we have interviewed. Besides, she is committed to living in town because of her family situation. If we don't make her a good offer and soon, she's going to join one of our competitors, guaranteed. If she joins us, we put a noncompete clause in her contract that prohibits her from joining a rival practice in the region for at least two years. I think she will be more motivated than most to conform to our partnership requirements."

Jason agreed with Richard's logic. Besides, it wasn't like they had a large pool of female candidates to choose from, Jason thought. With these issues in mind, Jason offered an annually renewable contract to Beth, which she accepted. She would start with the practice in three months. This time would allow her to finish the last few weeks of her residency and settle in her new community. Jason and the partners anxiously awaited Beth's start date. It would help the practice schedule to have another physician on board. Jason also actively promoted his new hire by placing advertisements in local newspapers announcing Beth's position at the practice. He even had one of the local papers run a biographical article introducing Beth to the community.

Although Jason and the partners knew that Beth would want to have children one day, they were completely caught off guard when she announced to them that she was pregnant two weeks after starting at the practice.

Jason was prepared to expect the worst. He thought that Beth would approach him soon to request a lighter work schedule. But contrary to his expectation, Beth seemed to work extraordinarily hard. In fact, Beth was tremendous, Jason thought.

Each physician in the practice was responsible for meeting patient appointments, making hospital rounds, assisting partners in surgery, and updating patient charts during the weekdays from 7:00 A.M. to 6:00 P.M. Each doctor was also scheduled to be on 24-hour call for labor and delivery at least twice a week. The practice work schedule was very tight. If a physician's on-call duties in labor and delivery fell on a weekend, that physician received no time off during the week. In order to receive a day off during the week, the physician would have to make a request weeks in advance to Sabrina, who was responsible for managing the physicians' work schedules.

Jason was pleased that Beth seemed to effortlessly adapt to her new work environment. She volunteered to see extra patients during the week. She often stayed as late as 10:00 P.M. to complete patient charts. She also volunteered to fill in on the call schedule for partners needing vacation or leave time. Jason recalled a conversation he had with Richard Worthy in the hospital cafeteria six weeks after Beth joined the practice.

As they sat down for a late dinner in a quiet corner of the room, Jason inquired, "So, Richard, what do you think of our new hire?"

"Beth? At the rate she's going, she'll make partner in a shorter time than I did," Richard laughed as he dove into his salad. "Makes me want to spend less time with my 3-iron."

"Yeah, I was a little concerned about hiring her," Jason confided. "But she seems like a very dedicated doctor. The office staff tell me she's also great with patients."

"Speaking of new hires, have you thought much about our fifth hire?" Richard hesitated a little before he added, "I was thinking since we started diversifying the practice we might want to consider hiring a minority physician."

"Whoa. Slow down a little, partner." Jason chuckled, nearly spilling his coffee. "I'm just getting comfortable with our first diversity experiment. Besides, Beth is working as hard as two doctors. Do we really need a fifth since we've hired her?"

"Yeah, but . . ." Richard started.

"Don't worry," Jason cut in. "I will handle it when the time comes. Speaking of 3-irons, the office is closed for the holiday. Want to hit the links?"

"Sounds like a plan," Richard said, relieved to change the subject. "I'll give Dwight a call to see if he wants to join us."

"Speaking of golf," Jason said, "I ran into Donald Mack at the country club last week. You should've seen his face when I told him we just hired a woman! You could see the envy in his face. His practice has been trying to snag a woman physician for the past six months."

Richard rose to leave. "Yeah, well, let's just keep our fingers crossed. Remember, she's pregnant."

"I guess we'll cross that bridge when we come to it," Jason said.

## The Trouble Begins

Seven months into her pregnancy, Beth developed preterm labor and was confined to bed rest for the next two months. Everyone at the practice was relieved when she gave birth to a healthy baby girl. But most of all, they were all anxiously looking forward to Beth's return after maternity leave. It was tough on all the partners to take over Beth's patient schedule and labor and delivery call while she was out for 12 weeks.

But those problems weren't as bad as those that arose when she returned. Beth seemed irritable and distant with the partners and office support staff.

Jason wondered, with concern, how she was interacting with patients. While pondering the problem, Jason thought back to a conversation he had had just last month with Sabrina. According to Sabrina, Beth had yelled at one of the receptionists for sending home a patient who was 30 minutes late for an appointment. "Office policy clearly states that late patients lose their assigned time," Sabrina said in defense of her assistant. "She was just following our policy."

Jason had met with Beth in his office to ask her to explain her behavior. After a brief exchange of pleasantries, Jason inquired, "I understand you had some words with a receptionist about a late patient appointment." Pausing for effect, he continued, "Beth, what's going on?"

"I took the time on one of my rare days off that I scheduled weeks ago just to come in to the office and see that patient," Beth snapped. "This woman had a very long drive and had to bring along her 92-year-old mother, whom she supports. The receptionist sent her home when she was only 20 minutes late. She didn't even bother to tell me that the patient was here!"

"That may be the case, but you can't treat the office staff this way. It's not professional. You'll have to apologize," Jason said sternly.

"You're right," Beth conceded. "I'll apologize for my behavior, but what happened inconvenienced both me *and* the patient. I understand the need for a policy, but had the reception staff told me the patient was here, all of this could have been avoided." Beth was getting worked up again.

Pausing to control her emotions, Beth said, "It's just...I haven't been myself lately. Jason, my schedule is killing me. The baby has colic, and I haven't gotten a good night's sleep since she was born."

"Beth, I'm sorry to hear that you're having adjustment problems, but that isn't an excuse for the way you treated my office staff," Jason said disapprovingly. "Don't you have family to help you out?"

"Doug's family is here, but they're all working," Beth explained. "Things might get a little easier when Doug is out of his residency program in Atlanta, but that's still six months away."

"You know, my wife raised our four boys. If you need some parenting advice, I'm sure she would be willing to help you out."

"That's very *kind* of you," Beth said with an edge to her voice. "But I really think the problem is with the work schedule. Jason, my schedule has to change. Right now."

Exasperated, Jason said, "I'll arrange a meeting with Richard and Dwight. Any request to change the work schedule will have an effect on them too," Jason explained. "Beth, a good doctor keeps her problems at home. Do you understand me?"

A week later, a meeting was called during the lunch hour with all of the physicians in the practice to discuss Beth's request. Jason remembered what high hopes he had had that the scheduling problem could be solved and things would get back to normal.

At an oval table, with himself at the head, Jason tried reasoning with Beth. "Look, I know things are tough being a first-time mother, but there's no way we can give you two days off in the middle of the week. The practice is far too busy for such a luxury."

Beth pleaded, "Gentlemen, if you want to hire women doctors you need to know how to work with them. And you probably should have realized that women, indeed, have babies. How could you of all people not be sensitive to this! The reality of my situation is that I am alone in this town with an infant daughter. My contract states that I work Monday through Friday from 7:00 A.M. until 6:00 P.M., in addition to the call schedule. Right now I'm working weekdays until 8:00 P.M. If I'm lucky I get a Saturday or Sunday off. But if my two on-call days fall on Saturday and Sunday, I get no time off during the entire week. I never see my daughter, and she is only six months old! I need a little extra time. It doesn't have to be long term. This is important to me!"

"Beth, most of us here have children," Jason countered. "At the same time, we've made a professional commitment to the practice. We are only asking that you do the same. The *reality* of the situation is that this is a growing practice that requires dedicated doctors." He stopped and looked around at all the partners before he began. "We all know you're under emotional strain. Have you thought about counseling? You know, just to help you get over the rough spots?"

They had debated for over an hour, but in the end they conceded to giving Beth an additional half day off on Thursdays. Jason thought it was a generous offer and he, as well as the rest of the partners, had looked forward to things going back to normal.

Later in his office, as he reflected on the meeting, Jason was pleased with himself to have resolved the issue but a bit annoyed that Beth had talked them into an extra half day off. Still, he thought, maybe this is the best solution for now.

Then Sabrina had walked through his door again.

## What to Do?

Is she ever going to get with the program, Jason thought, staring bleakly out of his office window. I can't lose loyal staff members just because she has a temper tantrum, he thought. But I also don't want to lose our only female doctor. We would be a laughingstock. The only practice to hire a woman, fires a woman. Even though her contract prohibited her from joining a rival practice, it was in force only for two years. Beth's lawyer could also challenge that arrangement. She could conceivably join one of our competitors within the year, he lamented. Donald Mack would love that!

## Dr. Swenson's Perspective

"Your baby looks just fine, Mrs. Gandy. If you go to the front desk, they will schedule you for your next appointment." Beth smiled at her patient, but it masked the turmoil she was feeling inside. She held her stomach, which always seemed to be upset these days.

She had seen Sabrina Ramos enter Jason Mortensen's office and close the door. I really did it this time, she thought, as she rubbed her bloodshot eyes. Another long night on call in the labor and delivery ward last night had nearly sapped her strength. It is only 10:00 A.M., she thought. How many patients were scheduled this morning? At least 20, she remembered. I never should have yelled at Sabrina this morning, she considered as she removed her latex gloves and started to wash her hands. I'm a nice person, she told herself. So why am I yelling at everyone?

When Beth joined private practice, she thought the long hours typical of her residency program were over. She recalled times when she would be on call in labor and delivery for 72 consecutive hours and worked 90 hours per week. The position at Advanced Womens Health Care Associates seemed ideal. The practice had a strong reputation, and it served some of the town's most prominent women. Advanced Womens Heath Care Associates had also offered the highest salary. But the most important reason for her accepting the offer was that the position was ideal for her husband, too. She knew Doug was excited to come back home. Anxious to start living a normal life, she and Doug had managed to juggle their residency schedules and get a few days off to go house hunting. They had bought their first house a month after signing her contract.

She remembered Jason's warning about the practice growing at a fast pace. The town of her husband's youth had changed from a sleepy southern hamlet to a major suburb dominated by office buildings, strip malls, and car dealerships. At first, the busy schedule was not a problem. Beth thought back to how she tried to show her commitment to the practice by working extra office hours and taking additional on-call duties. Since her husband was away, she enjoyed the extra work. Moreover, she didn't enjoy going home to an empty house. Unfortunately, she worked so hard it sent her into preterm labor.

## The Problem Begins

When she returned to work after the birth of her daughter, it seemed that her workload only increased. On average she was delivering three to five babies a week. Just two weeks ago she had delivered 13 babies in three days. It was not uncommon for her to work the entire day and then return to the hospital for a delivery that lasted until midnight. She hardly had any time to spend with her daughter.

There have been too many times of going 36 hours without sleep, she told herself. It was after one of those long stretches that she first snapped and yelled at the office receptionist for sending a late patient away. Don't they see how that hurts our reputation with patients? She cringed when she thought that the worst part was never seeing her baby, who was being raised by a nanny and a procession of babysitters. I wonder what she's doing now, Beth thought sadly. Is she smiling, cooing, wondering who her mommy is?

Beth moved quickly to scan the chart of her next patient waiting in another examination room for at least 30 minutes. As she rushed down the hallway to meet her next appointment, she thought part of the problem was that she was the only woman physician in this practice.

Here I am, fresh out of residency, and women are lining up to make appointments with me instead of the other partners. While this development was flattering, it was also making her life hectic. Some of the problem could be alleviated if they would just hire a fifth doctor, preferably another woman. But they kept dragging their feet. She wondered, are they reluctant to hire a woman or are they reluctant to have to pay a fifth person? The physicians, including Beth, made very good money. She knew that a fifth doctor's pay would cut into profits; she wasn't naive. Jason also seemed reluctant to make any scheduling changes. He doesn't really want to hear my problems, she concluded before she stepped in to greet her next patient. He is just interested in the problem going away, she thought glumly as she opened the door to the examination room.

"Good morning Mrs. Halley," Beth said brightly, trying to mask her fatigue. "I'm sorry you had to wait so long. How have you been?" Beth hurried through the exam as she chatted with her patient about the weather. She noticed that Betty, the nurse attendant who assisted in the exam, remained strangely quiet through the entire appointment.

## From Bad to Worse

Another problem being the only woman in this practice is the way the office staff treats me, she thought. She often saw the nurse attendants joking back and forth with her partners during examinations. It had a way of making patients feel at ease. But they never joke around with me, she recollected. Even worse, the front office staff ignored her.

How many times have I told Sabrina not to schedule patients past four o'clock? Sabrina's answer was always the same. "The other doctors don't mind seeing extra patients." Beth also wanted to retort, "But the other doctors have stay-at-home wives to raise their children, do the shopping, fix the dinners, and clean the house." Of course, she never said this to Sabrina. Rather, she just thought it and held her anger in.

Once she approached Dwight about the issue privately. He might have some sway over Jason, she surmised. Moreover, since she and Dwight attended the same church, she felt that he would be sympathetic to her dilemma. One day after service she approached him.

"Dwight, I really need your advice about work," Beth implored. She explained to him the problem with Sabrina ignoring her scheduling requests.

"Beth, as a family man and friend, I'm telling you this," said Dwight. "When you look back on your life, the most important thing you should remember is your family. Your child should be your first priority. Have you considered other work options?"

"Like what?" Beth inquired curiously.

"We need someone on staff at our new clinic," Dwight said. "Of course, you wouldn't be able to do surgery or obstetrics, but you wouldn't have to worry about being on call or working late hours," Dwight reasoned.

Beth felt deflated. "You mean I would be doing the work of a nurse practitioner. Would I be paid as one as well?"

"Well, yes. It would be a significant reduction in pay from what you receive now. On the other hand, it would solve your scheduling problems. Do you want me to mention it to Jason?" Dwight asked.

The implied demotion angered Beth. But instead she said, "I appreciate the thought, Dwight. But I went to medical school to learn how to be a surgeon. I would also lose money, my partnership, and my surgical skill. My family really can't afford for me to take that kind of cut in pay. Doug is only making about $30,000 in his residency. We just bought a house that has a large mortgage." She shook her head sadly. "I just don't see it happening. Please don't mention our conversation to Jason."

"Just remember the offer is there if you change you mind," Dwight said as he turned to leave.

But Beth never took him up on his offer. Instead, she fought with the rest of the partners and managed to keep one lousy, half day off on Thursday on a permanent basis. Even that isn't helping me, she thought despairingly. That half day is filled with me taking patient charts home to complete because there is no other time to do it during the week. And Dwight, the man who told me children were the first priority, wouldn't even look at me during that entire meeting when I practically begged for a more humane work schedule! I just don't get it, she thought. They knew when they interviewed me that I wanted to start a family.

### What to Do?

As Beth rushed to get the chart for her next patient, she noticed a Post-it* note on her office door. With hesitation she read it; "I need to see you tomorrow morning at 6:00 A.M. Jason." Beth knew what this meeting was about. She had better think long and hard about her job here. Could she afford to take the job at the new clinic? Could she afford not to? Getting her lawyer to challenge the noncompete clause in her contract would be expensive. She could leave the region, but how could she tell her husband? He was looking forward to being back home. Even if I do manage to get out of the noncompete clause, the other practices in town will wonder why I'm leaving, Beth thought. Potential employers would inevitably ask Jason for a reference. I can just imagine what he would tell them, Beth thought. "She's a skilled physician who doesn't want to work and has a hard time getting along with people," she envisioned Jason saying. Jason won't let me go easily, Beth lamented. He's just way too competitive.

These thoughts plagued Beth as she realized that the next patient had been waiting for over 40 minutes.

CHAPTER 36

# A Case of Mistreatment at Work?

## Mary M. Meares and John G. Oetzel

Jessica Martinez* stopped at the stoplight and tried to blink back her tears. What was she going to do? This job had started out as her ideal dream job.

A few months ago Jessica had graduated from a well-respected, local university with a degree in communication. She had several job offers, but the most exciting and lucrative, not to mention the one closest to home, was with TechnoloComm. TechnoloComm was a research organization that created a variety of new communications technologies. The location had been one of the best things about the job offer. Jessica was very close to her family, and the thought of moving far away was not attractive. If she worked at TechnoloComm, she could continue to live at home, save money, and have her parents' support as she made the transition from being a student to working full time.

Jessica was hired in the human resources office to work on internal newsletters and publicity. She even knew a few people who worked at TechnoloComm, including her mother's aunt, who had been there for 17 years. Auntie Maria warned her that the organization was not the ideal one that she imagined. Over dinner at her grandmother's one Sunday her great aunt had said, "Don't be too naive, Jessica. TechnoloComm has some good things and some bad. For example, there are a lot of times I've been treated badly there by the higher-ups."

Jessica remembered now that she had discounted this vague warning, thinking every workplace had some people who were not great, but surely it would be only a few. She told her great-aunt, "Oh, I'm sure that I won't have any problems like that—Tom, my new boss, is really nice." Now Auntie Maria's comments seemed more realistic. "I should have paid more attention to what she said," Jessica thought.

---

*This case has been developed based on real organization(s) and real organizational experiences. Names, facts, and situations have been changed to protect the privacy of individuals and organizations.

Everything had started out fine, even though Jessica quickly noted that she was one of few employees in this part of the organization who was not European American. Jessica had a cubicle in an office with Peter, Alex, and Susan. As the communication team, they were responsible for creating newsletters, press releases, communication training, and maintaining the website. The team was one of several within the HR department, and their office was part of a suite of offices in the building that housed many of TechnoloComm's administrative functions. Jessica liked the fact that she got to see lots of people from different offices, and since her work included writing the newsletter, she had a chance to talk to people about their jobs.

Everything went fine for the first week or two, and then something happened that made her question her job and the organization. She was getting a cup of coffee one Monday morning and joined a conversation between two of her teammates, Peter and Alex. She had not had much of a chance to get to know them because she spent most of her time the first few weeks learning her job and going to mandatory organizational training. In the few instances when Jessica actually did the work her job required, she tended to work more with Susan. Peter and Alex were working together on other projects. So, when she saw them in the break room, she thought this was a great time to talk with them.

"Hi, Jessica," said Peter. "We were just talking about the big street party last weekend."

"Yeah," said Alex. "I was really frustrated because I couldn't get into my neighborhood. Did you experience the same problem?" After pausing, he added, "I guess not, since you probably don't live on the north side of town."

"Yeah, you must live in the el barrio, right?" questioned Peter, making sure to try to give a Latin twist to "el barrio."

Jessica nodded, felt her face flush, and faked a laugh. She lived with her family in a traditionally Hispanic area of town and would never want to live anywhere else. Her neighborhood was *home*. It was where she had grown up and where she knew everyone.

Before she could think of a good response, the men headed back to their desks, chatting about the day's work, seemingly oblivious to her embarrassment and anger. Jessica sat down at her desk and thought, "Why do they assume I live in the barrio? I *could* live anywhere, I just don't want to. And I certainly wouldn't want to live in their neighborhood with people like that!" After thinking about it for a while, though, she decided to try to forget it, thinking, "It might be a misunderstanding and they probably didn't mean anything by it."

Later that afternoon, while Jessica was participating in a seminar to learn about TechnoloComm's retirement package options, Susan, Alex, and Peter used their break to discuss the new addition to their office.

"What do you think of Jessica?" Susan said.

"She seems nice enough and she does great work," Alex replied.

"Yeah. She's a little too serious though," added Peter. "But that's probably because she's new and worried about making a good impression. We'll just have to loosen her up a bit so that she can relax and fit in."

The next week, the four of them were working in the office and Jessica decided to try again to get to know Peter and Alex better. The two of them were talking to Susan when Jessica walked over to join them.

"Hey, guys. How was your weekend?"

Alex replied, "Great! Peter and I got together with our families and had a huge barbecue."

"Oh, sounds good. What did you have?"

Alex said, "We had surf and turf—you know, steak and seafood. It was delicious. Peter really knows how to cue it up."

"Sounds good. I love barbecue."

Peter responded, "I'm surprised to hear that."

"Why is that?" Jessica asked, surprised and innocently.

"Well, you know I always heard that Hispanics don't like to barbecue."

She asked somewhat disgustedly, "And why not?"

"Well, the beans fall through the grill."

Alex and Peter started laughing as Susan grinned and shook her head. "You guys are terrible."

Jessica turned around and walked back to her desk feeling very annoyed. She was really starting to get angry and thought that maybe the exchange last week wasn't a misunderstanding after all. She needed to talk to someone. Luckily, she had already planned to get together with her friend Jennifer over lunch. Jennifer worked in another part of HR. They had been peers at school, graduating the same semester, and they were hired at about the same time. Jennifer was a great listener and Jessica felt really comfortable with her. Over their salads, she told Jennifer about Alex and Peter's comments.

"Wow! I can't believe that they would say something like that. What jerks! You should do something about this."

"What?"

"I don't know, Jess. I hope I've never said anything to offend you. I don't know how to tell you to deal with this kind of problem. I guess maybe you should just confront Alex and Peter and tell them to not say things like that."

"What if I don't feel comfortable doing that? I'm not sure I could say that to them directly. Plus there are two of them and only one of me—and they've both been here a long time and have Susan on their side. She thought their stupid joke was funny."

"Well, then maybe you should talk to Tom. Since he is your boss, maybe he can help you figure out what to do. Maybe he can talk to them for you."

"I would hate to get Peter and Alex in trouble," Jessica replied cautiously. "And I don't want to be labeled a troublemaker. But on the other hand, they made me feel really bad." With renewed confidence in her voice, Jessica concluded, "They had no respect for me. Tom does seem really supportive. I don't want him to fight my battles for me, but maybe he can help me figure out what to do. Thanks, Jen."

"Good luck, Jess."

That afternoon, Jessica tentatively approached Tom's office.

"Um, Tom, do you have a minute?"

"Sure, Jessica. Come on in and have a seat. How is everything going with that newsletter?"

"Well, the newsletter is fine, but there's something else I want to talk to you about."

"What's that?" Tom asked as he motioned for Jessica to sit down.

"Well, I've had a couple of difficult things happen in the office." Jessica explained the conversations over the past week as well as she could without getting too defensive or angry. Then she waited to see his reaction.

"Oh, Jessica. I'm sure they didn't mean anything. Alex and Peter are both great guys. I'm sure they were just joking around. That is their way of including people. You've only been here a short time, so don't take it so personally. They do it to everyone."

"But–"

"No," Tom implored. "Don't worry about it. They're both great guys. When you get to know them better you'll understand. Now, are there any other problems?"

"No."

"Well, you had better get back to work then. That newsletter has to be out by tomorrow."

As Jessica walked back to her desk, she felt frustrated, angry, and discouraged. How could he minimize everything she felt and let those guys totally off the hook? She was even angrier than before she talked to Tom. "Why did I even go to Tom? Now I know that I can't count on him for support," she thought. Jessica sat down at her desk. She had a newsletter to get done. Looking at the pictures of her family that decorated her cubicle, she decided that she would show them—her work would be excellent!

Over the next two months, Jessica received compliments from Tom, Alex, and Peter on the work that she did with the newsletter and the website. However, the compliments did not make her feel better. Although she smiled in response to the praise, internally she kept evaluating the comments for hidden meanings or any sense of their surprise that she, a Hispanic, could do a good job. Jessica found it hard to concentrate and relax. She felt jumpy and anxious, especially when she had to work with Peter and Alex without Susan being present.

As the weeks wore on, Alex and Peter continued to tease her about a lot of things. Many of these were not cultural references, but they still made fun of the barrio and also some of the foods she ate. They worked hard and knew their jobs, but personally she just did not like to be around them.

One day at lunch in the cafeteria, Susan, Peter, and Alex sat together, joking and giving each other a hard time. When there was a lull in the conversation, Susan asked Peter how things were going with Jessica.

"Ah, I get along fine with Jessica. We give her a bit of a hard time, but she really needs to loosen up. She just needs to learn to tease us back."

"I don't know, guys. Your jokes don't bother me, but I get the impression that your teasing may be making things worse," Susan replied. "She really looks offended by a lot of your comments. I don't know, but maybe you guys should actually *talk* to her, rather than just tease her."

Peter stated, "I think you're crazy, Susan, but we will talk to her."

Except for Susan, who was working on a deadline, Alex, Peter, and Jessica left the office that afternoon at about the same time. As they were heading to their cars, the guys took the opportunity to confront Jessica.

Peter said, "Hey, Jess, Alex and I have been talking and it seems like you're upset with us. Do you have a problem with us?"

Startled, Jessica replied, "I don't have any problem."

Alex added, "Susan thinks you're upset with us."

Jessica felt a little uneasy about confronting them and simply said, "No, not really."

Peter asked, "So, we are cool then?"

"Um, yeah, I guess."

"OK then, we will see you tomorrow."

As Jessica drove away, Peter said to Alex, "I told you nothing was wrong."

Alex nodded. "I guess you are right."

As Jessica was driving home her heart was pounding. She wanted to tell them what was wrong, but she was scared and hadn't prepared anything to say. She felt cornered and didn't feel safe, especially knowing that she was still in her probationary period at work. Even if she wasn't afraid, how could she say exactly what she felt so they would understand? Tom hadn't understood or even really listened. Why could she expect Alex and Peter to understand?

The next afternoon after work, the team–minus Jessica, who didn't want to spend any more time than necessary with them–went to work out in the TechnoloComm gym. Alex and Peter were lifting weights and Susan was riding the bike when Tom walked in to work out. Seeing Susan alone, Tom thought, "Great, Jessica's three-month probationary evaluation is coming up next week, and here is a chance to find out how things are *really* working out with her in the communication team." He went over to the stationary bike next to Susan's and climbed on. "Hey, Susan. How's everything going down in your office? Is everyone getting along okay?"

"Well, things are interesting," she replied with a smile.

"I'm not sure I like the sound of that. Interesting in what way?"

"Well, there's a lot of tension, to be honest. I really like Jessica and think she is doing great work, but there is some kind of problem between her and the guys. I can't figure out exactly what it is. She hasn't talked to me about it, but it is clear that there is tension between them. I told the guys that maybe they shouldn't tease her so much... you know how they are," Susan continued. "But they said they talked to her and she said that there is no problem."

"Hmm... with Alex and Peter, teasing is their way of making people feel comfortable. Usually they don't tease people they don't like. Maybe I need to encourage Jessica to be more a part of the group. Well, I appreciate your input, Susan. How many miles are you riding this afternoon?"

The next Friday morning, Jessica had her evaluation meeting with Tom. She was especially anxious as she sat down in the chair across from him and tried to take a deep breath.

"Well, Jessica. I'm not sure what to make of your performance. Your newsletters and websites are great, and I'm ready to give you additional responsibilities. But before we discuss task issues, I want to talk about some relationship issues that have surfaced." Without giving Jessica a chance to respond, he continued, "You don't seem to be part of our team here in human resources. When I talked with your coworkers, a couple of them mentioned that you aren't as much of a team player as we would like. I'm going to recommend a second three-month probationary period. As you know, six months is standard, so no need to get worried. I'm going to mark your evaluation to indicate that you are making satisfactory progress. For me to change it to excellent at the end of six months, well, I will need you to work on your teamwork skills. Let's talk about those."

But instead of letting Jessica explain her perspective or provide a response, Tom continued to talk. First he talked about the importance of the team concept at TechnoloComm, and then he addressed the communication team specifically... how well everyone has always gotten along, and how he expects everyone to be a team player.

Jessica just partially listened to Tom as she thought, "I don't get this. I'm doing excellent work, and that is what should matter for my evaluation. He just doesn't understand how hard it is to work with Peter and Alex. I bet they're the ones that told him I wasn't a team player. If I was on a different team, I wouldn't have this problem. I have always prided myself on my teamwork skills. I like this job and I don't want to leave it. But I can't live with the current situation, so I have got to do something. But what?"

At the end of the meeting, Tom asked for Jessica's agreement that she would work on getting along better with her team. Not knowing how else to respond, Jessica agreed by shaking her head up and down...but she couldn't look Tom in the eye. She left Tom's office dejected.

After mulling her evaluation over for a few days, she decided to talk to a few of the other employees whom she thought might share her perspective. She wanted to know about their experiences. First she approached Jamal, who worked in HR. He had spoken to Jessica only once before, but Jessica believed it important to gain insight from someone who had been with TechnoloComm so long.

As she told her story, Jamal said, "You're not crazy for feeling angry. This organization is rotten, but then so are most organizations." Then, pausing for effect, Jamal's voice became more dramatic. "We people of color are never going to be treated with respect. It is the system, and the people in power are never going to give up their power and position. They say everyone should be treated fairly and not mistreated, but they don't really mean it. Damn the people and damn the system."

Getting more of a response than she expected, Jessica waited a moment before asking, "So, how do you deal with it?"

"Oh, I'm just waiting to retire. I go up to my cabin and chop firewood. That gets some of it out of my system. I don't talk to anyone about it though–it wouldn't be fair to my family to complain to them. I just deal with it on my own. If you go to your boss or to anyone else in the organization, you get labeled a troublemaker."

"Then why do you stay?"

"The truth? I have a family to support. I can't just quit my job because I don't like the people here. It would be hard to find another job that pays as well as this one, and I have two children who are in college. When I started things were pretty much okay, but in the last few years... well, it has really deteriorated. I'm just not in a position to make a change, though. I will stay here until I can retire. Until then, I just keep to myself as much as possible."

Jessica thought of Auntie Maria's comments about the problems at TechnoloComm. That afternoon she stopped by her office and brought up the topic of mistreatment and what had been going on in HR.

"Oh, honey," Auntie Maria said after closing the door to her boss' office so she and Jessica could talk more privately. "People have been disrespectful to me, too. I try to educate them, teach them some manners, but sometimes it doesn't make a difference. You have to realize that when someone has a lot of power, it doesn't matter what they say–powerful people are not going to be fired or disciplined, or even reprimanded. I've seen some of these people really mistreat their support staff, but TechnoloComm–for some reason–believes they can't be replaced very easily so they are not going to get fired."

"Is it hopeless then? Should I start looking for another job if I don't want to put up with this?" replied Jessica.

"Well, I don't think it's always hopeless. One time a group of us were able to get together to deal with it. A few of the women in my office were singled out for a problem that was really an overall office problem. We talked about it and we got mad that the men weren't held responsible. We went as a group to the supervisor's manager... because we acted together, they listened to us and took us seriously. If I hadn't had those other women to back me up, I doubt that I would have had the courage... but that time it worked out all right. You have got to pick your battles. Why don't you talk with my friend Rosa in accounting? I think you met her once before. She has worked with the diversity office on some of these issues."

Jessica met with Rosa and described the situation to her.

"You know, we have a policy against mistreatment," Rosa said. "I think this qualifies."

"Is this the diversity policy they talked about in our training?" Without waiting for an answer from Rosa, Jessica continued, "What should I do?"

"Well, that is a really good question–both of them. We don't really have any procedures to go along with the policy. I was talking to one of the women in procurement, and she said she thinks it is ambiguous on purpose, so TechnoloComm looks good but no one can really do much. She thinks it is management's strategy to make people happy, but really it masks the problems and keeps people from having a place to report them to."

"Then what should I do?" groaned Jessica.

"Well, maybe you should go to the diversity office and file a grievance claiming that this is a case of mistreatment. Who knows, maybe that would *encourage* their efforts to provide some procedures and some action to go along with the policy."

Jessica couldn't help but notice the way Rosa's voice changed on the word "encourage." She thanked Rosa for her time . . . but she was still uncertain about what to do. She thought to herself, "This is terrible. Surely I can do something to improve my situation. After all, they hired me to work in the HR office to deal with people. There must be something I can do to convince them to listen to me and everybody else who feels like this. I wonder if I should go to the diversity office?"

As Jessica was pondering her next move on the drive home, Tom, Alex, and Peter were meeting for happy hour. The guys often hung out together after work, and today Tom decided to bring up his concerns about Jessica. "Hey, you guys," he said as he sat down to join them. "What is going on with Jessica?"

Shaking his head, Peter said, "I think she is just too uptight."

Alex added, "We asked her if anything is wrong and she said no."

"Well, you can cut the tension with a knife whenever the three of you are together. I talked with Susan, and she thinks you guys are teasing her too much. Jessica came to me when she first started and said something to the same effect. I dismissed it then . . . I don't know . . . something needs to be done. She *is* pretty uptight, but she is a great worker and I don't want to lose her."

Alex explained, "We don't want her to leave either, but don't blame this on us. We have put a lot of effort into trying to help her fit in with our team. We have treated her like everyone else."

Peter added, "Yeah, and when we did try to talk to her about it, she said everything was okay. What else can we do?"

"I don't know exactly," Tom admitted, "but you need to think of something. Well, I gotta go. See you boys tomorrow."

"Later, boss." Peter turned to Alex and said, "What is going on here? We try to be nice and we just get in trouble. Man, I'm pissed."

"Calm down. Maybe we should talk to her again. She is definitely upset. Maybe we have teased her too much and should back off."

"Maybe you are right, but she needs to meet us halfway and talk to us about what's bothering her rather than just running to the boss."

"Yeah, in a perfect world, I agree. But what should we do?"

CHAPTER 37

# The Penis People

## Diane K. Sloan

I t was not her first consulting job or even the largest firm for which she had worked. Her résumé as an independent consultant and trainer was solid and filled with successes, including, among many, her work with two of the largest insurance companies in the country. But this was the biggest and most lucrative job Emma* had taken on. The fee from it would help support her family in some comfort for two years and give them some much-needed breathing room.

Emma had entered into a contract with a plumbing manufacturer that had plants located throughout the United States. The agreement called for her to develop and deliver leadership training to the organization's 300 or so managers. It was a plum assignment, and Emma was grateful for it.

Because of the size of the project, Emma had asked Sheila, another independent consultant, to work with her. Over the years, Emma was pleased to have discovered a network of independent consultants who called upon each other when projects were too large to handle alone and who were willing to travel to where the work was. These consultant-to-consultant relationships were loose and flexible, and they served Emma well, allowing her to remain her own boss while drawing on the expertise of others when the job was complex, long-term, or particularly demanding.

For this job, Bruce, the CEO of the plumbing fixtures corporation, had decided to bring his managers in groups of 50 to the home office rather than send the consultants to them. It was his hope that the mangers would benefit from spending time with each other as well as from the time in the classroom. He also hoped that managers would build a sense of camaraderie from working together and from working together with home office management.

---

*This case has been developed based on real organization(s) and real organizational experiences. Names, facts, and situations have been changed to protect the privacy of individuals and organizations.

278

So Emma had agreed to a year contract requiring her to be a half continent away from her family for six to eight months of that time, a condition that caused her great loneliness and more than a little guilt. She, her husband, and their 17-year-old daughter had, as a family, talked through the pros and cons of this lucrative offer. And they had all agreed she should proceed.

Yet Emma realized the preciousness of lost time together, that each day family history was being written without her participation. It was, as she knew it would be, incredibly hard, a hardship barely softened by the occasional trips home and the luxury corporate hotel suite that was her temporary home, even though it had a sweeping view of the city lights. Tonight, looking down at those lights, Emma knew that she had never been more miserable in her work and she had never doubted herself more.

Nevertheless, it was time for her evening meeting and debriefing with her partner. Tonight she and Sheila had arranged to meet for drinks in the hotel bar. Entering and squinting to adjust to the darkness, she saw Sheila sitting at the far end, in the darkest corner, her head in her hands.

"Let me guess," said Emma, sliding into her chair. "Bad session?" While the two often team-taught, they had also built into the schedule sessions for which only one consultant was needed. And this afternoon had been Sheila's turn at the solo session. Emma bit back any further small talk when she saw Sheila's tears as her partner raised her head.

"I think I'm going to have to kill them all," said Sheila, her words slow and measured. "They aren't men, they aren't human, they are bloody monsters."

"Tell me what happened," said Emma softly.

"It was a really good class. At least I thought it was. They were attentive, did their group work well. I thought maybe we had passed some sort of test and that things would be all right. So right before the class ended, I asked if there were any questions. One guy raises his hand and I see him waving something pink in it. 'Yeah,' he says, 'I have a question, Sheila, baby. Did you forget something when you left my room last night?'

"Emma, he's waving panties, women's underwear, at me. And then another guy raises his hand and he's doing the same thing. All of a sudden there is a whole room full of men waving women's panties and saying vile things about me in their rooms. And they're laughing and thinking this is great."

"Ohmigod. What did you do?"

"The truth, Emma? I don't remember. I don't even remember leaving the room. I just sort of went blank, you know? And it is just so humiliating. Here I am thinking what a good job I'm doing and that we're finally getting somewhere, while they're just waiting to pounce. Oh, geez, where do you suppose they got them? The panties, I mean. I don't even want to think about that."

"Don't," suggested Emma. "Listen, I need to tell you about something that happened to me two days ago. I didn't talk about it earlier because . . . well, because I didn't want it to spook you like it did me. And I guess I just wanted it all to go away."

She paused and took a deep breath. "I went down to get the room ready for my session, early like I usually do, around 7:00. So I go into the empty room, get my overheads in order, and turn on the machine. The glass base is covered with a piece of cardboard, you know, like the back of a yellow pad. I move it aside and…" Emma had to pause to take a breath. "There's a transparency under it, and showing up on the screen is a large erect penis with the written message 'Suck my d–.'"

"Oh, no, and if you hadn't come in early–" said Sheila.

"I guess everyone would have had a good ol' boy laugh and I would have been mortified–totally thrown off, probably for the rest of the morning. It's so sick."

"So what did you do when the class started?"

"First, I washed the porno picture off the overhead and then when they all came in, I just acted as if nothing had happened, ignored the whispers and looks, started talking, and didn't stop until noon. Four hours, no questions, no breakouts, no breaks, and I was out of there."

Neither said anything for a while, each fiddling with her drink.

"We have to do something, don't we?" asked Sheila thoughtfully.

"Yep, we do," said Emma. "I've thought about taking it all to Bruce. But then I try to imagine what I'd say. 'Hey, Bruce, I know you are putting out a great deal of money to have two highly trained and respected consultants do their magic in these dog and pony shows. But, golly gee, the guys are talking dirty and we wondered if you could just come in and tell them to knock it off.'"

"Right, and 'While you're at it, could you slay a couple of dragons for us too?'"

"Exactly," said Emma. "You know, I don't even know why they're doing this kind of crap. I don't know if it is completely hostile or if they just think this is all a bunch of fun. Or do you think the guys believe it is cute?"

"I think my brain just shut down. I'm exhausted," said Sheila.

"Me too. Tomorrow?"

"Tomorrow," agreed Sheila. Since the managers would be touring a local plant the next day, they agreed to meet for breakfast to see if they could come up with some ways to resolve this.

Later, in her room, Emma fixed a cup of tea, positioned herself on the sofa facing the lights, and thought hard about the four weeks or so she and Sheila had worked with this first group of managers. It started slowly, the sexual humor as a part of their class discussion, and seemed harmless at first. Sheila and Emma had talked about it but decided that making an issue might just inspire more and worse.

The fact that all 50 of the managers in this group were males could be an indication of the gendered nature of the company, Emma considered. It was also possible that this kind of talk had developed as a norm–one that developed just among this group. Emma continued her reflections. "We took the safe route, didn't we? For the most part, we ignored the sexual comments. When we did acknowledge them, I had hoped that our facial expressions would convey an 'Okay, back to business, guys.'"

But Emma knew one thing for sure. They had been careful not to join in, although at times Emma found it especially difficult not to verbally respond to the demeaning references to women with terms such as bimbos, broads, and worse.

"Do all sexist names for women start with the letter B?" she remembered Sheila whispering to her when the class was doing individual work.

"Let's hope so," Emma had answered.

But it hadn't slowed down. Emma and Sheila took some comfort in the fact that the daily evaluations from the class members were quite good and seemed sincere. But their time with the group became more and more difficult as the talk became raunchier and more obscene. The men focused, almost obsessively, on the male genitalia. In one morning session, she and Sheila had counted the number of times the word "penis," or their preferred term "d–," was said. They stopped counting at 25. Jokes were about penises, and casual talk filled with references. She remembered one guy saying to another, "If your d–is as short as your memory, no wonder your wife keeps calling me."

There was one incident that Emma still had trouble believing. She had organized breakout groups and sent them out of the room to do some work. When they came back, she asked how they had done on their assignment. The highest-ranking guy in the group, a vice president in the organization, said, "Great, we learned a lot." He then proceeded to tell the whole class that they had learned all about how one of their group members liked to "do it" in a variety of positions, some of which could be considered, uh, unusual. A vice president, no less.

In one class, while Sheila was teaching and Emma observing, Emma remembered how her anger filled her, and she started writing notes to herself. She wrote, "These guys are pigs. They look like pigs. They eat like pigs. They drink like pigs. They are the Pig People." And then she wrote, "No, they're not pig people. They're the Penis People. They're like some primitive tribe that worships the almighty penis. Everything is about their penis, their d–!" That's why, when she discovered the porno picture on her overhead, the first thing she thought was, "They have struck. The Penis People have struck again."

Okay, enough, she thought. Time for sleep. One thing was certain, though. She and Sheila would have to think of something fast. This was only the first group and if things got out of control, word would spread fast to those managers scheduled to attend in later sessions and this job, with all it meant to them, would crash and burn.

# CHAPTER 38

# Navigating the Limits of a Smile

## Sarah J. Tracy

### SETTING THE (BACK) STAGE

With a weathered emery board, Cassie Donners* smoothed a jagged edge of one red fingernail before grabbing a new pair of nylon thigh highs and carefully tugging them up her long tanned legs. As she had done every Monday evening for the last three weeks, 24-year-old Cassie was prepping for the Welcome Cocktail Party, the first formal night of the trans-Panama Canal cruise on the *Radiant Spirit*, one of the largest ships of the Spirit Cruise Line. Her roommate and fellow junior assistant cruise director, Sally, was currently occupying the tiny bathroom in their cabin, so Cassie made do with the closet mirror to fluff her highlighted, shoulder-length blonde hair and apply mascara to the long lashes lining her amber eyes.

As Cassie donned her starched "creams"—fitted ivory-colored polyester suits issued by Spirit—she thought about the whirlwind world upon which she had embarked just three weeks ago. Cassie had interviewed for the cruise staff position a month after graduating from a small college in Oklahoma. She was hoping to improve her communication skills, acquire international experience, and visit exotic locales before settling down into a *real* job.

During her land-based one-day training with Spirit, Cassie was introduced to the central responsibilities of the position. As a junior assistant cruise director, Cassie would be part of the ship's five-person cruise staff team—the smallest but perhaps most visible departmental team on the ship. Cruise staff, whose job it was to keep the ship's 1,600 passengers entertained at sea, were required to wear uniforms and name badges whenever they were in passenger areas and thus could be on duty for up to 15 hours a day. A typical day at sea included refereeing table

---

*This case has been developed based on real organization(s) and real organizational experiences. Names, facts, and situations have been changed to protect the privacy of individuals and organizations.

tennis and shuffleboard tournaments, calling bingo, creating and orchestrating trivia quiz games, running swimming pool Olympics, teaching line-dance classes, leading karaoke sing-alongs and other theme nights, performing on the main stage, and, most important, interacting with passengers. Cassie really looked forward to this last activity. She had always considered herself to be a people person and had especially enjoyed college classes that included small group activities.

Besides these basic duties, land-based management also provided Cassie with a training manual that outlined ship policies and procedures. Among other things, the training manual admonished, "Do everything you can to meet a passenger's request." Indeed, the manual warned that "discourteous work performance and/ or service to passengers" warranted an official warning to the crew member, and three warnings constituted grounds for dismissal. And if crew members had any troubles fulfilling their service requirements, The Spirit complaints procedure indicated that a staff member who felt he or she had a "genuine grievance" should report it to his or her direct supervisor.

Indeed, the land-based director of passenger programs advised Cassie that the ship management was run military style, saying, "If you have any questions or complaints, talk to the cruise director, and then he will contact us at headquarters if necessary. We just have too many employees on too many ships for you all to be calling us directly." Cassie nodded her head in eager concurrence. She could not imagine that she would have anything to complain about on a cruise ship! The director also warned Cassie, "Remember, you are never off-duty, especially when you are in a passenger area. On a cruise ship, you are basically public property."

Cassie shook off the warning, smiled warmly, and reassured the director, drawling sweetly, "I can take it. In fact, I'll love it." At the time, Cassie never could have imagined the extent this *public property* mentality would take on the ship.

Cassie's tour of duty began in Vancouver, British Columbia, Canada, a turn-around port for many Alaskan itineraries. Now into her third week, the ship had just begun to make its way down the west coast and into the Mexican Riviera. During her six-month contract, the ship would take Cassie from Alaska, to several Mexican ports of call, to parts of Central and South America, through the Panama Canal and throughout the Caribbean. She was assigned to the *Radiant Spirit,* a 70,000-ton floating paradise. At 14 stories, it would be the largest high-rise she had ever lived in, or upon. The job environment was also different from her past experience. She was one of only five Americans working on the ship, and most of the employees were men. Cassie estimated a 6-to-1 ratio of males to females. As a blonde American female, Cassie felt different and special.

Cassie pondered her uniqueness as she ran a brush through the tangles of her sea breeze-tousled hair. Her eyes drifted from her own reflection in the closet mirror to the alarm clock, and upon seeing the time, Cassie suddenly realized she needed to hurry up. She was surprised Sally was still in the bathroom. Sally, also a junior assistant director, was taking a break from graduate school. And it was Sally who was usually the more responsible one. The two had become quite close over the last three weeks. In fact, because they looked so much alike, fellow crew members had begun to call them the "little blonde American twins." Cassie checked the clock again. They were going to be the late and yelled-at little twins if Sally didn't hurry up. Cassie yelled through the bathroom door, "Hey, Sally, we only have five minutes before the Welcome Cocktail Party. Get your butt in gear!"

Sally emerged from the tiny bathroom with hair dripping wet. "Get your own butt in gear," she said with a smirk.

Cassie paused for a second, seriously considering Sally's comment. Peering at her backside in the closet mirror, Cassie conceded, "You know, you're right. I should get my butt in gear. It's just gotten bigger and bigger since I've been on this ship." It was one of the many self-deprecating comments Cassie would make about herself every day.

Sally shook her head and said, "Shut up, shut up. If you are fat, what does that make me, a beached whale?" Both weighed less than 120 pounds. Cassie was curvier, Sally a bit more athletic.

Cassie rolled the waistband of her skirt up a couple of times, a maneuver that loosened the skirt around her hips and thus masked the curviness of her supposedly big butt. Rolling the waistband also raised the skirt's hem several inches—something most of the female cruise staff agreed made the uniform appear more modern. She smiled at her reflection in the mirror; "Ahh, much better."

Meanwhile, Sally frantically turned over dirty clothes littering the 10- by 12-foot windowless cabin and muttered under her breath, "Where is my rhinestone hair comb? I just need to put my hair up and I'll be ready."

Ignoring her, Cassie said, "Listen, I'm assigned to trail Blake tonight to supposedly learn more about swanning, so I'll just go on ahead." *Swanning* was cruise staff speak for floating around and making conversation. As assistant cruise director Blake had informed Cassie upon her maiden voyage, "Our job is our personality." That was just fine with her.

Rushing around with rhinestone comb in hand, Sally said, "That's cool, go on. Blake will make some sarcastic comment if you aren't exactly on time, so I will just meet you there." Cassie began to leave, but just before the door shut, Sally yelled out, "Wait, Cassie! Where is your service pin?" Cassie caught the door with one cream-colored two-inch-heeled pump.

"Shoot! I always forget that darn thing." Cassie was still getting used to the cruise ship's dress standards, which, among other things, required all crew members to wear a small lapel pin etched with the ship's customer service credo. Supervisors could write up a crew member who was caught in a passenger area without the pin.

Also as part of the program, two copies of Spirit's service credo were affixed to the inside of crew members' cabin doors and bathroom doors. The credo included mandates such as "We never say no," "We smile, we are onstage," "Never express negative opinions, argue, or be discourteous with passengers," and "We are ambassadors of our cruise ship when at work and at play." In addition, backstage crew areas of the ship were plastered with posters reading "Always greet passengers; say 'Hello, ma'am,' 'Good morning, sir,'" and "We always are cheerful and say 'Please' and 'Thank you.'" Crew members largely echoed these mandates in their own talk; one staff member warned Sally on her first day of work, "When you wake up in the morning, turn your smile on. Don't turn it back off again until you go to sleep."

As cruise staff understood it, management basically wanted crew members to be at the beck and call of passengers for their every request. Most staff complied without complaint. As Blake liked to remind the staff, "Passengers pay our salaries." Indeed, cruise staff's main evaluation technique was through passenger comment cards: Cruise director Tim kept a detailed record of the number of passenger comments each employee received, subtracting negative ones from positive ones, and used this as a basis for cruise staff evaluation and promotion. As such, staff engaged in a number of activities to ensure they received good comments. Paul, the deputy cruise director, performed cartwheels—literally—at all his activities in the hope that passengers would remember to name him in the comment cards. Sally eventually cut her hair to distinguish herself from Cassie and thus potentially be named more often in the comment cards.

Cassie frantically poked the service pin through her cream blazer. "Ta-ta, I'm off to the party. See you at dinner if not before!"

## FACING THE AUDIENCE

Cassie pushed open the swinging doors that separated the crew area from the onstage passenger area, and on cue a smile spread across her face. She walked up the stairs to the ship's grand atrium, the open showcase area of the ship, spanning decks five through seven. Scanning the chandelier-lit space, she spotted Blake, the Donny Osmond look-alike assistant cruise director she was assigned to trail. He stood surrounded by female passengers, flashing a smile, his helmet of brown hair slick with mousse. Blake was a 30-year-old high school dropout, ex-car salesman, and chess wiz. He had worked more than two years for Spirit and seemed to gain pleasure in telling Cassie what to do.

Seabreeze Jazz, one of the ship's six bands, accompanied the evening with piano and guitar. Passengers dressed in evening gowns and tuxedos stood huddled in groups, furiously sucking down cocktails provided free of charge during the half-hour party. Cassie sidled up to Blake and the group, trying to decide whether the women were a group of divorcées, widows, or wives with tardy husbands. In his sing-song voice, Blake announced, "Ladies, ladies, let me introduce you to *Radiant Spirit's* newest employee. And this," he motioned grandly, "is Cassie." Cassie smiled.

A woman wearing lots of sparkly eye makeup turned to Cassie and said, "So, where are you from...England, I bet."

Cassie gently corrected her, saying, "Actually, I'm from the United States—Oklahoma." Cassie continued, "So how are you ladies enjoying the cruise so far?" Swanning was easier if you got the passengers to talk.

Another woman, this one wearing a large emerald choker that perfectly complemented her green-sequined dress, said, "Wow, I didn't think there were any American crew members on this ship." Cassie began to explain how the ship employed few Americans, largely because most Americans would not put up with working for six to eight months without a day off. Suddenly, Cassie felt Blake's disapproving stare, and she abruptly stopped.

He changed the subject with a flash of his teeth, querying, "So, did you all have a nice time in Cabo San Lucas today?"

Without hesitation, Sparkly Eye Shadow jumped in and said, "Actually, I've been there three times before, so instead I went to the bridge tournament here on the ship. Do you play bridge, honey?" She winked at Cassie.

"Uh, no...but my mom and grandmother do." Then she added with great enthusiasm, "I can play Go Fish!" Immediately she recoiled. Cassie thought she sounded as stupid as Blake, but no one else seemed to mind.

The ship suddenly lurched. The room lost balance en masse, and a gentleman from an adjoining group stumbled into the ladies' space, taking center stage. He adjusted his black satin cummerbund, appreciating the instant audience, and declared, "And I have only had one drink so far, ha, ha, ha. Maybe I will be able to stand straight after I'm drunk!" The ladies and Cassie giggled. A pained expression broke through Blake's smiley mask. Cassie would soon learn that passengers continually made this same *original* joke, all seeming to believe they were the first to think it up.

At last, the dinner bell rang. Passengers quickly gulped the remainder of their drinks and scurried toward the elevators to go up the one flight to dinner. Blake and Cassie headed for the stairs, ready to meet other cruise staffers in the officers' mess for dinner of their own. On their way, a couple stopped and asked them which way it was to dinner. In unison they explained that the dining room was "up one deck and back to the aft of the ship," but the couple still seemed confused. The woman, with a gray beehive, pointed to the elevator and tentatively asked, "Does this elevator go to the *back* of the ship?" Cassie stopped, thought for a second, and realized she had no idea how to answer this question.

Blake obviously didn't care, and with another toothy grin said, "Yeah, honey, on the *Radiant* we have special high-tech diagonal elevators." Cassie laughed nervously, trying to cover up her embarrassment at Blake's sarcasm.

Feeling a little sorry for the woman, she began to explain away Blake's tone to Beehive by giving her more detailed directions. But before she could finish, Blake grabbed her arm and whispered in her ear, "They will get it. We are out of here." Cassie consoled herself; he *was* the expert. Cassie was ready to turn off her smile and relax, and at this point the passengers had already wandered into the elevator.

Blake and Cassie made their way to the backstage crew galley, finally out of sight of passengers. As they walked through the long hallway to the aft of the ship, various male crew members whistled and made comments in Italian as the duo passed. Blake yelled back, "Hey, you never whistle at me when I'm alone."

One of them teased in accented English, "That is because we are not whistling at you." Then, directing his gaze on Cassie, he continued, "Ooh, la, la, look at those legs!"

Cassie was becoming increasingly aware that she served as a sex object for the male crew members and the male passengers. While she usually enjoyed being the center of attention, she was not used to blatant innuendo. She leaned over to Blake, saying, "I don't know whether to be flattered or insulted."

Blake replied, "Well, you don't have any control over it, so I would just learn to live with it."

In the officers' mess, Blake and Cassie met up with the other cruise staff. Compared with the menu of macaroni and cheese that Cassie was used to at college, the meal was a delectable delight—escargot swimming in garlic butter, French onion soup with a thick gooey layer of mozzarella cheese, and hazelnut soufflé with hot amaretto cream sauce. As she spooned in the last of her dessert, Cassie declared, "I swear, I'm going to get sooo fat on this ship!" As usual, the others ignored her. Instead, they began one of their favorite backstage rituals—swapping stories of stupid passenger questions. Cassie was proud to have one of her own to share. "You know, a couple just asked us if our elevators go to the back of the ship. It's like, 'give me a break!'"

## THE UPS AND DOWNS OF CUSTOMER SERVICE

Two months into her contract, Cassie had heard an uncountable number of stupid questions. She had become adept at dealing with them, and almost as good as Blake at ignoring or subtly deflecting passenger criticisms and complaints. However, her probationary review was quickly approaching, and she knew that she needed to keep a clean record, or better yet, receive a lot of positive passenger comments in order to receive a favorable review and be eligible for promotion at the end of her contract. It also made sense to make nicey-nice with the cruise director, Tim, someone with whom Cassie had not hit it off very well. Tim, a 45-year-old Los Angeleno, considered Cassie to be a dumb blonde, a part she herself admitted playing when it helped to get her way. As she explained to Sally, "Sometimes it is just easier to smile and laugh off stuff like you don't get it." Cassie continued, "*But*, that doesn't make me dumb. For goodness sake, I have a college degree–something Tim doesn't have. I may not be part of his little group of friends, but I don't want to have to be a brown-noser to get there."

Sally said, "Believe me, I don't like Tim much either. At the same time, though, keep in mind that it may be easier in the long run just to kiss up to him." Cassie sighed. Maybe she *would* suck it up for the next couple of weeks, at least until she got through her probationary review.

Three hours later, Cassie and the rest of the cruise staff raced around backstage preparing for Cruise Fun Night. Tim, already onstage, boomed over the show-lounge microphone, "Welcome to Cruise Fun Night, the show where *you* are the show!" The lounge was packed with nearly 800 passengers. Cassie and Sally were double-checking the prizes for the fun night games when Jean, the ship's exercise manager, limped over, having sprained her ankle earlier in the day while teaching aerobics. "Hey, guys, I'm not going to be able to do the balloon game tonight because of my ankle. Can one of you do it?"

A grimace spread across Sally's face. "Hey, I'm willing to be Naughty Nursie and stuff two balloons in my blouse for the cruise staff skit, but I'm not up to the balloon game."

Jean said, "You think I *like* getting jumped on by passengers week after week?"

Dan, a new assistant cruise director in training, approached the threesome and asked, "Hey, what is this about getting jumped on?"

Sally explained. "See these balloons here?" She pointed to two industrial-size paper bags, each stuffed with eight balloons, and continued, "They are for the balloon game. Earlier in the day, Cassie and I blew them up. And we blow them up in a special way–first as big as we can, and then we let out a lot of air. That makes them really stretchy and difficult to break. Well, during the show, we get eight female and eight male passengers to volunteer for the game. We line them up on opposite sides of the stage and give each of them a balloon. The passengers have to stick the balloon between their legs and kind of jump or skip over to either Blake or Jean– whoever is of the opposite sex–and break the balloon by sitting down and bouncing it between their butt and Blake or Jean's lap. Whichever team gets done first wins, and the thing is, it usually takes a while. Because the balloons are so stretchy, they usually have to bounce five or six times before the balloon pops!"

Dan grinned, beginning to understand as the mental picture formed in his mind.

Cassie added, "And what Sally failed to mention is that Tim tells the passengers that they have to sit forward, *straddling* you to break the balloon. It's *totally* disgusting."

Blake walked by and interrupted. "It is only disgusting if you get peed on, like I did two weeks ago. Now *that is* gross."

Cassie's face contorted in disgust. "I'm sorry, but I just don't want 60-year-old, dirty old men jumping up and down on me simulating sex."

Neither did Sally, and she was smart enough to convince Cassie to do the game. "Come on, Cassie, you will be great at it. The passengers love you. Anyway, I have to hand out balloons and prizes to the contestants." It was a lame excuse, and both of them knew it. Sally added, "Anyway, you're going up for your probationary review soon...this could win you some points with the passengers and with Tim."

Cassie exclaimed, "I just wish they had put this in the job description!"

"Yeah, right, would you have signed up for this job if they had?" Sally muttered, "If only my feminist friends back at graduate school could see me now."

With a deep sigh, Cassie agreed to be bounced upon. When it came time for the balloon game, Cassie and Blake took their positions on opposite balloon game chairs and braced themselves for what was to come. The audience screamed with laughter as the lineup of male and female passengers ran across the stage and frantically bounced on their laps, trying to break the balloons. Cassie's face was crimson. Her hands gripped the seat, and with every bounce a slight wince leaked through her ear-to-ear smile. Finally she could stand it no longer. For the last four men in line, Cassie did not allow them to bounce up and down more than twice before she herself pricked and popped their balloon with her fingernail. The game, which usually lasted at least four minutes, continued for only two. Tim, emceeing the evening, grabbed the microphone and merrily announced that the male passengers were the winners in this *Battle of the Sexes*. When he turned from the audience toward Cassie, though, his eyes were narrow in anger. In her haste to rid her lap of bouncing men, Cassie had ruined the game. She knew it, and it was clear now that Tim knew it too.

The show continued without ado, and the passengers gave a standing ovation. The cruise staff, sweaty, tired, and satisfied with the show, trotted backstage.

Cassie and Sally were peeling off their costumes when Tim approached them. "What the hell were you thinking, Cassie?" he barked in her face.

"What are you talking about, Tim?" Cassie whipped her head around but tried to sound nonconfrontational.

"That balloon game was freakin' ruined. If you can't do it right, why the heck did you do it? Are you so stupid that you didn't see you were popping the balloons twice as quickly as Blake's? Are you blind? Stupid? Or both?"

Cassie's eyes began to blaze. Sally silently pleaded for her to just leave it all alone. "Let's go, Cassie," she whispered.

## NEGOTIATING THE DARK SIDE

The next evening, Sally and Cassie prepared for the Fifties Sock Hop theme night, dressed in denim blue miniskirts and cheap white T-shirts with "Spirit Sock Hop" silk-screened across the front. Sally was "Bambi" for the night; Blake was "Rocco"; Cassie was "Trixie." Passengers were beginning to wander into the ship's disco, the home of this and various other theme nights the cruise staff held to keep passengers awake and buying revenue-producing drinks. Engineered entertainment. They came to watch. The cruise staff's job was to get 10% of the passengers involved, so that the other 90% would have something to watch. The disco's glitter globe cast shadowy illuminations upon about 30 passengers sitting at tables and a handful of couples who were dancing the swing on the sunken dance floor.

As the band finished, Blake took center stage. Unsuccessfully trying to appear fifties-ish in rolled-up jeans and a semitransparent Spirit tee, Blake grabbed the microphone and in a stupid tough-guy accent heralded the crowd into motion. "Good evening, ladies and gentlemen. My name is Rocco, and those are my girls down there, Bambi and Trixie." Blake gestured to Cassie and Sally, who twirled and bowed on the dance floor. Blake continued, "Now, this is a fifties sock hop, and a sock hop can't be complete without a twist contest, so if you're already on the dance floor, stay there, and if you're not, come on down." Couples who minutes before happily danced the swing made a beeline for the dance floor exits.

Sally blocked one of the exits, literally sitting on one exit post and kicking her feet up to the other, and told passengers in wide-eyed innocence, "There is an invisible laser barrier here, and if you pass it, you will blow up into a billion pieces." Two of the couples smiled at Sally's attempt at humor and agreed to participate in the game. Another couple turned and left through another exit.

Blake continued to explain the contest. "Now, this isn't just any twist contest, it is the balloon twist. Just watch Trixie and Bambi demonstrate." Cassie and Sally sprang onto the small disco stage, placed a balloon between their chests, and began to wiggle. Sally whispered to Cassie, "I've done this so many times that I am actually kinda *proud* of my balloon twisting abilities." Cassie rolled her eyes but kept smiling.

Blake continued, "Now the goal is to keep the balloon pressed between you and your partner, and you can't use your hands. If it falls to the floor, you are out. Now come on down, ladies and gentlemen. There is nothing to be afraid of." The room was still, silent. "Did I mention that we will give a bottle of champagne to the winners?" Three more couples straggled to the floor, likely unaware that the champagne prize cost Spirit about 50 cents.

The contest began. A couple won. The cruise staff delivered the champagne with a cheer and continued with a hula-hoop contest. Blake closed the theme night with a beach party line dance, providing an opportunity for all the single women to come to the floor. Sally and Cassie danced along with the passengers, egging them on to spice it up with turns and hip shakes. Blake finally turned over the evening to the disc jockey, and Sally and Cassie made their way up to the passenger bar, ready for a drink and a break.

A tall man who appeared to be in his mid-60s approached the bobby-socked duo. "Hi, gals. You sure were looking fine out there on the dance floor. Can I buy you a drink?"

After quickly examining the man with a long thin ponytail of gray hair, dressed in an expensive-looking black suit, Cassie and Sally responded in unison, "Sure." Passenger-bought drinks were one of the perks of the job, and staff were usually quick to take up offers. Drinking with passengers was a way to relax and swan at the same time. Cruise director Tim usually made the rounds of the various ship lounges throughout the evening to ensure that the cruise staff continued to "work" the passengers until at least 11 P.M. Sally glanced at the new watch she had bought in St. Thomas earlier that day. It was 10:30 P.M.–only a half hour to go.

The three of them gathered at a small table near the dance floor. Cassie and Sally quickly learned that the man's name was Fred. As he leaned in close to hear them over the beat of the music, they also learned that he had cigarette breath and sickeningly sweet cologne. After some small talk about his day in St. Thomas, Fred asked Cassie to dance. Female cruise staff were not technically required to dance with passengers. However, it usually made for positive comments in the comment cards, and quite simply it was sometimes less effortful to dance than to make conversation. Cassie agreed. The man, almost three times her age, triumphantly grabbed Cassie's hand. As he tugged her to the dance floor, Cassie looked back at Sally and mouthed the word "Gross."

In return, Sally mouthed "Yuck." Then she quickly looked around to make sure none of the passengers had noticed this interchange. No one had. Sally sank back into the chair, quietly sipping the $8 glass of wine Fred had just purchased for her. She was relieved that he had chosen Cassie rather than her–a perk of being the more athletic and less curvy of the little blonde American twins.

Once on the dance floor, Fred and Cassie began to move in rhythm with the beat of the disco music. Tired of feeling his sweaty grip, Cassie tried to break free of Fred's hand. She twirled out and away from him, but the moment she began dancing on her own, Fred somehow grabbed on again. Cassie resigned herself to being firmly anchored to Fred throughout the dance. As the song continued, Fred pulled Cassie closer and closer. Cassie pushed back and playfully quipped, "Aren't you a little devil? I'd actually like to dance further back, like this." She pointed to four inches of space she had managed to squeeze between their bodies.

Fred smiled slowly, saying, "I know girls like you. You're just a tease, like when you were wiggling with that balloon between you and that other girl."

Cassie began to feel uneasy. "That was a performance," she thought. "That is not me–the *real* Cassie."

Fred pulled her close again and, brushing his lips to her ear, said, "Come on now, tell me, would you ever consider me if you came over to the dark side?"

The dark side? Cassie's heart began to race. She did not know whether to laugh or to run. She decided to play dumb. "Huh? What do you mean?"

He persisted, "You know, the dark side. Would you consider being with me?"

Cassie again said "Huh?" and pretended not to hear him by holding her hand to her ear. But while she was able to ignore his words, it was more difficult to ignore his gyrating body pressed against hers. The smell of his sweat was beginning to leak through his heavy cologne. Pushing back the anger that stung her eyes, Cassie thought to herself, "Don't act offended, or he will win this game." She endured the last 20 seconds of the dance, disentangled herself from Fred's embrace, and ran back to the table where Sally was sitting.

"Come on. We are leaving *now!*" Cassie pulled Sally into the hallway and then through the swinging doors into the crew elevator area. She leaned against the hallway wall, slid down into a huddled figure, and looked like she was about to cry. Perplexed, Sally slid down and sat next to her. "Cassie, what? What is it? What is wrong? I know he was ugly, but..."

Taking a ragged breath, Cassie interrupted, "He kept rubbing up against me and actually asked me if I wanted to come to the 'dark side.' What the hell? I swear these passengers think when they buy the cruise, they also buy us–that we should be entertaining them in all areas. I feel like a freakin' call girl!"

Attempting to get Cassie out of her funk, Sally cracked, "Call girl, huh? Yeah, I wonder how the passengers ever get that impression, with us running around in short skirts and you letting men jump on top of you and all."

Sally's last comment perturbed Cassie; she did not find it funny. She protested, "Geez, Sally, you think this is my fault?"

"No, no, no, I didn't mean that. Gosh, I don't know," Sally responded.

Cassie reflected, "It is weird, because he wasn't saying anything blatant, like 'Come to bed with me,' but I just felt so violated, like I had no control. I was trying not to say anything mean to him, but…"

"You were being offended in making sure he wasn't offended," Sally finished Cassie's thought.

Cassie nodded vigorously. "Exactly!"

Sally paused and then continued. "So are you going to do anything about it?"

Cassie shrugged her shoulders, bit her lower lip, and thought about her options. She had accepted a drink from and agreed to dance with the guy. Did this make her a tease? Did this make her responsible? At the same time, she was angry. Her amber eyes narrowing, she said to Sally with more certainty, "You know we do *not* have to touch these guys, we do *not* have to dance with them, and I should *not* have to deal with this."

Sally said, "Well, you could just march up to him and tell him that."

"Yeah, right, and he would just march up to the comment card drop box and write something nasty about me," Cassie said. "I definitely don't need that right before next week's probationary review. Anyway, I don't feel like seeing that guy again, let alone confronting him."

Sally continued, "Well, maybe you should talk to Tim…"

Cassie exclaimed, "Yeah, I'm sure he is going to be real understanding after last night's balloon fiasco!"

"Well, maybe you could go above his head?" Sally questioned uncertainly and then quickly recouped, answering her own question. "Actually, no, that probably wouldn't be good considering the rumors of other staff who have gone over their supervisors' heads."

Cassie agreed, "Yeah, there is no way I'm going to do that. Remember, we are not supposed to contact headquarters directly, and anyway, Tim would make my life hell." She bowed and shook her head. "I don't know, Sally, I just don't know."

CHAPTER 39

# Putting My Best Foot Forward

## Aparna Hebbani

Straightening his new bright red tie as he looked out of his eighth-floor office
window on a snowy Wednesday morning, Scott Holmes* wondered whether
the advertised position would be filled. Scott was head of IT services at IT-Webdesign, a specialized IT firm providing web-based design services. Located in a
large metropolitan city in the United States, IT-Webdesign was founded four years
ago and was suddenly in high demand with increasing business volume. Scott, now
in his mid-30s, was relatively young to be the head of IT-Webdesign. He was lucky
to land this job with an MIS degree and a few years' experience as finance manager
in a local engineering firm.

The current staff, consisting of five full-time web designers, was starting to
feel the stress of increased workloads, long hours, and tight project deadlines. As
a result, Scott placed an advertisement in the local newspaper and on a job search
website for a web designer with a university degree in a computer-related field and
previous experience designing websites. He needed to fill this position as soon as
possible.

As Scott continued to look out of the window, a loud knock on his office door
caught his attention. He turned around to see Brad Jones, the HR manager, walk
in. "Morning, Scott, how's it going?" asked Brad, with files tucked under his left
arm. In his mid-50s, Brad spent the last 20 years as an HR manager for an agricultural equipment firm in Cedar Falls, Michigan. Brad was a bit nervous because he
was still new to the IT industry, having joined IT-Webdesign just five months ago.
Taking a seat at the long and polished conference table, he glanced around Scott's
plush office with contemporary furnishings and an excellent view of the snow-
covered mountains. "Not bad. How about yourself?" replied Scott as he cleared

---

*This case has been developed based on real organization(s) and real organizational experi-
ences. Names, facts, and situations have been changed to protect the privacy of individuals and
organizations.

his throat and took a seat at the head of the conference table. Soon the scheduled interviews would begin. "Perhaps we can take a few minutes to look over these résumés?" suggested Brad, "And prepare a few questions for each applicant?" Both men got to work immediately looking over the two applicants' files that Brad had brought along.

## MAKING FIRST IMPRESSIONS

Getting out of bed early at 5:30 A.M., Sunil (Sunny) Pandit was nervous about his interview today. As a matter of fact, he was so nervous that he had barely slept through the night, thinking about what questions he might be asked and how he might respond. In his early 20s, Sunny had arrived two years ago from India to pursue his master's studies, just like so many others before him. He was about to graduate from the local university and now desperately needed to get a job.

Then two weeks ago, he saw an ad in the classified section for a web designer. Saying a loud prayer, Sunny emailed his résumé and was thrilled to get an interview call. "I have to do really well at this interview today," he thought to himself as he dressed up in the only black suit he had. It was a bit faded, but with limited finances, he had taken the trouble to brush and iron it, hoping no one would notice. Taking care to groom himself properly, Sunny headed out the door determined to get this job.

Traveling on the train, he knew his interview was at 9:00 A.M., but the office was farther away from the train station than he had anticipated. Running as fast as he could through the snow-covered streets with a briefcase in his left hand, he hoped to arrive at the interview on time and wished they wouldn't notice his shoes, which weren't so clean anymore.

## TIME IS OF THE ESSENCE

Meanwhile, Scott and Brad were ready to welcome their first interview candidate. As the clock struck 9:00 A.M., Scott walked out into the foyer ready to greet their first interviewee, Mr. Pandit, only to notice that he had not arrived yet. Scott could not comprehend how a candidate could be late for a job interview. "This is just not right—coming late for an interview. He should at least have called to inform us that he was running late," thought Scott to himself. After instructing Barbara, the receptionist, to call him when Mr. Pandit came in, an irritated Scott returned to his office.

Taking the elevator up to the eighth floor, Sunil caught his breath and tried to tidy up his appearance by readjusting his tie and combing his hair by looking at the mirrors in the elevator. He looked at his watch—9:15 A.M.—he had finally made it to the office of IT-Webdesign, even if it was just a few minutes late. "What matters is that I am here," he convinced himself. Walking through the glass doors into the reception area, he smiled and introduced himself to Barbara with a noticeable east Indian accent. "Hello. I am Sunny. I am here for my interview."

## IT'S A DONE DEAL!

Half an hour later, as Sunil took the elevator down to the first floor, he was thoroughly pleased with his performance at the interview. In fact, he was so confident that he had a big smile on his face and walked with extra confidence. Knowing that he had all the qualifications the position announcement had asked for and that he answered all questions asked, there was no way he wouldn't be offered the job. He had stronger educational qualifications than the job required and a good GPA. As part of his coursework, Sunil had also designed a few websites, so he could clearly perform the job duties expected of him.

Meanwhile, up in his office, Scott shook his head and looked at Brad after Sunny had left the room. "We still need to keep looking—hope the next one does better," said Scott as Brad shook his head in agreement.

## NOT SO SURE

Scott had been slightly apprehensive from the moment he saw Sunny walk in through his door even though he had expected that Sunny would be of east Indian descent after looking at his résumé. That fact aside, Scott had invited Sunny for an interview based upon his résumé and qualifications. After all, Sunny was about to graduate with a master's degree from the local university and had a high GPA. His résumé also showed some experience in web design, even if it was part of his coursework. There were a few grammatical errors in his résumé, but nothing out of the ordinary. All in all, Scott had anticipated the interview to go well.

But now as he reflected on the interview, he had already made up his mind that Sunny would not be offered this position. Not only had Sunny walked into the interview 15 minutes late, which was rude enough, but also he didn't even apologize for not being on time. After Scott became accustomed to Sunny's Indian accent, he was taken aback by his short, to-the-point responses. Sunny had several opportunities when he could have sold himself, like anyone truly wanting a job would, but instead replied only in brief. For example, when asked, "Do you have any experience in web design?" Sunny replied, "Yes, I do" and did not elaborate. It seemed like Scott had to prompt Sunny to expand on his responses, and if it was this hard to get Sunny to talk in an interview, how would he be able to carry on a conversation with other colleagues, even if it was small talk about the weather? Scott thought that Sunny's poor verbal communication was due to sheer nervousness and lack of self-confidence.

Scott had also noticed Sunny's soft handshake and slightly bowed, meek posture. "Sunny also kept his gaze down to his hands placed in his lap and barely looked me in the eye," reflected Scott. "Perhaps there was something Sunny was trying to conceal?" And what was Scott to make of Sunny's head movements from side to side every time he asked a question? Was that a yes or a no?

Brad, too, had his doubts about Sunny's hireability. He was critical of Sunny's appearance. Couldn't Sunny have worn a newer suit? After all, this was his only chance to make an impression and land the job. Brad also noticed that Sunny barely kept his hands on the table or gestured. Sunny's nervousness was also evident in his posture as he sat upright and did not appear at ease. He simply wouldn't be a good fit in this office, concluded Brad.

"Well, our next candidate should be here in five minutes," said Scott as he reached for his mug of freshly brewed coffee. They hoped that the next candidate would be someone they both would be more comfortable with.

## THE NEXT CANDIDATE

A few minutes later Scott was greeting their second applicant, Tara Singh, who was a tall, east Indian woman in her 30s dressed in a well-tailored black suit. On second thought, Tara was quite pretty, with large, black eyes, long, black, thick hair that came down to her waist, and a figure well-maintained on a strict exercise regime.

Arriving right on time, Tara was looking forward to this interview. Having worked in the IT industry for the last five years, she had the experience needed. With a bachelor's degree in IT, she had the educational background for the job. Originally from Bombay, Tara came to the United States six years ago to live with her brother after completing her undergraduate degree. "Hi. My name is Tara, and I'm glad to be here," she said confidently as she introduced herself to Scott in an American accent. Tara was eagerly looking forward to knowing more about the position and job duties. Scott, too, was looking ahead to this interview as he noticed Tara's attractive figure.

## AFTER THE FACT

Walking into Scott's office, Tara greeted Brad with a firm handshake and sat down in the chair that Scott indicated. To her surprise, he sat next to her rather than across the table with Brad, which she thought was a bit odd. Trying to push this thought aside, she decided to get her mind back on the interview. "So tell us more about yourself," started Scott, to which Tara talked at length about her educational and work qualifications, much to Scott's satisfaction. The three of them talked at length about the nature of the IT industry, and Brad realized that he was learning more about the IT industry from this smart woman. Scott and Brad were pleasantly surprised and at ease with Tara's American accent.

Meanwhile, Tara felt distinctly uncomfortable with the way Scott looked at her throughout the interview, gazing at her and sitting in such close proximity. He could almost lean over and touch her if he wanted to, so she tried to reposition her chair as if to give herself more space. "How rude is he to sit so close to me?" she thought to herself. And what business did Brad have asking her if she watched Bollywood movies—just because she was Indian?

After politely finishing the interview an hour later, Tara thought to herself, "There is no way I'm taking this job. I'm just glad to be out of there." She just didn't have a good feeling about working in this office, especially with Scott's behavior. Even as she got up from her chair at the end of the interview, Scott walked out with her. Not only did put his arm on her shoulder, but also he had the nerve to clasp her hand with both of his! What did he think he was doing? Tara was distinctly uncomfortable with the way Scott behaved throughout the interview. Didn't he know not to touch an Indian lady?

---

**Mr. Sunny Pandit**

---

5637 Crowden Avenue                          Tel: (836) 432 1172
Cedar Falls, MI 43005                     Email: spandit@yahoo.com

**Objective:**
I want to do a job where my experience and skills can be effective.

**Education:**
- ➤ At present pursuing master's degree in computer engineering at the University of Cedar Falls
  GPA is 3.75, graduating end of this semester
- ➤ Pursued bachelor of computer applications (May 2006) at National University, India

**Computer/Technical Skills:**
- ➤ HTML, Illustrator CS2, Java, Servlets, JSP, PHP, SQL, XML, XSL, JavaScript
- ➤ Graphic design and photo editing
- ➤ Proficient user of Macromedia Dreamweaver, Adobe Photoshop, Fireworks MX, basic knowledge of Macromedia Flash
- ➤ Web servers: Apache Http Server, Apache Tomcat 4.0
- ➤ DBMS used: MySql, Oracle 8I, Access

**Relevant Experience:**
- ➤ Graduate assistant for technical support, School of Business, the University of Cedar Falls, August 2007–present. Responsible also for daily maintenance of their website.
- ➤ Web developer (internship) India.
  Duration: 1 April 2006–1 August 2006
  Tools/languages used: HTML, DHTML, Macromedia Dreamweaver, Microsoft Front Page, Flash-8, Adobe Photoshop, and many other graphic design softwares. Helped design a complete company website.

**Personal:** Enthusiastic, hard working, on student visa
**References:** References are available upon request.

**Figure 39.1** Mr. Sunny Pandit

## Tara Singh

624 Barrister Ct., Cedar Falls, MI 43005
Tel: (836) 432 2189
Email: Tara_s@hotmail.com

### Objective
- To obtain a position in web design/development that is challenging and will contribute to the success of my career.

### Technical Skills
- Database: PL/SQL, Oracle 9.0
- Languages: HTML, XHTML, DHTML, XML, Java, JSP, ASP, C, PHP Python, Perl
- Operating systems: MS DOS, UNIX (Solaris, HP-UX/AIX), MS Windows (98/NT/Vista), VAX/VMS
- GUI tools: Visual Basic, Developer 2000, and Visio 2000
- Packages: MS Office, Netscape, IE
- Experienced in hosing websites and downloading/uploading contents on server
- Knowledge of site compatibility, usability and accessibility issues

### Education
- Bachelor of engineering in computer science from Bombay University (2002)

### Previous Employment Details
- Company name: Web Design Ltd.
  Web designer
  From: December 2007 to present
  Technical skills used: Dreamweaver, MySQL
  Developed a site for online shopping for several occasions like Christmas, Valentine's Day, Thanksgiving etc. This site contains a shopping cart and detailed information and images of various products.
- Company name: IT Design
  Web developer
  From: May 2002 to November 2007
  Technical skills used: Created web designs, created HTML, various graphic materials (mailers, signature, banners, etc.) using Photoshop and Dreamweaver

### References
- Available on request.

**Figure 39.2** Tara Singh

## A FAIRYTALE ENDING?

On the eighth floor, Scott and Brad did not realize how time flew by, and before they knew it, they had finished Tara's interview. Both were pleased with Tara's performance. She had come across as an attractive, smart woman who would fit in with others at IT-Webdesign.

Both were in agreement about offering her the position. They couldn't see why she might turn their offer down and congratulated each other that the position was filled.

A week later Brad were puzzled to learn that Tara had turned down their job offer.

In another part of town, Sunny checked his mailbox and voicemail everyday hoping to receive news of an offer with IT-Webdesign.

Scott and Brad were back to the beginning of the search process. Would they ever find the right candidate?

CHAPTER 40

# Berating the Bow

## Andrew Jared Critchfield

**"Y**ou cannot bow to the American clients! It always puts us in a weaker position to negotiate! How many times must you be informed?" yelled Ayako's boss. His outburst was surprising because politeness and indirect communication are highly valued within Japanese organizations. In Ayako Ishigaki's native Japanese language, most conversation utilizes the concept of *tatemae* (literally, façade), or the masked feelings that will not interfere with social relations or group harmony. Rarely was it appropriate to share the *honne* (true feelings or desires).

"I understand. I am very sorry for embarrassing you, the organization I am honored to work for, and myself" Ayako cowered.

"I will do better every time in future client presentations, with your continued, helpful, and necessary guidance."

She bowed deeply as she stepped away from his desk. Her departure bow—which accompanied her apology—did not instigate further frustration from the boss.

This was the third time she had been yelled at this month concerning bowing to foreigners at the conclusion of a presentation. The month had been punctuated by additional outbursts. The boss did not appreciate her assertiveness in meetings. Her responsibility in meetings was to listen silently. If she had a suggestion or comment, it should wait until after the meeting, so he would not be embarrassed. Her emails, while usually appropriate, were sometimes too forceful, or direct, in request. That was rude and condescending. Her vocal qualities, including intonation and tone, often lacked the highly regarded Japanese feminine quality, making her words sometimes sound vulgar. And finally her English ability was poor. A native speaker of English would rate her English ability higher than that of her

---

*This case has been developed based on real organization(s) and real organizational experiences. Names, facts, and situations have been changed to protect the privacy of individuals and organizations.

boss. However, that was the problem. Although she was hired by her company, and then transferred to Tokyo, for her bilingual English and Japanese abilities, her superior use of English was an embarrassment to her boss. She too often had demonstrated her command of English to others, including foreigners, and it was unacceptable to make the boss look inferior in any respect.

"In the U.S., I was a good employee. But will I ever be a good employee according to a Japanese manager again?" Ayako wondered aloud.

She began to doubt whether she possessed any cultural competence whatsoever. She was having difficulty remembering how she was expected to communicate in each given situation and felt overwhelmed with remembering the appropriate behaviors of each culture she experienced. Her male, Japanese boss expected her to use the strictly feminine style of Japanese language and to bow to him and her colleagues at all times. Her assertiveness, learned while studying in the United State, was to be forgotten—except when interacting with foreign clients. She too often confused her role within the interaction and the communicative behaviors expected of her.

While Japanese as a whole is more indirect than English, Japanese women also use a slightly different version of Japanese than men. The women's version is more tentative, submissive, and polite and uses special vocabulary and verb forms. Women are also expected to use a distinct tone of voice and intonation to communicate. To speak Japanese without the accompanying requirements for women would render Ayako culturally incompetent. Bowing to foreign clients after a presentation was also culturally incompetent, according to her boss, regardless of how the clients perceived the bow. Constantly code switching between English and Japanese and each language's nuances and nonverbals was overwhelming.

A few years earlier Ayako had decided to study in the United States. As an account executive in her mid-20s, she decided to leave her public relations position in Tokyo. While she enjoyed her job and was skilled at marketing new electronic products, she recognized how she was viewed within the organization and understood she would have to leave in order to be promoted. Her career path, according to the organization, would soon end so she could get married. Traditional Japanese societal beliefs hold that women should work until they are married, preferably in their early to mid-20s. Not ready for marriage and seeking further opportunities, Ayako decided that a graduate degree from a U.S. school and some U.S. work experience would allow her to circumvent the career-ending marriage path. She also contemplated subtle changes in Japanese society, which were more permissible of women delaying marriage and family, and wondered if by the time she returned to Japan it would be more acceptable to pursue a career *and* a family. But the society's permission to delay marriage comes at a price: Ayako and others who choose to delay those "duties" are referred to as "parasite singles." Ayako also understood that even though she would pursue graduate studies and leave Japan for a while, she might return to get married and raise a family without further pursuing her career. Many Japanese women went abroad expecting to focus on their careers and returned to Japan instead to solely raise a family. Ayako also remembered the media coverage concerning a member of the royal family, Masako, who returned from her studies at Harvard University and ended her promising diplomatic career in order to start a family.

Ayako had arrived in the United States and immediately took an English course to help her adjust to the forcefulness of spoken and written English. Compared with Japanese, native English speakers spoke directly, including their true feelings, which can be rude or offensive. Ayako knew that to be successful in graduate school in the new culture of the United States, she would have to be much more assertive in speaking and would need to unlearn her Japanese politeness. She did well in her English and graduate studies. However, she was constantly reminded of her foreigner status. Sometimes faculty and student peers would tell her she needed to speak more in class and share her ideas and concerns more confidently.

Her professor suggested she was "unlike most Japanese women," meaning she was more assertive than he expected her to be. Ayako did not consider that a compliment, and it frustrated her that many of her acquaintances in the United States saw her as little more than an extra in the movie *Lost in Translation*, or even as a lead actress in *Memoirs of a Geisha*.

The suggestion, "So, basically stop being so submissive, like a geisha," offended Ayako. Her female peer offered the biting comment in class one day. This expectation, that she assert herself, was different from her university studies in Japan, where asking questions may be interpreted as a challenge to the authority and knowledge of the professor. The silent student who takes some notes but mostly sits in rapt attention during lectures represents the prized Japanese pupil.

Conversely, she also was reminded of whom she was to others and of their expectations of her communication behaviors when they would comment they were surprised that a Japanese woman would speak so confidently or assertively. In the United States Ayako rarely bowed and tried to be cognizant of all nonverbal behaviors. She understood that bowing in the United States would merely convey that she was foreign and different from her student peers and faculty instead of convey the respect that it communicates in Japan. Because she received so many messages, implicit or explicit, as to how she was expected to behave as a foreign, Japanese, female student, she began focusing specifically on Japanese communication patterns for her class assignments. It frustrated her that some believed she absolutely had to be interested in Japan-related studies or theories because she is Japanese. Sometimes those same peers assumed that all studies or theories with an Asian author or study site should be of interest to her. She also realized that some of her peers criticized her because focusing solely on Japan-related research topics was too cliché, or expected, as well. Her paper on Ouchi's Theory Z was both praised for giving an in-depth look at Japanese management styles and criticized for not delving deeply enough into the theory's underpinnings, as apparently any Japanese person should have an understanding of Theory Z.

Ayako recognized the competing demands for her expected behaviors and sometimes indulged those demands. However, she was in the United States primarily to increase her ability to do well at work back in Tokyo by improving her English ability, mixing theory and practice, and competently communicating with foreigners. During her graduate studies she gradually became more and more confident in her English speaking and writing abilities. She was less constrained in sharing her opinions in class and was more assertive in communicating in all situations, including at the grocery store.

"Please do not smash my bread!" Ayako exclaimed to the bag boy. She surprised herself with this demanding, direct outburst—communication she would have avoided in Japan.

After finishing her graduate studies she worked at an American company in Washington, D.C., that had multiple transnational locations, including Tokyo. Her intent was to transfer to the Tokyo office after one year in the D.C. office.

Her work in Washington was enjoyable, and she felt appreciated. It seemed that her coworkers understood her abilities and recognized what she added to the team, how she worked with them, and how comfortable she was sharing her ideas and insights for new product development. She worked with mostly U.S. citizens, but there were also some female and male Japanese employees. Ayako enjoyed working with all of her peers and felt she was seen as an equal, even by the Japanese men. She presented herself and her ideas confidently, both in written English and in presentations. She was excited to transfer to the Tokyo office and reacquaint herself with her native, beloved Japan after working and studying the in United States for three years.

However, the new office experience in Tokyo was not as enjoyable. Ayako struggled with the new job because she often felt more foreign at work than she did as a graduate student in the United States. She also wondered if she was still working for the same company because the business practices in Tokyo were extremely different from those in Washington. While she felt very confident in her work abilities in Washington, she had been slightly unsure of her English ability. In Tokyo, she used mostly Japanese language at work. Being a native speaker, she should have been completely confident. But she was in a new environment and was expected to be more reserved in her suggestions and comments. She was expected, regardless of her job title or skill set, to embody a Japanese female employee, one who is submissive to the male employees. When Ayako was hired in Tokyo, she was informed that she would speak in Japanese except when writing to, or speaking with, foreign clients. She had not realized that her command of English and U.S. experience had changed her communication style so greatly or that she had so readily adapted to the demands of the national and organizational cultures of her foreign study and work experiences.

Within the first month back in Tokyo, Ayako was both elated and saddened. She had not realized how much she missed Japan, so the elation was all related to being in Japan and experiencing it as a Japanese citizen. While the United States was a great experience, she really had missed the excitement of Tokyo and the opportunity to be deemed "local" in others' eyes instead of so foreign and different. In Japan, she could be somewhat "invisible" to others and was able to ward off some expectations in that manner, whereas in the United States she was always foreign and sometimes the "token" foreigner. The sadness Ayako felt in Tokyo was all related to work and her coworkers' expectations for her, which she felt were too low. It seemed that her three years of intense study and work in the United States were not appreciated by the new boss and her new office. In fact, quite possibly her time abroad was a detriment to her being promoted within the Tokyo office. She recognized that who made decisions and who was allowed to communicate decisions were more tightly controlled in the new office. And her inability, or possibly lack of effort, to manage all of the expectations of her as a Japanese, English-speaking, foreign work and studies, female employee was resulting in unpleasant outbursts from the boss.

Ayako returned to her desk and bowed her head slightly. Still within sight of her boss and her coworkers, she knew she must carefully guard her true feelings of *honne* and let her face—poised and pleasant—show, in *tatemae*, only that she was content to have been yelled at, knowing she should do better. She preferred to have a few private moments and wanted to leave the room but knew others would assume she was crying in the bathroom. She did not want to appear weak. Instead, she opened her folder and began looking at her next presentation, pretending to be riveted and interested in doing better, including not bowing, the next time.

However, Ayako was thinking about the past several years and how her actions were perceived, both while in Japan and the United States, and how the expectations concerning her communication behavior differed, depending on individuals she was interacting with. She was unprepared for all of the cultures she would straddle and the expectations of each. She thought of the differing national and societal cultures of Japan and the United States. She then thought of the organizational cultures of her organization and how they differed, depending on the trans-national location. She thought of her office culture and how the boss' most recent outburst made her uncomfortable. While all of the other employees witnessed the outbursts and were also likely uncomfortable, they steadily continued to work and politely ignored the altercation. She wondered if a different combination of cultures, such as working at a Japanese company in Austria, would impact the expectations of her as a Japanese woman more positively. Finally, she wondered if she should quit her job and look for another or succumb to societal suggestion and search for a husband.

## CHAPTER 41

# Islamophobia at Work

## Shawn D. Long

## SEPTEMBER 11, 2001

### 7:00 A.M.—"Have a Blessed Day"

It was a typical Tuesday morning for Antara* in Jonestown, America. She had finished her 7:00 A.M. treadmill workout at her local Squares gym and was walking purposefully next door to Moonstruck to get her regular morning cup of latte.

"Good morning, Jackie," Antara greeted the woman who usually provided her morning coffee.

"Good morning, Ann," replied Jackie. "I see that you are your usual chipper self this morning."

"Jackie, you know I always get excited about seeing my smiling Jackie each morning and, of course, my love child ... triple caramel, latte frappe."

"I know, Hon. I know," Jackie replied.

Antara quickly paid for her coffee with her gift card, which she loads every payday as part of her monthly expenses.

"I will see you this afternoon, Jackie."

"I'll be here Ann ... as usual. Now you have a blessed day!"

"You, too, Jackie," whispered Antara.

Jackie's "have a blessed day" initially made Antara uncomfortable. When she moved to her building five years ago from Empire State in the northeast, she thought Jackie was friendly but a little too intrusive. "Have a blessed day," "God is good," and, "I'm praying for you on your new job," were constant do-good gestures that Antara thought were inappropriate and downright personal, particularly given the nature of their relationship.

---

*This case has been developed based on real organization(s) and real organizational experiences. Names, facts, and situations have been changed to protect the privacy of individuals and organizations.

"Just give me my damn coffee, and leave your god out of our transactions," thought Antara. But just like everything else in Antara's life, she adapted to her new southern home and treated these exchanges as a new cultural experience.

Antara returned to her condo and did her daily prayer. Don't get Antara wrong. She believed in God, but she was not fanatic about it. Her Allah was her "private" Allah. This was the dawn of the new century, and she was not her grandparents' Muslims. Anyway, as she often told her friends, "How many Muslims are CEOs in America? My point exactly. Individuals climb the corporate ladder, not kneel down in prayer on the way to the top." This approach upset Antara's family members because they were very proud of their religion and religious background and thought it was shameful for Antara to try to "pass."

## 8:00 A.M.—"It's My Lucky Day"

Antara pulled out her "lucky" black suit. It was a well-tailored charcoal gray power suit. "I cannot wait to spend my bonus on that new handbag and that contemporary living room sectional I saw at Upscale's Boutique last weekend," Antara confidently contemplated her spending after she would receive confirmation from her manager about her quarterly bonus.

"Oh, my gosh, it's almost 8:25! I'm missing the morning news and stock reports," Antara said loudly to herself.

Antara turned off her radio and turned to her favorite morning television program, *Empire City This Morning*, which she subscribes to via satellite from Empire City. "Ugghh. I hate commercials!" Antara begin to prepare her work clothes and her shower.

"Oh, my gosh. The cleaners *did not* get out that stain." Antara, visibly upset, reached for another shirt in her closet that clearly needed to be pressed.

"I don't need this headache this morning. I have bigger fish to fry today. Better yet, I'm trying to land a shark." Antara joked to herself as she plugged the iron into the outlet to press her second-choice blouse.

"I'm walking on sunshine yeah, yeah. I'm walking on sunshine yeah, yeah, and don't it feel good!" Antara sang along to the catchy commercial jingle.

"OK, Antara. Time to focus," she said to herself. "I have my performance appraisal with Joe today, and I need to hit all my verbal targets."

*Empire City This Morning* was back on. Her favorite morning anchors were just as chipper as ever.

"Oh, my gosh, isn't the weather just beautiful in Empire City?" gushed the weatherman. Antara had settled into her ironing pattern, and her coffee was just at the right temperature.

"Jackie talks too much, and I wish she wasn't there most times I'm there, but she can make a good coffee!"

Antara noticed the steam coming from her bathroom. Her shower was ready.

**8:35 A.M.**

"I need to hurry up. My meeting with Joe is at 10 o'clock, but I left my notes at the office, so I will need to be out the door by 9:15."

The broadcast headlines scrolled at the bottom of the TV screen were:

"Former presidential candidate Elizabeth Dole is expected to announce her run for the U.S. Senate in North Carolina."

"It is primary election day for some states in the United States."

"Michael Jordan has given the biggest hint that he may return to the NBA as a player."

## 8:46 A.M.—"All Hell Breaks Loose"

The usually calm and upbeat demeanor of the morning newscast soon was interrupted by a statement by surprised and puzzled anchorman Justin Pembroke:

"We are getting sketchy information and unconfirmed reports that it appears that a small commuter plane has just crashed into one tower of the World Trade Center. It hit the side of one of the twin towers. Clearly something relatively devastating is happening on the south end of Empire City. We can see the pictures…unconfirmed reports that a commuter plane has just crashed into one of the towers of the World Trade Center."

## 9:03 A.M.

It could have been an odd but minor accident until Justin Pembroke, the usually even-tempered anchor, shouted:

"We just saw another one. … We just saw another one…another plane just flew into the second tower. This has to be deliberate, folks. This is *Not an accident!*"

Antara watched in disbelief. Her eyes were glued to the television.

"What is going on?" Anatara shouted intensely to the television.

Her phone immediately began to ring.

On her answering machine she heard, "Antara, this is your father. I am watching the television and seeing if you are OK. I hope this is not your Empire State travel day!"

"Hello, Father. This is Anatara." Antara quickly picked up the phone, still bewildered.

"I don't know what is happening," her father stated. "But I'm glad you are safe. Let's pray together and hope for the best."

"Dad, I'm shaking like a leaf. I've got to go. I love you." Antara quickly hung up the phone.

"Oh, my god. I think Tom and Barbara are traveling today. I have to get to the office."

## 9:10 A.M.

Antara quickly turned off her shower and grabbed her Blackberry. "Tom. Tom. Tom." Antara quickly scrolled through her contact list. Antara dialed Tom's number. There was no answer.

"Damn it," shrieked Antara. Next she attempted to reach Barbara.

"Hi. This is Barbara. Leave your details." Barbara's phone went straight to voicemail as well.

Antara returned to the television to try to make sense of all the chaos. "What is happening in my former city? Are Tom and Barbara OK? Why isn't Justin Pembroke telling us what is going on?"

Immediately the following events took place:

**9:10 A.M.**
The U.S. Federal Aviation Administration shut down all New York area airports.

**9:21 A.M.**
Bridges and tunnels leading into Empire City were closed.

**9:25 A.M.**
All domestic flights were grounded by the Federal Aviation Administration.

**9:45 A.M.**
American Airlines Flight 77 crashed into the Pentagon.

**10:05 A.M.**
The South Tower at the World Trade Center collapsed.

**10:10 A.M.**
United Airlines Flight 93 crashed into a wooded area in Pennsylvania.

**10:30 A.M.**
Antara received a global email message informing her that all employees of the Bank of the New South were not to report to work today. Antara attempted to call the office but was notified that the office was closed and and that she should contact her immediate supervisor. Antara grabbed her bags and rushed to the office. Antara soon arrived at the bank, which was now in complete lockdown.

A police officer quickly approached Antara and asked her to leave the area.

"Sir, I work here!"

"Ma'am, we cannot let anyone enter this building. I need you to leave this area immediately."

"Sir, I work here, and I need to check on my friends."

"Ma'am, I understand, but this building is on lockdown, and I need you to leave immediately."

Antara soon realized she would also be leaving her former life behind.

**1:00 P.M.**
Tom sent a global email to everyone. It read, "I'm OK. No travel day for me, team! God bless everyone and America. We are going to get those bastards!"

## NOVEMBER 2001—"MOVING FORWARD, LOOKING BACKWARD"

Two months after the dreadful day in September, things had settled down considerably. People were still somber and mourning the loss of freedom, friends, and family; but things were started to get back to normal, except for Antara.

Due to the attacks, the Bank of the New South, as well as other financial institutions, lost massive revenues; national and international travel was at an all-time low; and tensions between Americans and non-Americans were noticeably uncomfortable and even intolerable at times. Taking the advice of her family, Antara thought it would be appropriate just to lie low for now.

"Be careful, Antara," her father would always close their weekly conversation.

Although Antara tried to insulate herself until tensions died down, Tom made it point to always antagonize her and her "culture."

"How are your cousins doing, Ann? Are they plotting the next round? Have you heard that new Charlie Daniels song?" Tom would make these remarks quite frequently in front of others.

"I like your dress, Antara. Do you have a matching rag for your head?"

"Tell your peeps, 'This ain't no rag. It's a flag!' Remember that, Antara."

"Are you an insider cell informant, Anatara? Are you infiltrating our financial units? I don't trust you or your kind, Anatara!"

This type of behavior was characteristic of Tom. People either loved or loved to hate Tom. He was a hard worker and a valuable asset to the team, but he certainly was considered the immature frat boy of the organization. He drank heavily on weekends with male coworkers, made inappropriate sexual comments to the women on the team, and made gay and racist jokes frequently. Tom was an equal opportunity offender, but he was productive, and he was one of "Joe's boys."

"Tom, I have had enough of your nonsense. I find your statements pretty offensive, and I don't want to take it to Joe. We are all hurting right now. I know you are just joking, but I think you are teetering on crossing the line," replied Antara.

"Antara, baby, you and your cousins crossed the line already. You have just got me started! I'm not afraid of you or your rag-headed peeps. This ain't no rag. It's a flag." In addition to his remarks, Tom flashed Antara his now ever-present American flag lapel pin.

Antara was visibly upset. She went to her office and shut the door.

"Dear Joe I would like to log a formal complaint against Tom," her terse email began. Antara was frantically typing away, detailing every incident that had led up to this point.

"Tom finally crossed the line today," she wrote to close her three-page email. Before Antara could hit "send," she was interrupted when Jan knocked on the door.

"Anna, I have the reports you wanted to look at before our holiday break." Jan immediately saw the frustrated and angry look on Antara's face.

"What's wrong, Anna?"

"I'm fed up with Tom and his shit. Joe must fire Tom *now!*"

Jan quickly jumped in, "Hold on, Anna, don't jump the gun!"

"I hope you are not sending an email to Joe. You know Tom is one of 'Joe's boys', and sending an email sends the wrong message. Joe may think that you are serious. You should go talk directly to Joe. He is a reasonable man, and he knows how valuable you are to this team. Plus, you don't want to screw Tom up right now. He can't get another job, and he and Becky just had their first baby. Tom is an asshole, but he doesn't mean anything by it," closed Jan. Antara told Jan, "Maybe you're right. I'm not out for blood, and I just want him to act right. We are a great team, and I'm just trying to be a good team player, too, but he needs to stop busting my chops. He just crossed the line. It was probably the heat of the moment, so I probably took his joking as a threat. His baby daughter is so precious and beautiful. She should not suffer for her insufferable father. I couldn't sleep at night worried about her and Becky. Why do good women pick bad men? I cannot wait until the holiday break. We all need one."

Jan replied, "Anne, delete that email and save us all a headache. What would we do without that air bag around here anyway? I think you two are actually in love. Women love bad boys," laughed Jan.

"Oh, by the way, Anna, it's actually 'Christmas break,' not 'holiday break'! See you around, Anna."

Anna was curious about Jan's last comment, but she had too much on her plate to try to deconstruct it now. She decided not to send the email this time.

"I will have to save this for a rainy day," she thought and pulled out a jump drive from her purse and saved the email and quickly returned the drive to her purse.

Antara moved to schedule a meeting on Joe's public calendar. She needed to reschedule her performance appraisal before the end of the quarter, but she knew a raise was not coming because the bank was doing so poorly. But she thought it would be a chance to talk with Joe about Tom's behavior and keep Joe in the loop about her progress on the major project.

"Great, Joe is available December 15. It's a date!" Antara filled in her name on his schedule and marked it in her daily planner.

## DECEMBER 15

**10:00 A.M.**

Antara had on her "lucky" suit again for her delayed performance appraisal meeting.

"Knock, knock, Mr. Joe."

"Come on in, Antara. Have a seat," offered Joe.

"So, how have you been, Joe?"

"I've been busy as ever, Antara. Struggling to keep all the trains coming and going. We haven't had a chance to chat since our last scheduled meeting. We both know why! However, things seem to have settled down somewhat. Boy, big changes can come in a few months. 'Whew,' is all I can say. Enough about me. How about you? How have you been?"

"Well, Joe, to be quite honest with you, I have been better, and I guess this is a great segue for my issue before we jump right into the appraisal."

"What's the problem, Antara?"

"It's Tom and some of the other members of the team! Since 9/11, Tom has crossed the line and quite frankly made me incredibly uncomfortable with his inappropriate comments."

"What comments, Antara? This is the first I am hearing about this. Are you being sexually harassed or something?"

"Not sexually harassed, Joe, but how can I put this…ethnically intimidated."

"Hold on now, Antara, that is a pretty strong accusation about Tom. What do you mean…'ethnically intimidated'. I've never heard of that before."

Joe took off his glasses and placed the ear piece in his mouth. He began to rattle his ink pen nervously as he leaned back in his chair. He soon replaced the ink pen with a stress ball, staring intently at Anatara.

"You know how Tom is with his crude remarks sometimes, Joe. They are usually funny, but he has been accusing me and my family of being terrorists."

Joe slightly chuckled.

Antara continued looking surprised, "And asking me to clarify my last name, telling me that I am on his and the FBI's watch list, asking me do I send my money back home to support the Taliban. Just things like that which I find problematic."

Joe, with a sly smile, interjected, "Oh, Antara, you need to relax. Tom is just being Tom. If I thought you were a terrorist, I would have fired you months ago." Joe began laughing and wiping away a slight laughter tear. "You have to admit that was a good one!" stated Joe.

"Look, Antara, I will talk to Tom and tell him to chill out a little. I don't think they cover any of the Muslim sensitivity components in our diversity training, but I'll see what I can do to sensitize Tom a little. You know the prayer room kind of makes everyone a little uncomfortable around here these days, and Tom is probably just trying to break the ice.

"Look, Anatara. Here is an American flag pin to wear. It may help that you blend in just a little better with the team, just so we are all on the same page. I meant to give you one of these a while back but haven't had a chance to catch up with you." Joe extended his open hand with an American flag pin.

"Is there anything else, Antara?" asked Joe.

"What about my performance evaluation?" asked Antara.

"Let's not worry about that right now. The bank is strapped, and no one is getting a bonus. We should all be worried about keeping our jobs, not getting a raise. Should I walk you out?" asked Joe.

"No, I'm fine," responded a confused and puzzled Antara.

"Please shut the door behind you, Antara, and it was great catching up with you. I will check on the diversity training. Maybe I should suggest they add an American sensitivity training to their list as well. See ya around, Antara," added Joe.

Antara left Joe's office even more confused than when she entered.

"What just happened?" Antara thought to herself.

"I've got to get out of here. I can't do any more work today. I'm going home. An American sensitivity training? What is that about?"

Antara briskly walked to her office and logged off her computer and changed her voicemail indicating she would be away from the office the rest of the day.

## DECEMBER 16

Antara wanted to call in sick the rest of the week, but she knew that she was taking off from December 20 until January 4 to be with her family. As she prepared to go to work she reflected on her life. After she had left college, she had been determined not to be "just a Muslim," but a strong working woman. She tried to downplay her ethnic and religious background, never mentioning it at work, never showing pictures or mentioning her family in her home or work spaces. She loved Moonstruck, worked out, and loved drinking and hanging out with her friends. She avoided other Middle Eastern individuals professionally and personally, and they equally did not favor Antara. However, despite her behavior it seemed she was viewed as a "Muslim woman."

Antara had an important team meeting this morning to discuss strategy for the upcoming quarter. She was running five minutes late. Antara dreaded seeing and interacting with Tom. She could not believe Joe's reaction to her complaint. The rest of the team members seemed to distance themselves by not inviting her to the regular dinners—the group dinners that she started! Antara wondered what had happened to her friends.

"Good morning, everyone," Antara said, trying to put on an upbeat face in spite of her inner turmoil.

"Good morning, Ann," responded two of her eight teammates.

"Sorry I'm a little late, guys. My Jackie had a line this morning."

"Your Jackie?" said Tom.

Antara ignored Tom's comments and reached for a bagel.

"Oh, these look delicious. Did anyone pick up my favorite pineapple cream cheese?"

"I thought dairy and cows were sacred to fundamentalists. I mean 'Muslims,'" quipped Benjamin, kicking Tom under the table.

The rest of the team began to chuckle.

Antara ignored the comments and found her seat.

Joe entered the room.

"Good morning, everyone."

"Good morning, Joe," the team members responded. Joe glanced across the table and placed his eyes on Antara.

"Antara, what are you doing here?"

"Joe, I'm here for the strategy meeting. I have outlined a number of initiatives we should undertake next year that will help our vendor relations and streamline our processes simultaneously. Do you want me to begin the meeting?"

"No, you shouldn't," interrupted Joe.

"Have you not checked your inbox mail?"

"No, I haven't, Joe; I was running a tad bit late this morning. Is there something that I missed or a change in the agenda in a memo in my box?" inquired a puzzled Antara.

"I think you should check your box immediately," replied Joe.

"Can it wait until after the meeting?" asked Antara.

"No! This is quite uncomfortable, Antara, but you have been reassigned to another team. Your services with us are no longer required."

"What team, Joe?" Antara asked frantically.

"Check your mailbox for your assignment, but you will be relocating next week. It's all in the letter. I don't have time to explain the details here. I have a meeting to run. Take care and show yourself out," snapped Joe.

Tom and the rest of the team sat in silence and watched Antara leave. As she shut the door, there was a large sigh of relief from the room. Antara looked back through the window and saw the team members smiling and gesturing toward the door. Antara ran to the restroom. Jan quickly ran out the conference room after Antara.

**10:15 a.m.**

Antara tried to hold it together in the mirror, but the tears began streaming down her face.

"I'm going to quit. I can't take this anymore. I'm going to quit and sue."

"Antara, I'm so sorry. I hope you know they didn't mean anything by it. You know how we all joke around and give each other crap. Tom is an asshole, I know, but he's like the big brother we never wanted," consoled Jane as she handed Antara a paper towel from the electronic wall dispenser.

"Take care of yourself, Anatara."

A composed Antara didn't say a word. Her silence was deafening.

# Organizations and Their Stakeholders

CHAPTER 42

# Inviting Public Input

## Stephen C. Yungbluth and Zachary P. Hart

### A WELCOMED INTERRUPTION

Darryl* had been staring blankly at his computer screen for the past five minutes, trying to figure out how he was going to retrieve a file he deleted two weeks ago. He had run a search three times, each one coming up empty. At that moment, a new message window popped up on the screen. Feeling relieved to look at something less frustrating, he opened the message. It was from his friend, Stan, who worked on another floor of the Cerulean Consulting Group. The subject heading read, "Wanna take this one?"

Darryl wondered what kind of new work he was going to be asked to do, as if he needed more to add to his plate. Still, he decided he would rather read the email now than go back to looking for the missing file. The message was a request from the Moss Utility Company. Apparently the company was involved in some kind of legal situation with the Environmental Protection Agency (EPA) and was planning to meet a requirement to seek public input through the formation of a community council. Stan indicated Moss needed a facilitator to help run these council meetings. Darryl thought about it for a moment and then noticed that George, his office neighbor, had also been copied on the message. "Well, it might be a lot of work for one of us, but maybe we could do this together," he thought.

Figuring George had been reading the email, too, Darryl got up, tapped on his colleague's door, and asked, "Hey, George, what do you think of this?"

George turned away from his computer and motioned for Darryl to come in. "I don't know. It sounds interesting," he replied. "The fact that it deals with environmental issues is intriguing, but I wonder what is really going on and what they would want us to do."

---

*This case has been developed based on real organization(s) and real organizational experiences. Names, facts, and situations have been changed to protect the privacy of individuals and organizations.

Darryl walked into George's office and sat down. "Yeah, it seems like it would draw on our skills of organization and facilitation, especially when you look at the expectations for membership on the community council. It seems like they anticipate some heated discussions."

"It looks like they want real input from the public," George said as he turned to read the community council application form that had been attached to the email. "The council members have to agree to demonstrate a serious commitment to meaningful participation with an emphasis on thoughtful discussion, collaborative problem solving, a respect for diversity of opinion, and a common desire for continued success of the local region."

Darryl smiled and said, "It's good they established this expectation from the beginning, but we both know it can be hard to adhere to this type of commitment, particularly when the discussion starts to uncover people's personal agendas."

George laughed a little bit, then turned back to the application and commented, "Well, look! They reserved the right to remove anyone from the process if they 'do not behave in a manner consistent with the expectations of membership.' Hopefully that doesn't mean we will need a bouncer at the meetings!"

Both men chuckled, and then Darryl pondered, "Seriously, do you suppose we will be able to be impartial enough, given some of our own environmental views?"

George quickly responded, "I think I'm more worried about whether we have enough technical knowledge to manage the conversation. We should talk to them and get more information to find out what this is all about."

"That sounds like a good idea. I'll go set up the meeting," said Darryl as he got up to return to his own office, glad to have something else to focus on instead of that pesky missing file.

## A MEETING AT MOSS

The following week George and Darryl met in the lobby of the Moss Utility Company. After about 10 minutes, Mary, the public relations director, walked off the elevator and greeted them. George and Darryl signed the visitor's log, picked up their guest badges, and followed Mary to the conference room.

While George and Darryl were hanging their coats, Rob, the CEO, and Jasmine, the chief engineer, walked in together. "Thank you so much for coming," said Rob as he shook George's and Darryl's hands. "We are very much looking forward to getting your input on this entire process."

Jasmine introduced herself to George and Darryl as well. Everyone then exchanged business cards and sat down in the comfortable leather chairs surrounding the oak table.

Rob began the meeting by explaining the purpose of the community council. "We recently entered into a legal agreement with the EPA that provides guidance for how our utility can reach compliance with their required environmental standards," he said. "This agreement will require the expenditure of over $1 billion over the next 20 years to upgrade and repair the current utility infrastructure."

He went on to describe how this legal agreement represents the first of its kind anywhere in the country. "Most similar utilities in other cities usually wait until they are sued before making the needed repairs," said Rob, "but Moss is taking a proactive approach to develop a plan that would help the utility avoid the costs associated with lawsuits. We are required to obtain public input on our plans, so we came up with the idea of gathering key stakeholders to form this community council—a very unique approach."

"How many people will be involved in this council?" asked George.

"We will have around 50 people, including some government officials, developers, environmental advocates, and average citizens as well," replied Mary. She then explained how Moss had requested applications through advertisements in the local newspaper in order to reach as many community members as possible. They had hoped they would select a representative sample of the applications for membership on the council.

"Unfortunately, we received only about 60 applications, so we decided to accept everyone who applied," Mary said. "It's probably not a representative sample of the community, since many of those who applied have a very specific interest related to the environmental issues we are addressing."

Rob jumped into the discussion at this point, nodding his head, and added, "Most customers don't understand the nature of what we do at all, so they have zero interest in this council. As long as they get their services, they don't think much about paying their bill, unless the rates really jump."

Darryl laughed and said, "Yeah, I noticed my bill seems to go up about $5 a month, but I just think, 'oh, well,' and pay it."

Rob agreed, "Darryl, you are a typical consumer. The truth is, only a handful of people in the area really keep a close eye on what we do, and all those individuals applied and will be on the council. They tend to fall along two sides—those who think we don't do enough to protect the environment and those who think we are constantly cutting into their earnings."

Everyone was quiet for a minute, and then Darryl looked up and said, "It sounds like this could produce some heated discussions, right?"

Rob gave a sly smile and said, "There are a few people who applied that have given us some difficulties in the past. Actually, we only know about one-third of those who applied. We have some familiarity with another one-third based on the positions they hold. And then there's another one-third we don't know at all. It should be an interesting mix, and we aren't sure what to really expect."

"Are you really OK with everyone who applied to the council participating in the meetings?" George asked.

Rob looked directly at George and said, "Well, we certainly want the feedback, but we do worry a bit about some individuals coming in with an agenda and trying to dominate the discussions with issues that are irrelevant to the council's objective of providing input on the infrastructure improvement plan. We haven't figured out how to handle that piece, and that is part of the reason we asked for your help."

Jasmine raised her hand enough to get the group's attention and then added, "We are also hoping to use this council as an opportunity to educate the community on the reasons why we need to take the actions that we are planning to take. It seems a lot of people don't understand the amount of time and effort we put into trying to maximize the changes that we can make with the budget that we have. We need advocates in the community."

Darryl and George sat back in their chairs and looked at the notes they had been taking. Both got ready to speak, and George motioned to Darryl to go ahead.

"Well, given the broad range of people who will be represented on the council, I think you will want to take some time in the first meeting to allow people to introduce themselves and explain what their interest in the council is, and hopefully we can try to establish some common ground among them, so we can start to build an effective working relationship," said Darryl.

"That sounds like a good idea. It would be good to try to uncover why some of these people are there," replied Rob, "and we want to make sure that we set some ground rules about the nature of their involvement in this council."

Jasmine chimed in, "I think we need to take some time to explain the nature of our 20-year plan and tell them what we're going to be doing."

Realizing the meeting's discussion was about to end, George shifted in his seat and then asked, "OK, is there anything else that needs to happen at the first meeting?"

After a moment of silence and glances exchanged around the room, he proposed, "What if Darryl and I take some time to talk about this and perhaps put together an agenda for the meeting and send it to you sometime next week?"

Rob started to stand up and said, "So, it sounds like this might be something that you can do for us?"

Darryl and George gave a tentative nod, and Rob continued, "Well, we really appreciate you guys coming down here to meet with us and giving this some consideration."

Then Rob left the room after shaking hands with George and Darryl, followed by Jasmine close behind him. After George and Darryl gathered their things together, Mary escorted them to the lobby. "We are so glad you will both be working with us on this," she said as George and Darryl returned their guest badges to her. "We're looking forward to seeing the agenda you develop. See you soon."

George and Darryl silently walked out. As they approached their cars, which were parked next to each other, George looked at Darryl and said, "I'm wondering how much input they really want from the council."

Darryl replied, "I was thinking the same thing. Let's go get a cup of coffee and talk it over."

## COFFEE SHOP DISCUSSION

About 20 minutes later, George and Darryl sat down at a small table located next to a roaring fireplace in a nearby coffee shop. Each was holding a warm cup of java, trying to ward off the coldness of the snowy weather they had just driven through.

"So, what did you think?" asked George.

Darryl blew on his coffee a bit before taking a sip and then said, "Well, on the one hand, they seem to be expressing a genuine desire to be collaborative by taking this proactive approach; but, on the other hand, it sounds like their 20-year plan is pretty well set in stone, and I wonder what they really hope to gain from the council."

"They are going to such great lengths to ensure participation from various factions of the community," commented George. "Don't you think it is somewhat unlikely that this is just some sort of public relations effort to ward off lawsuits?"

"Yeah," Darryl agreed, "it seems like they are going above and beyond what is required to be in compliance with their legal agreement."

George removed the coffee stirrer from his cup and asked, "So, are you interested in doing this?"

"I think so, but there were a couple of times in that meeting where I felt a little lost when they started describing the technical aspects of their work," said Darryl as he scratched his chin and then gestured to George. "What about you? Do you think that might inhibit our ability to be effective facilitators?"

"Well," said George, "I agree that it might make it difficult to determine if the conversation is on track and whether expertise is being applied appropriately, but I think we have enough background in scientific reasoning; and we are certainly intelligent enough to read between the lines."

They were both silent for a moment, and then George continued, "Besides, we deal primarily with the emotional components that can reveal when people are expressing genuine issues. In some ways, I think a lack of content specialization gives us a certain advantage as neutral parties in the matter. We can ask questions in a way that would be less likely to produce defensiveness from any of the parties."

"I suppose so," replied Darryl a bit hesitantly. "Do you have a sense of how we should structure the meeting? Do you think they will want to start by welcoming everyone to the council and introducing the role that we will play at these meetings?"

George lifted his cup and took a drink before saying, "I would prefer if we start things off in order to assert our role as the ones who are facilitating the meetings, but I guess we should check with them first. Let's go ahead and write up an agenda and send it over to them and see what they say."

"OK, I can do that when I get back to the office," said Darryl as he finished his coffee and started putting his coat back on.

"All right, sounds good," said George. "I will catch up with you later. I have still got a couple of errands to run before I head back. I hope traffic isn't too bad—that snow is really coming down now."

## A SHORT NOTE FROM MOSS BEFORE
## THE COUNCIL MEETING

A few days later Mary sent an email to George and Darryl. The message read, "After discussing your proposed agenda for the first community council meeting, we all agreed that we would like to take more of a hands-off approach with the council to make it seem more independent. We understand your point that the council needs to feel as if its input will have a significant impact. Otherwise, many of the members may see no point in being there. Let us have a conference call a few days before the actual meeting to go over the finalized agenda and make sure that everyone is on the same page. Let me know what your schedule is."

## THE COUNCIL CONVENES

The day of the first community council meeting arrived, and George and Darryl arrived at the banquet hall about an hour beforehand. As they walked into the reception area, they were greeted by Mary and Jasmine.

"A few people are here already. Let me introduce you to our consultants, who will be taking notes on what transpires during the meeting and be available to provide expertise," said Mary as she motioned George and Darryl into the dining room where the meeting would take place.

Three men dressed in dark suits were standing in a corner quietly talking. Mary walked up to them and said, "Gentlemen, I'd like to introduce you to our facilitators for this evening."

Introductions were exchanged, and Darryl asked the men, "What do you hope will happen at the meeting?"

Charles, an environmental engineer, answered, "Well, hopefully we will create support for our plan. Most of the people here will not really understand the technicalities of the plan, and we will be here to provide expertise if needed. We have worked on this for quite a long time and believe it is really the best option for our area. I think the council will agree once they hear all the facts."

The conversation continued for a few minutes, and then as the council members began to arrive, George and Darryl headed back to the reception area to greet them. Over the next half-hour, they met a wide variety of community members: developers, environmental activists, county and city officials, academics, college students, retired citizens, and several small business owners, including one who claimed to know everyone in the area.

As George and Darryl sat down to eat dinner before the meeting began, George quietly commented to Darryl, "I am really impressed by the range of perspectives that are represented on this council. This should be quite interesting."

About 30 minutes later, after almost everyone in the room had finished eating, dinner, George and Darryl walked up to the podium and requested the attention of the crowd, now numbering around 75. This number included about 45 council members and 30 Moss employees and consultants, who were observing the meeting. The staff and consultants stood at the back of the room as the meeting got under way. A few of the council members gave curious looks at them to determine what they were doing back there.

After briefly reviewing the evening's agenda, George introduced Rob and asked him to make a few comments about the 20-year plan and the process of public input. "Thank you, George," said Rob, who then turned to face the council members. "Tonight I am quite excited to see this council meeting for the first time. You all represent a first in our country, the active involvement of community in planning the next 20 years of projects for a utility. We value your input, and we know that you will all take your role in this council very seriously. Your participation will improve the quality of the work and help us to serve the best interests of our community. For too long we have allowed lawsuits to be the main tool for interacting with and responding to our citizens. This council represents a far more positive approach."

As many council members nodded in agreement, Rob went on to describe some of the details of the 20-year plan that Moss was developing and identified areas where public input was needed. When he finished his presentation, George and Darryl came forward and told the group to divide into two smaller groups for its first activity.

"We will be using the next several minutes for you to introduce yourselves and to explain why you decided to join this council," explained Darryl. "We want you to get to know each other a bit and to understand the perspectives that are represented on this council."

After all members had a chance to introduce themselves and describe their interests in the council, George and Darryl reconvened the large group and noted some of the similarities and differences among the participants and their interests. In particular, they noted a common concern for meeting environmental standards, although there were differences in the orientations to these standards. Some were concerned about the costs associated with satisfying current regulations. Others questioned whether the current regulations were sufficient for improving the environmental impact of current development. This was followed by a brief question and answer session that clarified what Moss had done to date. Then they discussed the future direction of the council and provided details pertaining to the next meeting.

After the meeting concluded, a number of people lingered to connect with people they knew or to introduce themselves to those they would like to know better. George and Darryl each spoke with several council members and then checked in with the Moss staff members to get their initial reactions. The response seemed to be generally optimistic, with only a few reservations. Rob seemed a little uncomfortable with how enthusiastic and empowered the council appeared to be. He said, "I hope they're not thinking they are going to create the plan. We have pretty well established what the plan will be. We are simply looking to them for any reactions that may improve it, so we can ensure that we are being responsive to the needs of the community."

George asked, "Are you concerned that they will want you to change direction?"

Rob answered, "No, I just wouldn't want them to feel misled."

# CHAPTER 43

# Give Me Information or I Will Blog

## Patty C. Malone and Keri K. Stephens

Heather* was shocked when she picked up the morning newspaper to see the following article:

> **ATTENTION, ALL PET OWNERS (March 16, 2007)**
>
> "A major manufacturer of dog and cat food sold under Wal-Mart, Safeway, Kroger, and other store brands recalled 60 million containers of wet pet food Friday after reports of kidney failure and deaths. An unknown number of cats and dogs suffered kidney failure, and about 10 died after eating the affected pet food, Menu Foods said in announcing the North American recall. Product testing has not revealed a link explaining the reported cases of illness and death, the company said. However, the recalled products were made using wheat gluten purchased from a new supplier, a spokeswoman said. Menu Foods did not immediately provide a full list of brand names and lot numbers covered by the recall, saying they would be posted on its website early Saturday."—Associated Press, Washington

Heather was worried about her own dog, Star, and wondered if that was the same kind of food she gave her. "Oh, no," she thought, "I just bought some dog food a couple of days ago and have been feeding it to her. I need to find out if those cans are part of the recall." She immediately went to her computer and found several pet food websites. There were certainly a number of brand names listed, including the one she had just purchased, but she had a lot of questions and wanted some answers. She found a phone number at the bottom of the pet food

---

*This case has been developed based on real organization(s) and real organizational experiences. Names, facts, and situations have been changed to protect the privacy of individuals and organizations.

manufacturer's website, called it, and got a busy signal. Heather continued calling the number throughout the course of the day and continued to get a busy signal. As she became more frustrated she thought, "I can't believe this! I've been calling all day and gotten a busy signal every time! I don't know what to do. Star is getting hungry, and I don't know whether to give her what I have in the pantry or not. She doesn't seem sick. How can I get more information?"

Heather then decided to go back to the Internet and search for further information. She quickly found some other websites and then some blogging sites where other pet owners were sharing their concerns and giving each other information about brands and lot numbers of contaminated foods as well as descriptions of symptoms their pets were exhibiting. She tried one more time to call the pet food manufacturer but got the same busy signal.

## SUMMARY OF THE CRISIS

The pet food industry initiated a recall of pet food beginning in March 2007 after numerous cats and dogs were reported ill or dead after eating certain brands of pet food. Dozens of organizations beyond the pet food manufacturer became involved in the crisis, including the Food and Drug Administration, pet food distributors, animal organizations, media organizations, stores, and the general public. Much of the information distributed to the public was confusing and contradictory. Early press releases claimed the cause of the contaminated food was unknown. Later the contamination was blamed on chemicals added to the pet food. As the crisis continued to unfold, the public wanted more information, which it was not receiving from the organizations issuing the recall. Since the manufacturers were not providing this information, people affected by the crisis began to seek information and support by turning to websites and blogs where they found others with the same concerns.

## THE BLOGS

Tony had been following the news about the pet food recall since his dog, Bex, had become very sick. He was angry that he was not hearing from the companies responsible for the food contamination as to how this could happen or how to help his dog. As he watched the latest news report on TV he thought, "Why isn't a company spokesperson explaining what happened, how it happened, and what we should do?! No one has issued an apology, taken responsibility, or explained anything. I will never trust the company that manufactured the pet food or the store where I bought it again. I will not buy any of their products or anything else from them."

Since Tony was not able to get any information from those responsible, he had found another source of information as well as a source of comfort—blogs. Tony (Blog World, 3/18/07):

Tony (Blog World, 3/18/07)

"I'm sorry to tell our friends that we took our beloved pet dog, Bex, to the vet this morning. The vet tells us he is suffering acute renal failure and the outlook is not good. We fed him several of the brands of dog food we have now found out were contaminated. We tried to call the 'pet food recall hotline' but have not been able to get through. We cannot get a person on the phone, only a busy signal or a voicemail referring us back to the website with the list of contaminated pet food. Despite the fact that MANY MORE brands and lot numbers have been added to the list, they are still posting the original list that has been up there since Monday! They are not providing us with ANY INFORMATION! My friends, be careful what you feed your pets. They are still saying some are safe that are now on the recall list."

## THE PET FOOD COMPANIES

That same week pet food company executives were trying to decide how best to handle the developing crisis. Ted Hammond worked for the conglomerate that owned a number of the pet food manufacturers that produced the contaminated brands. He was concerned about the deaths, the suffering of the families, and the role his company played in the distribution of the contaminated pet food. As vice president of public affairs, he was also worried about how the public would view his company after this crisis and was considering how to repair the damage.

He approached the CEO, David Robinson, and said, "Dave, I think we need to think not only about the pets and the families who have suffered losses but also how these people are going to see us in the future. We need to consider their feelings if we want to keep them as customers. We can't alienate the public by ignoring this crisis. I think we should take a direct approach and offer them an apology, remind them of our product guarantee, and refund their money at the very least."

Dave didn't need to think too long about it and agreed. Ted issued the following press release and distributed it to the media:

(March 16, 2007):

"P&G Pet Care has announced a voluntary recall in the United States and Canada on specific 3 oz., 5.5 oz., 6 oz., and 13.2 oz. canned and 3 oz. and 5.3 oz. foil pouch 'wet' cat and dog food products manufactured by Menu Foods Inc. with code dates of 6339 through 7073. There have been a small number of reported cases of cats from the US becoming sick and developing signs of kidney failure. The signs of kidney failure include loss of appetite, vomiting, and lethargy. This voluntary product recall involves discontinuation of all retail sales and product retrieval from customers. Consumers should stop using the affected products immediately and consult with a veterinarian if any symptoms are present in their pet. All IAMS and Eukanuba products carry a 100% guarantee, and consumers can retrieve a refund for recalled products. P&G Pet Care is taking this proactive step out of an abundance of caution, because the health and well-being of pets are paramount in the mission of IAMS and Eukanuba. P&G Pet Care has informed the Food and Drug Administration and the Canadian Food Inspection Agency on this issue. The company regrets any inconvenience to its consumers and retail customers."—PR Newswire

Only a couple of organizations responsible for the recall issued apologies and offered to reimburse customers. These organizations also turned to the Internet and used websites to communicate with pet owners and the public. However, numerous other organizations responsible for the recall did not issue any statements or apologies or take advantage of the Internet to communicate with their customers. Pet owners found this to be extremely frustrating. As the recall continued over the next several weeks, manufactureres involved in the crisis gave conflicting information about which foods were contaminated and what caused the contamination. This complicated and contradictory information ended up in the hands of the media, who then publicized it. Many of these press releases appeared on various websites and blogs.

## DESIRE FOR INFORMATION

Katy felt completely at a loss and confused by what she was reading on the websites and blogs and did not know which foods were safe for her cat, Lucky. She thought, "Why isn't someone telling us clearly what we should do? They aren't responding to us, and they are giving out conflicting information. I don't know who to believe." She had most recently read two conflicting statements posted on different websites:

(March 23, 2007):

"ABC News has learned that investigators have determined that a rodent-killing chemical is the toxin in the tainted pet food that has killed several animals. A source close to the investigation tells ABC News that that the rodenticide, which the source says is illegal to use in the United States, was on wheat that was imported from China and used by Menu Foods in 100 brands of dog and cat food. Scientists at a food laboratory in Albany, New York, made the discovery a week after a massive recall of 60 million cans and pouches was issued. The chemical is called aminopterin."—ABC News Press Release

Blogging for Justice (Legal Website, March 24, 2007):

"A chemical has turned up in the ingredient 'wheat gluten,' which is commonly used in pet foods. The chemical is melamine, and according to the Environmental Protection Agency melamine is a byproduct and contaminant associated with numerous pesticides. This is a toxic chemical in high doses and when used in tests on rats resulted in bladder tumors. Melamine was found in the urine of sick cats as well as in the kidney of a cat that died after eating the recalled pet food. Federal agencies testing the pet food failed to find aminopterin, used in rat poison, and earlier blamed for the pet food contamination. Researchers now can't confirm that finding when looking at tissue samples taken from dead cats."

## DESIRE FOR SUPPORT

Katy felt frustrated at the lack of information available and the conflicting reports. Katy soon found that her best sources of information were the blogging sites.

"I don't know where to get accurate information or who to trust, except for this blogging site and the other pet owners like myself that I have met here." She began to develop online friendships with other pet owners like herself who were trying to protect their pets from the tainted food as well as those who had suffered losses.

Megan was one of those who had lost her cat. She found the blogging sites to be a great place to lean on others for comfort and support. She found many others experiencing the same things that she was experiencing. Many of the blogs she read were personal stories from other pet owners expressing the sadness of losing their pets, whom they considered members of their families. Others were looking for information or clarification. Many other blogs she participated in provided an emotional outlet to express sadness, anger, and frustration, including her own.

> Megan (3/25):
>
> "I had to put my seven-year-old cat to sleep a couple of days ago after she became really sick. She stopped eating and could hardly get up. I can't believe this has happened. What's really sad is you don't know they are that sick until it is too late. It happens really fast once the symptoms appear."

> Jared (3/25):
>
> "I am so angry. My cat is still in the emergency pet care clinic with renal failure. No one will tell me what caused this! I want to know how this happened!!! I want my cat back. She is only three years old. No one from the pet food company will return my phone calls...and there is no help from them for any of us!"

> Matt (3/26):
>
> "Our 8-year-old Shelty, Lady, had to be put to sleep due to liver failure. We still have some of the same cans of dog food we fed her before she got sick. These cans have older dates, which makes us think the wheat gluten supplier is not what caused the contamination. Is there some way we can help figure this mess out?"

> Missie (3/27):
>
> "These companies are so selfish. All they care about is making their MONEY while their pet food is poisoning millions of pets, and people have no idea they are feeding the pets (family members) they love POISON!! I WILL NEVER BUY FROM THESE COMPANIES OR STORES AGAIN!!!"

## TECHNICAL EXPLANATIONS

Although Heather had received a lot of information from other bloggers as to which brands to avoid, she was still confused about conflicting information since nothing had been clearly explained by the responsible companies. She thought to herself, "I still don't really know what caused the contamination or exactly how to keep Star safe. I am getting just about all of my information from Tony, Megan, and others on the blogging sites. At least I can go to them to ask for help. I wish someone would clearly explain exactly what happened. At least my dog is still alive and not sick like so many of the others."

Megan was heartsick about the death of her cat and was still searching for an explanation. She continued to search through the blogs, where she found links to websites that led to more complex technical information and explanations about what happened. She found that the blogs were the primary source for advice and opinions. She shook her head in disbelief as she read through entries from others like herself who were frustrated with the lack of information from the responsible companies. She was grateful that some of them had tips and advice. She thought, "At least that's something."

Anonymous (3/17/07):

"A long list of pet food brands and lot numbers came out this morning for the pet food recall. PLEASE check out these links to make sure you are not feeding your pet any of the brands on this list! I've got the links for you below."

Pam (Blog, 3/19):

"I am so sorry, all of you who have lost your beloved pets. I saw something about milk thistle being used for detoxifying the kidney and liver. It has been used as a natural remedy for certain types of poisoning in humans...maybe it could be used to help the pets as well. If anyone could put me in contact with the right person or group I can give them the link to this information."

Josh (3/24):

"The pet food is not made of what you think it is. They are taking meat from dead animals that have died from various diseases, and their tissue still contains chemicals such as phenoberbital, which is used to euthanize them. These animals are then put into vats of chemicals and later grinded up together and eventually ends up in the pet food. THIS IS DISGUSTING AND SHOULD NEVER END UP IN PET FOOD!!"

Jolene (4/5):

"You all should really check out a great website I found that has the most and best information I've seen anywhere: www.pamperyourpet.com Please look at it. I think you'll find a lot of what you are looking for!"

## DEMAND FOR LEGAL ACTION

The more Megan read, the angrier she got. She realized that this blogging site not only was a great place to share experiences and information but also provided a forum where pet owners could unite and respond to the food recall. She decided it was time to organize and form a collective group to demand remediation and legal action. Before blogging, she thought to herself, "We should help each other find lawyers and consider the possibility of filing a class action lawsuit."

Megan (3/28):

"Somebody is responsible for this and must pay. They owe us for our vet bills, not to mention our pain and suffering. I think we should form a group and consider taking legal action."

Annie (3/28):

"Tony, I'm so sorry to hear about Bex and his poisoning from the dog food. Just know that my family and I are thinking about you and all the others who are experiencing similar pain right now. I hope everyone affected is thinking about some sort of lawsuit or class action suit. This is not something I would normally suggest…but the pain and suffering have affected so many there must be something that can be done legally to help compensate for it."

Lisa (3/29):

"I am going to SUE THE COMPANIES RESPONSIBLE FOR THIS!!!! We have to get together and take action!!"

Kelley (3/29):

"On March 8 my wonderful baby died…she was only five months old. Like all the other pets she was weak, could not eat, and was vomiting. My vet said he was certain it was related to the tainted pet food. We were feeding her the same brand as everyone else that has since been recalled. The lot numbers matched those on the recall list. You have no idea how devastating this is to us. To lose my princess to somebody else's stupidity and greed…I am sick to hear of all the other losses, and my heart goes out to every one of you. I am so angry about this company's lack of response, total denial of any accountability. Everyone is blaming everyone else. Has anyone planned legal action? I would love to hear from other pet owners who are also suffering to see what we can do!"

Although Heather's pet managed to escape the sad fate so many others had not been able to escape, she pondered how a similar situation could be prevented in the future. It was still not clear to her what had caused the contamination, exactly which foods were safe to feed Star, and what, if any, compensation would be provided for all those who had suffered losses. Now what was Heather going to feed her dog?

# CHAPTER 44

# Community Civility

## Rod Troester

## THE COMMUNITY

Imagine that you are a member of the chamber of commerce for a Great Lakes community of 250,000. Your community has seen its economy transition from one based in manufacturing and heavy industry to one that is based in the service sector; you have watched several large employers who had provided good-paying, family-supporting jobs close shop and others reduce their workforce significantly; you see your town struggling to accept the fact that the "good old days" of plentiful jobs that last the span of one's work life, a stable tax base, and a sense of stability are in jeopardy. Like that of most chambers, your mission focuses on economic development as you seek to attract new businesses and to support, maintain, and expand the current business base of the community. In the best of times, your task is challenging. And since these are not the best of times, events are conspiring to make your job even more difficult.*

## NEW LEADERSHIP CONFRONTS THE OLD BOYS

In January 2002, a new mayor was sworn into office in Great Lake City. Only in his mid-30s, Mayor Smith was preceded in office by two long-serving mayors—one who died in office after 20-plus years and Smith's immediate predecessor, who was term-limited to eight years. Smith inherited a cash-strapped, Rust Belt, "shot-and-a-beer" city with a declining population, shrinking tax base, and a city council dominated by a bunch of "good old boys" (literally) whose philosophy and political careers were established in and remained focused on the "good old days"—when heavy industry was booming, jobs were plentiful, and the future looked bright or at least stable and predictable.

---

*This case has been developed based on real organization(s) and real organizational experiences. Names, facts, and situations have been changed to protect the privacy of individuals and organizations. The case is based on more than 100 news reports on the events described.

Almost immediately Mayor Smith and the city council began butting heads. The 30-something lawyer-mayor wasn't going to tell the seasoned politicos how to run their city. The old guard politicians became a constant thorn in the side of Smith. Proposals and initiatives advanced by Smith were generally met with either skepticism or the council's attitude of "that's not the way we do things here in Great Lake City." For his part, Smith made his share of naïve political mistakes, projecting an air of arrogance because of his apparent preference for imposing rather than proposing initiatives. Each side dug in its heels more with each passing week; antagonism, insult, and animosity colored nearly all of the interactions between the mayor and council. Since each side perceived that getting anything done was giving in to the other and losing political face, the city seemed to stagnate while the negatives continued to spiral downward. As a member of the chamber of commerce, you are obviously concerned.

## A PLUM ECONOMIC DEVELOPMENT OPPORTUNITY

A year or so prior to the new administration taking office, a major manufacturer had announced the closing of a large 100-plus-year-old lake-front manufacturing facility that put hundreds of long-time union workers out of their jobs. Located within the city limits, the vacant manufacturing property is viewed as a prime site for future economic development. Economic development officials, including members of the chamber of commerce, see the site as a prime location for a number of potential enterprises.

One of the leading enterprises interested in the site is a gaming-resort development company that proposes to locate a "racino" (a combination horse racing track and gambling casino) on the former industrial property. This gaming-resort company has pitched its proposal to several municipalities at several times, depending on which governmental entity is willing to provide the most lucrative and attractive tax-rebate, infrastructure-incentive package.

## THE INTRIGUE BEGINS

Several months after his election Mayor Smith and his chief of staff were approached privately by the gaming-resort company to discuss locating the racino at the recently abandoned industrial site. Around the same time a land-investment/speculation partnership was formed by several of Smith's former and current associates. A year later this partnership attempted to begin buying properties adjacent to the former industrial site, thinking that if the development happened, the partnership would profit from the acquisitions.

By late 2003, Smith publicly acknowledged that he had been in talks with the gaming-resort development company, at which time the local newspaper became interested and began investigating the story. The state attorney general and even federal authorities launched investigations into the relationship between Smith, his current and former associates, and the gaming-resort development company.

Curiously, private contact between the mayor, his former associates, and the gaming company allegedly continued during the spring of 2004. By the fall of 2004, the state attorney general had convened a grand jury, which would later return charges against Smith and several of his former associates.

## THE CHAMBER OF COMMERCE GETS INVOLVED

As a member of the chamber, you have followed all of these events carefully. In the last three or four years, you have watched several municipalities in the area try to entice the gaming-resort development to their locations with various tax-rebate and infrastructure-incentive packages. The stakes in terms of jobs and economic impact are significant for the successful municipality and the entire region. Your concern and the chamber's overall goal are to help land the development for the region regardless of the specific municipality. As the stakes increase, the political discourse among and between the various governmental bodies becomes more stressed and uncivil.

Depending on the stage of the negotiations, which municipality was involved, and the news agency reporting on the situation, accusations and charges flew between politicians, the negotiator representing the gaming-resort company, and other interested municipalities and elected officials. Chamber members attempted to establish joint negotiating teams to prevent the developer from playing municipalities against each other, but the lack of trust and respect between and among the parties foiled these efforts. Some of the negotiations were carried out in public; other times there were allegedly private meetings that include both elected officials and private parties. Inevitably these private meetings became public, and a new round of charges and accusations began. In short, things were going nowhere fast, and the tone of the political discourse was becoming a serious concern for members of the chamber.

## THE COMMUNITY CIVILITY INITIATIVE

During the fall of 2004, your fellow members of the chamber recognized a growing concern that incivility among and between members of various governing bodies was hurting the reasoned discussion of the public's business—and making economic development efforts difficult. Your basic concern was that the climate of incivility evidenced among elected officials was having a detrimental effect on your efforts to maintain and attract new business to the area. As one board member explained, "If a potential company were to watch a broadcast of a city council meeting or read newspaper accounts of our elected officials, what's the impression it would form of Great Lake City?" Your challenge was to formulate a strategy that can restore civility to local political discourse and thereby make your task of economic development easier.

Members of the chamber sought advice and assistance from several social service agencies in the area as well as two local colleges that have institutes and have sponsored initiatives devoted to community civility. Not surprisingly, members of the chamber were looking for an easy and efficient means for turning around the political climate of incivility to facilitate economic development efforts. Several meetings between the various parties from which the chamber sought advice took place during late 2004 and early 2005. The chamber discovered a similar community civility effort that had been undertaken by another chamber of commerce and with permission decided to pattern its efforts after that campaign.

In one of the final meetings with the outside advisers, members of the chamber expressed a desire to be a catalyst for change in the community but stated that following the initial efforts they would look to other entities to assume responsibility for any long-term civility campaign. Following these meetings and discussions, the chamber's marketing staff took responsibility for designing and executing a public information campaign on community civility.

In mid-spring 2005, the chamber rolled out its civility initiative using the theme "Joining Together for the Common Good of Great Lake City." A key element to the campaign was for business and political leaders to sign a civility pledge as their public affirmation of a desire to chart a new course for public discourse in the community. The pledge points were based on and drawn from P. M. Forni's book *Choosing Civility* (2002). The civility pledge points included actions such as being inclusive, listening to others, showing respect, keeping an open mind, taking responsibility, celebrating new ideas, getting the facts, and staying involved. Clearly these actions were not controversial, but the proof of the campaign would be in its ability to initiate change.

The chamber's marketing staff did an excellent job of producing print materials explaining and detailing the civility pledge, creating a strong web presence, and even featuring the civility campaign in promotional publications. Significant funds from the chamber and local businesses were committed to the effort. Local political officials and business leaders were invited to affirm their support for the initiative by participating in formal pledge-signing events. Eventually dozens of elected officials—who were the real target of the initiative—along with hundreds of local business and organizational leaders in the area would "take the pledge." Touting the success of the initial program, one fellow chamber member commented, "Business and industry leaders seem to really believe in civility. This is great publicity and not just a publicity stunt."

The local paper was less enthusiastic. It ran the front-page headline "Business and Political Leaders Pledge to Be Nice." Choosing to characterize the civility initiative as simply "being nice" seemed to diminish or minimize the true intent of the chamber's efforts. With the positive efforts by the chamber in place and spreading throughout the business community, political events in the community seemed to conspire against the best intentions of chamber members.

## GOOD INTENTIONS MEET POLITICAL REALITIES

Unfortunately, your chamber's civility initiative took place against the backdrop of the spring municipal primary election and the mayor's preliminary hearing on corruption charges. Fortunately for Mayor Smith, legal wrangling over the selection of a judge to preside in his trial delayed the hearing until after the primary election. Civility had been problematic to economic development efforts. The chamber of commerce sought to address the problem in a public and positive way. The challenge would be to see if any sense of civility could be maintained during a municipal primary election as the office of mayor and several city council seats were up for grabs.

The same mayor and city council members who were constantly at odds during the previous three years and who were essentially the target for the civility initiative of the chamber and who had signed the civility pledge continued their bickering as they campaigned for reelection. In the weeks leading up to the primary, the city council increasingly challenged the decisions of the mayor and demanded detailed explanations before paying any bills. City hall insiders claimed that city workers were being bullied by the council and the various state and federal investigators. Accusations of patronage hiring by the mayor and questions over the role that the racino developer might be playing in the primary election through campaign contributions were playing out. So much for pledges of civility on the part of these elected officials.

In one particularly nasty and festering situation, Mayor Smith—over the city council's objections—took the bold move of hiring a minority individual as his director of public safety. As the highest-ranking minority in city administration, he was hired to oversee and bring diversity to the city's police and fire departments, which were historically white and male. Any attempts at reform were greeted by the council threatening to cut funding for the position, the minority community crying foul and charging racism on the part of the council, and the mayor stopping just short of characterizing members of the council as acting in a Klan-like manner.

In the spring primary, candidates for mayor and city council were repeatedly asked to explain their position on the pending racino development project as well as whether they had received campaign contributions from the developer. In the several candidate debates and forums that were held, tempers flared, charges were made, and accusations were exchanged; in short, it was politics as usual. Maybe politics and civility don't mix.

Interestingly, several mayoral candidates specifically emphasized civility in their campaigns and even in their print campaign advertisements. At one point in the run-up to the primary, the local paper ran a headline claiming "Civility Major Primary Issue." The article noted that all of the candidates commented on civility during the debates and forums, that several first-time candidates explained that uncivil discourse was in part a reason for their running for office, and finally that the tenor of public discourse was hindering the city's ability to grow. Not surprisingly, the mayor blamed the council, and the council blamed the mayor, in effect; the continuing bickering amounted to "I'll be civil if you will."

## THE ELECTION RESULTS

Members of the chamber closely followed the returns on the evening of the primary election. Incumbent Mayor Smith was soundly defeated, coming in fourth in a six-person Democratic primary race. The winner of the mayoral primary was a first-term city council member who had the endorsement of both the police and fire unions and considerable grass-roots support. For all practical purposes, given the politics of Great Lake City, the Democratic nominee would likely become the next mayor. As for the city council, two incumbents were defeated, and for the first time in history the council would include three minorities—an incumbent and two newcomers. Ironically, the one city council candidate who explicitly featured "civility" in his advertising was not elected.

## EPILOGUE

The day after the primary Mayor Smith had his preliminary hearing on public corruption charges, and the public's attention once again shifted to the racino and economic development. As the mayor went on trial, perhaps thankfully, the judge issued a gag order in the case. A week or so following the primary, rumors circulated that a defeated member of the city council had allegedly been approached by the racino developer to do some legal work and might have accepted a personal loan from a member of the opposition political party. Several months after the primary election the winner of the Republican primary dropped out of the race and threw his support to the Democratic candidate—ensuring his victory in the fall general election. In explaining his withdrawal, the candidate acknowledged that he had little chance of winning and that the political bickering of a general election would not serve the interests of the city. As for the racino, the project was eventually built in an adjacent municipality but outside of the city limits of Great Lake City. As a member of the chamber watching all these events unfold, you can't help but think that sometimes fact is better and stranger than fiction. How can civility thrive and economic development take place in such a negative political environment? The chamber's civility initiative appears to be a one-shot effort with no planned follow-up or longer-term goals.

## REFERENCE

Forni, P. M. (2002). *Choosing Civility: The Twenty-Five Rules of Considerate Conduct*. New York: St. Martin's Griffin.

CHAPTER 45

# The Sago Mine Disaster

## Carlos E. Balhana and Deanna F. Womack

A t 4:37 Friday afternoon, January 5, 2006, Kimberly Young* is sitting at a
desk in her apartment surrounded by blueprints, technical reports, legal
affidavits, and newspaper clippings. Kim's company, a public relations and crisis
management firm, has just been hired by the International Coal Group (ICG) to
develop a strategic communication plan in response to the disaster that took place
on January 2, 2006, at the Sago mine in Sago, West Virginia. As one of the consultants assigned to this account, Kim is reviewing the mine's history, the industrial
elements of its operation, and the recent flurry of media coverage containing a
series of erroneous reports.

### THE DISASTER

At approximately 6:00 A.M. on January 2, 2006, two crews of miners, known as
"One Left" and "Two Left," descend into the Sago mine as a powerful thunder-
storm approaches the mine's location. About five minutes later the control center
gauges show that one of the mine sensors is detecting elevated levels of explosive
carbon monoxide (CO) gas. The sensor operators decide that the sensor in question is probably malfunctioning, and they send one of the on-site electricians to
examine the device. At 6:26 A.M. lightning strikes nearby, and a large explosion
occurs inside a sealed and abandoned part of the mine. The carbon monoxide
monitors on the conveyor belts immediately detect high levels of gas. As the One
Left crew starts to evacuate the mine, one of its workers reports that there has been
an explosion in the area where Two Left was drilling. The control center cannot
contact the missing crew, and, as One Left emerges from the mine's entrance, Two
Left remains trapped inside.

---

*Although the character of Kimberly Young is fictional, the timeline and all case facts are part of
the public record of the Sago mine disaster.

## THE RESCUE EFFORT

Kim cannot ignore the amount of time lost due to communication failures and a halting rescue effort. At 7:00 A.M. on January 2, the mine dispatcher contacts the assistant safety director and alerts him of the incident. After conferring with the mine superintendent, the assistant safety director decides to contact the inspector of the West Virginia Office of Miners' Health, Safety, and Training and the Barbour County Mine Rescue Team. The initial call to the inspector leads to a disconnected phone number, and the initial call to the rescue team goes unanswered. The Sago mine does not have an on-site rescue group.

The assistant safety director places several calls to the Mine Safety and Health Administration (MSHA) officials, but no one answers the phone. Finally, at 8:30 A.M., about two hours after the explosion, the assistant safety director manages to speak with an MSHA inspector, who gives an order that no one is to enter the mine until the rescue teams arrive. The Barbour County Mine Rescue Team arrives at the mine at 11 A.M. Other rescue teams have also been contacted. However, a command center is not set up until about noon on January 2. At 4:45 P.M., more than 10 hours after the explosion, the MSHA approves a rescue plan. The first rescue team is deployed at approximately 5:30 P.M. after the original plan has been revised. A bore drill is used to excavate the area around the presumed location of the missing crew, and additional rescue teams are sent in later in the evening. After 11:45 P.M. on January 3, 2006, nearly 40 hours after the explosion, the rescue team finds the Two Left miners.

## MISCOMMUNICATION

The first report to the command center states that all 12 miners are alive. This information is soon communicated to the rest of the Sago staff, the emergency personnel, the families of the missing workers, and the media. However, the report contains an egregious error—only one of the miners has survived.

To prevent the media from obtaining information about the tragedy through their investigations, the rescue team has been instructed to use a code: The team is ordered to say "items" instead of bodies and to use identification numbers instead of names when referring to the individual miners. The rescue team soon contacts the control center and explains that it has recovered one miner and 11 "items." The control center operators and company officials think that the team has misapplied the code. After much confusion, one of the officials asks for a clarification in plain language, and the rescue team relays the news that 11 miners are dead. At about 1 A.M. Wednesday, January 4, the lone survivor reaches the surface. By 10 A.M. the rescue teams have recovered the 11 bodies. Like the mine authorities, the media are slow to learn the real number of casualties but quick to blame Sago officials after the full situation is understood.

## EQUIPMENT FAILURES?

Kim is concerned that all of the misinformation and procedural hang-ups will make matters only worse for ICG as it deals with charges of inadequate equipment and structural negligence. According to the accounts of the rescue team and the sole survivor of the incident, the crew members had set up an emergency curtain to help quarantine themselves from the deadly smoke. The crew members had access to portable emergency breathing devices known as "self-contained self-rescuers" (SCSRs), but at least four of them initially appeared to malfunction. The miners did not have sufficient air supply to try to escape and had to share the remaining working devices. Laboratory tests on the recovered SCSRs revealed that the faulty devices had indeed been working when the miners discarded them. According to the investigative reports, the miners did not know how to activate and use the breathing devices properly. However, even if the SCSRs had all been used, each could provide a maximum of only four hours of breathable air, too little to have saved all 12 miners.

## SAFETY VIOLATIONS

Kim also learns that the International Coal Group acquired the Sago mine from another company in October 2005, just three months before the explosion. Kim starts to wonder whether the safety problems that contributed to this tragedy might have existed before ICG acquired the mine. Indeed, in 2005, prior to the ICG acquisition, inspectors from the Mine Health and Safety Administration cited 208 safety violations, 98 of which were deemed "serious and substantial." Inspections in the fall of 2005 showed that the number of violations was reduced to 46 violations, with 18 "serious and substantial" cases under ICG management. Still, mine operators had been aware of the incoming storm, and, at the very least, it was common for the carbon monoxide sensors to malfunction during bad weather. When the carbon monoxide alarm was first activated about 20 minutes before the explosion, the dispatcher disregarded it as a false alarm and ordered an electrician to inspect the sensor.

## KIM'S CHALLENGE

At almost 5:00 o'clock on the evening of Friday, January 5, Kim is distraught. For every well-executed action, there appears to be a burden of several bad decisions, a poorly defined rescue plan, and a frenzy of misinformation. Kim has to present a reliable public relations strategy to her client—the same client who used a code to withhold information from the media and whose representatives claimed that many of the safety violations were likely to be inspection-reporting errors that did not contribute to the disaster.

# Organizational Crisis

## CHAPTER 46

# More Questions Than Answers

## Amanda M. Gunn

Dorothea Dix Hospital (Dix)\* is the oldest state-run mental health hospital in North Carolina. It is closing its doors. The loss of 400 beds for the mentally ill in the capital city of Raleigh is a blow to the community surrounding the hospital, the patients served by the hospital, and 1,200 employees who are facing job loss. The reasons for the closure have been contested. Some argue that the land that Dix sits on, a pristine 300-plus-acre, rolling hill estate overlooking the city skyline, should be used for condos or parks. Some argue that the hospital is so old and outdated that starting over somewhere else is in the best interest of the patients. Some cite the state's Mental Health Reform Act of 2001, which demands a shift in psychiatric treatment from state-funded and-operated mental health hospitals to local community services and private industry, as the reason for the upheaval of the organization and its stakeholders. In the midst of the debates about why the hospital will be closing, there are numerous questions regarding how the closing will happen and what will happen to the organizational members. The employees are scared about their impending employment changes and feel excluded from the process. The director expresses his frustration with limited information sharing by those in power at the state level. Both perspectives are worth exploring in detail.

## THE FIRST FEW WEEKS

### Department Director Knight's Office

**EMPLOYEE:** "Nobody at work told me. I had to hear it from the news."

---

\*The information in this case is real. The dialogue has been constructed out of data that resulted from 55 in-depth interviews with Dix employees facing job loss as a result of the closing and more than 250 newspaper articles collected during a two-year period. The names have been changed, and the timeline is not exact. The emotions, concerns, and overall sensemaking reflect themes that emerged from the transcribed interviews.

**EMPLOYEE:** "Me, too. Ms. Knight, why did Tom and I have to hear about the closing from the TV?"

At that moment three other dietary workers walk into Ms. Knight's office with looks of concern. In hushed voices they each express the fear that has been building in them during the last 14 hours.

**EMPLOYEE:** "My husband told me last night when I got home that the hospital is closing. Is it true?"

**EMPLOYEE:** "Ms. Knight, I am scared. What am I going to do without a job?"

**EMPLOYEE:** "Please tell us what is going on."

**MS. KNIGHT:** "At this moment I do not know what is going on. You know there have been rumors for months that the hospital will be closing. I, too, heard on the news last night that the Department of Health and Human Services secretary (DHHS) stated that the hospital will close in the next two years."

**EMPLOYEE:** "What does that mean for our jobs? For my job? I am two years out from retirement."

**MS. KNIGHT:** "Karen, I do not know any more than you do at this point, but I will find out as quickly as I can."

As the five employees leave Ms. Knight's office she reflects on their fears with discomfort and frustration as she picks up the phone to call the hospital director, Dr. Carrol.

## From Another Important Office

**MR. TRUNE:** "Could I please speak with Dr. Carrol?"

**MR. TRUNE:** "Hi, Dr. Carrol, this is Mr. Trune from Housekeeping. I was hoping we could talk for a few minutes about the rumors regarding the closing of the hospital. My staff is in an uproar, and I would like to share with them any information I can."

**DR. CARROL:** "Mr. Trune, hello. I just got off the phone with Ms. Knight. I realize the news report last night has hit our organization like a boulder. The truth is that I do not have a lot of information either. I am meeting with the secretary in two hours. Can you be here at 3:00 o'clock to meet with me and the department directors?"

**MR. TRUNE:** "I can, Dr. Carrol, but I must say that I need to tell them something to keep them focused on their work for the next several hours."

**DR. CARROL:** "Yes, yes, I understand. We do have a hospital to run. Tell them about this conversation and that we are doing all we can to have the information to them before they go home today. Remind them that we have 400 patients to take care of who cannot take care of themselves, and that we and they need them. I will see you at 3:00."

## Break Room

**SANDRA:** "John, I have been working here for 25 years, and they did not have the decency to come tell me that I am going to be out of my job."

**JOHN:** "I know, Sandra. My mom and uncle worked here all their work lives. I came on 15 years ago. You would think they would have some loyalty to us. We sure have had it for them."

**BETH:** "Being an aide at a hospital is all I know how to do. Where am I going to go; what am I going to do? I don't have a college education."

**SANDRA:** "I don't want to have to start over at 45. I sure don't."

## Secretary of Health and Human Services and Hospital Director

**SHHS:** "Yes, we will be closing the hospital, Dr. Carrol. We have been talking about it for years. I have shared with you along the way. The final decision was reached in the legislature yesterday afternoon. I am not sure how the news got the story as quickly as they did. It is true. We will close Dix within the next two years. We will build a new hospital to replace this one."

**DR. CARROL:** "Oh, so I can tell my employees and the parents of the patients that they will be moved to the new hospital once it is built? Where will it be located?"

**SHHS:** "I do not have all of the details, Dr. Carrol. I will let you know as I know. There are lots of decisions left to be made."

**DR. CARROL:** "Secretary, I have got to give my employees more information than that. The rumors and gossip are already taking over. I need to offer them some information that will calm them down and keep them working."

**SHHS:** "Again, I will let you know as I know. Tell them they are still expected to provide the best care possible for our patients. The patients are, and will remain, the most important stakeholder."

**DR. CARROL:** "I need to know everything possible as soon as I can to maintain a functioning, safe, and supportive hospital for those very patients."

**SHHS:** "I will be in touch."

## Hospital Director and Department Directors' Meeting

**DR. CARROL:** "OK, here it is. Yes, the hospital is closing. There will be a new hospital built. We do not know when exactly, but it looks like two years. We do not know where exactly, but it will not be in this county. We do not know how many beds or positions it will have. I heard just a few minutes ago that we may be combining resources with another state hospital that is being closed."

**MS. KARNS:** "Dr. Carrol, how am I going to share with my nurses and aides all of the 'unknowns'? How am I going to keep them coming to work after they learn about what is happening and what we still do not know about? It is so hard to get good nurses. I cannot afford to lose any more because we don't have answers. How are we going to keep them for two years?"

**DEPARTMENT DIRECTOR:** "I agree with Ms. Karns, and I want to add that my workers are already asking me about whether they are going to get severance and about what is going to happen to their retirement and health benefits."

**DEPARTMENT DIRECTOR:** "The employees are scared, frustrated, and feel excluded from any and all information sharing. We have got to tell them something."

**DR. CARROL:** "No question, this is a mess, but it is a mess we have to deal with together. Here is what I would like to do. I am going to send out a memo that will explain what is going on. Then I would like to hold an open forum for people to talk with one another about what is happening."

**MS. KARNS:** "Dr. Carrol, that sounds like a good idea, but you should be ready for the anger that many of them are feeling."

**DR. CARROL:** "Yes, Ms. Karns, we should all be preparing for that and more."

## Open Forum Between Director and Employees

**DR. CARROL:** "We are going to close Dix, and a new hospital is going to be built that will combine the patients from Dix and those from John Umstead."

**EMPLOYEE:** "What is going to happen to our jobs?"

**EMPLOYEE:** "Yeah, what about us, and when are we going to close?"

**DR. CARROL:** "We do not know exactly when it is going to close. We are projecting two years from now. So, we will need for everyone to keep up the hard work until then."

**EMPLOYEE:** "Hey, is there going to be a job for all of us at the new hospital? What about the folks who work at Umstead?"

**EMPLOYEE:** "What is going to happen to the patients?"

**EMPLOYEE:** "Where will the new hospital be? I don't have a car."

**EMPLOYEE:** "There are many of us who work here who depend on the bus system to get to work. Where are they building the new one?"

**DR. CARROL:** "We do not have a lot of answers at this point. I wanted to meet with you today to let you know that I am here for you to talk with, that I am trying to find out the answers, and to let you know that we are going to meet on a regular basis and I will send out memos to inform you."

## SIX MONTHS LATER

### The Hospital Director and a Friend

**DR. CARROL:** "We are going to move the hospital out of the county; one of the fastest-growing counties in the state. The greater Triangle area has over a million people now, and Dix is the *only* facility available for people who are indigent or who don't have insurance. *And* a lot of people who are middle class don't have insurance for mental illness. It is absolutely contrary to the interest of the public to build the new hospital in Butner, 50 miles away from the Virginia border."

**FRIEND:** "How many beds are they going to have for the patients at the new hospital?"

**DR. CARROL:** "Well, there are going to be only about 400 beds for the current 800 patients when you combine the populations of the two hospitals."

**FRIEND:** "What will happen with the other patients?"

**DR. CARROL:** "They will be taken into the private system or the emergency rooms or in some cases the street."

**FRIEND:** "What is going to happen to the employees at Dix?"

**DR. CARROL:** "The people who are going to be hurt the most by this are the lower-paid employees. The dietary personnel, a lot of the health-care techs, and the housekeeping staff; they're going to be fired. And when they lose their jobs, they are not going to be able to find anything that is comparable with the ones they have because the ones they have are state positions that have health insurance, retirement benefits, and group life insurance. They are going to end up as custodians for private contractors, making probably less, with no benefits. There are probably 500 people in that class."

**FRIEND:** "Will they receive anything to get them through the transition?"

**DR. CARROL:** "None of the employees who are going to lose their jobs, and certainly many will, and a lot of people don't realize it yet, are going to be able to get any severance pay, because the new hospital is 33 1/2 miles away from Dix."

**FRIEND:** "Why does that make a difference?"

**DR. CARROL:** "Because if the state offers you a job at the same level within 35 miles of your current employment, and you choose not to take it, then you give up your rights to a severance package."

**FRIEND:** "Wow. And the new one will be just under 35 miles on a two-lane road."

**DR. CARROL:** "It makes me so angry, so frustrated, because I think it is a gross example of government doing probably the worst it can for the people most in need, both as employees and those who are mentally ill."

**FRIEND:** "How are the employees handling all of this?"

**DR. CARROL:** "They keep coming to work and doing the best they can. I think many of them continue to hope that the closure is not real. It is real, and they are going to wake up to it at some point. I feel for them and the organization when that happens."

**FRIEND:** "Surely some of them are finding other jobs and leaving?"

**DR. CARROL:** "We are losing more nurses than I would like due to the shortage. In fact, I have recently had to start hiring contract nurses, and that poses a lot of different problems."

**FRIEND:** "What about the housekeepers and the health technicians?"

**DR. CARROL:** "Most of them have stayed, and I think they will for a while at least. I sure hope so."

**FRIEND:** "Are you offering them any incentive to stay?"

**DR. CARROL:** "Not at this point."

## A YEAR LATER

**DR. CARROL:** "I know the planning process by the department and division doesn't appear to involve any thought at all.

"When this all started, I told my staff that I would periodically provide them with a memorandum on what was transpiring.

"I did that, I tried.

"I sent one and then six months went by, and another one, and I only sent two memorandums because I didn't have any new information to tell them.

"Had nothing I could tell them about what would happen to them or their future at all.

"I'm sure they feel like I have not been truthful, and I was keeping things from them, and I am sure that generated lots of suspicion and rumors and paranoia about what is going on.

"But the reality is, I didn't know either."

## Break Room

**EMPLOYEE:** "We still don't really know why."

**EMPLOYEE:** "I think it's the land. It's a money thing."

**EMPLOYEE:** "Yeah, this hospital sits high on a hill that overlooks the city. They want it. They want it bad."

**EMPLOYEE:** "I keep hearing that it may stay open."

**EMPLOYEE:** "It ain't gonna stay open. Where did you hear that?"

**EMPLOYEE:** "I heard some people down in the shop talking about it."

**EMPLOYEE:** "Well, they were pulling your leg. The hospital is going to close. They are going to sell the land, and we are going to be looking for jobs."

**EMPLOYEE:** "Why haven't they brought anybody in to talk with us, to help us in finding another job?"

**EMPLOYEE:** "Shoot, why haven't they come and talked with us about anything?"

**EMPLOYEE:** "I do wish they would have sat us down and said, 'Here is what is happening, and this is what we are going to do to get you through it.'"

**EMPLOYEE:** "It is not like I want them to give me a job. I just want to be treated with dignity."

**EMPLOYEE:** "What kinds of resolutions are being talked about?"

**EMPLOYEE:** "Right now nothing has happened. The director did tell me the other day that within the next year there will be some effort to establish on-site, departmental special human resources offices for people to see if they can find other jobs in state government or provide them with counseling on how to find other jobs."

EMPLOYEE: "Why are they waiting another year, until right before the hospital closes? That seems pretty close to call for me."

EMPLOYEE: "They need to keep us here."

EMPLOYEE: "But don't we need to find a job?"

EMPLOYEE: "I do get frustrated that nothing has been done at this point. The employees still have no information."

CHAPTER 47

# Ethics in Big Pharma

## Alexander Lyon and Robert R. Ulmer

In 2004, the U.S. Senate held a hearing on Merck Pharmaceutical's controversial pain drug, Vioxx.* The hearing was buzzing. Senator Grassley (R-IA) scolded Merck executives, "Consumers should not have to second-guess the safety of what's in their medicine cabinet!"

Raymond Gilmartin, chief executive officer (CEO) of Merck, defended the company, "Senator Grassley, many patients counted on Vioxx to help them when no other medicine would help...Merck has been driven by ethics for more than 100 years. Merck puts patients first."

David Graham, from the Food and Drug Administration (FDA), interjected in disbelief, "Let's put this in perspective. You've got a drug that's increasing the risk of heart attacks fivefold. We estimate that there were 88,000 to 139,000 deaths caused by this drug. And Merck is saying, 'We put patients' safety first.' To me, that's very disturbing."

Dr. Singh, an expert on Vioxx, ridiculed the company, "Apparently, Merck's decisions were made for marketing reasons and for PR reasons. In my opinion, ladies and gentlemen, it is still better to kill a drug than kill a patient."

For the rest of the hearing, Gilmartin defended Merck's marketing of Vioxx and insisted that the drug was safe. As members of the press followed the hearing, they asked themselves the same question: How did such a financially successful company that promoted itself as ethically sound end up in of one of biggest pharmaceutical crises in history?

---

*This case shows the actual events surrounding Merck's Vioxx crisis. It was developed from congressional testimony, internal Merck documents made publicly available by Congress at http://oversight. house.gov/features/vioxx/documents.asp and through Merck's published studies, and public statements from Merck executives. Also, some technical terms and interactions were simplified for the sake of clarity. For example, "myocardial infarction" was changed to "heart attack." Some lengthy talking turns and statements, particularly during the Senate hearings, were shortened or compressed to save space and aid readability. In each case, the authors preserved the original meaning of participants' statements.

## PROMOTING A POSITIVE REPUTATION
## FOR SOCIAL RESPONSIBILITY

Ten years earlier Gilmartin had become Merck's new president and CEO. He came from a company that sold medical devices. Pharmacy veterans considered him an outsider to drug sales. Gilmartin used to smile to himself when people asked, "Who is this guy?" During his time at Merck, the company was one of the top five pharmaceutical companies, with $20 billion a year in overall revenue. This financial success put Merck in the same category as other "big pharma" giants such as Johnson & Johnson, Pfizer, and Glaxo-Smith-Kline.

Under Gilmartin's leadership, the company grew to over 60,000 employees and launched more new drugs than over before. Vioxx was meant to treat people with acute joint pain caused by injuries or aging. It was similar to the popular drug Celebrex and the over-the-counter drug, Aleve, which contained naproxen (pronounced na-PROX-en). Merck pitched Vioxx to the FDA as safer than these other pain drugs because Merck's studies showed that it had a unique advantage: It caused less incidents of stomach bleeding than its competitors. Gilmartin and others at Merck hoped this advantage would help Vioxx become a blockbuster drug in the highly competitive pain medicine market.

Unlike some companies, Merck also took a clear public stand on ethics. The company website stated, "We seek to maintain high ethical standards and a culture that values honesty, integrity and transparency in all that we do. Company decisions are driven by what is right for patients." Gilmartin often quoted George W. Merck, son of the company's founder, "Medicine is for people, not profit." Gilmartin once explained his passion for ethics during a visit to the Harvard Business School. He asked, "Will our company be seen as one whose workers not only did great research, but also conducted themselves with the highest standards of integrity? These are the kinds of questions that are important to me." More than most CEOs, Gilmartin publicly held Merck to a high ethical standard.


## FDA FAST-TRACKED VIOXX'S APPROVAL FOR MERCK

Most of Merck's earliest studies on the drug showed that it (1) helped patients with pain and (2) showed a lower risk for stomach bleeding than similar drugs. These initial studies, however, were short-term and lasted from as short as six weeks to three months. As a result, the data on the drug's side effects were unclear. Some data suggested that Vioxx patients may have had a slightly higher risk of heart attacks than those taking other drugs. However, Merck executives explained that the numbers were low enough that they could have been due to statistical random chance. With the safety of Vioxx still in question, Merck pushed for the drug's quick approval. The FDA accepted Merck's explanation about the drug's safety and fast-tracked its approval in 1999.

Merck began marketing the drug heavily in 2000. The company promoted the drug as the premiere drug of choice for pain. Early advertisements showed former Olympic figure skater Dorothy Hamill enjoying a refreshing and pain-free skating workout. Merck spent a record $500 million-plus marketing Vioxx. It quickly became the blockbuster drug Gilmartin had hoped for and earned Merck $2.5 billion a year. Before Merck released Vioxx, its stock was trading between $50–$60 per share. When Vioxx sales were in full swing in 2001, Merck's stock went as high as $90 per share.

The financial success of Vioxx and other drugs allowed Gilmartin to pursue one of his other priorities for Merck—to give generously to communities in need. With Gilmartin in charge, Merck developed a public image of corporate responsibility through its donation of vaccines and medicines. For example, the company has an ongoing effort to fight river blindness in Africa, and it donates financial and research support to fight HIV/AIDS in China and Africa. The company also contributes to many domestic health-care concerns such as support for a network of health-care professionals committed to treating childhood asthma. While many companies give, Merck also employed staffers to publicize its good deeds in order "to make sure that stakeholders know about the company's good work." Merck's public reputation was based primarily upon promoting the positive examples of its social responsibility.

Vioxx's early financial success, however, was met with a growing concern about its cardiovascular safety. Those outside the company claimed that Merck had downplayed the potential cardiovascular risks of the drug in the data it showed the FDA. Further, some experts claimed that Merck's marketing spun the data to hide the drug's potential risk for causing heart attacks. Some Vioxx patients had heart attacks and died. Members of the scientific community began harshly criticizing Merck and Gilmartin for not living up to its own stated ethical standards. Stories in the press began to question Vioxx's safety and wondered if Merck and Gilmartin's claimed desire to help patients was truly driving the company's actions. Or was it something else?

## SCIENCE SELLS

Merck continued doing studies on Vioxx to help market the drug to physicians. "Science sells!" as one executive dangerously explained Merck's motivation for doing additional studies. The company paid researchers to conduct various studies with catchy titles such as *Advantage* or *Approve* and *Vigor* to help promote the unique benefits of Vioxx.

*Vigor*, Merck's best-known study, was a nine-month study that supported Merck's claim that Vioxx caused fewer incidents of stomach bleeding than existing drugs. However, the study also showed that the elevated risk of heart attacks indicated in earlier studies for Vioxx patients persisted in the long-term study. In fact, patients taking Vioxx were five times more likely to have a heart attack than those taking the alternative drug in the study, naproxen. Merck explained away this risk by using creative language to flip the interpretation of the data upside down. Peter Kim, president of Merck's research laboratories, claimed in technical terms, "The most plausible explanation for the *Vigor* results is that naproxen was exerting a *cardioprotective* effect" on its patients. In other words, Kim concluded that Vioxx was absolutely safe. Naproxen patients were simply five times *less likely* to experience heart attacks than the average person. As Merck saw it, naproxen had a benefit. There was no problem with Vioxx.

Despite a harsh *New York Times* article about Vioxx, Merck's aggressive, mul-timillion-dollar campaign rolled on. Much of the marketing was done by Merck's 3,000 drug representatives. Merck trained them to "sell" the drug to physicians or convince the physicians to prescribe Vioxx. Merck executives told them to insist that Vioxx was safe and to end with a strong close, "Doctor, based upon the efficacy, safety, and convenience of Vioxx, is there any reason why you wouldn't choose Vioxx *first* for your patients?"

Merck provided drug reps with a printed brochure called the "Cardiocard" that emphasized the drug's safety with impressive graphs and charts. The FDA, however, told Merck that it should not use the brochure because it used old, hand-picked data that made Vioxx look safe by omitting data from the more recent *Vigor* study. The FDA warned that the pamphlet hid risks that should be communicated to physicians. Merck ignored the FDA and instead sent out a press release claiming, "Merck confirms favorable cardiovascular safety profile of Vioxx" in response.

The company continued its aggressive marketing of Vioxx as a drug that pro-vided "superior pain relief" with "excellent tolerability" or low side effects. Merck repeated its claim that Vioxx was safer than competing drugs. Merck's main mes-sage was spelled out for drug reps to repeat word-for-word to physicians: "Doctor, let me say that based upon all of the data that are available, Merck stands behind the overall efficacy and safety profile of Vioxx."

Public criticism and doctors' questions about the drug's risks continued. Behind the scenes, Merck told its drug reps, "Do not initiate discussions on any of the recent articles in the press on Vioxx." The drug reps were told literally to "dodge" doctors' concerns such as "I am concerned about the cardiovascular effects of Vioxx."

Company leaders forbade reps to discuss the drug's cardiovascular risks. Inter-nal memos stated forcefully, "DO NOT DISCUSS" the drug's risks. Publicly Merck executives dismissed claims that their judgments were being clouded by the drug's enormous financial success. Peter Kim, the president of Merck's research laboratories, assured the FDA, "Merck is a data-driven company" and "We put patients first."

## SCIENTIFIC TRANSPARENCY OR RUNNING FROM RISKS?

As time when on, others in the scientific community disagreed with Merck's claim that Vioxx was safe. Many physicians saw problems in the data and unusually high rates of heart attacks for their own Vioxx patients. FDA rejected Merck's claims about Vioxx's safety as "simply incomprehensible" given the data. The FDA ordered Merck to change the warning label on the Vioxx bottle to include the clear risks of heart attacks, which were "five times higher" than alternative medications. Merck, however, refused to change the label for two years while it continued to market the drug's safety heavily. After two years, Merck executives finally gave in but insisted on their own ambiguous language for the label. Dr. Singh, a professor at Stanford's medical school and expert on Vioxx, criticized Merck executives' actions during Congress' investigation of Merck:

> Rather than warning about cardiovascular risks...the label says, "Vioxx is not a substitute for aspirin for cardiovascular risk prevention." Ladies and gentlemen and physicians in the audience, let me ask you, do you know of a single physician, one physician in the world, who has ever prescribed Vioxx for cardiovascular risk prevention? What are we about here? Why not also say on the label, "Do not use Vioxx for erectile dysfunction, it doesn't work like Viagra"?

Dr. Singh, who used to work for Merck and had a friendly relationship with executives, reported, "I asked Merck repeatedly for more data, including information on high blood pressure and heart failure rates." Merck ignored his requests.

An internal email shows Merck members privately acknowledging the legitimacy of Dr. Singh's claims about Vioxx's safety:

> Dr. Singh...reports product information that is not favorable to Merck...and although we may not like to hear about it, his information is scientifically accurate.

Still, instead of providing data and responding to Dr. Singh's concerns, Merck executives threatened Singh and contacted his boss at Stanford. In an email to another Merck insider, an executive wrote,

> Tell Singh that we've told his boss about his Merck-bashing. And should it continue, further action will be necessary (don't define it).

Like Singh, physicians and researchers all over the country reported being threatened and pressured when they publicly criticized Vioxx. Company executives argued that they were committed to transparency, "We have long recognized the importance of open dialogue and two-way communication."

Executives explained that those who criticized Vioxx's safety were simply "anti-Merck" and had personal gripes against the company. Gilmartin eventually apologized to Singh for the harsh treatment and assured critics, "We encourage healthy debate" about Merck's medicines.

## WITHDRAWING THE DRUG AND FALSIFIED DATA

Under growing public and governmental pressure in 2004, Merck eventually withdrew Vioxx from the market. Gilmartin was clear, however, that the decision was precautionary. This was a "voluntary withdrawal of the drug."

Around the time of the withdrawal, researchers and journal editors made fresh allegations that Merck executives and researchers falsified the data about

Vioxx's safety. Editors from the *New England Journal of Medicine* who published *Vigor*, for instance, discovered that some Vioxx patients' deaths were "deleted from the *Vigor* manuscript two days before it was initially submitted to the journal." The editors slammed the authors for being deliberately "misleading" and stated that the "calculation and conclusions of the *Vigor* article were incorrect." The *Vigor* authors deleted all of the Vioxx deaths that occurred in the 10th month of their study, the most deadly month. Instead, they claimed they did a "9.0 month" study in the paper they sent the journal editors.

Further, Merck's marketing department designed, paid for, carried out, and wrote a study entitled *Advantage* that reported Vioxx had no cardiovascular risks. After its publication, members of the scientific community learned that Merck executives tampered with the data. In total, eight patients taking Vioxx in the study had heart attacks. Before the study was sent to the journal, Merck executives had labeled three heart attack deaths as having unknown causes and edited them out of the paper to make the drug look safer. An internal email between Merck scientists show them discussing one of the patients' deaths:

> Common things being common, the clinical scenario for the patient's death is likely to be a heart attack.

Merck's vice president for clinical research, however, asked that the cause of death be changed,

> I would prefer [it to be described as an] unknown cause of death so we don't raise concerns.

As public reports of patients' deaths climbed into the ten thousands, Congress opened an official investigation into the marketing and safety of Vioxx. By 2004, Gilmartin, CEO, was under serious scrutiny. He maintained throughout his remarks that the withdrawal was purely precautionary. He asserted that Merck's scientific process was completely transparent and that Vioxx was safe.

> We extensively study our medicines both before and after the medicines are approved... We promptly disclose [our data]. When questions arise about our medicines, we quickly analyze the available data, explore their meaning within the company and in scientific forums...Our ethical standards are the foundation of our company...We believe that our actions surrounding Vioxx are consistent with putting the interests of patients first.

In an interview with a magazine in 2005, Gilmartin insisted more boldly about Vioxx, "There's no risk, no increased cardiovascular risk" and suggested that Merck might decide to sell Vioxx again in the near future.

Congress' investigation gained media attention when it released all of the internal documents Merck had turned over to the government. These memos, voicemails, and training materials showed Merck's preoccupation with Vioxx's main competitor, Celebrex, a constant emphasis on the company's financial success, and the routine disregard for physicians' concerns and patients' health. Gilmartin, CEO, resigned from his position just days after Congress made Merck's internal documents public. As investors lost confidence in the company, Merck's stock sank from a high of $90 per share to a dismal $30 per share. The press blasted Merck's actions for being driven by a concern with its public image and sales numbers at the expense of patients' safety.

The press covered the story as an ironic crisis because of Gilmartin's continued public statements that Merck was an ethical company that was concerned only with science and patients' health. It makes one consider the veracity of those public statements in light of the company's communication about Vioxx. Since then the family members of deceased loved ones have filed thousands of lawsuits against Merck. Merck's lawyers scramble to reach settlements and reduce the financial losses to the company. Senator Grassley concluded the congressional hearing on Vioxx with the statement, "I will continue the committee's investigation on what happened with Vioxx. It seems clear to me that there is more to learn about this drug disaster."

# CHAPTER 48

# Forced Collaboration

## Beth Eschenfelder

### THE TRAIN IS COMING

As Muriel* walks into the meeting room at the Children's Funding Board (CFB), a staff member is working at the front of the room preparing for today's board meeting. He fumbles around with some cords and a laptop, struggling to get the LCD projector overhead to make a connection. As Muriel walks toward her seat, she watches with interest, waiting to see what would be displayed on the screen that hangs above the board's seating area. The projector comes to life, and the usual images of smiling children's faces fill the screen. The words "*CFB Strategic Plan Report*" float above the heads of the smiling children. That is hardly enough to give Muriel any clue about what will be presented by the CFB staff at today's meeting.

As a director of the largest neighborhood family center, which receives substantial funding from CFB, Muriel regularly attends the CFB monthly board meetings. CFB is her largest funder and the largest funder for all the neighborhood family centers in the county. Today's meeting is one that could have a significant impact on the future of her organization and that of the other neighborhood family centers.

Muriel mentors and works closely with the other neighborhood family centers, including their work last year to formalize a planning collaborative composed of all the neighborhood family centers: the Neighborhood Family Centers Collaborative (NFC Collaborative or Collaborative). Muriel is honored to be serving as the first president of the Collaborative, and she tries her best to balance her allegiance to her own center and to the Collaborative. When she attends the CFB meetings, she wears both hats, looking out for the interests of her agency as well

---

*This case has been developed based on real organization(s) and real organizational experiences. Names, facts, and situations have been changed to protect the privacy of individuals and organizations.

357

as those of the small neighborhood family centers that can't spare a staff member to attend a meeting.

The board room is packed with other agency directors. Like Muriel, some are there to hear what the board has to say about key strategies that might impact their agencies in the coming year. Others are there simply to *be seen* by their funder and the elected officials who serve on the board. There also are a few people who attend only because the CFB meetings have become *the best show in town—the show* being the conflict that routinely erupts at board meetings since its composition began to change in the past several months due to new appointments to the board.

Political viewpoints are often at the forefront of board discussions, disguised behind the veil of *providing quality care to our county's children.* The CFB board is responsible for allocating more than $34 million in local tax revenue to child-serving agencies throughout the county, and board members take their responsibilities seriously. The next budget cycle is around the corner, and today's board meeting largely will focus on implementing strategies from the strategic plan that was approved by the board last month.

Larry is already seated when Muriel arrives to the meeting. Larry is a former neighborhood family center director who recently accepted the challenge to work as the first executive director of the NFC Collaborative. Muriel takes her seat next to him. They always sit in the row of chairs that borders the back wall. Sitting in the middle of that row, they have a clear view of the board members who sit at the U-shaped tables at the other end of the long room. Muriel likes to watch the facial expressions of some of the board members and CFB staff, especially when the newly appointed "good old boys" (and girls) start doing their thing to push their personal agendas forward at the expense of county taxpayers.

As more people file into the room exchanging their usual greetings, Muriel and Larry focus on the board's strategic plan document that was distributed with the meeting notice. They read through the goals and objectives trying to predict how things will shake out at today's meeting. The neighborhood family centers are the most vulnerable of all the agencies because so many of the centers are small, grass-roots agencies that grew out of local neighborhood initiatives. They depend on CFB funding to survive, and this particular collection of CFB board members is not endeared to the neighborhood family center model like some of the previous board members had been.

Muriel opens her strategic plan to page 7, where all the adopted goals are listed. Right in the middle of the list is the big one that concerns her:

Goal #3: Increase the efficiency of CFB's work by actions such as:

**a.** program consolidation;

**b.** elimination of contracts where economies of scale are not achieved;

**c.** continued elimination of poor performing programs;

**d.** internal restructuring to support strategic direction;

**e.** examination of new business models such as lead agencies; administrative service organizations, or other means.

Larry looks over at the document Muriel is holding in front of her. She moves it closer so he can read the list. Some of the words jump off the page as if they are speaking directly to them both: "program consolidation," "elimination of contracts," "new business models," "administrative service organizations."

At the last CFB meeting, several motions were made to support the new goals and strategies, including a motion to reduce the number of funding contacts and to fund only agencies with budgets greater than $500,000.

Muriel flips through the next few pages of the plan, which includes detailed strategies drafted by CFB staff to operationalize the goals charged by the board. Her eyes zip down every page looking for words such as *neighborhood* or *family center*, but that level of detail has not yet been incorporated; that likely is being saved for discussion at today's board meeting.

The board members get seated and ready to begin the meeting, while audience members continue to flow into the back of the room looking for available seats. Today's is an exceptionally crowded meeting because of the important agenda item, which still projects above the heads of the board members: "*CFB Strategic Plan Report.*" The smiling children's faces are still there, as if to warmly greet all the guests.

"I'd like to call this meeting to order," says the board president. "If all members have reviewed their board packets, I'd like to accept a motion to accept the agenda."

The meeting continues in its usual manner with small business items filling the early part of the agenda. Muriel zones in and out, sometimes listening to the board discussion about minutes, program reports, and workgroups, but mostly she watches—she studies the movements and expressions of the board members, the CFB staff, and the other members in the audience, mostly other nonprofit directors. She scans the faces she can see, wondering who else is there because they fear that their agencies might be at risk.

Finally the *Strategic Plan Report* is next on the agenda. No one stands at the podium to make the presentation. Ken, the executive director of the CFB, can run the presentation by remote control. He stays seated at the U-shaped table and begins the presentation. The audience focuses on the projection screen overhead, while the board members focus on the high-resolution big-screen monitor in front of them. Ken reviews the board's approved strategic plan goals and provides an overview of related studies identifying relevant county facts, themes, and key findings. Finally one slide comes up that reads "Proposed Actions." Muriel and Larry both perk up—now sitting at full attention. Muriel quickly scans the bulleted list, but nothing stands out as being out of the norm for CFB planning; everything focuses on child welfare and general strategies for enhanced coordination of effort.

The slides continue to flip, one after the other, and Muriel continues to scan for dangerous bullets:

Heading—*Other Activities*: "Maybe it's hidden in there," thinks Muriel. Heading—*Evaluation of New Initiatives*: "Maybe that's it."

Nope. Nothing.

The presentation begins and ends without the carnage everyone expected. "What about follow-up actions on the crazy motions made at last month's board meeting?" Muriel silently asks herself. "Reducing the number of contracts? Funding only large agencies? Where is the list of agencies to be cut?"

Nothing.

Then a CFB staff member walks up to the lectern to continue the presentation.

"Uh oh," Muriel thinks. Speaking from the lectern always means bad news is coming. "Here comes the train," she says, leaning over and whispering to Larry. "And it's coming at us at 140 miles per hour."

Consolidation of contracts is the discussion item being brought forth, and the staff members roll out their recommendations to implement the board's directive to achieve efficiencies. Most strategies address ways to have large agencies serve as fiscal agents for smaller agencies, which seems like a logical approach to keep some of the small agencies afloat.

Ken takes the next item: "We are also proposing to consolidate the funding contracts for the nine neighborhood family centers into one. We hope to work with the center directors to form an administrative service organization that can manage the consolidated contract, monitor program performance, and implement strategies to achieve efficiencies through economies of scale."

"What?!" Muriel and Larry look at each other, wide-eyed, but in only partial disbelief. They knew this was coming; the writing has been on the wall for some time. But hearing it said out loud—being presented for all to hear—is a different thing. Muriel cannot believe her ears.

"Will the neighborhood family centers agree to this proposal?" asks one of the board members. "Will they all sign on to participate in this new model?"

Staff members assure the board they will work with the neighborhood family center directors to seek their buy-in, but they also request time and funding support from the board to help implement this new integration model. Because they are a board of successful business leaders, this concept they understand.

"When you start up a new business, it takes some capital," says the board president. The other board members nod in agreement, and they express a willingness to support the staff's request for adequate time and resources to implement the new model.

The board members also put forth some conditions: "We're going to expect some things from you. One of the things we're going to expect is a better functioning body—a body that can get more done than they can individually."

"We expect savings," says another member "spending less to do the same work or better."

"You've got to be kidding me," thinks Muriel. Now she is squirming in her chair. She has been sitting for a while, but her discomfort is an uncontrollable physical response to the discussion taking place.

The board members want to know more about the staff's plan, and they want confirmation that all the neighborhood family centers will participate in this new model. They request staff to make a follow-up presentation at the next board meeting to provide details, a budget, and a timeline for how this project will unfold.

"Muriel, how are we going to make this happen?" asks Larry. "There's no way our center directors are going to agree to do this. There's no way."

Muriel nods in agreement. "It's like they gave me 40 acres and a mule, and now they want to take my mule and the 40 acres away."

They continue to talk as the meeting breaks up. At the front of the room, Reilly stands up, looking to seeing if Muriel and Larry are still in the back of the room. Reilly is the CFB staff member who works most closely with the neighborhood family centers, and he will need to work with them throughout the next month to get them to agree to the integration. He knows it isn't going to be easy.

He grabs his meeting materials and starts to make his way toward Muriel and Larry.

Audience members and board members flow out of the room, passing by Muriel and Larry, but they hardly notice. They are still stunned about what is happening.

Reilly approaches Muriel and Larry: "Ok, I don't want you to panic. We can make this happen."

"Easy for him to say," thinks Muriel.

"Reilly, there's just no way," Larry says. "This is being forced upon people who have been functioning well and independently for quite some time. There's no way our center directors are going to go for this."

"Well, they're going to have to," says Reilly. "I hope you realize that. If the centers don't agree to this, they will be at grave risk of losing their funding. In fact, all the centers may be at risk of losing their funding."

Muriel and Larry look at each other, shaking their head in disbelief.

Reilly gently puts his hand on Muriel's arm. "Look, I have to go talk with Ken. Call me when you get back to your office, and let's talk about the next steps for how we're going to do this. We'll have to move pretty quickly."

"That's for sure!" says Larry.

Reilly heads back to the front of the room, as Muriel and Larry begin slowly walking out the door. Muriel knows they'll have to call an emergency meeting with the center directors. Larry is right, they are not going to come along willingly; they will fight this with every breath they have. The new model will likely require center directors to give up some of the control they have over their funding and contracts, and that will not be an easy sell.

It is evident from today's presentation and board discussion that if neighborhood family center directors don't work together to institute this administrative service organization, their centers will lose their funding.

Muriel and Larry divide up the list of center directors, and they agree to call them immediately to set up a meeting for the next afternoon.

"Well, the message is pretty clear," says Muriel. "The message is, 'Get on board or get run over.' That's what the message is, all right."

## GETTING EVERYONE ON BOARD

Muriel, Larry, and Reilly agree to meet before they go into the conference room to meet with the center directors. "I don't mind breaking the news to everyone," says Reilly.

"Break the news?! Are you kidding?" says Larry. "Every service provider in town already knows what is happening. You won't need to break anything...although a few things may get broken, nonetheless."

Larry is trying to joke. He's nervous, and he's trying hard not to show it. A proposed integration would completely change the scope of his job and his relationship with the center directors. He was hired to help them, to strengthen the Collaborative, and to increase opportunities available to them as a collective of neighborhood family centers. Now he may have to become an enforcer—a contract manager. It's not a role he's comfortable filling with people who had previously been his peers.

Muriel also is concerned about the reactions from members and about keeping the group unified. "Ok, what's the plan?" she asks.

Reilly provides a quick overview of what needs to happen. The most urgent need is for the center directors to agree to the proposal. The proposal will require the centers to turn their funding contracts over to the NFC Collaborative and to work together to form a new umbrella organization to oversee and manage their contracts. The directors have one month to agree to the proposal and to communicate their acceptance of the proposal to the CFB.

The second huge task for the directors will be to create the new structure—an administrative service organization—and to have it up, running, and fully functional within 14 months.

"How is this going to be funded?" asks Larry. "I assume we'll need more than just me on staff to do all this work."

"Well, yes, you will," says Reilly. "And as you heard yesterday, the CFB board agreed to give you some time and some funding to get this new organization up and running, but after that the Collaborative will have to pay the costs."

"Oh, this is going to be good!" says Larry, still laughing nervously. "And you're going to explain this to them...how they'll need to give up some of their funding to pay my salary? Oh, man; some members are going to hit the roof!"

"Well, it's completely up to you and them how you accomplish it, but it has to happen," says Reilly.

Muriel starts picturing the reactions from each of the members. She has worked with most of them for many years, and she knows this is going to be hard case to make. She starts thinking through her strategy of how she will handle the directors who will be most strongly opposed to the proposal.

The three agree that Muriel will open the meeting and then turn it over to Reilly to provide an overview of what the CFB is expecting and requesting of the centers. Muriel and Reilly leave the office and head toward the conference room. Larry momentarily lingers behind, still chuckling nervously to himself about the discussion about to take place. "This is going to be interesting."

They start walking down the hall toward the conference room. As they approach, they can hear several members yelling—not at one another but rather about what CFB is doing to them. The loud accusations don't subside as the trio enters the room, but members take their seats, anxious to hear what Reilly has to say.

"Where is Ken?" asks one member. "Why isn't Ken here to meet with us?"

"Ken plans to come talk to you at your next meeting," explains Reilly. "He just couldn't be here today."

"He needs to be here!" exclaims one center director. "We shouldn't be having this meeting without him."

Another member chimes in: "This is big! We need to hear this from the horse's mouth."

Reilly is caught off guard by the comments. "Ken asked me to come talk with you on his behalf today. He really wanted to be here…"

"Well, he needs to be here!" repeats the director. "He is disrespecting us as directors by not coming to tell us this news himself."

Several members chime in in agreement.

Reilly had known the center directors were going to be upset, but he had not expected this type of reaction to Ken's absence at the meeting. He is momentarily stunned and unsure what to say next.

"We can't wait for Ken to be here," says Muriel. "We have some decisions we need to make right away, and we need to start this discussion and this process *today*."

"All the more reason why Ken should be here," says the other director.

"Please…," continues Muriel, "give Reilly a chance to explain this to us. We've got a lot of business to address, and it's going to take us some time to get through this; so, please, let's allow Reilly to speak to us about what's happening right now."

She turns to Reilly, who clearly is relieved that Muriel got the group focused.

Reilly provides an overview of what transpired in the past couple of months that led to the recommendation to form the administrative service organization. He reviews the strategic planning goals and corresponding motions adopted by the CFB board last month, specifically the directive to reduce contracts and fund only large agencies. He provides an overview of the proposal for the integration model and the next steps required for the process.

"It's important for you all to know that CFB staff value the work of the neighborhood family centers…especially Ken," says Reilly. "And Ken is committed to finding a way to make sure all the neighborhood family centers stay intact. This was the only way staff could come up with to save all the neighborhood family centers—to work with you to form an administrative service organization."

"What exactly is an administrative service organization?" interrupts one of the center directors.

Reilly takes a deep breath and begins his explanation. "Well, an ASO is when you create a new organization that serves as an administrative clearinghouse, of sorts, for several other organizations—for example, to do bookkeeping, payroll, benefits, and contract management... or anything you want. The goal is to increase the administrative efficiency of participating organizations."

"Ooh, I like that," responds the director of one of the smallest neighborhood family centers. "No bookkeeping. No contract management."

"Yeah!" says another member. "That would be a huge relief. Then I can focus on my programs and services instead of paperwork."

"Yes, that exactly right" says Reilly, excitedly pleased that some members see the benefit of the integration plan. "Those are some of the benefits you can incorporate into your model."

"No way!" says another member. "No one is going to take over my contracts or bookkeeping or payroll—not nothing! My agency can do those things ourselves."

"Well, you don't have to turn over all those things," Reilly says. "It's completely up to you."

"So, this won't affect me then," one director assertively proclaims. "I've got one of the largest centers in the county, and my CFB contract is well over $500,000. I don't have to participate in this."

"Yes, you do have to participate," says Reilly. "Let me be very clear about this. In order for this to work, everyone needs to participate, or you may be at risk of losing your funding. Ken will tell you the same thing when he meets with you."

Reilly continues, referring to all the directors, "But here's the great part about it: You will have complete authority over the ASO because it will be the NFC Collaborative that fulfills that role."

"Wait a minute! This is ours! We created this Collaborative," exclaims one member. "CFB's got nothing to do with it. CFB shouldn't be putting their hands in *our* Collaborative."

"It will still be *your* Collaborative," explains Reilly. "And you'll still run your own agencies, the same way you always have. The only thing that has to change is how your CFB contract is administered if you want to continue receiving funds."

"I'm not going to believe any of this until I hear it from the horse's mouth," says one member, referring to Ken as *the horse*. "I don't need some other entity—let alone the Collaborative *we* created—to manage my contract! I'm perfectly capable of managing my contract on my own."

"We're not saying you can't," says Reilly. "No one is saying that any of you aren't capable of managing your own contracts. You're all strong, capable directors, and you've proven that. This just is the mandate that we have to adhere to." Reilly continues to explain that six of the nine neighborhood family centers are under the $500,000 contract limit and would lose their funding under the board's directive. He rattles off the list of the challenged neighborhoods being served by the small centers, and he lists the different programs and services being offered:

after-school programs, tutoring, emergency financial assistance, parenting skills training, and much more.

Reilly is trying to make a connection with the directors of the larger centers. Surely they understand the importance of these programs. "All of these centers and programs are important. You know that! That's why CFB is offering this opportunity to consolidate the funding—so all the centers can continue providing services."

"I don't care whether the small ones make it or not," says a director from one of the large centers. "I have to be concerned about my own agency, and my board of directors *is not* going to go for this."

"Well, that's really nice!" says the director from the small center, who is clearly upset by the comment. "It's easy for you to say because you've been in existence for a while. The work we do is important, too, and we need to keep our CFB funding or we *will* close."

"That's not my problem."

"Hold up, everyone! Wait a second," says Muriel. "You're all making this personal. It's not personal. We gotta keep this at what it is, which is something we have to work through as a group."

"Yes, please," agrees another member. "Let's not personalize this. If we personalize, then we're not going to get along, and we won't get through this."

"She's absolutely right," says Larry. "We all have to work together on this."

"Well, I don't need these small centers," says one member. "Our agency could take over their contracts and services."

Muriel leans forward, propping her elbow on the table and pointing at the members. "Let me tell all of you, I would survive, probably over everyone, but I choose to be part of this group. I choose to save everyone, not just two or three of you. I choose to save everyone who's willing to be saved."

The group is silent and attentive to what Muriel has to say. Her ability to always say the right thing at the right time is instrumental in keeping the group focused on the important issues before it.

"Wow!" thinks Reilly. "You know, how do you fight that?" He's thankful that Muriel is chairing the meeting and serving as president of the Collaborative.

Everyone continues to pay attention to Muriel and Reilly.

Reilly begins again, now feeling a little desperate for the group's cooperation. "Look, you know, guys, we're in a situation here. If we don't pull this off—if we don't agree to execute the single contract, and if we don't get this ASO up and off the ground within the next year—then the CFB board is going to start saying, 'Ok, they're not willing to work together.' There's a risk that the CFB board may take away all of your funding if that happens."

"That's a threat!" yells one director.

"No, it's a fact," assures Reilly. "It's what could happen if the group doesn't agree to do this."

"Well, who's going to pay for this new A—S—O?" asks one member with a clear tone of disgust in his voice.

"Oh, boy!" thinks Larry. "Here we go."

Reilly explains that the CFB is going to provide temporary funding to hire additional staff to help Larry and that the Collaborative members will need to pay for operation of the ASO after that period of time.

One member jumps up in distress at this news. "What! No way, no way, no way! There is no way I'm giving up some of my funding to pay for this."

"That doesn't make sense, Reilly," says another member. "We can't afford to pay all our expenses now. And that just doesn't make sense to give up our funding to pay for work that CFB staff is already doing."

"This is like having to give CFB blood!" exclaims one agitated member. "To give them our money for something we don't even want or need."

"I think we have to realize," says Larry, "that there's nothing we can do about the single contract. That's a done deal. The question for the group is do we want the Collaborative to fill the role of administering the single contract, or do we want to throw ourselves at the mercy of fate?"

Reilly sits back and takes another deep breath. The room is silent as members contemplate the situation. Reilly looks over at Larry, who is scanning the faces in the room. The emotions displayed range from hostile to relieved and from helpless to empowered. Others are clearly hurt and upset by comments made by members.

Muriel leans forward again to remind people of the bottom line. "Well, you all have two choices: CFB has said they're going to give our money to the Collaborative. So, you can either be a part of this, or you can choose not to be a part of this—you can either ride on the train or get run over by the train—that depends on whether you want the money or not. I would prefer to have the money."

Members continue to sit silently, listening to Muriel. A few members are now nodding their head in agreement, supporting what Muriel is advocating to the group.

"The bottom line is," continues Muriel, "most of us want to continue doing what we're doing; so, we have to figure out a way to make this happen. We gotta get on board, and we must choose to make this work."

# ABOUT THE EDITORS

**Joann Keyton** is Professor of Communication Studies at North Carolina State University. In organizational communication, Keyton focuses on organizational culture and sexual harassment. In group communication, Keyton explores the relational behaviors that organizational group members engage in while addressing task concerns. Her research appears in *Communication Studies, Communication Theory, Communication Yearbook, Journal of Applied Communication Research, Management Communication Quarterly, Small Group Research, Southern Communication Journal,* and numerous edited collections, including the *Handbook of Group Communication Theory and Research.* She is the author of *Communication & Organizational Culture* (Sage) and *Communication Research* (McGraw-Hill). Keyton was the editor of *Journal of Applied Communication Research* (volumes 31–33, 2003–2005). Currently she is coeditor of *Small Group Research* and editor of *Communication Currents.*

**Pamela Shockley-Zalabak** is Chancellor and professor of Communication at the University of Colorado at Colorado Springs. She is the author of seven books and over 100 articles and productions on organizational communication, and her research interests include organizational cultures as they relate to individual employee values and overall organizational effectiveness. Prior to assuming chancellor responsibilities, Dr. Shockley was Vice Chancellor for Student Success and the founding chair of the University of Colorado at Colorado Springs Communication Department. Dr. Shockley is the recipient of the University of Colorado Thomas Jefferson Award, President's Award for Outstanding Service, Chancellor's Award for Distinguished Faculty, and the Colorado Speech Communication Association Distinguished Member Award.

# ABOUT THE CONTRIBUTORS

**Donald L. Anderson** (Ph.D., University of Colorado, Boulder) is a faculty member at the University of Denver and manages employee communications at a high-tech company.

**Julie Apker** (Ph.D., University of Kansas) is associate professor of communication at Western Michigan University.

**Colleen Arendt** (M.A., Purdue University) is a doctoral student in organizational communication at Purdue University.

**Carlos E. Balhana** is a graduate student in the Department of Linguistics at Georgetown University.

**Christina M. Bates** (J.D., Boston University; M.S., Boston University) is a doctoral student in the Hugh Downs School of Human Communication at Arizona State University and an associate with Booz Allen Hamilton.

**Ryan S. Bisel** (Ph.D., University of Kansas) is assistant professor of communication at the University of Oklahoma.

**Jensen Chung** (Ph.D., SUNY at Buffalo) is professor of speech and communication studies at San Francisco State University.

**Cheryl Cockburn-Wootten** (Ph.D., University of Wales, Cardiff) is senior lecturer in the Management Communication Department at the University of Waikato.

**Christine E. Cooper** (Ph.D., University of Texas) is assistant professor of communication at the University of Alaska, Fairbanks.

**Andrew Jared Critchfield** (Ph.D., Howard University) is assistant professor of communication and organizational sciences at George Washington University.

**Jennifer D. Davis** is a doctoral candidate at the University of Texas at Austin.

**Linda B. Dickmeyer** (Ph.D., University of Nebraska) is associate professor of communication studies at the University of Wisconsin–La Crosse.

**Scott G. Dickmeyer** (Ph.D., University of Nebraska) is associate professor of communication studies and a trainer with the Small Business Development Center at the University of Wisconsin–La Crosse.

**Scott C. D'Urso** (Ph.D., University of Texas) is assistant professor of communication studies at Marquette University.

**Beth Eschenfelder** (Ph.D., University of South Florida) is assistant professor of communication at the University of Tampa.

**Stuart L. Esrock** (Ph.D., Bowling Green State University) is associate professor of communication at the University of Louisville.

**Heather Gearhart** is president of Gearhart Public Relations in Flagstaff, Arizona.

**Adelina Gomez** (Ph.D., University of Colorado, Boulder) is associate professor of communication at the University of Colorado at Colorado Springs.

**Amanda M. Gunn** (Ph.D., University of North Carolina, Greensboro) is assistant professor of communication at Denison University.

**Melissa Gibson Hancox** (Ph.D., Ohio University) is associate professor of communication at Edinboro University of Pennsylvania.

**Joy L. Hart** (Ph.D., University of Kentucky) is professor of communication at the University of Louisville.

**Zachary P. Hart** (Ph.D., Michigan State University) is assistant professor of communication at Northern Kentucky University.

**Aparna Hebbani** (Ph.D., University of Memphis) is a lecturer at the School of Journalism and Communication at the University of Queensland, Australia.

**MJ Helgerson** (M.S., University of Portland) manages training at a high-tech company.

**Mary Hoffman** (Ph.D., University of Kansas) is chair and associate professor of communication and journalism at the University of Wisconsin, Eau Claire.

**Marian L. Houser** (Ph.D., University of Tennessee) is assistant professor at Texas State University.

**Cynthia A. Irizarry** (Ph.D., University of Nebraska) is assistant professor of communication at Stetson University.

**Jessica Katz Jameson** (Ph.D. Temple University) is associate professor of communication at North Carolina State University.

**Lori J. Joseph** (Ph.D., University of Kansas) is associate professor and chair of communication studies at Hollins University.

**Erika L. Kirby** (Ph.D., University of Nebraska) is associate professor of communication studies at Creighton University.

**Joy Koesten** (Ph.D., University of Kansas) is a lecturer of communication studies at the University of Kansas.

**Michael W. Kramer** (Ph.D., University of Texas) is chair and professor in the Department of Communication at the University of Missouri–Columbia.

**Robert L. Krizek** (Ph.D., Arizona State University) is associate professor of communication at Saint Louis University.

**Greg B. Leichty** (Ph.D., University of Kentucky) is professor of communication at the University of Louisville.

**Laurie K. Lewis** (Ph.D., University of California, Santa Barbara) is associate professor in the Department of Communication at Rutgers University.

**Shawn D. Long** (Ph.D., University of Kentucky) is associate professor of communication studies at the University of North Carolina at Charlotte.

**Alexander Lyon** (Ph.D., University of Colorado, Boulder) is assistant professor of communication at the College of Brockport.

**Patty C. Malone** (Ph.D., University of Texas at Austin) is assistant professor of communication studies at California State University–Fullerton.

**Steven K. May** (Ph.D., University of Utah) is associate professor of communication studies at the University of North Carolina at Chapel Hill.

**Jeanne S. McPherson** (Ph.D., University of Colorado, Boulder) is principal of McPherson Organizational Consulting and teaches at Washington State University Tri-Cities.

**Mary M. Meares** (Ph.D., University of New Mexico) is assistant professor of communication studies at the University of Alabama.

**Caryn E. Medved** (Ph.D., University of Kansas) is assistant professor in the Department of Communication Studies at Baruch College, City University of New York.

**Amber S. Messersmith** (Ph.D., University of Kansas) is assistant professor of Communication Studies at James Madison University.

**Carol B. Mills** (Ph.D., Purdue University) is assistant professor in communication studies at the University of Alabama.

**John G. Oetzel** (Ph.D., University of Iowa) is chair and professor of communication and journalism at the University of New Mexico.

**Leslie Reynard** (Ph.D., University of Kansas) is assistant professor at Washburn University.

**Nancy M. Schullery** (Ph.D., Wayne State University) is professor of business information systems at Western Michigan University.

**Craig R. Scott** (Ph.D., Arizona State University) is associate professor in the Department of Communication at Rutgers University.

**Elayne J. Shapiro** (Ph. D., University of Minnesota) is associate professor of communication studies at the University of Portland.

**Astrid Sheil** (Ph.D., University of Tennessee) is assistant professor of communication at Cal State University–San Bernardino and president of Sheil & Associates.

**Mary Simpson** is a doctoral candidate and lecturer with the Management Communication Department at the University of Waikato.

**Diane K. Sloan** (Ph.D., University of Nebraska, Lincoln) lives and writes in Sioux City, Iowa.

**Keri K. Stephens** (Ph.D., University of Texas at Austin) is assistant professor of communication studies at the University of Texas at Austin.

**Sarah J. Tracy** (Ph.D., University of Colorado, Boulder) is associate professor at the Hugh Downs School of Human Communication at Arizona State University.

**Rod Troester** (Ph.D., Southern Illinois University) is associate professor of communication at Penn State Erie, the Behrend College.

**Paaige K. Turner** (Ph.D., Purdue University) is associate professor of communication at Saint Louis University.

**Robert R. Ulmer** (Ph.D., Wayne State University) is professor and chair of the Department of Speech Communication at the University of Arkansas at Little Rock.

**Mary E. Vielhaber** (Ph.D., University of Michigan) is professor of management at Eastern Michigan University.

**Melinda M. Villagran** (Ph.D., University of Oklahoma) is associate professor of communication at George Mason University.

**Heather L. Walter** (Ph.D., State University of New York, Buffalo) is associate professor in the School of Communication at the University of Akron.

**Maryanne Wanca-Thibault** (Ph.D., University of Colorado, Boulder) is a principal in SDL, an organizational development consulting firm.

**Deanna F. Womack** (Ph.D., University of Kansas) is professor of communication at Kennesaw State University.

**Stephen C. Yungbloth** (Ph.D., Northern Kentucky University) is assistant professor; Department of Communication at Northern Kentucky University.

**Theodore E. Zorn Jr.** (Ph.D., University of Kentucky) is professor in the Department of Management Communication at the University of Waikato.

# DETAILED CASE CONTENT INDEX*

*W = case available on the book's website at www.oup.com/us/keytonshockley

| Subject | Cases |
| --- | --- |
| New employees | 1, 22, 27, 32, W3, W5, W19 |
| Nonprofit organizations | 6, 7, 12, 48 |
| Nonverbal communication | 38, W15 |
| Organization exit | 25, W8, W12 |
| Organization mission, vision | 38, W7 |
| Organizational awards | 27 |
| Organizational change | 1, 2, 3, 4, 6, 7, 10, 12, 13, 19, W2, W4, W7, W14 |
| Organizational commitment | 23 |
| Organizational control | 1, 5, 7, 18, 38, W3, W8 |
| Organizational crisis | 19, 45, 46, 47, 48, W20 |
| Organizational culture | 1, 2, 3, 4, 5, 6, 7, 11, 27, 40, W3, W4, W5, W6, W7, W14, W16, W18, W19 |
| Organizational ethics | 5, 21, 22, 29, 31, 47, W8, W12, W20 |
| Organizational identity | 5, 9, 30, W16 |
| Organizational learning | 12, W2 |
| Organizational performance & productivity | 2, 3, 13, 47 |
| Organizational structure | 3, 4, 9, 13 |
| Organizational values | 1, 5, 19, 22, 29, 30, 35, 38, W3, W7, W19 |
| Performance evaluation | 25, 31, 32, 36, 38, 41, W11, W18 |
| Personnel issues | 6, 29, 31 |
| Play/fun at work | 5, 27, W15 |
| Politics | 7, 8, 17, 18, 22, 24, 25, 28, 29, 30, 31, 32, 33, 41, W12 |
| Power | 5, 10, 18, 28, 37, 40, W12 |
| Professional etiquette | 8, 28, 30, 31, 37, 40, 44, 48, W17 |
| Public relations | 17, 22, 27, 42, 43, 45, 47 |
| Quality of work life (QWL) | 26 |
| Racial/ethnic discrimination | 24, 36, 26, 41 |
| Rumors | 46, W5 |
| Sexual harassment | 37, 38 |
| Staffing | 6, 29 |
| Status | 27, 30, 35, 36 |
| Stress & burnout | 25, 26, 33, 35, 41 |
| Supervisor-subordinate relationships | 2, 5, 11, 22, 24, 25, 26, 27, 28, 29, 30, 31, 32, 33, 38, W12, W17 |
| Teamwork | 2, 11, 13, 14, 15, 16, 27, W2, W9, W11, W15 |